THIS BOOK IS WRITTEN FOR HIS GLORY!

MAY YOU BECOME A PART OF GOD'S END-TIME RECONNECTION.

MUCH LOVE IN YESHUA/JESUS

BLESSINGS & SHALOM

**THEOLOGICAL OVERSIGHT BY
DR. DANIEL JUSTER**

ROMANS
911

TIME TO SOUND
THE ALARM!

A COMPREHENSIVE STUDY BOOK IN THE
RECONNECTION OF THE ONE NEW MAN

GRANT
BERRY

Published by HigherLife Publishing & Marketing, Inc.
    PO Box 623307
    Oviedo, FL 32762
    AHigherLife.com

Front cover image by Emily Conforti with Bill Johnson of Digg
Reconnection Key art design by Joel Wilbur
Reconnecting Ministries: http://www.Reconnectingministries.org

ISBN: 978-1-951492-83-0 (Hardback)
ISBN: 978-0-9998197-7-7 (Paperback)
ISBN: 978-0-9998197-8-4 (Ebook)
ISBN: 978-1-7326377-6-4 (Audiobook)
LOC Case #1-10660447841

Printed in the United States of America.

DEDICATION

This book is dedicated to the Heart of the Father, His most precious Son, Yeshua/Jesus, and His Holy Spirit, who has inspired me to write Romans 911. Lord, I love You with all my heart and don't want to do anything without You.
Please continue to teach me this principle.

ACKNOWLEDGMENTS

I WOULD LIKE TO recognize my beautiful wife, Hali Berry, who is my lover and best friend. You are the most wonderful companion and partner, and it is my honor and privilege to share our lives together. Thank you for all your love and support to help bring *Romans 911* to life and for *The Reconnection* to go forth into the family of God – and for all of your editing input.

To my father Joseph Philip Berry, who went home to Glory during Passover in 2018 as I was finishing this book. Thank you for all your love and support to me; it is an honor to be your son.

To the Recon Warriors group of watchmen and watchwomen in Brookfield and Norwalk, Connecticut, God knows you by name. Thank you for your love, dedication, and commitment to help initiate the Reconnecting Ministries' focus through *"Pure Intercession."* Thank you for trusting me with God's vision to Reconnect His family spiritually in *The One New Man*. And thank you for many of the spiritual insights and revelations that have come through us as a group in the Holy Spirit to help write this book.

To my apostolic leadership, Dr. Daniel Juster of Tikkun Global Ministries, and to Che Ahn of Harvest International Ministries (HIM), thank you for your ministry oversight, guidance, and spiritual covering.

Most importantly, thank you for your heart and spirit in wanting to help promote this Reconnecting ministry message to the Church and Messianic bodies at large so that we can reunite at this time.

To my ministry board, Pastor Don Wilkerson, Rabbi Barry Feinman, John Maclean, Abner Suarez, Al Sanchirico, and Rabbi Robert Wolff, thank you for watching over me and for all your spiritual contributions to Reconnecting Ministries and to Messiah's House.

To my pastors, Glenn Harvison, Nick Uva, Joe and Alicia Adevai, thank you for all your love and support.

A special thank you to all our ministry partners and to John and Judy Maclean, Stephen and Claire Frieder, Angel and Sarah Suarez and to Jewish Voice Ministries—we could not have done this without you.

A special thank you to all the leaders who have endorsed *Romans 911*, for recognizing it as a most crucial work to help reunite the Body of Messiah/Christ in *The One New Man*.

A special thank you to the prayer leaders, the prophetic intercessors who have prayed for this book and encouraged me to write it. To Gregg Healey, Jonathan Friz, Jason Hubbard, Dai Sup Han, and John Robb, thank you.

A special thank you to Dominick and Leslie Crincoli, and Guerney Hunt, for their input and to HigherLife Publishing and their editing team.

PREFACE

A S PART OF my ministry experience with *The Reconnection*, I often confront obstacles. One day when I was at Congregation (January 2015), I was in the spirit worshiping the Lord but was feeling particularly discouraged by one of these obstacles. I very clearly heard the Holy Spirit laughing, which continued for quite some time. I was challenged by this because of what I was dealing with, so I asked the Lord, "Why are you laughing?" The Lord quickly replied, "These are strongholds; you can't break them, but I can!"

This message from the Holy Spirit was to be life changing for me. Immediately, I knew exactly what the Lord was saying, in light of the intense intercessory experience and spiritual warfare I had been immersed in for the Russian Jews in the 1990s, when I led missions to the former Soviet Union. These spiritual battles and the thousands of Jewish and Gentile souls that were won to the faith were fought and won first on our knees, through the Holy Spirit's leading, and then through a special type of prayer and intercession that cleared the spiritual skies, allowing our evangelistic work to proceed. With a similar directive and focus, *The Reconnection* must be bathed through prayer and intercession as a means to properly deal with the strongholds in its way, to create more of a pure intercessory environment for the Holy Spirit to do this type of bidding through His prophetic intercessors.

This required stepping back and refocusing to bring this Reconnection message forward through the Lord's directive. First, to raise up and mobilize an army of intercessors throughout the Church and Messianic bodies with this new intercessory prayer strategy. Second, to increase the insight and revelation on *The Reconnection* teachings so that the watchmen and watchwomen called into it could gain a deeper sense of how to flow with the Holy Spirit's directives.

I have spent five years of my life working on this book project. I spent numerous hours on a daily basis and some in the middle of the night as the Holy Spirit prompted me to write this. I have honestly felt like a scribe of the Lord writing *Romans 911,* and I never touched the work without bringing my heart into right alignment before a Holy and righteous God. I have wept, I have cried, I have laughed, but most often I have been personally amazed at the great revelation and insight the Lord has poured out into the creation of this book. On many occasions, *The Reconnection* breaks new ground to help reunite His family.

Visit ReconnectingMinistries.org for my author video commentaries and chapter outlines that will help you with the reading of this book.

May the God of Israel richly bless your experience of reading *Romans 911.* I hope and pray it connects you personally with its message.

With lots of love in Yeshua/Jesus and for His Glory!

BLESSINGS AND SHALOM,
GRANT BERRY,
FOUNDER RECONNECTING MINISTRIES,
AUTHOR, AND PRODUCER OF *THE ROMANS 911 PROJECT*

AFTER THE CORONAVIRUS

N 2017/5778, ON Shavuot/Pentecost, I launched the first edition of *Romans 911—Time to Sound the Alarm!* In the book, I wrote in two places that God will create the natural circumstances to bring about His Reformation and Restoration in His Ekklesia/Church to make way for His coming (see chapters 4 and 12). Then, in 2020, the world found itself in the midst of the Coronavirus epidemic (COVID-19), which is nothing short of a plague. Both the Church and the world have been dramatically impacted and forever changed.

MERCY TRIUMPHS OVER JUDGMENT

In the past, many of us might have asked the Lord, "Father, with all that has gone on in our world, why don't you show Yourself more? And why don't You act?" Well, I think we have our answer. I don't want to get into a detailed discussion about exactly who is behind this, but rather I prefer to focus on the greater picture as to what this shaking can produce. But I will say this: nothing happens in our world without God's foreknowledge (see Job 2). And God wants none to perish, but all to come to the knowledge of the truth (see 1 Timothy 2:3–4).

So, if you ask me why this has happened, I would say that it is also an act of God's mercy. Why would I say that? Because both the Church and the world need to awaken—the judgment is close and is coming!

God says to be more fearful of the one that can take the soul, and it is evident that we all need a wake-up call, but for different reasons. First, this is necessary for His Ekklesia/Church to become the radiant Bride that we are called to be, for us to reach the lost. Second, the world needs to be awakened to salvation before it is too late.

Hebrews 12 says it best: *"His voice shook the earth then, but now He has promised, saying, 'Yet once more I will shake not only the earth, but also the heavens.' Now this phrase, 'Yet once more,' shows the removal of those things that are shaken—that is, created things—so that what cannot be shaken may remain. Therefore, since we are receiving a Kingdom that cannot be shaken, let us show gratitude—through this we may offer worship in a manner pleasing to God, with reverence and awe. For our God is a consuming fire"* (Heb. 12:26–29 TLV).

Since the turn of this century, we have experienced 9/11 in 2001, the financial crisis in 2008, and now the Corona plague, mass rioting, political division, and unrest.

In the midst of the Coronavirus crisis, I posted a prophetic vision in *Charisma* magazine from a trusted Messianic brother who has chosen to be nameless. It is called "Wrecking Balls!" (You can read this article on the ministry website in the Charisma section.) The vision outlines this attack on the world as the first of five shakings, all created to shatter the idols of humankind. The vision doesn't speak of any specific time, except to say they are spread out pretty evenly, with perhaps a wider space of time between the first and the four consecutive wrecking balls. However, it is clear that once the wrecking balls are finished, our current world as we know it will be severely impacted and dramatically changed.

While these wrecking balls may appear to be acts of judgment from God, they will be nothing compared to the final judgment that is coming upon the world because of sin before the Lord returns, which is spoken about in the books of Daniel and Revelation. This is why I state that they are actually acts of mercy because while loss and suffering have obviously been experienced during this first wrecking ball, about which we mourn and pray, the vast majority of us have remained safely tucked away in our homes with nearly all the provision and comforts of life. And it is apparent now, at least to those of us who know the Lord, that He wants to get our attention. An alarm is being sounded, and we must hearken to its sound!

Interestingly, it was during Passover and the celebration of the resurrection (2020), while we were shut away in our homes, that probably more prayer for protection and deliverance was going up to the heavens than at any other time in history.

With Israel's awakening and the end-time harvest in mind, I believe there are two main focuses from the Lord that we need to take a serious look at to properly process. The first has to do with His Ekklesia/Church arising, coming out of Babylon with all of its influences, and being restored and reformed to prepare for His coming. The second has to do with the end-time harvest awakening that is reached through a transformed Bride.

NOT QUITE YET

During the crisis, I heard a good number of our leaders in the Church make statements that this is the beginning of the great awakening and outpouring of the Holy Spirit. And without question, a huge amount of prayer is being offered, which is what helps to usher in revival. My sincere hope is that it will continue afterward. While I believe we could see several revivals on the path to the last great awakening (I call them "pockets") as a result of increased prayer, we are not there yet. This is because the Ekklesia/Church is not ready and must now enter a period of sincere repentance, purification, and Restoration to be made whole.

Simply put, the Church has been stifled; and it is not operating on all of its cylinders, as it needs to be. Pray to God, in all humility, that we will be able to recognize this alarm and warning from the Lord and begin to move the Body of Messiah/Christ into the necessary Restoration and Reformation needed to prepare the Body for what is coming.

At the beginning of the last Jubilee period (fifty years) on the

Earth, on Rosh Hashanah in 2017/5077, the Lord gathered hundreds of His watchmen in the State of Connecticut to blow a prophetic shofar to proclaim three major shifts and changes for His Ekklesia/Church, which you can read about in more detail in chapter 12, the last chapter in the book. They were:

1. The Restoration of *The One New Man* between Jew and Gentile.
2. The Church moving into the fullness of the fivefold ministry.
3. The Preparation of the Bride for the Lord's return.

I believe that the Glory our Lord Yeshua/Jesus spoke of in John 17 comes about as a result of the love and unity in God's family so that ultimately, we will be able fulfill His great commission (Matt. 28:18–20). Before He can send the fullness of that power and Glory upon us, His Ekklesia/Church must be properly restored. Presently, this is not the case, and while we are beginning to awaken to greater prayer, which is a good thing, we cannot and must not ignore our present state and the division and separation that exists in the Church and the Messianic bodies, and the repentance and humility that will be required to get us back on track. The fear of the Lord must return to His Church, for the God of Israel is a consuming fire! (See Hebrews 12:29.)

In this light, we must return to the Lord wholeheartedly and remove any idols. The world is coming under judgment, and our feet must be steadfast upon the Rock of our salvation (Yeshua/Jesus) in all we do, without compromise. Let us remember that judgment begins in the house before anything else (see 1 Peter 4:17). Let us always remember that He chose us and that we are saved to serve Him rather than the other way around (see Matthew 20:25–28). Let us also remember that there were only two characters who made it into the Promised Land from the first generation of Israelis who came out of Egypt: Joshua and Caleb. It was because they followed the Lord *wholeheartedly* (see Numbers 14:24; 32:12). It is one thing to be saved, but quite another to enter in, and we must be transformed during these days and made ready for the Bridegroom.

(Please note the emphasis in Numbers 14 on Caleb, who had a different spirit to the rest of Israel.)

For sure, these days will be most glorious as we come into the fullness of love and unity in the family of God. But they will also be most challenging. Like the virgins, we must be filled with the oil that will cause our lamps to be running over; otherwise, we might not make it (see Matthew 25:1–13). While we are coming into and drawing closer to that time of the great outpouring of the Holy Spirit on the Earth with a huge end-time harvest (see Joel 2:28), at the same time, there will also be a falling away from the faith (see Matthew 24:10; 1 Timothy 4:1). I believe now that the spiritual forces of light and darkness are going to heat up even more, and we will need to be deliberate in all we do.

So if this love and unity need to be rebuilt between us and God and among one another, and if it is a prerequisite to the fullness of the Glory of God coming upon His Ekklesia/Church to restore the unity in God's family, where do we start?

WE MUST REBUILD THE WALLS

There is a good picture here that can help us in the story of Nehemiah. There are some wonderful comparisons between the physical walls of Jerusalem that Nehemiah was called to rebuild and the spiritual walls we are called to rebuild, of love and unity in the family of God.

First, he had to face reality and take an honest hard look at where Israel was. The walls were broken down, the gates burned, and Jerusalem was disgraced (see Nehemiah 2:17). If you look up the word "disgraced" in the dictionary, it means to lose honor, respect, and esteem. Well, wouldn't that be a very real picture of where the Church is today from a worldly perspective? But then look carefully how Nehemiah goes about rebuilding, and there is a focus on two hands—one to build and one to fight (see Nehemiah, chapters 3–4).

Isaiah cries out, *"Build up, build up, prepare the road! Remove the obstacles out of the way of my people"* (Is. 57:14). So how do we build?

We build up with love in the natural, the same way Yeshua/Jesus does. But at the same time, we fight and contend, which should be done in the Spirit, in prayer.

This book is about this preparation, this supernatural love, this supernatural contention, and aiding the Body of Messiah/Christ for perhaps what will be known as the greatest time on the Earth for the Kingdom of God before Yeshua/Jesus returns. This is the goal of *Romans 911* and *The Romans 911 Project*: to rebuild this love and unity in the family of God and to prepare us for what is coming so the Father and Yeshua/Jesus can release the Glory upon us.

However, to achieve this healing and Restoration, we must be willing to look back, especially now as Israel awakens, and to come into agreement with the Father and Yeshua/Jesus to mend all breaches and divisions in the family of God that started with the Church breaking away from Israel and its Jewish roots and heritage. There are deeper issues here that we have only just begun to touch. These are complex matters and require a great deal of unpacking and understanding to help move the family of God into this healing and Restoration between Jewish and Gentile believers and between the Church and the Remnant of Israel. However, I believe without a shadow of doubt that if we can give our Father a restored *One New Man* between Jew and Gentile, then we take back something strategic in the spirit from the devil, called "division," that will empower us to pray and seek healing in all other areas of division in the Body of Messiah/Christ.

THERE IS NO SUBSTITUTE FOR THIS MESSAGE

We must come to understand that there is no substitute for this message of renewed love and unity. There is a plan here for us to follow so the Father can move His holy tabernacle (the Body of Messiah/Christ) back to Jerusalem. There is a bridge for us to cross now, called "Restoration," that will lead us to a "Realignment" with Israel that will help to heal these divides and lead us on a pathway to God's end-time plans for His Ekklesia/Church.

I call this *"The Reconnection!"* Are you ready to be Reconnected? Come join us on this journey, along with the many thousands and millions of believers who are to get on this pathway to the Lord's return.

Repentance and renewal in the familial relationship between Jew and Gentile will help to restore a pathway to John 17 love and unity and rightly lay the groundwork for healing and Restoration of other divisions in the Church. This is the goal of *Romans 911* and *The Romans 911 Project*.

THE RETURN

As I put the finishing touches to the editing of this second edition of *Romans 911*, we have just completed the Fall Feasts bringing in the year 5781 on the Jewish Calendar (2020). We just experienced 10 Days of Awe and "The Return" event in Washington, D.C., established by Jonathan Cahn and Kevin Jessip.

"The Return" was the most amazing, incredible, wonderful event focused on repentance prayer for the Ekklesia/Church and our world, which is so desperately needed. It was most probably one of the most-watched spiritual events in all time, experienced by untold millions upon millions of people across the globe. But what is crucial to point out about this gathering is that it was totally focused upon bringing the Ekklesia/Church into deeper repentance and this Restoration in *The One New Man*. An alarm was sounded into the heavens and throughout the globe, and when Jonathan Cahn gave his prophetic message, it actually thundered three times in the skies above. I heard these rumblings with my own ears.

This day will go down in history as a sovereign move of God to bring about His purposes upon the Earth, and spiritual doors were opened in the heavens to help prepare the way. We need to understand that we are on God's timetable here for His plans to come forth for His Ekklesia/Church and the world. But this move of repentance in His Church is just the beginning of this process. It will lead us into a Restoration, a Reconciliation, and a Realignment in the family of God to fulfill Yeshua/Jesus's Heart cry that will ultimately lead us to the end-time Revival. This is one of the main reasons why we capitalize the R's in all of these words. *The Reconnection* message helps to establish this pathway so God can send the Glory. Time will prove this process and the steps needed for His end-time Church to fulfill its destiny.

BLESSINGS AND SHALOM,
GRANT BERRY,
FOUNDER RECONNECTING MINISTRIES,
AUTHOR, AND PRODUCER OF *THE ROMANS 911 PROJECT*

CHAPTER OUTLINE & BACKGROUND

INTRODUCTION

Welcome to the interactive part of *Romans 911*, which you can view on our website in the *Romans 911* section. I wanted there to be a connection between the book and the website with live video feed, where readers could gain a deeper connection and understanding of the book. In the videos, I have personally explained the outline of *Romans 911*, the focus of each individual chapter, my approach, and why I wrote each chapter (https://reconnectingministries.org/product/new-romans-911/).

Romans 911 is definitely not a short read, but rather a comprehensive study book, fully unpacking *The Reconnection* in *The One New Man (TONM)*, between believing Jew and Gentile in Yeshua/Jesus, and Israel and the Church.

As you will discover, *The Reconnection* has huge end-time consequences for us all. While *Romans 911* definitely deals with some very delicate issues on both sides of the family between Jew and Gentile that move us into *The Reconnection*, its main purposes and functions are to help reunite us in *TONM*, to Reconnect the Church to Israel spirituality, and to restore the Ekklesia/Church to its original Glory. We must focus on all that this means and all that lies ahead for us, as a Body so we can help complete Our Father's end-time plan on the Earth to glorify Yeshua/Jesus.

The objective of *Romans 911—Time to Sound the Alarm!* Is to serve as a comprehensive study book on *The Reconnection* in *TONM*—to fully unpack all the issues involved, bringing greater clarity and understanding—so we know how to pray to help the rest of God's family receive and move into it.

The aim of *Romans 911* is not to be fully conclusive, but rather to help motivate the Body of Messiah/Christ into *The Reconnection* so we can discover the incredible love and Glory—the unity, power, and revelation—that await us as the Church now begins to connect spiritually with an awakened Israel. I have no doubts that the more we discover this spiritual Reconnection, the more we will discover about it. This is just the beginning. But it is time now to bring it forth; to put it all out on the table; and to enter a new era of unity, Reconciliation, and fresh dialogue on all these issues. The fullness of *The Reconnection* message and the love and unity it helps to bring opens the door to greater Reconciliation in the family of God that will lead us to the Glory. It is like a power equation for the Church and Messianic bodies, the golden key to help unlock the end-time revival and power of God that we are so hungry and thirsty for. It is heaven's spiritual equation that affects everything else we do for the Kingdom of God here on the Earth.

So hold onto your horses, for you are about to embark on an amazing journey of new revelation and understanding to move us into the end times. May the God of Israel richly bless you in Yeshua/Jesus's name. Amen.

FOUR PARTS

Romans 911 is divided into four sections. Part one addresses *The Reconnection*. Part two presents a picture of what it may look like. Part three deals extensively with the obstacles and hurdles that are keeping us from it, on both sides of the family between Jew and Gentile. And part four unveils the strategy to help us get there, both corporately and individually.

PART ONE FULLY ADDRESSES THE RECONNECTION

Chapter 1: The Purpose

The Reconnection cannot be defined in one or two sentences, as it is truly multifaceted and requires a great deal of unpacking to be able to fully comprehend it. For this reason, instead of writing a lengthier introduction, I decided to dedicate the first chapter of the book for this purpose: to summarize and overview *The Reconnection* in *TONM*, so the reader has a good understanding of where we are going with the book, right from the start.

Chapter 2: The Hour before the Wedding

Need I say more! The hour before the wedding can so often be a mess and a last-minute panic, with all sorts of things going wrong. But when that Bride walks down the aisle, in all her Glory, she is just beautiful, and everything is serene. This is how it will be for those of us whose oil is burning brightly when our Bridegroom calls us and returns for His Bride. But the hour before?! This is where we are presently in the Body of Messiah/Christ between Jew and Gentile in the faith, with lots of issues still affecting us, and some without us even knowing.

Chapter 2 is perhaps one of the most sensitive and delicate chapters for our Gentile family in the book, along with chapter 7. It exposes and effectively deals with all past generational bloodline influences through our Gentile family. And it makes a very good case for how the Church in the nations has been affected by the actions of its ancestry and the continuing influences of generational antisemitism. It further explains how these influences have affected us and why up to this point, we have not been able to see the end of days, as the Father and Yeshua/Jesus see them; and why there is still so much confusion with our differing interpretations. But in order for us to get totally restored and healed from all these past influences and the way the enemy of our souls has been using it against us, we must be willing to look back to move forward and find our destinies. I felt strongly that it was important to address these issues up-front because *The Reconnection* is much more about all of the incredible, wonderful, positive elements it actually brings about, rather than the negative issues. However, without addressing, confronting, and effectively dealing with them, we remain stained by the past, and the enemy still uses it against us. It is time for the devil to be fully exposed in this place.

Chapter 2 opens the doors to the hearts of our Gentile family, to begin to receive the mercy of God for Jew and Gentile to be fully reconciled. It is one of the most powerful chapters in the book.

Chapter 3: Who Is Israel?

The thought process behind this chapter is to try to bring greater clarity and understanding to exactly who Israel is. Is the Church Israel? Is Israel the Church? And what of the physical seed of Israel, the Jewish people? What of Jewish believers, and what of God's believing children from the nations? And exactly who is the Israel of God?

Chapter 3 addresses these issues and answers these questions. How and where do we all fit in? Especially now, as we come down to the period when Israel is to be fully awakened, and the Lord is to return to us. Israel comes into her fullness, and all the different pieces begin to fall into place.

Chapter 3 also brings a greater definition to the differing paths of Israel through the teachings of the Apostle Paul, in Romans Chapter 11; both believing Jews in Yeshua/Jesus, known as the Remnant and the broken off branches that ultimately, will be restored.

In the final part of the chapter, we begin to introduce our Gentile Family to their Jewish family, honoring those who have gone before us to help pave the way.

Chapter 4: A Taste of Milk and Honey

Chapter 4 presents a taste of milk and honey—a future picture of what the world may actually look like when the Lord returns to establish His throne on the Earth. Not just the excitement of it, but also its reality. This chapter presents a freshened perspective on eschatology (end-time theology), more from a Messianic perspective. But it also challenges the preciseness of our differing eschatological views, especially the divisiveness it causes. And it challenges all believers in Yeshua/Jesus to be more tolerant and open-minded toward each other regarding end-time views. Chapter 4 ends with the seeding of the strategies and battles that lay ahead of us and what it will take to aid in establishing God's Kingdom on the Earth.

PART TWO PRESENTS A PICTURE OF WHAT THE RECONNECTION MAY LOOK LIKE

Chapter 5: If We Want the Fire, We Have to Reconnect the Wire!

Ah, the chapter we've all been waiting for. What is *The Reconnection*, what is at the heart of it, how it may benefit us, and what it may actually look like as we may move into it? Chapter 5 puts legs and a face to *The Reconnection* between God's children from the nations and the re-emerging Remnant of Israel. It proposes practical ways for us in the Church and the Messianic bodies to reunite, connect, and move into *The Reconnection*.

This chapter also emphasizes the additional power that is to be loosed upon us from heaven into the family of God, as we fully embrace this spiritual transaction between us and the subsequent unity it will help to bring to the rest of God's family. As in the chapter's title, when we Reconnect the wire, the fire of God (greater power and blessings) is loosed upon us. Chapter 5 outlines two areas of focus to help bring about *The Reconnection* through His Body: practical changes and adjustments for the Church as a whole and additional changes for Churches located in more heavily populated Jewish areas. The chapter concludes by re-emphasizing the significance of *The Reconnection* and what we can expect through it in God's plans for end-time awakening and revival, petitioning prayer for the family of God to move into it.

Chapter 6: Two Branches, One Olive Tree

Chapter 6 is definitely the lightest chapter in the book. It presents a romantic portrait of the Apostle Paul's illustration of the Olive Tree of God in Romans chapter 11. From the time of the call of Abraham until this modern day, it takes us on a spiritual journey reflecting on the family of God through Jew and Gentile, from its beginnings through its transformations and its ultimate conclusions. As we yield to our Father's plans and love for His family to be one, it gives us a picture of what the olive tree can look like and of the new life and power that will be experienced as a result of this renewed harmony between the two groups.

Chapter 6 concludes by beginning to introduce the Messianic Body to the Church, giving outline to differing Messianic expressions and ministries that have emerged through the Messianic Movement.

PART THREE DEALS WITH THE OBSTACLES AND HURDLES KEEPING US FROM THE RECONNECTION

Chapters 7 and 8 deal with some of the most delicate sensitive issues in the book, on both sides of the family. Confronting these issues head on—so we can find the necessary healing and Reconciliation in *TONM*. *Romans 911* digs up all past negative influences to fully break them off, to help us find our future and our destinies during these days. Chapter 9 addresses fivefold gifts encouraging the Body of Messiah/Christ to fully embrace them; it also addresses some of the challenges that are holding us back from them. These are very powerful chapters for all of us in the family to address and confront. I pray that God will produce the choicest of fruit in us for the Kingdom of God, as we willingly embrace them.

Chapter 7: The Christian Lens

While chapter 2 addresses generational bloodline issues affecting our hearts and souls, chapter 7 focuses on theological barriers affecting our minds and thinking in the Gentile Church. Section one in Chapter 7 exposes the false teachings of Replacement Theology, both through Islam and Christianity. On the Christian side, it explains how these teachings have fueled the divide and separation in God's family between believing Jews and Gentiles. Section two exposes the residual negative influences of these teachings and how they are still affecting the Gentile Church as a whole. This includes the part of the Church wanting to bless Israel, but still not connecting with her, as she should through *The Reconnection* and *Alignment* and the fullness of her identity through Israel.

Chapter 7 addresses the many differing eschatological views in the Church that are missing *The Reconnection*, suggesting a greater openness to Messianic viewpoints. The goal is for us to find the balance in this most significant place, in the *Father's Heart* and plans for us to be one. Section 3 offers up prayers of healing, confession, and repentance for all God's children from the nations to break off these negative influences, to rid us fully of these teachings. It challenges our scholars and teachers to rewrite Christian theology and eschatology through a renewed and Reconnected lens, fully inclusive of the Jewish branches of the faith and to bring us into a new day of togetherness and love and unity with our firstborn family.

Chapter 8: The Messianic Lens

The issues separating Jewish believers from fully Reconnecting with their Christian family are quite different from those of Gentile believers. Chapter 8 lays out these issues in the hope of bringing greater healing to the Messianic branches. Chapter 8 is also written in three parts. Part one addresses emotional and spiritual wounds that are holding Jewish and Messianic Gentile believers back from the fullness of *TONM* and fully Reconnecting with their Christian family, without any fears of losing their own identities. It also addresses false theology on the Messianic side. Chapter 8 helps to better define the call for Messianic Gentiles and encourages our Messianic family to become more united and focused on exactly what we do believe, to rid ourselves of the onslaught and confusion that is attacking the Body and dividing it. It also gets back to the basics of prayer and evangelism to win the balance of our people to Yeshua, which started the Messianic Movement in the first place.

Part two offers up prayers of healing, confession, and repentance for all Jewish believers, breaking off wounding and all negative spiritual influences, to correct Messianic theology and to fully re-embrace the believing Church and our Gentile believing family. Part three outlines the incredible blessings awaiting all Jewish believers and a Reconnected Messianic Body in *TONM*, as well as the roles we can expect to play, as Jewish believers with our Christian family.

Chapter 9: The Reconnection and the Fivefold Gifts

Chapter 9 is a most crucial chapter for our understanding in the end of days between *The Reconnection* and the fivefold gifts. It describes the connection between these two ministry focal points and shows how they are intricately linked. It also describes how the Church is now coming full circle—not only to return to its Jewish heritage in and with Israel, but also to its apostolic roots. While *Romans 911* fully embraces the re-emerging Apostolic Movement as part of God's plan, it also recognizes the obstacles holding it back, preventing the rest of the Body from entering into its fullness. This chapter voices these concerns in the hope of creating a dialogue in the Body to find greater unity and Reconciliation in these places, to enable the rest of the Body to embrace it. Chapter 9 also identifies the emergence of some of the fivefold ministries in the United States Church, showing each of their unique connections to the unveiling Israel revelation and the great need for each of them to embrace one another in this regard. Chapter 9 also introduces the Church to the emerging fivefold ministry among the Jewish branches, both in Israel and the Diaspora (dispersion into nations), which is less known up to this point in time.

Chapter 9 concludes by stressing the great need for both Jewish and Gentile Apostolic bodies to unite during these days. This new-found unity will help to lay a stronger foundation for the Church and Messianic bodies to release a greater measure of the Kingdom's authority on the Earth, both through the proper equipping of the saints for the works of ministry and a more targeted prayer and worship focus to help impact the world around us. This fivefold influence will not just affect the local Church and Messianic bodies; it will also affect regions, nations, and the world at large. It will help to awaken Israel and the last great harvest of souls.

PART FOUR UNVEILS THE STRATEGY TO MOVE US INTO THE RECONNECTION

The final section of the book outlines the strategy to move us into *The Reconnection*, both corporately and individually.

Chapter 10: The Strategy

Chapter 10 focuses on the plans of God through a new corporate wineskin and the final reforms of the Ekklesia/Church through the fivefold. The goal is to help move us out of the pew and into the works of the ministry to release greater Kingdom authority upon the Earth, wherever we may live. This chapter outlines the strategy to mobilize the Church into a greater daily prayer focus, to align with the emerging prayer movement through the Tents of David and 24/7 houses of worship and prayer and for strategic intercession, to enter a more specialized targeted type of prayer to achieve the Holy Spirit's directives. It offers practical ways for us to get involved, bringing attention to some of the new prayer ministries that have arisen. The chapter ends by putting out a call to the intercessors to unite into this fray, to theologians to replace Replacement Theology, and to all leadership everywhere to unite into this vision.

Chapter 11: The Battle Belongs to Him

The battle truly belongs to the Lord and His plans to bring about the final Reformation. Chapter 11 unveils the fullness of John 17 unity, for all of us in *TONM*, and provides a glimpse of the additional love and Glory waiting, as we Reconnect as a family. This chapter further expands on the prayer and worship strategies through a renewed focus on Jerusalem and the nations through Isaiah 62:6–7, as part of the end-time Reformation for the Church and Messianic bodies. Chapter 11 provides details for a greater strategic intercessory focus known as *Pure Intercession*, which is a supplemental prayer model to *Harp & Bowl*, and explains how to implement and manage a Strategic Intercessory group. *Romans 911* challenges all believers to reprioritize prayer as part of their everyday lives, especially for men to join the women and respond to this call with our leaders. To lead by example, to move into this prayer Reformation.

Chapter 12: The Preparation of the Bride

While most of the book has focused on more of the corporate side of the Church and the Messianic bodies, this chapter focuses on the Bride being made ready for it through our own individual walks. It offers personal insights from my own experience of greater intimacy with the Lord and explains how to more effectively walk in the Spirit to overcome the flesh, to help prepare us for the days that are ahead (see Galatians 5:16). They may be challenging, but they will be glorious for sure! Chapter 12 closes out the book with an exhortation for both Jewish and Gentile believers to get it right. The book ends with a challenge for all believers to join the Ezekiel Generation and to count the cost of the commitment toward the Jewish people.

ENDORSEMENTS FOR ROMANS 911– TIME TO SOUND THE ALARM!

Romans 911 has been endorsed by *twenty-four* elders—
twelve from the Messianic Body and
twelve from the Gentile Church, plus *five* prayer leaders.

PLEASE NOTE WHEN READING THE ENDORSEMENTS:

- Endorsements from Messianic leaders follow on the **right side** of the pages with the Star of David logo.

- Endorsements from American Church leaders follow on the **left side** of the pages with the Cross logo.

ENDORSEMENTS FROM THE COMMONWEALTH OF ISRAEL (UNITED STATES)

1. *Romans 911,* by Grant Berry, illustrates the truth of Psalm 133, "Behold, how good and how pleasant it is for brethren to dwell together in unity!" Berry has made it his mission to sound the trumpets and bring revelation to the Church and the Messianic community the necessity for prayer to bring about the four R's: repentance, Reconciliation, Reconnection and ultimately revival. *Romans 911* awakens us to practical action toward *The Reconnection* of the two branches on the one olive tree (in Romans 11), which is unto the essential Reformation of the Church and the awakening of Israel to Yeshua/Jesus. *Romans 911* is full of poten-

tial to bring relational healing between both the Church and Jewish believers, of anti-Semitism, resentment, rejection, and misunderstanding. Grant Berry is timely with this truly powerful book, as not only is Reconnection at hand, but revival of the nations is at stake.

DR. CHÉ AHN
PRESIDENT, HARVEST INTERNATIONAL MINISTRY
FOUNDING PASTOR, HROCK CHURCH, PASADENA, CALIFORNIA;
INTERNATIONAL CHANCELLOR, WAGNER UNIVERSITY

2. One of the most incredible truths revealed by God to mankind was the Covenant that He made to Abram, who became Abraham—His offspring, His firstborn, a mighty nation, His inheritance. Many years later, God, through His own son, *Yeshua,* then offered all mankind the ability to enter this inheritance. Those who would be grafted into Israel; into the power of this inheritance that was created from God and Abraham's union, would have access to all the blessings of the agreement that was made between the two. Through the family of Abraham and the patriarchs, God had an incredible plan to bless mankind.

God's goal has always been to draw together men and women from every tribe and tongue and language. He wants

Endorsements from Israel (Land and Diaspora)

1. *Romans 911* is written from the heart of a prophetic intercessor with keen insight into the Bible. It is not just another message about the God's election of Israel and its salvation, rather it is about the nature of the preparation to the Church for its roles with Israel and the nations. The importance of worldwide revival, the harvest of the nations, and the Preparation of the Bride are all foundational. But none of this will take place without it being prayed into existence. My friend Mike Bickle of the international House of Prayer teaches that God works in history through prayer. He reveals his plan to us and then we are called to pray what He reveals into reality. We are his partners. So here is a book with vast vision with a call for

prayer on the largest level of world concern. Combining eschatology and prayer is a rare but crucial direction, and we have it in this book.

May God richly bless those who read this book and go forth in commitment to its vision.

DANIEL JUSTER, TH.D.
RESTORATION FROM ZION OF TIKKUN GLOBAL

2. This book provides a blueprint for Restoration and Realignment between the Church and Israel. It is a must-read for those seeking true unity and Reconciliation, which will result in the final harvest of souls, the greatest revival the world has ever seen.

JONATHAN BERNIS
PRESIDENT AND CEO,
JEWISH VOICE MINISTRIES, INTERNATIONAL

2. continued...
every expression of humanity to join in a great symphony of praise to God. He wants believing Jews and believing Gentiles to come together as "One New Man" in Messiah (Eph. 4), and walk together in Abraham's Covenant blessing through Israel.

This is an hour when God is shaking the Church into a new level of reality. Grant Berry is one who understands this key for the Church. ***Romans—911 It's Time to Sound the Alarm!*** is just the book to help you understand where God's Kingdom is headed in the days ahead.

DR. CHUCK D. PIERCE
PRESIDENT, GLOBAL SPHERES, INC.;
PRESIDENT, GLORY OF ZION INTERNATIONAL MINISTRIES

3. I have known and mentored Grant Berry since the middle 1980s. Even though "the Jews are back," both in the land of their inheritance and many coming to believe in Yeshua as their Messiah like never before since the first century, most of the Church is unaware of this amazing phenomenon and of its significance in God's end-time plan. Grant has taken what I call "the forgotten chapters" of Romans 9 to 11 to show what God has in mind for us now with the full Restoration of the

The One New Man between believing Jews and Gentiles and the intricate connection of Israel's spiritual awakening and the last great harvest of souls. May Grant's words be another powerful force to awaken the Church during these days.

DON FINTO
FOUNDER, PRESIDENT, CALEB GLOBAL,
"EQUIPPING THE CHURCH TO UNDERSTAND, EMBRACE, AND PARTICIPATE IN GOD'S BIBLICAL PLAN FOR ISRAEL AND THE JEWISH PEOPLE AND ITS RELATIONSHIP TO WORLD AWAKENING IN OUR DAY."

3. The olive tree parable in the Epistle to the Romans speaks of the mystery of the relationship between Israel and the Church. While the Apostle Paul wrote this almost two thousand years ago, its significance has grown as the prophecy has developed through history. Today with the international Church, the Restoration of the State of Israel, and the Messianic Remnant of

Jewish believers in Yeshua, the whole issue is coming to a fullness. Grant has dealt with the complexities of this prophetic revelation in a sensitive and well-thought-out manner and especially the focus on the emerging prayer movement to help bring it to pass.

ASHER INTRATER
FOUNDER REVIVE ISRAEL, PRESIDENT TIKKUN GLOBAL

4. This is God's time to favor Israel. This is God's time to evangelize Israel. This book will help the believing Jew and believing Gentile be one—so the world will believe!
SID ROTH
HOST, "IT'S SUPERNATURAL!"

5. Grant Berry's passion for the mutually honoring union of Jewish and Gentile believers in Yeshua pulsates with every page. This is a heart-born exploration of prophetic Scripture that brings fresh clarity to Romans 9-11. Berry calls us all to our strategic participation in God's end-time plan.
EITAN SHISHKOFF
FOUNDING DIRECTOR, TENTS OF MERCY NETWORK KIRYAT YAM, ISRAEL; VICE PRESIDENT OF TIKKUN GLOBAL

4. "I met Grant Berry in 1986, first in New York City when I was on prayer missions with Dick Simmons of Men for Nations. Grant was a young believer at that time and was just beginning to learn the art of intercession. Then later on in the 1990s when we were both on an intercessory mission to Moscow, Russia, in a burned, broken-down synagogue that we visited for prayer. By the leading of the Holy Spirit I helped to position Grant into what turned out to be a prophetic proclamation and breakthrough of intercessory prayer for his future mission work among the Russian Jews through the Passover celebration.

Grant has a huge heart for the lost sheep of Israel, but also for God's family to be reunited in *The One New Man*, which is now his full-time missionary focus, to help lead us into God's end-time plans and purposes. His latest book, *Romans 911*, puts a face and legs to this renewed unity between believing Jews and Gentiles, which will help to lead to the fulfillment of biblical prophecy concerning Israel's salvation and the end-time harvest of souls. Grant takes us to the next level in

this process, addressing the issues that keep us apart while mobilizing strategic, informed intercession spawned on by the Holy Spirit. *Romans 911* is a great read for every believer who desires to see an end-time revival and Jesus Christ receive the rewards for His suffering.

JAMES W. GOLL
FOUNDER OF GOD ENCOUNTERS MINISTRIES,
INTERNATIONAL SPEAKER AND
AUTHOR AND LIFE LANGUAGE TRAINER

6. How can Jewish and Gentile believers become One New Man in the Messiah without losing their distinct identities—without Jews becoming Gentiles and Gentiles becoming Jews? Grant Berry takes seriously the Lord's prayer in

John 17 for our unity and offers practical, Holy Spirit-based solutions for coming together in Jesus/Yeshua. And rather than focusing on outward peripherals, he points us to the heart of God, speaking the truth in love.

Dr. Michael L. Brown

author, host "The Line of Fire" radio-TV program

7. As I read the manuscript of Grant Berry's book *Romans 911*, I could see a picture unfold in my spirit. I was observing the gathering described in 1 Chronicles 12, where those who knew it was time to make David King were gathered. As I watched the different discussions and debates that were taking place, I realized that something similar is taking place today. There are gatherings of men and women in the Body of Messiah/Christ who understand that much of the Church is failing to understand God's prophetic purposes for the Church and the Jewish people. They are the ones who realize how significant the Reconciliation between the Body of Messiah/Christ and the Jewish people is, not only for the advancement of God's Kingdom purposes but for ushering in the return of the Lord.

Grant Berry is one of the Jewish leaders in the Body of Messiah/Christ who, like his ancient predecessors gathered with King David to fulfill God's plans, has been called and anointed to further these Reconciliations and Restorations. His book should hold a prominent place in the discussions and debates revolving around the issues concerning the Restoration of God's present prophetic purposes. Addressing such subjects as anti-Semitism, Replacement Theology, prophetic intercession, and the emergence of *The One New Man*, Grant is rightfully and prophetically placing them as issues that the Body of Messiah/

5. "Reconnection" is a word that implies there was first a "disconnect." That is certainly true as regards the Church and Israel, Jew and Gentile. In this comprehensive study book, Grant Berry takes us through the issues and obstacles inhibiting us from Reconnection, from becoming *The One New*  *Man*, and proposes practical ways for the Church and Messianic bodies to reunite and become catalysts to aid in Israel's spiritual awakening. The end-time consequence of this Reconnection will be nothing less than worldwide revival and the greatest harvest of souls.

JANE HANSEN HOYT
PRESIDENT/CEO, AGLOW INTERNATIONAL

6. Grant Berry, a mature and experienced Messianic Jew of strong biblical conviction, has felt the Father's heart regarding the unity God longs for among ALL His people. In *Romans 911* Grant challenges conventional Christian thought that relegates to irrelevance Israel, the God-purposed other half of *The One New Man*. For the Body of Messiah to be fully functional in a needy  universe, Grant makes clear only mutual edification of Messianic Jews and Christians will send that unmistakable message of God's unity, love and anointing that will awaken mankind to Yeshua, the King of Israel and the Savior of all.

RAYMOND L. GANNON, PH.D.
VICE PRESIDENT FOR ACADEMIC AFFAIRS,
MESSIANIC JEWISH BIBLE INSTITUTE

7. continued...
Christ must address and rectify.

As one who has been on this battlefield since 1992, I recommend *Romans 911* for your study and discussion. I pray that what you learn from this book will inspire you to seek the Lord on a deeper

level and to respond in faith and obedience to what He shows you to do. May it help you to become one of the "sons (and daughters) of Issachar" who gathered with David because they *"understood the times and had knowledge of what Israel should do"* (1 Chronicles 12:32).

DR. HOWARD MORGAN
AUTHOR, PROPHETIC TEACHER, PRESIDENT, AND FOUNDER, HOWARD MORGAN MINISTRIES, AND KINGDOM MINISTRIES INTERNATIONAL

8. According to Isaiah 25:7–8, there's a veil over all the nations concerning the Nation of Israel that God will remove as He

takes away the reproach of His people and wipes away the tears from all faces in these last days. Grant Berry does a wonderful job in helping to remove the veil as he connects the grafted in branches back to the ancient olive tree, Israel.

PASTOR MARK BILTZ, EL SHADDAI MINISTRIES

9. With typical Grant Berry enthusiasm, *Romans 911—It's Time to Sound the Alarm!* certainly hits the mark. Grant has plowed the field of the *The One New Man* theology by utilizing every opportunity the LORD has provided to bring Messianic Jews and Christians together. *Romans 911* expresses a theology that goes beyond mere mental exercises and reaches into the very heart of G-D to demonstrate a dynamic spiritual existence that reflects the hope and life of New Testament writings. A must-read!

RABBI MARTY WALDMAN
EXECUTIVE GENERAL SECRETARY, TOWARD JERUSALEM COUNCIL II

7. In *Romans 911*, Grant gives a fresh and prophetic look at *The One New Man*. Paul calls this Jewish and Gentile connection a mystery that is now fully revealed (Eph. 3).

I don't think Paul ever imagined this truth would still be such a mystery to so many in our generation. This secret was out two thousand years ago, and Grant illuminates the practical ways Jewish and Gentile believers can honor one another and walk out their special callings and identities. I encourage you to prayerfully read this work and ask God to give you inspiring insights.

WAYNE WILKS JR., PH.D
ASSOCIATE SENIOR PASTOR,
GATEWAY CHURCH, JEWISH MINISTRY;
PRESIDENT EMERITUS, MESSIANIC JEWISH BIBLE INSTITUTE

8. There is much discussion about the need for Christian unity. However, almost all of it neglects the historic and foundational connections to God's work through the children of Abraham, the Jews. This neglect is sometimes due to theological implications, sometimes intentional, and sometimes by simple lack of awareness. But thankfully there is a move of the Holy Spirit in opening our eyes to our Jewish brothers and sisters and what it means for Jewish followers of Yeshua to be recognized, affirmed, and encouraged. Grant Berry gives us a readable introduction to the critical issues facing Jew and Gentile as we come together in the Body of our one Lord,

Jesus the Messiah. This book is informative, insightful, and engaging. Berry's approach affirms the rich heritage of Jewish and Gentile Christians and how we can benefit from how the Spirit is at work through us to reveal the Glory of God in our time.

DR. DOUG BEACHAM
GENERAL SUPERINTENDENT,
INTERNATIONAL PENTECOSTAL HOLINESS CHURCH

10. Romans chapters 9 through 11 chronicle the pinnacle of Paul's ministry. Grant meticulously guides us up this lofty pathway as he points out the stumbling stones of misguided theology, then directs us along the trusty trail where Yeshua's plans for Reconciliation and unity find their solid

foundations. Grant reveals how our God-given identity in Yeshua has been established to prepare His Body for the end times. *Romans 911* is an essential and timely resource to part the clouds of confusion regarding the person and purpose for *The One New Man*.

ROBERT WOLFF
CEO, MAJESTIC GLORY MINISTRIES

11. This book is a clarion call for the believing Remnant of Israel and the faithful Church to join together for the one thing that changes everything—prayer. Passionate, personal, and practical, this book is a comprehensive framework for how *The One New Man* can pursue its glorious fullness in the days leading to the end times. We know that prayer works, yet Grant proposes that the very catalyst for world redemp-

tion and for Yeshua's return is the unified and intentional prayer of the Bride. Don't just read this book for the solid theology, let it propel you to engage with your communities and cities in the prayer that will prepare for and hasten the day of Messiah's return!

BENJAMIN JUSTER
UNITED STATES, DIRECTOR, TIKKUN GLOBAL

9. In Revelation 2:7, Yeshua says, "Whoever has ears, let them hear what the Spirit is saying to the Churches." If you want to hear what the Holy Spirit is saying to His Churches today, a good place to begin is Grant Berry's book, *Romans 911—It's Time to Sound the Alarm!*

As I've traveled and ministered around the world, I've seen two issues emerge at the forefront of the Holy Spirit's work today. The first is *The Reconnection* of the Gentile Church with Messianic Israel to form the "one new man" of Ephesians 2:15. The other issue is the raising up of an apostolic wineskin where five-fold ministry can equip every believer to minister with power (Eph. 4:11-16). I believe the end result of these changes will be a Church that operates in supernatural power to birth worldwide revival—the "life from the dead" of Romans 11:15.

Grant Berry's cutting-edge book deals with both of these issues in a thoughtful and thought-provoking way, challenging both Gentile and Messianic believers to move forward in the Spirit into Reconnection and full Restoration!

I highly recommend this book.

Dr. Robert Heidler
apostolic teacher, Glory of Zion International Ministries

10. I highly respect and appreciate Grant Berry. He lives this message every day of his life. I have seen him with humility and grace along with boldness and directness communicate this message to the Gentile Church. I've also seen him with the Messianic Jewish believers stand out with courage and clarity in pointing them to Reconnection with the Gentile Church.

This book is laid out logically and comprehensively. It is a sharp prophetic tool that I believe God will use to cut out the cancer in the global Body of believers that will heal the division, mistrust, and pain that exists among both Jewish and Gentile believers.

12. At a time when cultural revolutions are sparking and the words of the the Lord Yeshua/Jesus and His prophetic voices are coming to pass, I could think of no better message to embrace than Romans 911. There are very few messengers who have imbibed this critical message with their   whole heart. Grant Berry is one who has been called and anointed for such a time and purpose as this. I wholeheartedly encourage every born-again believer to read and follow our brother on his journey of being faithful to call us to these critical, life-changing truths.

MATTHEW SMOLER
MISSIONARY, IHOPKC ISRAEL MANDATE INITIATIVES
AND TIKKUN GLOBAL AMBASSADOR

10. continued...

Grant writes with authority from experience, with vulnerability and rawness, and logic that is both simple and clear for the readers.

I highly recommend this book. I believe it is relevant for every believer on the Earth. I pray 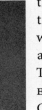 that this book will truly bring Restoration to the Body through Reconnection, which will then bring revival to Israel and all nations!

Tod McDowell
EXECUTIVE DIRECTOR,
CALEB GLOBAL MINISTRIES

11. Grant Berry, in his new book *Romans 911,* writes with intense passion as well as real depth of theological understanding about the crucial need for a true Reconnection of Israel and the Gentile Church in fulfillment of God's purpose for our time. Jesus' prayer of John 17 that we might be "one so that the world would believe" especially involves Jewish and Gentile believers coming into a familial unity that will have a catalytic impact, not only on reaching the rest of the Jewish people, but also on the remaining unreached peoples of our world. This healed and restored relationship, Berry maintains, will also help prepare the Bride of Christ for His second coming.

As an intercessor himself, Berry understands that united, authoritative prayer will play an all-important role for this Reconciliation and rejoining of Jews and Gentiles in the one eternal family our God is currently building. He calls on followers of Jesus to join the battle as "recon warriors" to love, pray and witness so that the Gospel may go "first to the Jew and then to the Gentile"  in order that the broken-off branches will be restored to their Messiah and to the end that "all Israel will be saved." You will find *Romans 911* a compelling road map for effective prayer and action toward this essential prophetic milestone in the fulfillment of God's purpose for all of humanity.

John Robb
CHAIRMAN, INTERNATIONAL PRAYER COUNCIL; FACILITATOR, WORLD PRAYER ASSEMBLY; CONVENER, NATIONAL PRAYER ASSEMBLY (USA)

12. We have the privilege of living in the greatest time in Church history. One of the keys to navigating this season is to embrace God's passion to position His Body correctly. In *Romans 911*, my friend Grant Berry gives an essential key in God's Restoration of the Church as expressed in the  Apostle Paul's epistle to the Church at Ephesus, "so as to create in Himself one new man from the two, thus making peace" (Ephesians 2:15). This book is timely, practical, revelatory, and a gift from Heaven to all who desire God's fullness in this season in the Earth.

ABNER SUAREZ
AUTHOR AND SPEAKER, FOR SUCH A TIME AS THIS

Endorsements From Prayer Leadership (United States)

1. The Lord has given Grant Berry profound understanding into the relationship of Israel and the Church!  *Romans 911* is a great gift to the Body of Christ and *The Reconnection* of Jew and Gentile, as we labor together in the power of God's Spirit for the Glory of God's name! May the Lord use this book to bring about a glorious Christ awakening and all for the Glory of the Lamb!

Dr. Jason Hubbard
EXECUTIVE DIRECTOR, LIGHT OF THE WORLD PRAYER CENTER

2. I recommend *Romans 911* to everyone as a window into the heart of God for Israel and the Jewish people. Grant is an incredible bridge-builder and catalyst for John 17 unity. He's so good at calling us to repentance in a spirit of love and gentleness, without condemnation. Through my friendship with Grant  and through this book, I've seen a personal breakthrough in my heart to pray for Israel. Whereas before, I prayed for them out of duty, the Holy Spirit has done a work in my heart and I now love to pray for the completion of God's purposes for his "firstborn" in the family of God.

Jonathan Friz
FOUNDER, 10 Days of Prayer

3. I highly recommend *Romans 911* to ALL fellow intercessors seeking our Father's deliverance and destiny of the nations.  This anointed book by Grant Berry provides practical insights into our critical role in prayer, *The One New Man* movement, the end-time harvest, and the glorious return of King Yeshua. "Now is the time to sound the alarm!"

Dai Sup Han
NATIONAL FACILITATOR, PRAYER SURGE NOW!

4. The importance of Reconnecting the purposes of the Church and the purposes of Israel in these last days cannot be overstated. In the book *Romans 911*, Grant has drawn from the deep well of age-old prophecies and has brought up to the surface a perspective that brings their intended impact to our current generation. This is not a book to be read casually but with reflection, expectation and response. The Holy Spirit is  orchestrating the "Great Reconnection" that will awaken both Jew and Gentile in Yeshua/Jesus, to the expressed will of God found in Ephesians 1:9 "bringing together all things in Heaven and on Earth together in Messiah."

GARY DePASQUALE
FOUNDER AND EXECUTIVE DIRECTOR, INTERNATIONAL HOUSE OF PRAYER, EASTERN GATE, NEW JERSEY

5. *Romans 911* is a wake-up call to the Gentile Church of God's amazing prophetic plan in *The One New Man* leading up to the Lord's return. God's chosen people of Israel remain the apple of His eye. We Gentile believers must be led by the Spirit into the Father's ways for how all of Israel will be saved rather than presume what it will look like (given the Church has been led by Gentiles for so long). As we see more Jewish people longing for Messiah, our mandate as Gentile co-laborers is: pray to the Lord of the Harvest for Messianic five-fold harvest workers  to come forth, lovingly introduce them to Yeshua Hamashiach, and help graft them back into their own olive tree, rather than into Gentile Church traditions. I thank God for you my brother, in writing such an important book!

GREGG HEALEY
PARTNER, NATIONAL HALL CAPITAL PRAYER,
AND UNITY CATALYST, IMPACT CONNECTICUT AND THE NEW ENGLAND ALLIANCE

WORDING AND TERMINOLOGY IN ROMANS 911

URING THIS TRANSITORY period in the Body of Messiah/
Christ in *The One New Man (TONM)*, it is helpful to create
terms that enable us to describe the process we are entering
into between Jewish and Gentile believers, and between Israel and
the Church. *The Reconnection* is one of these phrases, and it is used
as an umbrella term to incorporate all different aspects of this process that are reuniting the family of God. I also use the term to
communicate the heart of this transaction from the Father to personally reunite Jewish and Gentile believers.

For example, through *The Restoration* in *TONM*, we all receive
healing. Through *The Reconnection*, we reconcile and reunite with
one another. And through *The Realignment*, we begin to live and
act out our new roles and lives together as a united family under
the God of Israel. With this in mind, there are times that I use "*The
Reconnection*" phrase on its own, and there are times when I join
it to the others to better define the process. I also capitalize these
terms to highlight them and bring more attention to them.

DUAL LANGUAGE

In *Romans 911*, I use what I refer to as "dual language" when writing
Christian and Messianic terms. For example, with the use of the
name *Jesus* for our Lord, which is the Greek-translated name of
our Messiah, for our Jewish-believing brothers and sisters, I use
His Hebrew name, *Yeshua*. For *Christ*, I use *Mashiach* (Mashiach/
Christ), and for the *Body of Christ*, I write *Body of* Messiah/Christ.
You might also be surprised to hear that our Lord was never called
Jesus while here on the Earth and in His ministry; rather, He was
called by His Hebrew name, *Yeshua*.

Please understand that I personally have no problem with the use of Christian terms, and I have great love and respect for my believing Gentile family who uses them. However, from a Jewish persective, many of these names and terms have been used in the past against the Jewish people to persecute them. So what might be near and dear to us is most definitely not to them or to most Messianic (Jewish) believers who choose to relate to our Lord using Hebrew wording or other English terms. An example of this is the name for *Ekklesia* (Greek), which in English is translated as *Church*. Because of past persecution, most Jewish people will not go near a Church or anything associated with it. So Messianic believers in Yeshua will use *Congregation* in its place, and sometimes, when referring to the Body, they will use Ekklesia. For this reason, I use Church and Ekklesia/Church interchangeably, depending on my emphasis.

These are a few examples of the dual langauge I use in the book and in my other writings to be sensitive to this. To honor both my Jewish and Gentile believing family, I use both Christian and Messianic terms. Plus, when I teach Christians to share the Good News with their Jewish friends and neighbors, I strongly emphasize the use of Messianic terms in our dialogue, as it is important to defuse these barriers as much as possible when sharing Yeshua with them. The heart of the Apostle Paul might help here; he was a Jew to the Jews and a Gentile to the Gentiles (see 1 Corinthians 9:19–23). What mattered most is that Mashiach/Christ is proclaimed.

I think it is important during these days of Israel's awakening that we all learn to become more sensitive to this. I have written about this in more depth in this book.

Romans 911 is all about Jewish and Gentile-believing issues, so it is necessary in the book to use terms that help bring greater definition. For this reason, I do not often use the term *Christian* to describe believers, because this could include both Jewish and Gentile believers but instead, *Jewish (or Messianic)* and *Gentile believers* or *Gentile-believing Church* and *Messianic Body* for corporate references, so you know who I am referring to in the text.

When Jesus or Yeshua is possessive (Jesus's), I usually use one or the other or Yeshua/Jesus's.

OTHER WORDS OR TERMS

- **Antisemitism**—I chose to use this spelling from the *International Holocaust Remembrance Alliance* because it ties more effectively to antisemitism against the Jewish people, as opposed to all other Semitic races.[1]

- *satan*—I do not capitalize this name for the devil because he is not worthy of it.

- *The Reconnection, The Realignment, The One New Man (TONM), Pure Intercession, Strategic Intercession and The Galatians Process*—These terms and words are both capitalized and italicized, owing to their importance in the text. Also, after the term *The One New Man* is presented, I have abbreviated the term as *TONM* thereafter.

- All **God names** and terms are capitalized, as well as any terms that are associated with Him, such as Your or Glory, etc.

- All **R words** tied into the Reconnection such as Restoration, Reconciliation, and Realignment (including Alignment), are capitalized to bring greater emphasis to God's end-time plans.

- The word **Remnant** is used in a couple of different ways in Romans 911. First, to refer to the Remnant of Israel. These are Jewish believers in Mashiach/ Christ that Paul writes about in the first six verses of Romans 11. Second, to the Remnant in the Ekklesia/

Church and the prayer movement who are crying out in prayer for reform and change to come to the Body of Messiah/Christ.

- **Servitudel** – This is a new word created to describe how fivefold leadership should operate and function

FOREWORD

I AM VERY PLEASED to write this introduction and recommend this important book by my friend and colleague, Grant Berry. There are many books on the subject of preparation and the last days before the coming of the Lord. Grant Berry's book, *Romans 911*, is a preparation for the Restoration of the Church and Israel that rightly perceives Romans chapters 9–11 as the key texts for the last days. However, this book, written from the heart of a prophetic intercessor with keen insight into the Bible, is not just another message about God's election of Israel and its salvation. Rather, it is about the nature of the preparation to the Church for its roles with Israel and the nations. The importance of worldwide revival, the harvest of the nations, and the Preparation of the Bride are all foundational. But none of this will take place without it being prayed into existence. My friend, Mike Bickle, of the International House of Prayer, teaches that God works in history through prayer. He reveals his plan to us, and then we are called to pray what He reveals into reality. We are His partners. So here is a book with vast vision with a call for prayer on the largest level of world concern. Combining eschatology and prayer is a rare but crucial direction, and we have it in this book.

I have studied theology for many years and also write theology. However, after a lifetime of ministry and writing theology, I am looking for those books that ignite passion. Lasting passion and conviction are needed in this hour. So in this book, we have something that ignites fire in the heart and draws people into it.

May God richly bless those who read this book and go forth in commitment to its vision.

—DANIEL JUSTER, THD,

RESTORATION FROM ZION OF TIKKUN GLOBAL

CHAPTER OUTLINE

PART I: THE RECONNECTION

PART II: THE ONE NEW MAN, TOGETHER AGAIN

PART III: OBSTACLES TO THE RECONNECTION

or Replacement Theology in every Christian heart and throughout the Church.

Exposing false theology and barriers among Messianic Jews that prevent unity with their Gentile family and ownership of *The Reconnection*, including the remedy of identificational repentance. We all need healing.

Prayers of confession, renouncement, and repentance to break off all past negative influences in our generational bloodlines of any wrong attitudes toward our Gentile family and the Church.

What we can expect as Jewish believers who embrace *The Reconnection*.

A description of *The Reconnection's* emergence through the "Fivefold Ministry Gifts" across Church and Messianic Expressions.

PART IV: PRAY! PRAY! PRAY!

The strategy implemented to achieve *The Reconnection*.

Part I

THE RECONNECTION

CHAPTER 1

THE PURPOSE

BEFORE YOU START to read *Romans 911*, I want to be as clear as possible in stating the objective. While I focus mainly on this Reconnection in *The One New Man (TONM)* between Jew and Gentile, it is not the main goal. The objective is to fully restore the love and unity in God's family, according to John 17, so that Yeshua/Jesus can send His Glory upon us. I believe this will help lay down the pathway for the last great awakening, for the fullness of the Gentiles to come in, and for Israel's salvation, which ultimately will lead us to the Lord's return.

This is our mission; however, I believe that this Reconnection message is at the heart of this Restoration and is foundational to the rest. So, focusing on this part of God's plan first opens the door to the balance; this is our approach. It is like a golden key and needs to be recognized as such throughout the Church at large. Metaphorically speaking, embracing *The Reconnection* message in the love of the Father leads us onto a bridge we call "Restoration." This leads God's children from the nations into a Reconnection and Realignment with the Remnant of Israel relationally, which empowers the Body to greater healing in all other areas. This Reconciliation has everything to do with God's end-time plans coming forth during these days.

The Lord has given a number of us in the Body of Messiah/Christ a burden to communicate the need for a greater sense of unity and Reconnection between Jewish (Messianic) and Gentile believers in *TONM*, otherwise known as the *Israel Piece*. This is in fulfillment of God's end-time plans related to Israel and the Church. But we've been so focused on waving this banner in front of the Church, trying to get it to understand the significance of this connection, that very little has actually been written to help us move into it.

I wrote *Romans 911* for this purpose—to support the Church and Messianic bodies, from our leadership to our intercessors and laypeople, and to provide a comprehensive study book on this subject. The book will help us fully embrace *The Reconnection* in *TONM* by adapting it into our local Churches, Congregations, and communities. Israel's awakening has begun. Since the retaking of Jerusalem in 1967, more Messianic believers are coming to the Lord than ever before. *Romans 911* fully explains the *Father's Heart* in relation to *The Reconnection* and the great need for unity in *TONM* to be fully restored in accordance with Ephesians 2:14–22.

While I focus mainly on this Reconnection in The One New Man (TONM) between Jew and Gentile, it is not the main goal. The objective is to fully restore the love and unity in God's family, according to John 17, so that Yeshua/Jesus can send His Glory upon us.

Romans 911 simplifies and clarifies *The Reconnection* as a vital link for God's children from the nations to Reconnect with the Remnant of Israel and to our Jewish roots and heritage. I also wrote it to help Jewish (Messianic) believers Reconnect spiritually with their Gentile-believing family, even as the mystery of Israel's spiritual unveiling and the fullness of souls from the nations comes into being (see Romans 11:25–32).

A UNIQUE TRANSACTION

A unique transaction is about to take place in the Body of Messiah/ Christ as we reunite through the love of God in *TONM* between Jew and Gentile. It is a remarriage of sorts, with both sides contributing something unique and special, but it can be experienced only after the union has taken place.

Romans 911 emphasizes this spiritual Reconnection and the incredible power and blessings that await a Reconnected Church from the Heart of God. If their rejection brought Reconciliation to the world, what will their acceptance be but life from the dead? (See Romans 11:15.) The book helps us recognize all that is associated with the mystery of Israel's spiritual rebirth and how it affects us, as well as the adjustments we need to make to help bring it to fruition.

Romans 911 presents the *Israel Piece* (Reconnecting the Gentile-believing Remnant [Gentile-believing Church] to the Jewish-believing Remnant to awaken the balance of Israel and the fullness of the Gentiles) as a golden key—the final piece of the puzzle in our Father's plan to restore and reform the Church toward Israel that more fully ignites the rest. It also explores how the Church will be the catalyst to help bring about Israel's awakening. If we want the fire, we need to first Reconnect the wire! The Reconnection is a key to this end-time revival.

> *Romans 911 presents the Israel Piece as a golden key—the final piece of the puzzle in our Father's plan to restore and reform the Church toward Israel that more fully ignites the rest.*

Romans 911 unveils God's Glory plan to Reconnect His family through Israel's spiritual awakening. It helps us see the broken branches of Israel (Jewish people not yet believing in Yeshua) by faith, as the Word tells us they will be and not as they are at this time. It recognizes that the existing veil and blindness over them are temporal. It Reconnects the Church toward Israel and specifically to the current Body of Messianic believers (known as "the Remnant"), in a reuniting of *TONM*. And it Reconnects Jewish believers to their Gentile family in Mashiach/Christ.

Through *The Reconnection* in our *Father's Heart,* the joined Body of Jewish and Gentile believers becomes the *catalyst* and *salvific agent* to help bring about the fullness of Israel's rebirth, which, in turn, will help release the greater harvest and end-time gathering of souls from the nations. This will come through a fresh focus on love, unity, and praise and worship, intercessory prayer, and evangelism through the Holy Spirit's power and guidance. It will complete the family of God in these final days and prepare the Bride for His coming. *Romans 911* helps facilitate and introduce this topic through a fresh perspective of love, liberty, and tolerance for each other in how we express our faith and connection to God through Yeshua/Jesus.

UNDERSTANDING THE FULLNESS OF THE RECONNECTION

People often ask me to explain the fullness of *The Reconnection* in a forty-minute sermon. This is simply not possible, owing to complexities between Messianic and Gentile believers in the family of God and between Israel and the Church, which require a great deal of unpacking, not to mention the mystery, significance, and end-time role of an awakened Israel. An unraveling of these complexities is required before any simple explanation of *The Reconnection* can be attempted, including the history of *TONM*, the unity, the love, the power that changed the world, the schism, the wounding, the generational bloodlines, the sibling issues between Messianic and Gentile believers, the theology and eschatology, and many other related issues.

The Reconnection in TONM is fraught with obstacles and barriers on both sides of the Messianic and Church bodies that cannot be overcome in our own strength and ability.

The devil understands the significance of unity between Jewish and Gentile believers in God's family and with the Father and the Son. He understands the outflow of love, power, and Reconciliation that will come from it, and he shudders at the thought of full and complete Reconnection, even as his demise draws ever closer. For this reason, *The Reconnection* in *TONM* is fraught with obstacles and barriers on both sides of the Messianic and Church bodies that cannot be overcome in our own strength and ability.

Simply put, these mountains are too high for us to climb. But we serve a God of impossibilities Who has chosen this time of mercy for His family to reconcile and reunite. He has ordained for these mountains to tumble into the sea and that all things be put under His feet so His end-time plans can take place. He has ordained for His *mercy oil* to be unleashed on us so that we can find the healing and Reconciliation that are needed as a family to come together again in the fullness of *TONM*, in which the Church operated during the first century.

In this day, different from others, we will begin to see *The Reconnection* move toward center stage to see how God will use it to heal the divisions in His Church and Messianic bodies. This will shift us into His end-time plans. Although *The Reconnection* isn't all that God is doing on the Earth, we will begin to recognize its significance and how important it is for us to fully embrace it at this time. In addition to which, God will shift events in our world for all of this to take place, as it must come to pass and is a stepping stone to restoring unity in the balance of God's family. *The Reconnection* becomes a power source for the rest.

Romans 911 and its Reconnecting message will challenge you at some point, whether you are a Messianic or Gentile believer. But *The Reconnection* is drawn from the Word of God, informed with a renewed perspective based on a *unique hour* and time of history. This is a time that has been *hidden* from past generations and must be proclaimed into the heavenly realms to deal a death blow to the spiritual principalities that are misaligned with God's dominion and authority for His Kingdom to come upon Earth.

The Reconnection in the *Father's Heart* will transform God's family, along with a number of other reforms greatly needed in the Gentile Church and Messianic bodies. It does require repentance that will open the door to the changes God needs to make, both individually and corporately, in the Body of Messiah/Christ. In this light, we need to be willing to humble ourselves and open our hearts to receive all that God is giving out in this hour. We also must be *vigilant* to fully expose the real enemy, who is aligned against us to keep us apart.

As a result, my assignment from the Holy Spirit is twofold: first, to fully unpack *The Reconnection* message in *TONM* and simplify it so that anyone can understand it. Second, my task is to mobilize the Body of Messiah/Christ into this end-time fray to help complete the job.

I addressed many issues that tie into *The Reconnection* in my second book, *The Ezekiel Generation,* which introduces the message, especially the subtle influences of generational antisemitism on God's children from the nations. Both books work hand in hand to provide a complete picture. However, *Romans 911* trumpets *The Reconnection* and identifies the ways we should apply it in our everyday lives. It is the next step for the Body of Messiah/Christ.

THE DISCONNECTION

The title of the book, *Romans 911,* has a dual purpose. First, it refers to the focus on chapters 9–11 of the book of Romans, in which the Apostle Paul outlines God's plans and purposes for Israel and the Church. Second, it serves to blow a prophetic shofar (911)—a trumpet blast and holy alarm into the Body of Messiah/Christ, whose eyes are still veiled to *The Reconnection. Romans 911* exposes all aspects of antisemitism, blatant and generational, as well as the lasting effects of Replacement Theology on our Gentile family of believers. *Romans 911* demonstrates how this spirit has caused the Church to be in error regarding Israel and eschatology, and it exposes reasons why the Messianic family remains separated from our Gentile family.

Romans 911 sheds light on the unrighteous strongholds of the enemy in the spirit, moving us to break off his influence through prayer and repentance.

Romans 911 deals with the obstacles and barriers preventing Jewish and Gentile believers from finding *The Reconnection* in *TONM.* It addresses the spiritual, theological, and emotional challenges that continue to keep us apart, which we must be willing to face and overcome together. This is necessary for us to achieve the unity of Spirit that God desires for His family of Messianic and Gentile believers. *Romans 911* sheds light on the unrighteous strongholds of the enemy in the spirit, moving us to break off his influence through prayer and repentance. The book addresses Jewish believers in the same manner, but the issues of healing and repentance are quite different.

Romans 911 helps all believers face the past so they can find their destinies in the Kingdom of God and experience the power and blessing associated with this ultimate awakening and revival.

The Reconnection does not require God's children from the nations to become like the Jews, as explained in Acts 15. Rather, it blesses them as they have been called through the nations. It calls them to spiritually reunite with their Jewish brothers and sisters in relationship and intimacy and to track toward their original identity as a part of Israel. It also calls them to fully recognize and bless the believing Jewish branches of the olive tree that are now reemerging so the two can coexist and bless each other. Just as the Church was when God established His fivefold apostolic government through His Jewish apostles, where both branches of the faith dwelt together in unity and demonstrated His power, *The Reconnection* calls Jewish believers to embrace the Church and fully unite with their Gentile-believing family without fear of losing their identity.

> *Romans 911 helps all believers face the past so they can find their destinies in the Kingdom of God and experience the power and blessing associated with this ultimate awakening and revival.*

As the ancestral Church emerged and established itself as a world religion, it mistakenly severed this most crucial link (its Jewish roots), wiping out any differences between Jewish and Gentile believers in Church theology. The Roman Church separated Christianity as a separate and distinctive religion apart from its Jewish heritage, which has had significant effects on the Church's original identity, which remains to this day. This is true to the extent that as

Jewish people came to faith over the centuries, they had to follow the patterns and traditions of the Gentile Church, as this was the only branch available for them to the faith. In reality, there are two sets of branches to the faith, one for Jews and one for Gentiles, that both operate in *TONM*, especially now that Israel is awakening spiritually. *Romans 911* brings this needed course correction, for the true and proper extension of Judaism and Christianity is through Yeshua/Jesus without separation from its roots and heritage and its relational connection to Israel's Remnant in the love of the Father and Son. This will also help Jewish people be grafted back into their own olive tree more easily.

Romans 911 shows how this divorce took place and also encourages a spiritual reunion between Jewish and Gentile believers now that the Remnant of Messianic believers has arisen.

Romans 911 shows how this divorce took place and also encourages a spiritual reunion between Jewish and Gentile believers now that the Remnant of Messianic believers has arisen. It also discusses the criticality of this spiritual transaction between us as a family in this present day and hour. Like Ruth's connection to Naomi and her subsequent marriage to Boaz, "*...your people will be my people, and your God my God*" (Ruth 1:16).

The Reconnection and *Alignment* not only focuses on the Restoration in *TONM*, but also take us back to our family roots and helps to restore love and unity between Abraham's physical family, between Ishmael and Isaac, and between Arab and Jew where division and separation first began.

PERFECT ESCHATOLOGY

Romans 911 doesn't aspire to perfect eschatology. Although I might express my opinions passionately, I recognize as a human that I only "see in part" (see 1 Corinthians 13:12). When perfection comes, the full picture will be made known. *Romans 911* promotes a healthy balance between Jewish and Gentile mindsets regarding end-time views, one I believe has been mostly missing because of the separation that exists between Jewish and Gentile believers. This book definitely challenges end-time eschatology that excludes *The Reconnection*. I believe this spiritual reuniting in the family of God is one of the most significant transactions in the *Heart of the Father* for us to be one in accordance with His end-time plans.

I believe receiving the fullness of *The Reconnection* message will bring a natural change and correction to our end-time views, which up to this point have mostly excluded this from taking place. My hope is that prayer and intercession will remove and clean up a great deal of the confusion that currently exists in Christian eschatology.

WE NEED EACH OTHER

As we come into this final era before the Lord returns, which the Apostle Paul refers to as "the fullness of the Gentiles," all Israel will be saved, Israel's spiritual Restoration and the fulfillment of God's Covenants to restore them becomes the key element in God's Glory plan to unite His family and complete His plans through us (see Romans 11:25–32; Ezekiel 36:22–28), where Israel's spiritual awakening and the last great harvest are intricately linked and where the Church has a most crucial role to play to help bring this to pass. It is an end-time plan devised by the Father Himself to finally unite His family for His Son's return to the Earth.

This is all quite different from standard Church theology that keeps Israel and the Church separate spiritually until after the Lord's return. There are reasons for this that *Romans 911* brings to light and expounds on.

THE HOLY SPIRIT IS SHIFTING US

As a result, the Holy Spirit is now shifting His Church into this Reconciliation to restore *TONM* between Jew and Gentile. This is one of the main reasons why so many Christians are being drawn to Israel in some way or another at this time, without fully understanding why, yet wanting to bless Israel.

The Reconnection must take place for Israel's prophetic rising (all Israel will be saved) and to prepare His Ekklesia/Church for His coming—a victorious Church, a powerful Church, a Church without spot or wrinkle, a Church that has truly risen! God's spiritual family requires both branches of the faith to come together to be complete to achieve Israel's final regrafting and Restoration. This will enable His firstborn and His children from the nations to rule and reign together with Mashiach/Christ, a divine monarch whose authority will flow out of Jerusalem and Israel and its Commonwealth of Nations. We must not be ignorant to this mystery that is unveiling before our eyes.

INTO THE FATHER'S HEART

As you read *Romans 911*, you will quickly discover that the fullness of the revelation of *TONM* does not come from one side of the family or the other, solely through a Jewish or Gentile lens, but rather through the Eyes and *Heart of our Father* in heaven, who loves all His children equally. It is my hope that we, His end-time generations, will be united in His love and purposes so that His Kingdom will be glorified upon the Earth.

As you read Romans 911, you will quickly discover that the fullness of the revelation of TONM does not come from one side of the family or the other, solely through a Jewish or Gentile lens, but rather through the Eyes and Heart of our Father in heaven, who loves all His children equally.

Like a Church moving into the fullness of the Spirit or into its five-fold governing focus, *The Reconnection* presents various adjustments and Realignments for Church and Messianic bodies to move into to help us unite as the family of God. It explains that the fullness of this revelation of *TONM* cannot come solely from a Gentile lens/perspective in the Church but must be inclusive of the reemerging natural branches through the Messianic Body of Jewish believers known through Scripture as the Remnant of Israel (see Romans 11:1–6).

It encourages the natural branches of Israel to come forth with the Church's full support and blessing. Israel cannot be grafted back into the Gentile side of the tree but must be grafted back into its own natural branches (see Romans 11:22–24). And it encourages all believers to explore the full potential of *TONM* to experience the greater riches of their full inclusion (see Romans 11:12).

THE CHURCH

Romans 911 helps those who want to bless Israel, who are growing in this revelation, to find its fullness and come into a deeper understanding of God's plans and purposes in these days through His family and this Reconnection to make us one. It also encourages those ensnared by the deception of replacement or Fulfillment Theology to renounce it with a sense of urgency and to repent before it is too late.

A TIME OF MERCY

Romans 911 trumpets a prophetic message of God's *mercy* for all His family to be properly reconciled at this time. It ties into the Apostle Paul's final dissertation on Israel and the Church in the eleventh chapter of Romans. That message is that God's *mercy wave* would be unleashed on us all, to Jew and Gentile alike—to receive the Father's mercy, His love, His healing, and His Reconciliation back into the fullness of *TONM* to glorify His Son upon the Earth. However, the book also puts out a caution and a warning toward those who will not receive it.

WE MUST FIGHT

Romans 911 has been written to mobilize all Jewish and Gentile believers into this end-time fray, where the enemy has sowed numerous barriers and deceptions to keep us apart. The book calls for a greater movement and understanding of the end-time intercession and spiritual warfare that will be required to move the family of God into this fight, to help Realign us with our Father's end-time plans.

Romans 911 has been written to mobilize all Jewish and Gentile believers into this end-time fray, where the enemy has sowed numerous barriers and deceptions to keep us apart.

Romans 911 puts out a call to train and equip the watchmen and watch-women on the walls for the purpose of awakening the Church and Messianic bodies into the critical role of seeing Israel's salvation and the greater outpouring of the Holy Spirit into the nations.

ROMANS 911 BIBLE-STUDY BOOK

Restoration in *TONM* is a serious and timely message that should not be treated lightly. *The Reconnection* will require time and a fresh focus with renewed teachings to help bring its fullness to pass among Church and Messianic bodies. However, it will be difficult to measure or outweigh the amazing rewards, benefits, blessings, love, and power that will be poured out on us as we yield to our Father's will for His end-time Glory plans upon the Earth.

There are many issues here that need to be addressed, as out-lined in this introduction. For this reason, *Romans 911* is not a short book. I wrote it in an exhaustive manner to help deal with issues and bring necessary changes and Restoration among Jewish and Gentile believers, so we can come together and reunite in the Father's love.

With this in mind, we have prepared a video Bible-study teaching series called *The Romans 911 Project*, which is inclusive of *The Romans 911 Study Guide*. The video teachings are FREE with the purchase of the books. They are available on our website for download for believers, Churches, and Congregations everywhere to effectively teach *The Reconnection* message and help them apply it into our everyday lives.

DR. DANIEL JUSTER

When I first got the download for *Romans 911* from the Holy Spirit to spell out *The Reconnection* more clearly, I approached my Messianic Apostolic leader and good friend, Dr. Daniel Juster, with the burden that was on my heart. He responded that he would like to join me in this effort and provide oversight for the book. I rejoiced because I knew this book needed to be presented with great clarity and depth—not only in the full understanding of *The Reconnection,* but also in addressing its many obstacles with clear and sound theology to help both sides of the family move into it. I knew his experience and knowledge would be invaluable to the task of helping me find this balance: thank you, Papa Dan.

Dr. Daniel Juster is probably the most proficient Messianic theologian alive today. He has carried the burden for Israel and the Church for more than forty years as one of the main leaders in the Messianic Movement. He has written more than twenty books on Messianic Judaism and Israel and the Church. One of the many things I love about Dan is that he has great love for the Church and is extremely balanced in his theological approach between the two branches of *TONM.*

In addition, to bring further balance, *Romans 911* has been vetted by a number of Christian and Messianic leaders who also have a heart for *TONM.*

IT'S TIME TO EXPLORE THESE ISSUES IN GREATER DEPTH

I've used this chapter to outline the major issues that need to be addressed during these days, many of which are quite different from what most of the Church has been teaching, especially in its eschatology. There are reasons for this that we must now explore in greater depth to help us understand why we need to enter the fight.

In the next few chapters, you will gain a deeper understanding of how the Church became disconnected from Israel and our great need to Reconnect for *TONM* to be reestablished and for God's Glory plan to be initiated through us.

Now that Israel is awakening and the wave of Jewish believers continues to swell, we will discover our need for a renewed love and unity between the two parts of the family. We truly need to become *one* in properly representing the Kingdom of God upon the Earth.

LET US PRAY

I had a strong sense from the Lord that this book was to be a most thorough and excellent work in its approach to the entire Body of Messiah/Christ, both in the Church and Messianic bodies. *Romans 911* presents challenges to all of us in God's family for us to find this unity at this time. It can be likened to a huge ship at sea that must be turned about at this time to achieve our final purpose in righting the ship's course.

Please understand that the pursuit of *The Reconnection* is a most delicate matter for both believing Jews and Gentiles. I pray that the fullness of this message will play on our heartstrings and touch places deep within us, some of which we might not have recognized before. It might

> *It can be likened to a huge ship at sea that must be turned about at this time to achieve our final purpose in righting the ship's course.*

be uncomfortable for us at times. But we need to be willing to put many of our differences aside and to put our Father's will above our own. This might well become the driving force for many of us to move into this greater love and unity in God's family.

It is with great joy that I bring the fullness of this Reconnection work to you and all that God is going to do with it as He Reconnects us into this most special unity within His family between Jew and Gentile, reuniting us into His Heart for His family to become one.

Now, would you please pray with us and open your heart to prayerfully consider all that is written in it? Please pray about the impact it will have on end-time generations in the Church and

Messianic bodies as we Realign into our Father's plans to glorify His Son upon the Earth.

OPENING PRAYER

"Dear heavenly Father, Lord God of Israel, I come to you in the precious name of Your Son, Yeshua/Jesus. I ask you to show me about The Reconnection in TONM and about all the issues that surround it. Lord, if I have not fully recognized these insights and revelations yet, I ask that you would show me if this is of You or not. If it is, help me recognize it, fully receive it, and move into it according to Your perfect will. Amen."

CHAPTER 2

THE HOUR BEFORE
THE WEDDING

BEFORE I BEGIN this chapter, please allow me to address the issues of separation and disconnection because they are delicate. My reason for writing about them at the beginning of the book are two-fold: they not only need to be confronted and brought into the light so we can properly deal with them; they must also lay the foundation for us to accept and more readily embrace *The Reconnection*. Simply put, there is so much more for us to gain from *The Reconnection* that far outweighs anything else.

To delve into these issues adequately, I need to be very open, honest, and direct. I need to share my thoughts and heart as a Jewish believer from the Messianic perspective regarding how Jews and Gentiles have been impacted as a spiritual family. In these next several chapters, I ask for the liberty to express myself from this viewpoint in the hope of helping those on the Gentile side of the family to more fully understand and grasp these most sensitive issues. In a sense, we need to dig up the past to unravel it and break off any negative influences that might still be upon us. This is my goal in helping us to realize and fulfill our destiny during these last days.

My hope and prayer is that you will walk through this journey with me and begin to identify these issues more clearly and learn how they have affected us and how the devil has used them against us (the family of God). It is time for the enemy and his craftiness to be fully exposed!

My hope and prayer is that you will walk through this journey with me and begin to identify these issues more clearly and learn how they have affected us and how the devil has used them against us (the family of God). It is time for the enemy and his craftiness to be fully exposed!

CHRISTIANITY IS JEWISH

Please follow my line of thinking for a moment: if Yeshua/Jesus is the Messiah, then He is the only true and proper extension of Judaism. That means that the existing Jews who have not yet accepted Yeshua are still broken off and need to be grafted back into the olive tree, which has been prophesied to take place toward the end (see Romans 11:23–32). This stands to reason because Christianity is Jewish (see John 4:22). All the Covenants and promises were given to Israel first, including the New Covenant through Mashiach/Christ (see Jeremiah 31:31–34; Romans 1:16; Romans 2:6–11; Romans 9:4–5).

It is important to point out that we are not complete as a Body until the broken-off branches (Jewish souls yet to be saved) are restored and the full harvest from the nations has come in, which is the final mystery in the family that the Apostle Paul discussed in Romans 11.

Yeshua/Jesus was sent first to the lost sheep of Israel (see Matthew 15:24) because the Covenants, promises, especially the law had to be fulfilled through His death and resurrection. The Holy Spirit was then released and sent to the apostles and the Jewish believers, who not only founded the Ekklesia/Church but also continued to represent Israel (because the Lord had transferred His authority away from the priesthood to His apostles, see Matthew 21:18–27; Mark 11:12–21; Acts 2:1–4 and page 55, which addresses this issue in detail). In this way, the Gospel would be taken to the nations through them so His other children could be grafted into Israel's Covenants and promises to be joined together with them (see John 10:16). They became one with Israel's Remnant and now represented Israel as her commonwealth, which make up *TONM*. This fulfilled the first family mystery with the New Covenant regarding how the Gentiles would come to faith (see Ephesians 3:1–11; Colossians 1:26–27).

This was also a fulfillment of Scripture through the prophet Isaiah, who had declared that God would use Israel to be a light to the Gentiles so that His salvation would reach to the ends of the earth (see Isaiah 42:6; 49:6). However, it is significant to point out that Yeshua/Jesus is intrinsically linked to Israel and that we received Him through them and their Covenants, which makes us one. There is a significant connection here for us to grasp that is vital to our understanding, especially now with Israel's awakening and *The Reconnection* between the two groups. God looks to restore His family through the balance of Israel's Restoration (the broken-off branches Paul speaks about in Romans 11, as stated earlier).

Through Yeshua/Jesus and the Holy Spirit's guidance, the apostles cleared the way for Gentiles to be free of the law while continuing their own associations to it in the New Covenant (see Acts 21:20–25), which we discuss later on in the book. There was a definite connectedness between Jew and Gentile with a Jewish heritage and flavor that was apparent during those days, as they laid the foundations for the Ekklesia/Church through a fivefold governing focus of apostles, prophets, evangelists, pastors, and teachers to equip the saints for the works of the ministry. The power of the Holy Spirit flowed freely, accompanied by signs and wonders, and they witnessed everywhere the gathering of Jews and Gentiles into the faith. The world was forever changed.

It is also incredibly important to note that during these days, Gentile believers rejoiced and were incredibly grateful to become a part of Israel's rich heritage and history and to be grafted into their Covenants and promises as coheirs (see Romans 9:5). The Apostle Paul worked hard to convey this message to His Gentile family, which was a challenge at first, in light of Israel's rich heritage (see Romans 9:4–5; Ephesians 2:11–22).

Yeshua/Jesus created a beautiful harmony between believing Jew and Gentile in *TONM* that would now take the Gospel to the ends of the Earth. Ariel Blumenthal[2] from Revive Ministries in Israel writes about this mystery, making reference to three different Greek words the Apostle Paul uses to describe it: *synkleroma*, *sysoma*, and *synmetoka* (see Ephesians 3:4–6). All these words start with the prefix "syn," from which we get English words such as synchronize, synthesize, and synergy. New Testament Greek scholars tell us it is hard to capture the clout of these three words in other languages. They emphasize a great depth of connection, togetherness, and partnership that should never have been broken. And now that Israel is being restored, it needs to be repaired.

It is also important to note that as the Ekklesia/Church was emerging and being established, this unity was realized amid constant opposition from the broken-off branches of the faith—those who did not accept Yeshua but rejected Him. Persecution was initiated by Jewish leadership against the Ekklesia/Church, which affected these believers and the apostles who wrote about it in their letters.

This was only the beginning, however, for these tables were about to turn. By the time Rome took control of the Church in the fourth century, anti-Jewish sentiment had developed from within its ranks, which began to compound and greatly increase at this time. The sentiment was so strong, in fact, that the ancestral Church began to force itself on the unsaved Jewish population, doing everything in its power to break away from the Jewish roots of our faith received through the apostles. It also greatly misunderstood the plight and journey of the Jewish people, cutting away any options for the Jewish branch of the faith and introducing some of Rome's paganism into the Church.[3]

By the time Rome took control of the Church in the fourth century, anti-Jewish sentiment had developed from within its ranks, which began to compound and greatly increase at this time.

This persecution has mostly continued against Jewish people into the modern era. In a sense, from a family context between Jew and Gentile, this can be compared to the story of Joseph, whose brothers sold him into slavery. When you think about this, it's quite a picture, but thankfully, the story doesn't end there. So let's keep focused on the Restoration and incredible healing that all the brothers experienced and received when Joseph was fully restored because our God had other plans for His family.

Of course, entrenched mindsets against the Jewish people didn't happen overnight; we can see the growth of prejudicial attitudes and the theology that led to it in evidence during the second, third, and fourth centuries. However, this disconnection severed a most vital link to the faith, similar to a divorce, and established Christianity as a distinct religion away from its Jewish roots and heritage into a theology of replacement. This created a separation from its full identity in Israel that, for the most part, continues to this day. These mindsets have had dramatic influence over the Church, becoming fully interwoven into its fabric and dominating its thought and theology for more than seventeen hundred years—even among those in the Church who profess to love Israel.

Of course this was a great challenge to the Church and rather perplexing because the balance of Israel (now its majority) was still broken off, even though the Apostle Paul explained this in Romans 11 (verses 11–32). However, to this day, this disconnection from Israel has remained a fundamental part of the Christian Church, despite its Reformation up to this point in time.

From the Jewish-believing perspective, it was now as if the wild olive branches that were grafted into the vine had become the only branches (see Romans 11:17). And from that point on, all Jewish believers who wanted entry had no choice but to become like the Gentiles, following their traditions, because the Church taught that it had now fully replaced Israel without its original connection or its ultimate Restoration.

In this light, the *Israel Piece* appears to be the last piece that God will restore to His Church, in a final unifying of His family to help awaken Israel, so the end might actually come. And a spiritual *reunion* is needed between us through *The Reconnection*. This might be challenging for some of our Catholic brothers and sisters to embrace. However, please know it is written in truth and love so that we can find correction and repentance in this area, which are greatly needed.

We might be encouraged to hear that the Catholic Church is engaging the Messianic Movement at some of its highest levels to facilitate greater understanding today.

GOD'S RESTORATION MUST BE COMPLETE

Robert Heidler puts it best in his book, *The Messianic Church Arising,* which I have expounded upon with his permission. God's process of Restoration began with the Reformation in the sixteenth century, when He restored the Bible and doctrine of salvation. He began to reestablish a desire for holiness in the eighteenth century. He restored the gifts in the twentieth century. And in this present day, He is restoring the apostolic roots and foundations of His Church through *The Reconnection* and the fivefold governing focus. This is composed of both branches of the faith perfected in *TONM* between Jew and Gentile.

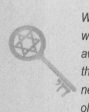

With all due respect and understanding, we must come to learn that an awakened Israel cannot be grafted into the Gentile branches of the tree but needs to be grafted back into its own olive tree through the natural branches, as Paul described in Romans 11.

This is the final piece to be restored. Otherwise, the present-day Restoration will *lack* its full authority.

As a result, we need to Reconnect spiritually, not only to aid in Israel's awakening, but also to prepare us for a Messianic Kingdom here on the Earth, to which we are inextricably linked with and through Israel, now that God is moving upon her once again. This is the time of *TONM!*

With all due respect and understanding, we must come to learn that an awakened Israel cannot be grafted into the Gentile branches of the vine but needs to be grafted back into its own olive tree through the natural branches, as Paul described in Romans 11. This olive tree was Jewish from the beginning and remained so during the expansion of the Ekklesia/Church during the first several centuries. If we are willing to accept it, the Jewish branches on the tree are now reemerging through the Messianic Movement and the many thousands of Jewish believers who are coming to faith. Please note, more Jewish souls have come to Messiah over the past fifty years since Israel took back possession of Jerusalem in 1967 than in the past nineteen hundred years put together.

What's more, spiritual Reconnection prepares and unites us for a Messianic Kingdom upon the Earth whose authority will go out from Israel through Mashiach/Christ, to the nations, to represent its commonwealth. The Church is not a separate entity, and it has not completely replaced Israel. Rather, it is intrinsically linked to it in more ways than it knows at present.

This act alone will make it easier for Jewish people to return to God because they will be returning to their own faith and not a foreign or disconnected one that has been presented through the Church up to this point in time. We must come to understand that the ancestral Church fell prey to the enemy's schemes regarding the Jewish people and was used to persecute and kill them. This fact still weighs heavily upon the Jewish psyche and generational bloodline, as was presented in my first book, *The New Covenant Prophecy*.

Due to the Church's disconnection from its roots and heritage, in its thinking and viewpoint, it has been Gentile for so long that even now, in the time of Israel's spiritual Restoration, the reemergence of the Jewish branches of the faith seem so foreign and alien for Gentile Christians to even contemplate. When you think about it, it's similar to the Jewish people of Jesus's time who couldn't fathom that God would reach out to the Gentiles, despite the clear teachings of Scripture. The same is true today, but in reverse.

We've come full circle in our understanding of each other when it comes to Jew and Gentile in the family of God. The mirror images between us in our humanity are enlightening. In these days, we need to have the hearts and spirits of our founding apostles, who, after recognizing the Holy Spirit's movements to awaken His other children from the nations, did everything in their power to make the transition easy when it came to loving and blessing their Gentile family into the faith, accepting them as their own.

It's no surprise, then, that the modern Church is in need of this Restoration and Reconnection and that our current view of the Ekklesia/Church is quite different from its intended state or its origins. Dr. Daniel Juster defines the Church this way: "*The Church is that Body of those from the nations that have embraced the Jewish King/Messiah and thereby become joined to the Messianic Jewish Remnant, who thereby have become attached to or rooted in the Jewish people and joined to the Jewish people in their destiny, even the redemption of Israel and the nations, the world.*"

> Dr. Daniel Juster defines the Church this way: "The Church is that Body of those from the nations that have embraced the Jewish King/Messiah and thereby become joined to the Messianic Jewish Remnant, who thereby have become attached to or rooted in the Jewish people and joined to the Jewish people in their destiny, even the redemption of Israel and the nations, the world."

To me, a Jewish believer, this is a very clear definition of how the Church is supposed to be, especially now that Israel has reemerged. God's children from the nations are grafted into Israel as its commonwealth, not the other way around. Due to the Church's disconnection from its roots, however, most of the Church does not view things this way and might even be offended by this definition. Herein lies one of our greatest challenges in this day we live in: Jewish and Gentile believers are divided, and the devil has ravaged any association between the two with the aim that they will never meet. But thanks be to the mercy and Glory of God, He plans to restore us and reform His Ekklesia/Church for His return.

WHERE DID WE GO WRONG REGARDING ISRAEL?

First, we must understand that the Church experienced a huge loss when it broke away from its Jewish roots and heritage. What might have appeared to be an amazing deal for the Church in national-izing the faith in the fourth century under Constantine actually stripped the Church of much of its spiritual power. This discon-nection was most probably the root cause and the beginning of the Abrahamic curse that would fall upon any who would come against Israel (see Genesis 12:3).

Not long after that, the Church became religious like its Jewish predecessors (Pharisees and Sadducees). This caused people to follow a religious system rather than connecting with the inti-macy the New Covenant promised through Yeshua/Jesus and the Holy Spirit—namely, that each of us would *know* God for ourselves (see Jeremiah 31:31–34). This was the main focus before the Church merged with Rome.

The Church then advanced into the Dark Ages. While it was sleeping, Islam was born, looking to steal away many souls who were connecting with Mashiach/Christ and adding greater confu-sion to teachings regarding the deity of Yeshua/Jesus.

Second, we must fully understand the devil's strategies against the family of God that enable him to keep dominion over the Earth. As blinded as satan might be by his own pride, he will never give up without a major fight, as evidenced by Scripture (see Revelation 12:7–9). In these end-time battles, we need to recognize the Jewish people and our association with them as his prime targets—not only to destroy them, but to also keep the Church separated from them and from us in terms of our great role to help bring them to spiritual life. This is his main goal because when the Jews finally come in, the family will be restored, and satan will be finished!

My dear friend, Arni Klein from Emmaus Way Ministries, who is one of the pioneers of worship ministry in the land of Israel, relates that in the Kingdom of darkness, there are three particular princi-palities to be encountered on the way to the Lord's return: the spirit of religion (legalism), rooted in Jerusalem; the Greek humanistic spirit (worldliness), rooted in Tel Aviv; and the spirit of false religions (New Age, witchcraft, and other spiritual religions), rooted in the Galilee.

> If we are going to get totally free from the enemy's influence on our past, we'll need to gain a deeper understanding of how he has actually influenced us in this area. We'll also need to be very honest with ourselves about what has transpired between Jew and Gentile in Church history and how this affects us today—not only in the Church at large but also individually as children of God.

This is one of the main reasons why the devil has launched his attack against the family of God between Jewish and Gentile believers: he understands how instrumental we are in God's plan to help bring redemption to mankind and true unity between Jew and Gentile in *TONM*. And if we are going to get totally free from the enemy's influence on our past, we'll need to gain a deeper understanding of how he has actually influenced us in this area. We'll also need to be very honest with ourselves about what has transpired between Jew and Gentile in Church history and how this affects us today—not only in the Church at large but also individually as children of God.

THE CHURCH BECAME ANTISEMITIC

Not only did the early Church break away from its roots and heritage; in the process, it became very antisemitic. I have referenced a website[4] that lists many comments against the Jews written by Church leaders, and I think it is important to view and read them, at least to understand how the Church misunderstood Israel's plight and moved in this direction against the Jewish people. I also strongly encourage you to read Dr. Michael Brown's book on antisemitism in the Church, *Our Hands Are Stained with Blood*, to gain a deeper understanding of this issue.

Please understand my heart here: it is not my intention to dredge up issues from the past to point the finger at anyone or any group, for there is no condemnation in our Lord. However, if the evil one is still able to exert his influence in light of past sins, as I believe to be the case, which I will explain in greater depth, then it needs to be addressed more fully to bring it into the light. This will help free and release us from its influence and any residual curses that might still be upon us.

It is easy for us to look back and ask the question, how could this have happened? Even though Scripture gave such clear direction to Gentile believers in how they should behave towards the Jewish people (see Romans 11). Perhaps Paul penned these instructions because he had a sense of what was coming regarding Christian treatment back towards the Jews.

Paul had a divine call to reach his own people—even to the point of being stoned and facing death (see Acts 14:19). No one had to convince him to reach his own blood, the Jewish people. However, those who were coming to faith from the Gentile side were not natural family because they were now being grafted in. In the process, and as the Church began to grow in the nations, they were also experiencing challenges and opposition from the Jews who did not accept Yeshua/Jesus. So the call to love Israel was never an easy one, right from the start.

Please understand my heart here: it is not my intention to dredge up issues from the past to point the finger at anyone or any group, for there is no condemnation in our Lord. However, if the evil one is still able to exert his influence in light of past sins, as I believe to be the case, which I will explain in greater depth, then it needs to be addressed more fully to bring it into the light. This will help free and release us from its influence and any residual curses that might still be upon us.

However, the ancestral Church clearly misunderstood God's action toward the Jewish people by interpreting His judgment on them as final, rather than as a *judgment*, a *dispersion*, and a

Restoration at the end, which Scripture points us toward (see Deuteronomy 30:4–6; Ezekiel 36:22–32; Romans 11:25–29).

Please also keep in mind that the ancestral Church had just witnessed and experienced God's judgment against Israel and the Jewish people with two major Roman attacks. The first one destroyed the temple in 70 AD, and the second, which occurred in 135 AD, killed and dispersed the balance of Israel throughout the nations, as Moses and Yeshua/Jesus had foretold (see Deuteronomy 28–30; Matthew 24:2).

Unlike the rest of humanity, God called Israel to face the law, which brought sin into account. As a result, Israel had to suffer the consequences of its disobedience. But most of the Church failed to discern God's unconditional love and His Covenants to ultimately restore Israel. The Church also failed to discern the numerous Scriptures and prophecies that support their ultimate redemption as His firstborn children in the family; God's gifts and call are irrevocable (see Romans 11:29). Indeed, as Yeshua/Jesus informed us, this ensured that the first would be last (see Matthew 20:16).

The most crucial point in our understanding here is not necessarily how our Church ancestors acted but rather how the devil was able to seduce the very vessels that were called to love Israel and use them to persecute and destroy them. What a despicable plan—yet, in our humanity, we fell for it. In Israel's humanity, they failed the law; but in the Church's humanity, they failed to love Israel.

This can be hard for us to process. But if we truly want to be free, we need to be willing to face our past before we can break off the unclean spiritual ties that might remain so we can be freed from the enemy's hold.

GENERATIONAL BLOODLINE INFLUENCE

It's hard to believe that Church patriarchs were behind many disparaging things that have been written and said about the Jewish people. But this is how deception works. What's more, we don't have to look far back in history, including our own Church history, to see how deceived we can be when it comes to treating certain groups with less equity than our own.

Take racism and slavery, for example, and how unfairly we have treated others based on the color of their skin. Observe how this was handed down from one generation to the next for hundreds of years and totally controlled the thoughts and actions of most white people, many who professed to be believers. On the other hand, we can't say that all under its influence were not necessarily believers, either. And what of the great fight and incredible challenge of the ministry of William Wilberforce and, later, of President Abraham Lincoln, to stand against slavery and break its hold over us?

This is significant to our knowledge and insight on this generational bloodline issue and how it has caused generational antisemitism in the Body of Messiah/Christ. And it could be one of the secrets to unlocking a deeper understanding of how the enemy has used it against Israel and the Church to keep us on separate tracks.

The generational bloodline influences were so strong that it took the efforts of several generations (who would impact and change the world) to finally put an end to it. Although these political actions changed the laws of our land, it was only the beginning of a heart change in this area because the remaining generational bloodline influences have to be broken off spiritually through identificational repentance to free us fully from this past.

This is one of the main reasons why racism still exists today. We must deal with sins of the heart from our generational bloodlines through identificational repentance and break off past influences through Mashiach/Christ to achieve full deliverance and complete freedom.

Education is an important tool, but it is not the only remedy to the problem of racism. We must also address issues of the heart and, specifically, generational bloodline influences if we want to get totally free from it. The same is true of antisemitism and the residual influence it has on our hearts and minds.

This is significant to our knowledge and insight on this generational bloodline issue and how it has caused generational antisemitism in the Body of Messiah/Christ. And it could be one of the secrets to unlocking a deeper understanding of how the enemy has used it against Israel and the Church to keep us on separate tracks. We do well to question whether this influence still exists and to explore how it might still be affecting us.

In my book *The Ezekiel Generation,* I discuss how satan has used generational bloodline influence to exert control in this area. I encourage you to read it and pray the prayers of identificational repentance as a significant first step in this process.

The challenge here is not necessarily explaining how this influence came to pass but rather the great delicacy required to help our Gentile family in the Church understand how they might still be under its influence and how the devil is still using it against us.

It takes a good deal of humility to admit that you are in need of correction. But if the enemy has deceived us in the way we think and operate without us even knowing it, shouldn't we at least be willing take an honest look at it?

Without question, I believe this to be the case. The effect of generational antisemitism on the Church has numbed our hearts spiritually in the way we relate to Israel and the Jewish people. But it has also influenced and clouded our theology, moving us away from the very people with whom we are called to connect and reach with the Gospel (see Romans 11:30–31). The Church must come to understand that through the irrevocable Covenants and promises spoken over the Jewish people by our Father in heaven, they will be restored back into the family of God (see Romans 11:29). Their spiritual awakening plays a strategic role and is inextricably linked to the final outpouring of the Holy Spirit and last great world harvest upon the Earth. These outcomes have huge consequences for all of us, and I pray to God that we will begin to recognize them.

The Covenants toward Israel have not been fulfilled yet, as some think and teach. This fulfillment cannot happen until the breath of God finally enters His firstborn children (see Ezekiel 37:9–10) and they recite the age-old blessing: *"Baruch Haba B'Shem Adonai— Blessed is He who comes in the name of the Lord"* (see also Matthew 23:39; Psalm 118:26). These Covenants are only now beginning to be fulfilled through Israel's awakening, as Israel is restored and more and more Jewish people come to faith through Yeshua/Jesus.

Allow me to explain how generational antisemitism has affected our past, how it operates, and how the enemy is still using it to wield influence. Please understand that generational antisemitism isn't the only issue that keeps us separated as Jewish and Gentile believers. But it is fundamental to exposing other areas that need to be dealt with—namely, the heart cleansing God wants to do through us in preparation for what is to come as the Lord reunites us in *TONM* between Jew and Gentile.

JEWISH BELIEVERS

This separation caused by generational antisemitism applies to the Gentile side of the family, but Jewish believers have also kept separate from the Church and their Gentile-believing family—though the issues that have kept us apart on the Jewish side are quite different. There needs to be a greater willingness and flexibility among the siblings on both sides of the family to get this right.

> *There needs to be a greater willingness and flexibility among the siblings on both sides of the family to get this right.*

You might be a Jewish believer reading this book who is in agreement with all that is written, not understanding why the Church has been unable to see and understand these things clearly. But what about the Jewish branches and our separation from our Gentile-believing family in the Church? *The Reconnection* applies to Gentile and Jewish believers in equal measure, so we all need to be willing to let go and forgive one another. While we are on this subject, I feel compelled to ask this question to my Jewish-believing family: What is stopping us from connecting with our Gentile-believing family and the many Churches around us, and what is in our hearts that might need cleansing and healing for us to fully embrace our Christian brothers and sisters?

GENERATIONAL ANTISEMITISM

Let me explain the difference between *antisemitism* and *generational antisemitism* and how satan has been using it. *Antisemitism* is blatant discrimination and hostility toward Jewish people; *generational antisemitism* refers to the spiritual influences in the generational bloodline that cause us to become antisemitic. You can be affected and influenced through generational antisemitisim without having acted on it. This is part of the devil's trickery and deception through the generational bloodline influence; it's part of the intergenerational inheritance that's spiritually conveyed to us as a result of sin, which we can't see because our thoughts have been affected.

For example, you might want to bless Israel because you recognize the truth of God's Word concerning concerning the Jewish people in Genesis 12:3: *"I will bless those who bless you, and curse those who curse you."* But generational antisemitism can still exert its influence through your generational bloodline until you pray and repent, inviting Him to break off any influence and to cleanse and heal you in this area. In this instance, the influence manifests in the form of a connected mind (intellect) but a stony (disconnected) heart, something I have witnessed and experienced so many times with my Gentile family in the Church, especially among leadership, regarding issues that relate to Israel and the Jewish people. It can manifest in the form of cold love or indifference and can stir up subtle antisemitic feelings and thoughts toward Israel or the Jewish people.

In fact, digging deeper into the concordance here in Genesis 12:3, a more literal translation reads: *"he who lightly esteems...treats you lightly ...I will bitterly curse,"* which puts much greater emphasis on exactly how we treat and care for the first-born in God's family.

Here's another example of generational antisemitism that can be easily overlooked: you might read the dual language used in this book when referencing Jesus or Christ (Greek/Latin background) and Yeshua and Mashiach (Hebrew) and feel offended or feel some resistance toward it. Without repentance, generational antisemitism is handed down from one generation to the next. It is inherited through the actions and words of those around us in subtle ways, such as family members—parents and grandparents—and through our friends and associates.

Scripture sheds light on this influence in the Second Commandment, saying that God will punish the children for the sins of the parents up to the third and fourth generations (see Exodus 20:5). From this text, we understand that sinful actions can be transmitted from one generation to the next through the generational bloodline unless we repent and break them off through prayer. We also can act on sinful actions through our own decisions and choices, which then travel down through our own lineage and become multigenerational.

Please do not misunderstand me here; I am not inferring that as believers in Mashiach/Christ, we are not forgiven. Yeshua/Jesus died once and for all sins (see Romans 6:10; 1 Peter 3:18). Rather, sin influences can still have an effect on us from one generation to the next, especially in the sanctification process that all of us go through as the flesh gets transformed by God's righteousness (see Romans 12:1–2). If you have *The Ezekiel Generation* please refer to the Tod McDowell story in chapter 5, which explains the depths of this lingering influence in the Gentile generational bloodline in much greater detail.

PERSONAL GENERATIONAL BLOODLINE ISSUES

It's interesting to note that over the past ten to fifteen years, the Church has developed a greater awareness of generational bloodline influences and how they can affect our walks with the Lord. Thankfully, as we recognize certain negative patterns of behavior in our hearts, we are able to break them off in Mashiach/Christ through prayer, confession, and deliverance.

But think for a moment about your own life and some of the negative behaviors and patterns your parents or grandparents might have practiced or indulged in. Look at your heart and those of your siblings to see if you have inherited these influences. This was true of my own life and family members. I also see some of my own characteristics evidenced in my children's lives. Let us give thanks to our most wonderful and merciful God, Who has the power to deliver us all. Amen.

A proper understanding of generational bloodline influence can also shed light on our understanding of the homosexual issue, which can also be inherited through the generational bloodline. God did not create man to be adulterers or homosexual—these are sin states. If someone in our family line practices these sins without repentance, they can travel to and influence the next generation. The same can be said of alcoholism or any other besetting sin issue. Sometimes generational sin will skip a generation or two and show up in later ones, which is why certain orientations and proclivities can be evident from an early age.

THE ENEMY CAN INFLUENCE THE GENERATIONAL BLOODLINE

Let me say this about the strongholds of the enemy and how they function: the devil has free reign to exploit any type of disobedience or sinful behavior that is outside the grace and protection of God. Demons or spirits can attach themselves in such instances. The greater the opening people invite to that sin, the greater the spiritual

Let me say this about the strongholds of the enemy and how they function: the devil has free reign to exploit any type of disobedience or sinful behavior that is outside the grace and protection of God. Demons or spirits can attach themselves in such instances.

influence over them. You can sense this when entering an area of a country that has been given over to a particular sin. The demonic influence can be seen and felt all around. Some influences are more subtle than others, but the principle is the same.

There is no greater sin influence than generational antisemitism through the bloodline because it has remained mostly undetected for hundreds of generations. This is one of the main reasons why much of our eschatology in the Church is out of balance and disconnected regarding Israel, because of these negative influences. The devil has preyed over our generational bloodlines and our separation issues. The enemy's erroneous influence over us against the Jewish people has gone undetected up until this time, especially regarding God's end-time plans to restore Israel *through us* and how we are connected to them.

Scripture tells us, *"Just as you who were at one time disobedient to God have now received mercy as a result of their disobedience, so they too have now become disobedient in order that they too may now receive mercy as a result of God's mercy to you"* (Romans 11:30–31). If the Church is the chosen vessel by the Father to breathe back this *mercy* and salvation to the Jewish people, and the enemy can prevent this from happening, then he (the enemy) remains in control, right? Of course, we know that all things are ultimately under God's control and sovereignty, but the devil never gives up without a fight. The enemy's influence must be discerned and exposed and then brought down in this critical area of unity in the family of God and *TONM*.

There is perhaps no fiercer battle to be fought than the one surrounding Israel's awakening, the Church's Realignment with it, and the last great revival/harvest of souls that's still to come—all of which are crucially linked to an end-time focus for the Church that's different from what prior generations have understood. This is the natural outflow of the *Heart of God* for all His family to be saved and for the Gospel to be proclaimed to the Jewish person first and then to the nations (see Romans 1:16).

HOW DID THIS DECEPTION OCCUR?

Furthermore, hasn't the Gentile side of the family in the Church been given edicts from God toward Israel? And wasn't most of Romans 11 written to the Gentile side of the family? *"I am talking to you, Gentiles..."* (see Romans 11:13). Here are the edicts: to draw Israel to jealousy, not to be arrogant thinking that we have now replaced them, and loving them on account of the patriarchs, despite their current rejection.

Yet the Church's ancestry moved in the opposite direction, opening the door for the enemy to deceive us in our lineage and position toward Israel. And who hasn't been affected by this spirit in the Church in some form or another? All Gentile believers from the nations were originally seeded from the Western Church, so they were sure to come under its influence and theology because it wasn't broken off through confession and repentance.

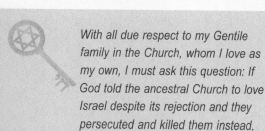

With all due respect to my Gentile family in the Church, whom I love as my own, I must ask this question: If God told the ancestral Church to love Israel despite its rejection and they persecuted and killed them instead, then how can we, the Church, expect to have an accurate understanding of eschatology toward Israel and the Church without having first broken off the disobedience and influences exerted through generational antisemitism? If the enemy was able to seduce the Church into severing the Jewish roots that connected us in the first place, shouldn't we be looking to address this area first, especially now as we come into the mystery of Israel's unveiling? (See Romans 11:25.)

Eastern Orthodoxy was not the first split in the Church (11th century);[5] it was preceded by the split between Messianic and Gentile believers (our Jewish roots and heritage) during the early centuries.

I must reemphasize that no one is pointing the finger or saying that we are directly responsible for the actions of our ancestors. But shouldn't we look to correct the past if the sins of our fathers and mothers are still having impact on our thinking and the devil is using them to keep us divided?

I can't fully explain why God has waited until now to shed light on the issue of Reconnection. Perhaps the timing wasn't right. Perhaps He wanted the pace for the Church's Restoration to be gradual, with the *Israel Piece* emerging at the end. But for sure, this couldn't begin until Israel's spiritual awakening commenced.

Indeed, as we come into the time of Israel's spiritual Reconnection, I believe God must effect changes in us before He can hope to make changes in them. Doesn't judgment *begin* in the House of God? (See 1 Peter 4:17.) The Jewish people are far more likely to connect with a Church that fully comprehends their Restoration than one that remains separated from its Jewish roots.

HOW HAS ANTISEMITISM INFLUENCED OUR THEOLOGY?

You might wonder how our theology has been influenced and affected by antisemitism. However, if the ancient Churches' actions toward Israel went in the wrong direction—away from the Heart of God in Scripture, and the Church continued in this vein throughout the centuries, as we have discussed—what would stop the Church from being lured away from the truth in this area? Is it hard for us to imagine that there would be consequences to the Church for having misjudged Israel?

Yeshua/Jesus said, "*With the measure you use, it will be measured to you*" in Matthew 7:1–2, and isn't this universal principle in play here? The judgment on Israel has been one of spiritual blindness and deafness. If we are supposed to love Israel despite its current rejection, and we persecuted its people instead, wouldn't the Church have received a measure of judgment back on itself (blindness and deafness), especially concerning our end-time view of Israel, where our theology would be blurred at best?

Arni Klein describes it this way: "For centuries the Church has been partially blinded. With the *Israel Piece* missing it could not have been otherwise...Israel is called the apple of God's eye (see Zechariah 2:8). The Hebrew word 'apple' means the 'pupil.' The pupil regulates the amount of light entering the Body. A Body without a pupil is blind. A Body with a dysfunctional pupil cannot rightly discern details—the vision is blurry at best."

Arni Klein describes it this way: "For centuries the Church has been partially blinded. With the Israel Piece missing it could not have been otherwise... Israel is called the apple of God's eye (see Zechariah 2:8). The Hebrew word 'apple' means the 'pupil.' The pupil regulates the amount of light entering the Body. A Body without a pupil is blind. A Body with a dysfunctional pupil cannot rightly discern details—the vision is blurry at best."

This analogy masterfully explains the level of blindness and confusion that exists in the Church toward Israel and why it has been so difficult for us to see Israel's awakening and unveiling up to this point in time. It's a bit of a quandary—sort of a Catch-22. The Church needs to awaken to see Israel, and the Church needs Israel to awaken. The answer, the only way through this maze, is in and through the *Father's Heart*. When His concerns are truly ours—when the blessing of His Heart is our number-one passion, then He will bring about the necessary correction. Right now, the Church is in need of divine revelation so it can see Israel the way the Father does.

Before Israel can fully awaken, the Gentile-believing Church must Reconnect with Israel in the Spirit through the *Heart of the Father* with His *love* and *mercy* for His family to be one. And we need to be willing to address all of the obstacles that might stand in the way of helping Israel come back to life!

This can be a challenge for the Church to accept, especially from the Gentile side of the family. But this is exactly how the enemy has been able to deceive and maintain influence over our eschatology and theology in this area. Through attaching to generational anti-semitism and all of its lingering influences and using it to keep us separated, we remain victim to the enemy in this place. This also underscores the urgency we have to fully expose this spirit and how the devil has been using this tactic against us.

This applies to our eschatology and the confusion that exists in how we view Israel and the Church before the Lord's return. The enemy schemes to keep the Church spiritually disconnected from Israel because helping the Father and Son bring Israel back to life is one of our greatest roles and callings.

This also explains why we're unable to see the full significance of this mystery yet and why many Christians have stony hearts in the area of Jewish evangelism. Most of the Gentile Church is still disconnected spiritually from the people of Israel and its Jewish roots and heritage. This breach must be fully repaired for us to find freedom and move into the role we will assume during the end times. In addition, we would do well to consider what the healing of this breach might contribute to the overall unification of the Church.

With all due respect, the majority of the Church is confused in its theology toward Israel, with most still believing it has fully replaced Israel (Replacement Theology). Few in the Church under-stand the difference in roles between Jewish believers and Gentile believers. Some no longer see any difference in the roles of Jew and Gentile. Others view Israel with varying degrees of significance and have not yet discerned the fullness of *The Reconnection* or their unique role in God's final plans to restore His Church. Some believe that Israel and the Church will remain separate until after the Lord's return. Some even believe that Jewish people do not need to receive Yeshua to be saved—something that's particularly hard to imagine since the New Covenant was clearly prophesied and ultimately given to Israel first through the apostles (see Jeremiah 31:31–34; Acts 2). The Apostle Paul could not have been clearer on this issue, even to the point of offering his own life for the sake of Israel's salvation (see Romans 9:3–4).

Our role in the Church is vital now to God's end-time plan and in the full cycle of God's family returning to Him. God used Israel (in this case, the apostles and other Jewish believers) to bring us life through Yeshua/Jesus, so now, in turn, (to complete the family circle) God's children from the nations will *breathe* that life back to them through the *mercy* they have received from God (see Romans 11:30–31). This is a major part of God's end-time plans.

If Israel's spiritual awakening and our refocus on their salvation is the final piece of the puzzle, then we can expect the devil to place numerous obstacles and barriers in the way of the Church receiving this revelation. Generational antisemitism is fundamental to these obstacles holding us back from *The Reconnection*, along with other issues and theological misunderstandings that we will discuss.

THE FATHER'S HEART

It might help to reflect on the biblical account of a father and his two sons known as the story of the Prodigal Son (see Luke 15:11–32). In comparison, Israel can be seen as the younger son, even though between Jew and Gentile Israel is the firstborn child, while God's children from the nations make up the rest of the family. However, when it comes to this story in the New Covenant, which of the two sons has more fully embraced it, and which of the two sons is now running the Father's House? Even though the Church was founded by a Remnant of Israel, most of them did not receive it and are still broken off from the New Covenant. So the prodigal's plight and journey can also be reflective of Israel's spiritual deficiency and their great need to be restored to the Father through Yeshua/Jesus.

The Father waited patiently, without compromising His love

and position toward His lost son. When the son comes to repentance, the Father's heart is full of compassion, and he immediately re-embraces him, restoring him to the full honor of sonship. The brother's heart is the opposite of his Father's heart. The older brother cannot rejoice or forgive because his heart is hard. He's in control of the Father's house and doesn't want to give that up or share it, using clever arguments to justify his position.

This is simply not fair and is totally unreasonable to him, and he is not able to see beyond this. However, it's the Father's desire for His Church to embrace His firstborn and welcome them back into the fold, blessing them as Jewish believers in the Kingdom of God and supporting their identity as restored branches. And it is only in the *Father's Heart* that we can secure this transaction. Historically, the Church has been unable to because we have tried to love Israel in our own strength (and in our humanity) and have been unsuccessful. Only the *Father's Heart* beating in ours can move us into our role to help our firstborn brothers and sisters come back to life.

> Sibling issues between Jewish and Gentile believers in the Body have played a huge role in keeping us apart. Great indifference among Gentile believers prevails toward the Jewish people, spurred on by spiritual influences of generational antisemitism, pride, jealousy, anger, and fear, which the enemy continues to use to keep us apart.

Sibling issues between Jewish and Gentile believers in the Body have played a huge role in keeping us apart. Great indifference among Gentile believers prevails toward the Jewish people, spurred on by spiritual influences of generational antisemitism, pride, jealousy, anger, and fear, which the enemy continues to use to keep us apart. These have caused a lack of humility on our part toward the Jewish people and even causes us not to want to reach out to them with the love of God.

Wherever I go and whatever type of Church I preach in with *The Reconnection*, I can discern a level of spiritual opposition among my Gentile-believing family due to these influences. We need to repent of what divides us spiritually before we can be fully united. We need to submit to the healing and cleansing that the Holy Spirit wants to bring to each of our hearts to fully break off all past influences and to make the necessary corrections and adjustments to a theology that keeps us separate. Jews and Gentiles in the family of God must be fully acknowledged and supported in this Restoration. From our Father's point of view, there has been little unity between Jew and Gentile; yet this is the cry of His Heart, as demonstrated by the prayer of Yeshua/Jesus in John 17.

God's Word tells us that a final Remnant of Israel (whose awakening has already begun) must be restored with those we will ultimately rule and reign with when Yeshua/Jesus returns (see Romans 11:25–32). Therefore, the healing and cleansing work that Abba wants to bring will prepare us to restore and unite His family and prepare the Bride (His Body of Jewish and Gentile believers) for His coming.

The concept of God's people as His Bride dates to Hebrew Scriptures through Solomon and the prophets (see Song of Songs, Isaiah, and Jeremiah). It is not just a New Testament concept. God called Israel His Bride long before Yeshua/Jesus came to Earth to inaugurate the New Covenant. Thinking the Jewish people will be excluded from the bridal call of the Bridegroom is a great deception to the end-time culmination of Jew and Gentile and of Israel and the Church.

THIS IS THE MESSAGE OF THE HOUR

I believe *The Reconnection* is the message of the hour and the final key to the Restoration of the Church. It's critical to the reestablishment of the Church's fivefold governing focus (see Ephesians 4:11—some apostles, prophets, evangelists, pastors, and teachers). Israel is the final piece of the puzzle that leads to the fullness of unity in the Church insofar that it is able to address the principalities and powers through prayer and intercession while proclaiming the Kingdom of God upon Earth as the Church once did for the Gentiles to come to faith (see Ephesians 3:6–10).

We want revival. We want power. But we have been seeking these things in the wrong places. Simply put, the Church as usual, or as it has been, will not do! It isn't enough to simply bless Israel. The Church must Reconnect spiritually first (and be grafted back into her), to re-embrace her, which includes the Remnant of believers, to love them as our very own. Then the Body of Messiah/Christ can step in as the intercessor, the catalyst, and the salvific agent to stand in the gap, prophesy to the breath (see Ezekiel 37:9–11), and begin to push and see this baby come back to life. Nothing less will do!

As alluded to earlier, Gentile believers have been given the Gospel to make Israel jealous (see Romans 11:11) and must now fulfill their role on the Earth to bring the Kingdom forth. This is God's will for us, both Jew and Gentile, and this is His Divine timing. This is God's Glory plan—that through His *mercy* He would reunite His family so the fullness of the Gentiles will come in through Israel's salvation and our focus on it (see Romans 11:11–12, 15, 23, 25–26). But we won't understand *The Reconnection* in its fullness until we Realign ourselves with the *Heart of the Father* in *TONM*, which includes both branches of the faith—*Jewish* and *Gentile* believers acting in love and supporting one another.

> Then the Body of Messiah/Christ can step in as the intercessor, the catalyst, and the salvific agent to stand in the gap, prophesy to the breath (see Ezekiel 37:9–11), and begin to push and see this baby come back to life. Nothing less will do!

I always say that the fullness of the revelation concerning this special unity will come about only as we move into it. Although I might be shedding light on this new path, I do not see it in all its fullness, and I believe more is to be revealed from within the unity and love that we will begin to share with one another in the family of God. Please understand that *The Reconnection* is not a fanciful message or something to simply contemplate; it needs to be acted on. It requires a response from us and a correction in our thinking.

In all humility, if our current eschatology excludes *The Reconnection,* it needs to be corrected. Without a doubt, the mindset of the Gentile Church has been affected because of the devil's influence in this area. The fullness of the Father's eschatology can only flow out of the very unity in *TONM* that He's now beckoning us into as Jewish and Gentile believers in Yeshua/Jesus.

Israel's awakening and our reassociation with it—both the Remnant of Jewish believers, as well as having faith for the broken-off branches—is the golden key that will help open the door to world revival. Absolutely nothing less will do! *This is the Word of the Lord for Israel and the Church at this hour.*

I'm not bringing a new revelation here but rather a fresh understanding of what is already written in Scripture, and one that I pray God will move us into. We are waiting and longing for our Lord's return, but this will not happen until we take hold of *The Reconnection* key! Church, it's time to take the key!

THE HOUR BEFORE THE WEDDING

The Reconnection isn't about what we've done wrong, but what we need to do right. It's a message of mercy and love from the Father for His children to finally reconcile in *TONM* because we have entered the time of Israel's Restoration, Reconnection, and Realignment. But without properly uprooting the past and exposing its influence, we are not able to move forward with a clean slate, which is the Father's will for His family during these days. As Jewish and Gentile brothers and sisters, we need to love each other without fear or pride, malice or control, and long for the unity that was planned for us through His most magnificent Son since the beginning of time. Our destiny is to rule and reign together with our King (see Revelation 2:26; 5:9–10).

The Reconnection can be likened to a wedding at which, often, the hour before the ceremony, there can be panic and confusion with some type of last-minute mess that needs to get cleaned up. This is where we are currently in the family of God and the hour we find ourselves in. But all Glory to the Lord, when the Bride walks down the aisle, she is just beautiful, and the Glory of God shines on her every step. There is a cleanup process God is wanting all believers to enter at this time so He can properly prepare us for what is coming.

We live in a broken world, where what is called right is wrong and what is called wrong is right. In our humanity, we so often fail and miss the mark, but thanks be to the Lord, Who delivers us from all sin that we have the strength and ability to get it right. In this picture and story between Jew and Gentile up until now, both groups have failed. But doesn't Scripture align in this area that God has given all men over to disobedience so that He may have mercy on us all? (See Romans 11:32.)

Don't you think that God foreknew all that would happen between us and that the devil would use it to keep us apart? And doesn't God love to show His power and Glory through us in all of our weaknesses when we humble ourselves before Him in wanting to get it right?

> *The Reconnection isn't about what we've done wrong, but what we need to do right. It's a message of mercy and love from the Father for His children to finally reconcile in TONM because we have entered the time of Israel's Restoration, Reconnection, and Realignment. But without properly uprooting the past and exposing its influence, we are not able to move forward with a clean slate, which is the Father's will for His family during these days.*

There is a window of opportunity, for us in the Church, to receive this message in God's mercy and to get our hearts right with one another. That's why the title of this book sounds a holy alarm and blows the shofar, the trumpet. As I believe, many of us will move into this Reconnection message, and it will indeed sweep across the Church and Messianic bodies, much like the charismatic movement at the end of the twentieth century. I believe the heart of this message is from the Holy Spirit, Who is guiding us into His end-time plans—God knows His sheep, and His sheep know His voice (see John 10:3–4).

However, there is also a caution in this message because as this window of mercy draws to a close, those who have not been cleansed, broken off past influences, and moved into *The Reconnection* will continue to come under its influence. But this time, the deception will be greater than ever before, as the devil comes into his final hour (see Matthew 24:10, 23–25). I would not want to be one of those who is still against or indifferent toward Israel when the Lord judges the world for its sins before He returns.

That's why it's so important for us to get this message of *The Reconnection* out to every Church and "every highway and byway," to be able to enter discussion and dialogue that will enable us to embrace it. This will help prepare the Body of Messiah/Christ for what is to come and move us into one of our greatest-ever roles, which is to help restore the family so that the Lord can take final dominion here on the Earth with His return. What an honor He is bestowing on His end-time Ekklesia/Church.

This will require a great deal of humility, love, and patience in each of us, especially in the hearts of our shepherds, to gently lead both sides of our believing family into this Reconciliation and prepare us for what is coming.

So what exactly is God requiring of us here, not just to get our hearts right and break off ungodly influences from our past? This is just the beginning. We must also spiritually Reconnect to our firstborn brothers and sisters in a relationship of love and intimacy, which will Realign us with Israel, with whom we are family. Through this Reconnection, Abba can work His wonders through us to shine His love and mercy back toward the rest of Israel to help bring its people to life. Of course, as we move on further in this book, we will fully explore this and all that it will mean to us— what *The Reconnection* is and the adjustments and changes it will bring.

Our greatest challenge here is our own associations and attachments to our many differing theological viewpoints in the Church (this is usually where we are so passionate) concerning the end times with Israel and the Church. These attachments will require adjustment and adaptation to the calling that is upon us in this generation and the ones that tarry before the Lord returns to us.

HIDDEN FROM PRIOR GENERATIONS

Isn't it interesting that the mystery of opening the Gospel to the Gentile world through Mashiach/Christ (see Ephesians 3:1–11) that made Gentile believers coheirs together with Israel was not made known to prior generations? (See Ephesians 3:5–9.) The same is true for us now, with the mystery to restore Israel (see Romans 11:25), as we move back into a time of Reconciliation and Realignment for the Church with Israel—namely, that our calling is different and was *hidden* from those who have gone before us.

With all humility and sincerity, it is not easy to speak to a giant (the Gentile Church) to suggest that they are in need of change. In the scheme of things, you might ask, "Who are you to address this topic?" My answer: no one, except one of the voices crying out in the wilderness from the Messianic part of the olive tree saying, *"Prepare Ye the way of the Lord."*

As I have already stated, the fullness of *The Reconnection* must come from both sides of the family, Jew and Gentile alike. Will you continue to take this journey with me to explore the greater depths of this Reconnection message and all it means to us as family in *TONM?*

CHAPTER 3

WHO IS ISRAEL?

To UNDERSTAND THE significance of *The Reconnection*, it will help us to better define exactly who *Israel* is, in light of confusion that exists theologically between physical Israel and spiritual Israel, which we will fully explore in this chapter.

When it comes to Israel and the Church, the Gentile Church is divided into two camps: those who believe the Church has fully replaced biblical Israel, known as *Supersessionism* or *Replacement* or *Fulfillment Theology,* and those who believe that the nation and people of Israel will ultimately be restored.

Interestingly, those who believe in Replacement Theology claim that *they are* the new *Israel*, while those who accept Israel's Restoration often hold to a *separatist* view between the Church and Israel, where the two come together when Yeshua/Jesus returns, or sometime beyond that point. As we explore further, we'll see that both views are in need of adjustment, especially the first.

The question *"Who is Israel?"* is a challenging one and rather complex to understand, especially in light of the *broken-off branches of Israel* that the Apostle Paul discusses in Romans chapter 11 (verses 7–24, those who did not believe in Yeshua/Jesus but were nevertheless Jewish and part of Israel). This was further complicated by the breach in the fourth century, when the Roman Church separated the Church from its Jewish roots and heritage. This breach caused the Church to develop a separate identity and mindset apart from its Hebraic origins; beforehand this was not the case.

As a Jewish person coming to faith in the Gentile-dominated Church and receiving this burden from the Lord for His family to Reconnect, I've realized that a good amount of our Christian theology and eschatology comes through a Gentile Christian lens and perspective. We will quickly discover, however, that our ability to fully understand *TONM* isn't dependent on either a Gentile or Jewish lens but rather on *the Heart of God* and a desire for His family to be one.

But without the Church opening to the Messianic viewpoint, this door will remain closed, and we will remain unbalanced in our theological and eschatological understanding of Israel in the last days. We'll see that we need to rediscover our connection to Israel, especially the *modern Remnant* of Israel (Jewish believers), with whom we share the Kingdom of God. However, we won't be complete as a spiritual family until the balance of Israel (those who remain broken off through unbelief) are grafted back into the olive tree. According to Scripture and in God's timing, *Israel* is composed of this believing Remnant, along with those yet to be restored. This is the great error of Supersessionism.

When it comes to Israel and the Church, the Gentile Church is divided into two camps: those who believe the Church has fully replaced biblical Israel, known as Supersessionism or Replacement or Fulfillment Theology, and those who believe that the nation and people of Israel will ultimately be restored.

By faith, Israel is part of who we are (both the believing Remnant of Israel and those who are broken off). But more importantly, *Israel is part of who we will be, owing to God's Covenants and promises to restore them before Yeshua/Jesus returns*. It is pivotal that we understand this, especially because we are at the door of their spiritual regrafting. Actually, Restoration of the broken-off branches is critical to our Father's end-time plan to glorify His Son upon the Earth (see Ezekiel 36:22–32).

WE ARE GRAFTED INTO ISRAEL

To understand this question "Who Is Israel?" more fully, let's go to the scriptural teachings of Yeshua/Jesus and the apostles, all of whom were Jewish. First, why did Yeshua/Jesus come only for the lost sheep of the house of Israel, as He stated when ministering to the Canaanite woman? (See Matthew 15:24.) And why did He tell us that salvation comes from the Jews? (See John 4:22.) The answer is that all things had to be fulfilled first, as we know that Yeshua/Jesus was at the end of the law for all who believed (see Romans 10:4).

However, there is another significant reason why this had to take place first. We do not hear about this reason too often because of the Church's disconnection from Israel. Most of the Church still teaches that Jesus made everything totally new. Although the New Covenant was definitely new through Yeshua/ Jesus (and all that He did as the Lamb of God), and one that both Jew and Gentile had to believe in to receive, it was still an extension and continuation of all the other Covenants and promises that He first gave to Israel. However, keep in mind, Gentile believers were not required to follow Jewish laws (see Acts 15).

This is why Yeshua/Jesus had to come to Israel first. It was not only to fulfill the law but also to reestablish Israel's authority through His Jewish disciples, fulfill Israel's call to be a light to the nations (which is now also the Church's call), and take His message out to the world (Isaiah 49:6; Matthew 28:19). This way, the rest of His family could be reached and grafted into the same promises and Covenants of Israel to become the other part of TONM.

This is why Yeshua/Jesus had to come to Israel first. It was not only to fulfill the law but also to reestablish Israel's authority through His Jewish disciples, fulfill Israel's call to be a light to the nations (which is now also the Church's call), and take His message out to the world (Is. 49:6; Matt. 28:19). This way, the rest of His family could be reached and grafted into the same promises and Covenants of Israel to become the other part of *TONM*.

THE CONNECTION

This connection is crucial but is also greatly misunderstood in the Church, especially when the ancestral Church taught that it had fully replaced Israel and broke away from its Jewish roots. During those days, the Church aggressively confronted any Jewish or Gentile believers wanting to associate with this heritage, ridding it of any of its influence. This went on for the next several centuries until there really was no Remnant to connect with anymore. And this separation has obviously remained until today, even as God is now reestablishing Israel. So even the part of the Church that blesses Israel needs to gain a deeper understanding and connection here because it has not yet fully spiritually Reconnected to its Jewish family as it needs to (now that Israel's awakening is upon us). It still sees the Church as a separate entity, apart from Israel, which it is not; rather, it is *intrinsically* linked.

Speaking from the Gentile-believing perspective, all the Covenants were given to Israel first, so ultimately we could receive them through Mashiach/Christ. When we believe in Him, we become a part of Israel, as its commonwealth, joined with it through Israel's Remnant as coheirs with full rights (see Ephesians 2:19). This is *TONM*.

THE ISRAEL OF GOD

Some of us in the Church use the term "spiritual Israel," or better yet, "greater or extended Israel," which is who we become when both Jew and Gentile accept and believe in Yeshua/Jesus. However, greater or extended Israel is not complete without its connection to the physical part of Israel—first toward its Remnant (Jewish believers) and then ultimately to the balance of Israel, who is yet to be awakened and restored. And this connection between believing Jews and Gentiles is essential; especially now as God looks to awaken the balance of physical Israel (to work His end-time plans through both groups) to complete His spiritual family—the *Israel of God*—and establish His Kingdom on Earth.

Isn't this exactly how God used the apostles and the balance of the Jewish believers when the Church began to foster this union, to bring the Gospel to the nations? We need to now regain a deeper understanding of this connection as the Lord looks to reunite us. We need to more fully comprehend who we are in Messiah, our connection back toward Israel, and how we can actually draw the balance of the Jewish people to jealousy the way the Apostle Paul intended it to be. This will reunite us into the fullness of *TONM* and everything that means. It will help us fulfill our end-time role in the Church and properly represent Israel throughout the nations here on Earth when the Lord returns.

Despite the Church's separation from the Jewish branches, we are still ultimately living, operating, and sharing in their Covenants, which now through Mashiach/Christ also belong to us. Scripturally, this is not vice versa, as the ancestral Church proclaimed it to be. This must be corrected now as the Jewish branches are reemerging.

Furthermore, speaking from the Jewish perspective of those who believe in Yeshua/Jesus, not all Israel is fully Israel. But rather only those who ultimately believe in Him and make up the Remnant of Israel (Romans 9), until the balance of Israel is brought in at the end, which ultimately makes us (Israel/Church) whole (see Romans 11:11–32). So greater or spiritual Israel still comes from physical Israel, through Mashiach/Christ and the Remnant of Jewish believers, whom His children from the nations are supposed to be connected with in *TONM*.

Regarding Scripture and the Heart of God, this has never changed, and it never will. In fact, the names of the twelve Jewish apostles and the twelve tribes of Israel will be forever etched and written on the foundations and gates of the New Jerusalem because the Israel of God has a Jewish heritage to which we are eternally connected.

The Apostle Paul writes about this connection in his letter to the Ephesian Church. He said that when we were separate from Mashiach/Christ, we were also excluded from citizenship or commonwealth from Israel and foreigners to the Covenants of the promise: *"For he came and preached peace to you who were far away and peace to those who were near. Consequently, you* [God's children from the nations] *are no longer foreigners and strangers, but fellow citizens with God's people* [Jewish believers from Israel—the Remnant] *and also members of His household, built on the foundation of the Apostles and prophets, with Mashiach/Christ Yeshua/ Jesus Himself as the chief cornerstone"* (see Ephesians 2:17–20).

Furthermore, in Romans 11, Paul teaches us that all God's children from the nations were grafted into the olive tree of Israel, not the other way around (see Romans 11:24). How can we be grafted into Israel when most of them have been broken off by not believing? Speaking from the Gentile perspective, this is a paradox to most of us, but one we can better understand when we can more fully identify with the nature of both physical and spiritual Israel and its separate journeys to faith. In this process, we will also begin to recognize the greater significance of our connection to them and how we are now a part of Israel, which Paul explains to us in this chapter.

There is a vital connection here (with the Jewish branches) for us that we lost a long, long time ago. However, as we come to the end and the Lord looks to restore Israel, this breach must be repaired between God's Gentile Remnant (the Gentile-believing Church) and His Remnant from Israel so that God's plans and purposes can be achieved through us and the end can actually come.

There is a *vital* connection here (with the Jewish branches) for us that we lost a long, long time ago. However, as we come to the end and the Lord looks to restore Israel, this *breach* must be repaired between God's Gentile Remnant (the Gentile-believing Church) and His Remnant from Israel so that God's plans and purposes can be achieved through us and the end can actually come. As I have already suggested, the *Israel Piece* and our Reconnection to it is the final act of Restoration for the Church to help reunite us, so that God's full blessings and power may come upon us!

YESHUA SHIFTS THE AUTHORITY OF GOD

To gain a deeper understanding of this connection, first let us take a look at how Yeshua/Jesus actually achieved this shift, in transferring Israel's authority from the Sanhedrin, which was connected to the Levitical priesthood to the apostles who founded the Church. Then let's reexamine the different paths of Israel from Jesus's time to the time of His return when the balance of Israel is restored, to help us see the full picture here regarding the whole Israel of God.

The apostles and prophets did not carry the authority of Yeshua/Jesus until it was given to them through the Holy Spirit at Shavuot/Pentecost. And first it had to be taken away from the Sanhedrin/Levitical priesthood because of their rejection of Mashiach/Christ, which is vital to our understanding. *"O Jerusalem, Jerusalem, you who kill the prophets and stone those sent to you, how often I have longed to gather your children together, as a hen gathers her chicks under her wings, and you were not willing"* (Matt. 23:37).

Please try to understand that before Yeshua/Jesus went to the cross, the priesthood still carried the authority of God that was given to them through Moses at Sinai. This is how He referred to them in this light. *"So you must be careful to do everything they tell you. But do not do what they do, for they do not practice what they preach"* (Matt. 23:2–3).

However, as we drew closer to His mission to take up the cross, look what happens to the barren fig tree that He curses: *"May you never bear fruit again!"* And immediately afterward, when He arrives in Jerusalem, the Pharisees and Sadducees confront Yeshua/Jesus over His authority: *"By what authority are you doing these things?"*

There are two accounts in the Gospel of this story regarding the fig tree. The first is in Matthew, and the second in Mark. Both of them precede issues of His authority being questioned by the

Pharisees and Sadducees. This is especially notable in Mark, where Yeshua/Jesus actually ransacks the temple (see Matthew 21:18–27; Mark 11:12–21).

I respectfully submit to you that this fig tree did not represent Israel, as a good number of Christian Bible teachers and theologians might point out. Rather, the Sanhedrin and Levitical Priesthood, the authority of Israel, had become so dried up by their own self-righteousness and religious pride that they were already completely barren and lacked any true life and spirituality. *"Woe to you, teachers of the law and Pharisees, you hypocrites! You travel over land and sea to win a single convert, and when you have succeeded, you make them twice as much a child of hell as you are"* (Matt. 23:15).

Please also try to understand that Yeshua/Jesus was incredibly popular among the people of Israel during His ministry years. This is why the Sanhedrin and many Pharisees were fearful of His influence. Many Jews were drawn to Him because they witnessed His love, His compassion, and the power of His miracles.

As we come down to the end, here are the missing pieces of the puzzle. The Israel of God will never be complete until God's children from the nations are connected spiritually to Israel's Remnant and until the broken-off branches are fully restored: "All Israel will be saved" (see Romans 11:26-27). The broken-off branches are still a part of us in light of God's Covenants and promises to restore them.

Consequently, we now find ourselves at the final juncture of God's mission with His Son. The confrontation heats up between Yeshua/Jesus and the Sanhedrin, culminating with His final rebuke and warning of pending judgment in Matthew 23 and 24 and their final act against Him to send Him to His death: *"Woe to you, teachers of the law and Pharisees...Look, your house is left to you desolate"* (see Matthew 23:13–38).

Spiritually speaking, through the cross and resurrection, Yeshua/

Jesus was about to move a *major mountain* and throw it into the sea. The authority of God that had been upon the chief priests and teachers of the law had come to an end: *"May you never bear fruit again!"* It was about to be removed from them and placed on the apostles and prophets by the power of the Holy Spirit. This would establish a new foundation on which the Ekklesia/Church (the Israel of God) would be built, through the Remnant of Israel and God's children from the nations, who were to be grafted into the tree with believing Israel, who would now fulfill Israel's call to be a light to the nations in a very special love and unity, specifically designed by God in *TONM*.

GOD'S COVENANTS ARE IRREVOCABLE

As we come down to the end, here are the missing pieces of the puzzle. The Israel of God will never be complete until God's children from the nations are connected spiritually to Israel's Remnant and until the broken-off branches are fully restored: *"All Israel will be saved"* (see Romans 11:26-27). The broken-off branches are still a part of us in light of God's Covenants and promises to restore them. These promises are based solely on God's Word and timing, rather than men, for these are *unconditional Covenants*.

The firstborn of Israel are a *Covenant* people and not just another national group, as most of the Church now perceives them to be. Indeed, we need to be reattached to them as family. We need to treat them as our very own, just like our Father does, for this to come to pass through us. This is what *The Reconnection* achieves in us as we embrace God's healing touch for His family to be one.

This is a great challenge for the Church presently, especially if it holds to Christian theology, that all of the Covenants have already been fulfilled through Christ. The presumption is that there is no longer any difference between Jew and Gentile in the faith, as the Church has taught for some seventeen hundred years.

ONE GROUP WITH DISTINCTIVE ROLES

This is definitely a misunderstanding. Although Yeshua/Jesus broke down the wall and the dividing partition to make us one in the Spirit, this did not eliminate our distinctive calls and roles from within this unity between Jew and Gentile (see 1 Corinthians 7:17–24; Acts 15).

Jewish believers (the Remnant) clearly continued an association to the law through the Torah, no longer with their understanding concerning salvation, which could come only through Mashiach/Christ, but to live as Jews and be a continuing light for their own people to help win them to the faith (see Acts 21:17–25). This is both a right and a liberty Jewish believers have to be connected to their heritage in a way that is different from God's children from the nations, who did not have the same requirement, but still operated in unity out of *TONM* (see Acts 21:25). And the same is true today for Jewish believers to help bring their own people back to the faith.

The Apostle Paul draws out this distinction in his epistle to the Galatian Church when teaching on this unity by using the analogy of a man and a woman. Although we might be one in the Spirit through Mashiach/Christ, we still perform different roles from within this unity. And the same was true then, even of a master and his servant (see Galatians 3:26–29).

Paul never taught us to eliminate these distinctions. In fact, he upheld them and earnestly sought the blessing and well-being of the Jerusalem Church (the Remnant of Israel) that existed in his day and the Remnant of Israel (see Acts 21:17–26). We need to do the same now, as the Jewish branches come back to life, through the modern Remnant, in light of Israel's salvation and the fulfillment of God's Covenants to them. As the Church Realigns to put Israel's salvation first once again, the natural outflow of this is the greater harvest to the nations. That's why our renewed focus on Israel's spiritual awakening is the *golden key* that helps open the door toward world revival—the unity of the Father and the Son in His *One New Man*. Opening up to the Messianic perspective is also crucial to this equation. This renewed union between us with its heart's cry will ultimately help make the Israel of God complete; a Bride readied for His coming.

THE PATHS OF ISRAEL

To better understand the different paths and directions that Israel took after Yeshua/Jesus came, let us take a deeper look at Romans 11. I firmly believe that the Apostle Paul wrote Romans chapters 9 and 10 to lay a foundation of understanding regarding spiritual election between Jew and Gentile. He writes this to help the Gentile part of the family better understand physical Israel's complexity that he explains to us in Romans chapter 11. The Remnant of Israel (Jewish believers) and those blinded who were broken off because of unbelief, but would be restored and grafted back in at the end.

As I was writing an article for *Charisma Online Magazine* on Romans 11, the Holy Spirit gave me a fresh perspective on this. In the first eleven verses of chapter 11, Paul asks us three questions, and each of them relates to a different direction and journey for the Jewish people—first, the Remnant of Israel who would believe in Yeshua; second, those who remained blinded to Him; and third, those who are ultimately restored at the end.

PATH #1 — AND THE FIRST QUESTION — THE REMNANT

Romans 11:1–6

> *"Did God reject His people? By no means! I am an Israelite myself from the tribe of Benjamin. God did not reject his people who he foreknew.... So too at this present time there is a Remnant chosen by grace"* (Rom. 11:1).

Here, Paul uses Elijah's experience with Israel, where he thought he was the only one left. But God explains that He has reserved seven thousand and at this time, there is a Remnant chosen by grace—the Remnant of Jewish believers in Yeshua/Jesus who founded the Ekklesia/Church. They included not just the apostles, but also the many Jewish believers who made up the Remnant of Israel at that time, with whom all the initial Gentile believers were united into *TONM*.

These Scriptures have also applied to a Remnant of Jewish believers coming to faith over the centuries, up until today. From the time of Yeshua/Jesus to now, there has always been a small Remnant of Jewish believers coming to the Lord. This can also apply to the reawakened modern Remnant of today.

PATH #2 — AND THE SECOND QUESTION — THOSE VEILED

Romans 11:7–10

> *"What then? What the people of Israel sought so earnestly they did not obtain. The elect among them did, but the others were hardened, as it is written: 'God gave them a spirit of stupor, eyes that could not see and ears that could not hear, to this very day'"* (Rom. 11:7).

THE TERM "ELECT"

First, *"The elect among them did"*—This reference relates to the Remnant of Jewish believers we have just discussed. (However, the term "elect" in itself applies to all believers, both Jew and Gentile alike, as it appears from New Testament Scripture that God knows exactly who will believe and follow Him and who will not. It can also mean "chosen.")

THOSE HARDENED

Second, much can be said about the hardening of Israel in this text, especially regarding our understanding of its timing. Did it come upon them because they rejected Yeshua/Jesus, or was it already on them before Mashiach/Christ came? In my second book, *The*

Ezekiel Generation, I dedicated a whole chapter to this subject of our understanding of the different veils upon mankind (chapter 8) and how they actually came about; I encourage you to read it.

While we can trace the explanation to this hardening of Israel to the Torah (five books of Moses) in the book of Deuteronomy (29:4), we are also aware that all humankind's hearts are veiled to God as a result of sin, which naturally hardens (see Isaiah 53:6).

However, it was not until Israel and Judah totally abandoned God for their idols that the Lord commanded Isaiah to proclaim a blindness and deafness upon them, which has remained to this day (see Isaiah 6:9–10). Even when Yeshua/Jesus appeared among them, they could not recognize Him.

I believe this is the Scripture the Apostle Paul is referring to here, but I should also point out that through the Sanhedrin's condemnation and rejection of Yeshua/Jesus, they led the balance of the people of Israel astray and permanently sealed their fate up until the end. Those of Israel whose eyes were not opened remained under this curse, *until* the appointed time, when the veil and the curse will be lifted (see Romans 11:25–26).

These Jewish people faced the judgment and dispersion that both Yeshua/Jesus and Moses forewarned about (see Deuteronomy 28–30; Matthew 23:37–24:2). Not one stone would be left upon another when Rome attacked Jerusalem, both in 70 AD when the temple was destroyed, and in 135 AD, when their dispersion (Diaspora) became final.

HAVE WE REALLY UNDERSTOOD?

We know that the people of Israel paid a great price for their disobedience. To whom much is given, much is expected. Israel was now scattered into a final dispersion, where the people's sufferings would be apparent for the ages to come.

However, I believe our viewpoint of them has been harsh in light of the ancestral Church's judgment of them and misunderstanding that we have had about their plight, which I also addressed in greater detail in *The Ezekiel Generation.* Did not the Apostle Paul challenge us to love them despite their present rejection? (See Romans 11:28.) In reality, who could have stood up to the law in their own strength? Only one person ever did, and His name is Mashiach/Christ.

ISRAEL CHOSEN TO FACE THE LAW

The people of Israel were called to face the law for all humanity so that sin could be brought into account and so that Mashiach/Christ could ultimately come to free us from its curse. God knew beforehand that they would ultimately fail even before they began (just as any other people group would have done). Please also read the Scriptures I have already referred to in Deuteronomy chapters 28–30, which clearly reflect this.

Although Scripture tells us that the Gentiles will not be judged by the written law but by the law they know naturally through their conscience (see Romans 2:12–16), what is it that would ultimately bring sin into account if the law (the Ten Commandments) hadn't been given first? This is also why Paul tells us that the law is a schoolmaster to bring us to

> The people of Israel were called to face the law for all humanity so that sin could be brought into account and so that Mashiach/Christ could ultimately come to free us from its curse.

Mashiach/Christ (see Galatians 3:24) and why not one letter of the law will disappear until everything is accomplished (see Matthew 5:17–18). It is only when we cross over with belief in Yeshua/Jesus that we pass from sin's curse, which the law exposed (see Galatians 3:13). Otherwise we remain under it and face the judgment against sin that the law introduced (see Romans 7:7–11; 4:15). *We need to gain a deeper understanding of how the law actually functions in this context.*

While it might have been possible for Israel to uphold the law, in its present state at that time, without the Spirit being in them (see Romans 8:1–4), its humanity could not possibly sustain it. They wanted to be like everyone else. However, because they were called out, the law still required consequences for their actions and held them accountable as a result. In reality, ultimately their only out was through Mashiach/Christ Himself, Who was at the end of the law for those who believed. As a result, look how God used the Remnant of Israel in this regard (the Jews who did believe) at that time to fulfill Israel's call and role; and look how He is using the modern Remnant now, as He looks to restore Israel. However, those who didn't believe and rejected Him during those days faced dispersion and the pending judgment as a result.

SOMETHING UNIQUE

Indeed, there is something quite unique and even hard to comprehend, or even put into words, between the suffering of Mashiach/Christ and the suffering of the firstborn of Israel that no other people were called to endure. I don't know about you, but as a believer in Yeshua/Jesus, and aware of my sinful nature, I would much rather be born and be alive under the New Covenant than under the Mosaic Law.

Isaiah cries out in this regard, *"Comfort, comfort my people, says your God. Speak tenderly to Jerusalem, and proclaim to her that her hard service has been completed, that her sin has been paid for, that she has received from the Lord's hand double for all her sins"* (Is. 40:1–2). I am not suggesting, either, that we compromise for their humanity, but rather that we would have more compassion and understanding for their plight and what they suffered—not just for themselves, but also for the rest of us in facing the law in bringing sin into account, which had to happen first, before Yeshua/Jesus could come.

Arni Klein puts this brilliantly: "God loved us so much that He

> *Arni Klein puts this brilliantly: "God loved us so much that He chose the least amount of people to have to face the law for the rest of us." Wow! That certainly puts this in a different light.*

chose the least amount of people to have to face the law for the rest of us." Wow! That certainly puts this in a different light.

This understanding should help change our perspective and give us a greater appreciation for all they have gone through in light of their own calling. After all, they still need to believe in Yeshua to be saved. In Paul's words, *"How, then, can they call on the one they have not believed in? And how can they believe in the one of whom they have not heard? And how can they hear without someone preaching to them?"* (Rom. 10:14). This should be our burden now, as it is the Father's and the Son's, and because without Yeshua/Jesus, they are still lost.

PATH #3 — AND THE THIRD QUESTION — ISRAEL RESTORED

Romans 11:11–32

"Again I ask: Did they stumble beyond recovery? Not at all!" (Rom. 11:11).

In this text, Paul questions us again for the third time. However, this time it relates solely to those Jewish people who have been hardened, who have still not believed and remain under the veil. Please note, however, that they are still referred to as "Israel" in this text (verse 11). Did they stumble beyond recovery? Not at all! And Paul makes clear to us that there is a future redemption for Israel that is still to come. What else can these Scriptures refer to? We also must ask why the Church fathers did not see this when Scripture is so clear concerning Israel's ultimate Restoration. Paul writes, *"How much greater riches will their fullness bring? For if their rejection brought Reconciliation to the world, what will their acceptance be but life from the dead? And if they do not persist in unbelief, they will be grafted in, for God is able to graft them in again. After all, if you were cut out of an olive tree that is wild by nature, and contrary to nature were grafted into a cultivated olive tree, how much more readily will these, the natural branches, be grafted into their own olive tree!.... I do not want you to be igno-rant of this mystery, brothers and sisters, so that you may not be conceited: Israel has experienced a hardening in part until the full number of Gentiles has come in, and in this way all Israel will be saved"* (Rom. 11:12–27).

THE AWAKENING HAS BEGUN

Without a doubt, the veil and hardening over physical Israel will be lifted. If we are willing to accept it, we can see a reawakened, modern Remnant of Israel through the arising of the Messianic Movement and the many thousands of Jewish believers who are coming to faith. This is the first part of this mystery to be revealed, and according to Scripture, there will be a mass awakening of Israel turning to the Lord toward the end with a great repentance (see Zechariah 12:10).

HOW IMPORTANT IS THE MODERN REMNANT?

Up to this point, we have not really understood the full signifi-cance of the Remnant of Israel. This is understandable because they have been cut off from us for so long. But now that Israel is being restored, our Reconnection to them in the Spirit moves center stage and needs to be unveiled.

This is the part of Israel we are supposed to be connected with now through Mashiach/Christ, even though the ancestral Church broke off this influence. However, now that God is in the process of restoring the Jewish branches, our reassociation to them becomes paramount to our understanding because the Remnant is our link to the rest of Israel. And for the balance of Israel to come forth, the Remnant needs to be strengthened, which we will explore further in chapter 5.

THE LAST GREAT HARVEST OF SOULS

So the first part of the mystery relates to the full awakening of Israel. Now, the second part of the mystery in Romans 11 relates to the last great harvest of souls relating to the link between the fullness of the Gentiles and Israel's final spiritual awakening. This is a *connectedness* that requires our utmost attention and has huge consequences for the Kingdom of God in these last generations. However, up until this time, *it has been hidden from us.*

POCKETS OF SPIRITUAL AWAKENING

I also believe that, as the Church begins to Reconnect more to the Jewish branches into the fullness of *TONM*, more and more of Israel will be restored through intercessory prayer and lifestyle witness and evangelism. The supplication that will be sent up into the heavens from this reunification in the Spirit will have its cause and effect. It will create greater pockets of spiritual openings among the Jewish people, similar to the beginning of the Messianic Movement (1967), when thousands upon thousands of Jewish people were sovereignly touched, beginning this awakening.

I also believe that, as the Church begins to Reconnect more to the Jewish branches into the fullness of TONM, more and more of Israel will be restored through intercessory prayer and lifestyle witness and evangelism.

As such, with the Church's full support, the foundation for Jewish belief in Yeshua will be made stronger once again, just as it was in the first century. This will help prepare the way for the salvation of the balance of Israel, which will be part of the final Body of Messiah/Christ. That will make both Israel and the Church complete.

NOT EVERY JEW

I do not see every Jewish person coming to faith in this final awakening, just like not every Gentile will come to faith, either. However, I do believe that a great majority of Israel will turn to the Lord at this time. The true Body of Messiah/Christ has always been a Remnant in and of itself, and unfortunately many will perish under the judgment. Plus, the wars of the end of time seem to indicate that many will die before Israel, in general, turns to the Lord. Nonetheless, the nation of Israel will turn to God in the end. I hope I am wrong on this point and that all will come to the knowledge of God. Amen!

THE FULFILLMENT OF HIS COVENANTS TO ISRAEL COMPLETES US

Israel's final awakening is the fulfillment of God's Covenants toward Israel and its commonwealth. A Kingdom of priests from every nation and tribe... (see Revelation 5:9–10). Israel's Restoration not only completes us a spiritual family; it completes Israel and the Church, which at this point are one and the same.

THE CHURCH IS ISRAEL

This is truly an interesting phenomenon. Is the Church spiritual Israel, and is the Israel of God the Church? Yes, in the sense of an extension of Israel, an expanded Israel, but not in a sense of replacement, and not without it being properly connected to the Remnant of Israel in *TONM* (Jewish believers), with an understanding that it is not complete until the balance of Israel is spiritually restored. Said another way, *through union with the saved Remnant of Israel, the Church is also connected to the Jewish nation, including those not yet born again.* Take a look back now and review Dr. Daniel Juster's definition of the Church. You will see that they are one and the same (chapter 2, page 21).

This is truly an interesting phenomenon. Is the Church spiritual Israel, and is the Israel of God the Church? Yes, in the sense of an extension of Israel, an expanded Israel, but not in a sense of replacement, and not without it being properly connected to the Remnant of Israel in TONM (Jewish believers), with an understanding that it is not complete until the balance of Israel is spiritually restored.

In conclusion, we have come full circle, both in defining the

Church and in defining Israel. The Church is not a separate entity and can never replace Israel without being fully connected to it. Similarly, Israel and the Church are not separate entities but are intrinsically linked through their destinies. This is true even though we have unique roles and paths to play out from within the context of *TONM,* culminating with the last great harvest of souls and Israel's ultimate spiritual Restoration.

DEREK PRINCE

Derek Prince, the great theologian from the twentieth century who loved Israel and the Church, worked tirelessly for us to understand that God's Covenants toward Israel can be fulfilled only through their spiritual Restoration. He pioneered many of the fundamentals that we have taken hold of now, in the part of the Church that loves and blesses Israel.

In the beginning of his ministry, he had a great challenge because at that time, most of the Church followed Replacement Theology. Therefore, they could not see any distinction in the Covenants toward Israel because they were taught that they were either fulfilled through Christ or applied to them now, instead of Israel.

While unbelieving Jews are still on their journey and most still remain broken off from their own olive tree, in light of God's irrevocable Covenants toward them, they are still a part of us through faith. Indeed, it is, in fact, through our faith that God will actually restore them. *We need to see them as Scripture tells us they will be, not as they are currently, and pray for them in this vein.*

THE JEWISH BRANCHES REEMERGE

Before 1967, there was hardly even a Remnant for us to be connected with, and up until that time, nearly all Jewish people coming to faith had no choice but to be assimilated into the Christian Church. The concept of Messianic Judaism was reborn about the same time as the rise of the Zionist movement and the Pentecostal awakening in the Church. Many missions failed at that time, but a few took root, such as Chosen People Ministries, founded earlier by Leopold Cohn, American Messianic Fellowship and Christian witness to Israel. In England, Churches Mission to the Jews (CMJ) was founded by William Wilberforce. It was not until much later in the twentieth century, after Israel took back control of Jerusalem, that this new movement was born.

> *"Very truly I tell you, unless a kernel of wheat falls to the ground and dies, it remains only a single seed. But if it dies, it produces many seeds"* (John 12:24).

THOSE WHO HAVE GONE BEFORE US

We should also honor the lives of many who have gone before us, both Jewish and Gentile believers who have helped our Lord give birth to the reemergence of the Jewish branches of the faith. From the Puritans to the Pietists, whose theology and prayers have had an untold effect and the Christian Zionists, to William Wilberforce, who was one of the founders of the CMJ well over 180 years ago (Church's Ministry among Jewish People). Count Ludwig Von Zinzendorf in the first part of the eighteenth century had a vision for the Jewish people to come to Yeshua and remain Jewish. Plus, there were a good number of Jewish believers whose spirits burned deep in their hearts with these truths: Joseph Frey and Joseph Rabinowitz in the nineteenth century; and Arthur Katz, Moishe Rosen, Manny Brotman, and Marty Chernoff in the twentieth century, among others.

Manny Brotman started the Young Hebrew Christian Alliance, which then became the Young Messianic Jewish Alliance. The Young Alliance influenced the larger Hebrew Christian Alliance toward Messianic Judaism, and they changed their names, respectively, to Messianic Jewish Alliance and Young Messianic Jewish Alliance, known as the MJAA (Messianic Jewish Alliance of America), which

Marty Chernoff then headed. Moishe Rosen founded Jews for Jesus, and Art Katz's prophetic teaching and preaching foresaw much of what is happening in these last days.

A PROPHETIC FULFILLMENT

It is also true that the reestablishment of the State of Israel in 1948, the awakening of many thousands of Jewish believers in Yeshua/Jesus, and the rise of the Messianic Movement are the beginning signs of the prophetic fulfillment of God's faithfulness to restore His firstborn back to the family by keeping His *Covenants* specifically to the Jewish people. The Messianic Movement has helped lay the foundation for all Jewish believers now coming to faith that testify that the *modern Remnant* of Israel has been reborn.

This is crucial to our current understanding and is different from the understanding of other generations. Today, it is the modern Remnant of Israel that God has chosen for His Gentile-believing Church to be Reconnected with so the Jewish branches of the faith can reemerge and flourish in *TONM*. This, in turn, releases the full blessing and power back on the rest of the Church.

Up to this point, this has been challenging for us in the Church because we have been looking at this through such a Gentile lens that there has been no room for us to even recognize the Jewish part of the family along with their views and differing expressions, let alone the call of the Jew, except for them to be the same as the rest of us.

You might ask why it is different now than the way it has been for so long. The answer to that question is because now is the time for Israel to come forth. Thus, we must adjust accordingly to prepare the way for their Restoration so our Lord's *Covenants* to them can be fulfilled.

However, since this awakening has begun, most of the Church has not yet recognized this *Remnant* properly.

WE CANNOT SEE THIS THROUGH A GENTILE CHRISTIAN LENS

Up to this point, this has been challenging for us in the Church because we have been looking at this through such a Gentile lens that there has been no room for us to even recognize the Jewish part of the family along with their views and differing expressions, let alone the call of the Jew, except for them to be the same as the rest of us.

THE JEWISH ROLE

As a result, we must come to fully accept and comprehend the role of the Jewish believer from within the context of *TONM* that has its own unique qualities that allow them to shine faith and light back to those of Israel who are still broken off and under that veil.

This is the calling for all Jewish believers, without exception, as it is also for Christians to draw Israel to jealousy. However, when a Jewish person remains Jewish with belief in Yeshua, it sends a bold statement back into the Jewish community that perplexes and challenges current Jewish belief, which is ultimately necessary to help win them back to Messiah. Instead of communicating and conveying that they have converted to Christianity, which has not only been used to persecute them but is also completely foreign to them.

These bridges are already in the process of being rebuilt, providing Jewish people a new and fresh option they might not have considered beforehand, to help win them to faith, for them to understand that belief in Yeshua/Jesus is Jewish. And as we will see, Jewish believers do not have to be religious to fulfill this calling and be a light back to their own people.

Indeed, didn't the Apostle Paul function and operate as a Jew, when ministering to his own people in Jerusalem? (See Acts 21:17–26.) So, in turn now, we need to bless our Jewish brothers and sisters into the fullness of their identities to help them win the rest of Israel (the family) back to faith.

Truth be told, many Jewish believers actually need a great deal of encouragement in this area, especially those who have come to the Lord through the Church. Sometimes they even deny and break off their own heritage to accept the Lord.

THE HOLY SPIRIT IS SHIFTING

For certain, the Holy Spirit is shifting us into this time, which is why so many more of us have some kind of Israel consciousness on our radars. There is no question that the time of Israel's awakening is upon us and that we are in the last days. However, for us to fully recognize this time, as well as our role to help awaken them, the blinders must be removed from us first so that we can fully see all that is in God's Glory plan, as we started to discuss in this book.

ROMANCE TOWARD ISRAEL

Some of us are now what I call "romantic" toward Israel, even thinking that Jewish people don't need to accept Yeshua/Jesus to find salvation. Although it is a good thing for us to bless Israel, both our support and discernment are in great need of refocus and improvement. The Remnant of Jewish believers must be our *first fruits* in how we support Israel financially before anything else; especially those in the land, and in the nations as well.

The enemy doesn't mind us blowing shofars, wearing tallit (prayer shawls), or even connecting to the Jewish calendar. But all hell is let loose when we get the fullness of this Reconnection revelation and all it means for us to move into it to help rebirth Israel spiritually. When we do, it is all very close to being finished.

When many Christians visit Israel, they take Christian tours through the land and visit historical sites but there is little connection to the actual believers there. There should be a balance here, and I believe this is going to change.

THE ENEMY—ANYTHING BUT THE MAIN OBJECTIVE

The enemy doesn't mind us blowing shofars, wearing tallit (prayer shawls), or even connecting to the Jewish calendar. But all hell is let loose when we get the fullness of this Reconnection revelation and all it means for us to move into it to help rebirth Israel spiritually. When we do, it is all very close to being finished.

I have had experience with certain Gentile groups in the Church wanting to become more Messianic in how they function and operate in light of the ancestral Church's actions against Israel and our Jewish roots. However, they have still lacked the most significant reason for our Realignment, which is to reunite us together into the *Father's Heart* for *TONM*, to win Israel back to faith. We must never lose sight of this. This Reconnection is at the heart of this transformation and is the power source for everything else in it.

ARE WE WILLING?

For us to hit the mark, there must be a greater openness and humility in us. We need to be willing to search our hearts, re-embrace our Jewish family as our own, and revisit and adjust our theology and eschatology, which keep us separated from the fullness of *The Reconnection*. This is one of our greatest challenges in this area. The enemy has many obstacles already in place, including our own pride, to either prevent or hold us back from finding *The Reconnection*. Some of these obstacle are theological, some are emotional, and some are spiritual, such as fear; there are even sibling issues between Jew and Gentile. The devil plays on all such issues through

> For us to hit the mark, there must be a greater openness and humility in us. We need to be willing to search our hearts, re-embrace our Jewish family as our own, and revisit and adjust our theology and eschatology, which keep us separated from the fullness of The Reconnection.

our heartstrings to keep control and prevent us from hitting the bull's eye with Israel's spiritual awakening.

A PROPHETIC PICTURE

There is a prophetic picture here that can help us identify our roles. It has to do with the battle Israel faced against the Amalekites when they first came out of Egypt. Every time Moses dropped his hands, the Amalekites advanced, so Aaron and Hur held up his hands on both sides and in this way they defeated the enemy (see Exodus 17:8–13).

This is a picture of the modern-day Church holding up the arms of the Remnant of Israel so that the enemy can be overcome and defeated. This is what it will take to hold up the Jewish branches, which are in great need of the Church's full support and blessings. We also need them to make us complete. God has designed this time to reunite us, and we are in great need of each other.

THE JEWISH BRANCHES NEED HELP

Like the Gentile Church, Messianic Congregations and Jewish believers are far from being perfect. Many are not even aware of this, but the Messianic Body needs a great deal of strengthening—not just financially but also spiritually.

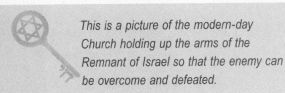

This is a picture of the modern-day Church holding up the arms of the Remnant of Israel so that the enemy can be overcome and defeated.

Up to this point, the Messianic Body has been caught between two main groups. As a result, it has grown up with some major insecurities. The Jewish Body tells them that they can no longer be Jews and believe in Yeshua, and the Church has told them, "You can't do that Jewish stuff anymore!" So they have been misunderstood on both sides, perhaps clinging to religion more than they should have out of fear of losing their identity. As with everything in the New Covenant, the Holy Spirit should always come first.

In addition, the people on the Gentile side of the family are not the only ones who need to Reconnect in this picture. Our Jewish brothers and sisters have also become isolated; that is not our Father's will, either. Many Jewish believers could greatly profit spiritually from some of the wonderful healing and deliverance programs that are offered in the local Church and be strengthened in the gifts of the Holy Spirit.

Just imagine for a moment a restored, healed Body on both sides, with the local Church and the Messianic Body working together in unity and love for the common good of all believers and more effectively reaching out to the Jewish communities around them to properly draw them to jealousy. This is the goal and aim of *The Reconnection* and *Alignment*, which we fully explore in *Romans 911*.

CHAPTER 4

A TASTE OF MILK AND HONEY

AS A JEWISH believer coming into the Church, I have come to love my Gentile family as my very own. I am also very grateful for learning a great deal of my spiritual gifting from the Gentile side of the family, who have been most open to the Holy Spirit. It is very apparent to me that we have much to offer one another.

UNITY

I believe this to be the Heart of Jesus's prayer in John 17: that both Jew and Gentile, all of us in the family of God, would know and taste more of the unity that Mashiach/Christ proclaimed and encouraged us into through His own relationship with the Father. I pray that we would be brought to a complete love and unity so more of the world can know the truth about God (see John 17:20–23).

It is as if something extra is released into us as we discover more of this unity in the Father and Son's love between us. As we rediscover greater fellowship and unity among Jewish and Gentile believers in *TONM*, we will gain a greater fullness of the love and character of God. This special gift from God awaits us as we draw more closely to it. We are calling this, "Liquid Love."

Unity is seriously important to the Heart of God and is one of the intrinsic principles that releases His power upon us. However, this needs to be achieved without compromising the truth of His Word, which in our modern day has already begun to separate the sheep from the goats. Let us pray for those who are more liberal among us that they will be awakened to truth and not compromise the Word of God for humanity's sake.

THE DEVIL'S TRAPS

The enemy is keenly aware of this principle through us. As a result, he works overtime to keep us separated and divided. This empowers the Kingdom of darkness around us and weakens the Body of Messiah/Christ. No area is more affected by this in the family of God than through our eschatology, with so many differing viewpoints on the end of days between Israel and the Church and the Lord's return to us. We become so strongly aligned with these beliefs that it makes it difficult for us to cohabitate in the Spirit. This is not healthy for the family of God.

A FRESH WAY TO LOOK AT ESCHATOLOGY

We can actually learn from religious Jews here in the way they study Talmud. This is the collection of the oral laws and traditions that were handed down through the rabbinic generations, which were recorded much later in time. I am not focusing here on the writings per se, but rather how they study and conclude with many differing views and interpretations. What's unique here, is that there is a greater love and unity among those who study to not only permit and tolerate each other's viewpoint, but also to accept and respect them, despite their own personal views (which might differ from their brothers' view). This permits them to enter a deeper dialogue on the actual issues they are discussing without experiencing division. This is something we must have more of in the Body of Messiah/

78

Christ to help us become more accepting of our differing views. We can then address the core issues that are at hand and prevent further division among us from the enemy.

NOT EVERY DETAIL CAN BE FORESEEN WITH PROPHECY

The Word of God gives numerous prophecies concerning all major events upon the Earth, none more than this time period before the Lord's return. Having said that, there are certain fundamentals to prophetic Scripture that we should all be encouraged to promote and teach, such as the Lord's return, because God has directed us to do so. However, it is important to note here that when it comes to the details of most prophetic Scriptures, they are almost impossible to predict 100 percent of the time, in light of the exact circumstances that will surround them. This is why they are prophetic. Only when they are fulfilled will we know for sure how they were to manifest. This is true of many prophecies concerning Yeshua's first coming as the Lamb of God, which the apostles used as evidence in their New Covenant writings.

However, this should not stop us from being passionate in what we believe and how we see these prophetic Scriptures coming to pass. All prophecy must be fulfilled, but we should also show respect and openness for other viewpoints in these areas, especially on the specific details that surround prophecy, this is my point here. I think it is when we try to get down to the infinite details that we can sometimes get ourselves into trouble in this area. We often attempt to lay out the exact circumstances that will take place, when in reality there are many variables to certain prophecies that can come into play that we simply cannot anticipate.

This is certainly true of much of the book of Revelation. So when it comes to the details, let's just present our thoughts and opinions without carving them in stone; most importantly, let's not permit any division to arise between brothers and sisters over our differing interpretations. *"Knowledge puffs up, while love builds"* (1 Cor. 8:1). We need to engage in dialogue to find the most significant aspects of prophecy, which might need to be applied to current events during these most crucial days.

This certainly applies to this Reconnection element between Jewish and Gentile believers that we need to enter, now that Israel's awakening is upon us. This all must be realized to complete the family of God and help prepare us for the Lord's return.

> I think it is when we try to get down to the infinite details that we can sometimes get ourselves into trouble in this area. We often attempt to lay out the exact circumstances that will take place, when in reality there are many variables to certain prophecies that can come into play that we simply cannot anticipate.

As we move closer to these times, I believe that God will orchestrate natural events to bring His family closer together. Let's agree to work on bringing greater unity between us rather than fueling our differences.

MESSIANIC ESCHATOLOGY

Having said all of that, with liberty and love, allow me to share with you a Messianic perspective on eschatology that might be somewhat different from your own. Please do not allow our differences to keep you from the rest of the message of this book. *Romans 911* is not so much about what we believe prophetically but rather the *Father's Heart* for us to be one.

> Let's agree to work on bringing greater unity between us rather than fueling our differences.

You might be surprised that most Messianic believers draw a great deal of their eschatological beliefs from certain Christian viewpoints, yet with one fundamental difference: we see the Church more through an Israeli lens, as opposed to seeing Israel and the Church separately. I address this in more detail later in this book.

So for a moment, will you take a journey with me into the land of milk and honey?

Can you imagine what it will be like when the Lord returns to Earth? Scripture is clear about two visitations of the Messiah—the first as the Lamb of God and the second as a roaring Lion, with both of them being portrayed prophetically through the Passover story. We believe that with His first coming, as the Lamb, He conquered sin and death in the heart through the cross and resurrection, taking back all spiritual dominion from the devil. When He returns as the Lion, the enemy will be bound, and sin will face its final judgment, as His rule on Earth will become absolute. The Bible refers to this time as the Millennium, the fulfillment of the next chronicled period upon the Earth, at which time the whole world as we know it will be changed.

Not a lot has been written about the Millennium, and when we look into the Word, we can get glimpses of what it will be like. Yet there are certain promises from Yeshua/Jesus Himself that should cause us to be greatly excited, especially now, as we draw so close to these times. There will be a thousand years of peace, when Yeshua/Jesus will rule and reign, with justice and mercy flowing from His throne to all nations. In the Millennium, satan and his demons will be bound (see Revelation 20:2–3). The Earth will be void of all spiritual resistances and opposition. With God, we will finally have the opportunity to get it right here on the Earth, to help establish Heaven's ways among us. This is all very different from this current world, where sin still abounds.

Prophetically speaking, it is as if the days of creation are reflected through this time; a day can be like one thousand years to the Lord (see 2 Peter 3:8). The Bible speaks of six thousand years of work, labor, and toil (see Exodus 20:11) and a thousand years of rest and peace (see Revelation 20:1–6).

This is our inheritance to all those who believe and endure, both Jew and Gentile alike. We are promised a great role in the

Millennium and beyond, of rule and authority over the nations (see Revelation 2:26).

> *"A Kingdom of priests from every tribe and language and people and nation to serve our God and rule on the earth"* (Rev. 5:9–10).
>
> *"The wolf will live with the lamb, the leopard will lie down with the goat, the calf and the lion and the yearling together; and a little child will lead them. The cow will feed with the bear, their young will lie down together, and the lion will eat straw like the ox. The infant will play near the cobra's den, and the young child will put its hand into the viper's nest. They will neither harm nor destroy on all my holy mountain, for the earth will be filled with the knowledge of the Lord as the waters cover the sea"* (Is. 11:6–9).

Sometimes it is difficult for us to even think that there could be such a life on the Earth, full of love and void of fear. In our view, if we believe in Scripture, God's hand and directive in all other historical periods assure us that the time of Mashiach/Christ to return is coming! (Historical periods: Eden, Adam, Noah, Abraham, Moses, New Covenant. Future Era: Millennium—New Heaven & Earth.) It is a time that we should all long for and greatly desire. As the old Church slogan goes, *"Come, Lord Jesus!"*

Over the past two thousand years since Yeshua/Jesus introduced the New Covenant (see Jeremiah 31:31–34), only our precious Lord and Savior has been raised from the dead into His resurrected Body. Not to compare us to His sovereignty, but when He returns to the Earth to sit on David's throne, we believe His rule will be absolute, and many of us will live and operate out of our transformed bodies and share in the Kingdom's authority, just as Yeshua/Jesus has promised (see 1 John 3:2). Although many on the Earth will still be in their natural bodies, those who are left after the Lord returns and who have

survived the wrath and judgment on sin will cohabitate and har-
monize the Earth.

> *"Listen, I tell you a mystery: We will not all sleep, but we*
> *will all be changed—in a flash in the twinkling of an eye,*
> *at the last trumpet. For the trumpet will sound, the dead*
> *will be raised imperishable, and we will be changed. For*
> *the perishable must clothe itself with the imperishable,*
> *and the mortal with immortality"* (1 Cor. 15:51–53).

When He appears in the clouds with all His Glory, in a flash, in
a moment, very suddenly everything will be changed, never to be
the same again. Not only will our bodies be transformed into an
eternal vessel that can transcend all the Earth's current physical
dimensions (see John 20:19–26), but we will also be free of the flesh,
which wages war against our souls and spirits. In the Millennium,
many of us will inherit the new life and become a light to those
who are left here on the Earth, still in human form.

And what about the land with all the animals? They also will
be freed of the curse. Scripture tells us that creation waits in eager
expectation for these things to take place (see Romans 8:19–23).

While Earth is full of beauty now, can you imagine what it will
look like when the curse of sin is lifted? The natural beauty of creation will be beyond imagination! The worship and sounds of joy
will be most lovely, and what about the heavens and eternity? So
little is actually written about it, but how beautiful will it be? No
more tears, no more sorrow–only light, peace, and joy throughout
the heavens, forever and ever.

Eternity is difficult for us to grasp, yet it is a spiritual reality for
all those who believe. As John Lennon sang, "You may say I'm a
dreamer, but I'm not the only one." This was the longing of a worldly
prophet that, in reality, can happen only when sin is dealt its final
blow and the Lord comes back to reign to establish Heaven's rule
upon the Earth.

HALLELUJAH!

"On that day his feet will stand on the Mount of Olives, east of Jerusalem, and the Mount of Olives will be split in two from east to west, forming a great valley, with half of the mountain moving north and half moving south.... Then the Lord my God will come, and all the holy ones with him. On that day there will be neither sunlight nor cold, frosty darkness. It will be a unique day—a day known only to the Lord—with no distinction between day and night. When evening comes, there will be light. On that day living water will flow out from Jerusalem, half of it east to the Dead Sea and half of it west to the Mediterranean Sea, in summer and in winter. The Lord will be king over the whole earth. On that day there will be one Lord, and his name the only name. The whole land, from Geba to Rimmon, south of Jerusalem, will become like the Arabah. But Jerusalem will be raised up high from the Benjamin Gate to the site of the First Gate, to the Corner Gate, and from the Tower of Hananel to the royal wine presses, and will remain in its place. It will be inhabited; never again will it be destroyed. Jerusalem will be secure" (Zech. 14:4–11).

Can you imagine the Glory of that day? God's dynasty that it is in the heavens will be established fully on the Earth, and the Lord will take His seat on David's throne in fulfillment of His promises (see 2 Samuel 7:13; Daniel 7:27; Revelation 11:15). He will rule and reign for a thousand years until the New Jerusalem comes among us, and all things will be made final. The fulfillment of David's throne on the Earth is a crucial part of Messianic eschatology, just as it was with Israel before Yeshua/Jesus came.

> The fulfillment of David's throne on the Earth is a crucial part of Messianic eschatology, just as it was with Israel before Yeshua/Jesus came.

"And I saw an angel coming down out of heaven, having the key to the Abyss and holding in his hand a great chain. He seized the dragon, that ancient serpent, who is the devil, or satan, and bound him for a thousand years. He threw him into the Abyss, and locked and sealed it over him, to keep him from deceiving the nations anymore until the thousand years were ended. After that, he must be set free for a short time. I saw thrones on which were seated those who had been given authority to judge. And I saw the souls of those who had been beheaded because of their testimony about Yeshua/Jesus and because of the Word of God. They had not worshiped the beast or its image and had not received its mark on their fore-heads or their hands. They came to life and reigned with Mashiach/Christ for a thousand years" (Rev. 20:1–4).*

"Then I saw 'a new heaven and a new earth,' for the first heaven and the first earth had passed away, and there was no longer any sea. I saw the Holy City, the New Jerusalem, coming down out of heaven from God, pre-pared as a Bride beautifully dressed for her husband. And I heard a loud voice from the throne saying, 'Look! God's dwelling place is now among the people, and he will dwell with them. They will be His people, and God Himself will be with them and be their God. He will wipe every tear from their eyes. There will be no more death or mourning or crying or pain, for the old order of things has passed away'" (Rev. 21:1–4).*

I personally see no reason why we cannot take these writings lit-erally and agree that sin is dealt its blow and the devil is bound for a thousand years and after that thrown into the lake of fire, espe-cially when the rest of Scripture backs this up and ties into it. This is fundamental to our understanding of the Word of God. We should not take Scripture out of context or overspiritualize it to meet our beliefs; ultimately, it must explain itself and flow with the balance. But I do understand and accept that there are differing views and interpretations of these Scriptures. *The great question that truly challenges us during these days is, can we possibly unite into the fight for this Earth, despite some of our differing views?*

A SHIFT IN OUR THINKING

We have so much to look forward to as believers and followers of Mashiach/Christ: a supernatural inheritance that is most real and extremely promising. This is the destiny of all those who believe. However, before all this can take place and before we can receive our inheritance, a great *battle* must ensue so that the evil one is finally bound and dealt his final blow. I believe this must happen before the Lord can return to establish His throne upon the Earth.

THE DEVIL STILL PROWLS

We know the beginning from the end and that ultimately the Lord finally deals with the devil. We know that in this phase of the New Covenantal order we are living in, through our own experience, that he never gives up without a fight. Unfortunately, this is the devil's nature, and he opposes all those who stand up for truth and God's will and ways upon the Earth (see John 10:10). It is only when satan is finally dislodged from his heavenly realm and from his current earthly domain and defeated by the Lord that the next phase and fulfillment of God's plan for us will take place (see Revelation 12:7–12).

>*"All authority in heaven and on earth has been given to me,"* Yeshua/Jesus said after His resurrection (Matt. 28:18).

Because the enemy was defeated at the cross and the door opened for humankind to return to God and find peace, we have victory and authority over the devil in our own lives and throughout the land as we proclaim it. We also know that within this current order, satan still prowls, and his influence is felt all around us, as well as through our individual walks in the battle for our own hearts and the areas of sanctification that all believers experience.

Plus, it is evident that his influence, strongholds, and dominion (that are actually cloaked to the world) affect many spheres of life, including religion, government, media, and entertainment so that the world will be led astray from the truth. As Scripture tells us, *"Wide is the gate and broad is the road that leads to destruction and many enter through it"* (Matt. 7:13).

THE CURRENT GENERATIONS ON EARTH

Will this ultimate battle between God and the devil for the world take place without any of our involvement? Or, during this day and hour, is God drawing us into the fray? These questions truly beckon answers. If we believe the battle to be true, it will change the way we think in the Church during the last days and impact our end-time strategy to help advance the Kingdom of God upon the Earth.

With all my heart, I believe that the generations we find ourselves living in before the Lord returns have a different call and purpose than for those who have gone before us. The final battles we are about to face will affect and change the world around us for the Kingdom of God to prepare the Ekklesia/Church for the Lord's coming.

> Will this ultimate battle between God and the devil for the world take place without any of our involvement? Or, during this day and hour, is God drawing us into the fray? These questions truly beckon answers. If we believe the battle to be true, it will change the way we think in the Church during the last days and impact our end-time strategy to help advance the Kingdom of God upon the Earth.

As mentioned in chapter 2, Scripture refers to *two mysteries* that relate to the gathering of God's spiritual family related to the New Covenant. The first was how God brought the Gentiles into Israel (see Ephesians 3:2–10; Colossians 1:26–27). The second mystery relating to Israel's reawakening is yet to come; it is being unraveled now in the current generation before our very eyes (see Romans 11:25–32). There is a mirror image here for us to grasp—the way both mysteries were and are being revealed is strikingly similar, between the timing of the spiritual awakening of both Jew and Gentile into the family of God and those believers in each generation who were called into the fray to help bring it to pass. Yet at the right time, this mystery of Mashiach/Christ was declared through His Church to the rulers and authorities in the heavenly realms, according to His eternal purposes (see Ephesians 3:10–11). And the same is true now, but our roles are reversed to bring Israel forth. A special type of worship and intercession is needed that is already beginning to arise in the Earth to fuel the heavens.

THERE MUST BE AN INTERCESSOR

When has God ever done anything on the face of the Earth without using humankind as His intercessor to help bring it to pass? So why would the end be any different from the beginning and exclude us from this role? From Adam to Noah, Abraham and Moses, to David and to Yeshua/Jesus Himself and to the apostles, God introduced new revelation and understanding into the world and then brought a shift and fresh direction to move us into it.

THE BATTLE CRY MUST GO UP

I believe one of the main reasons we are feeling so frustrated today in the Church and losing a great deal of our effectiveness to win souls is because we are not proclaiming our authority and moving in it, as we should be in the heavenly realms. This can apply both individually, through our own personal walks, and corporately, through the Church and Messianic bodies. God is trying to get our attention in the modern-day world we live in. *"The Kingdom of God suffers violence, and the violent take it by force"* (Matt. 11:12).

Sometimes God allows us to feel frustration, especially when we are missing something, so the discomfort will cause us to cry out and seek worship, prayer, and intercession that can change the world around us. This not only releases greater individual victory; it also causes His Ekklesia/Church to rise and take back what ultimately already belongs to it.

For we have been given heavenly tools to fight with that are not being properly or fully used; I discuss these later in this book. *"For our struggle is not against flesh and blood, but against the rulers, against the authorities, against the powers of this dark world and against the spiritual forces of evil in the heavenly realms"* (Eph. 6:12).

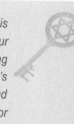

> There is a great deal of division in His Body, some of which is so petty that our authority is greatly diminished in affecting the world. This fuels the enemy's camp, empowering his strongholds and preventing us from making progress or shining light in the darkness.

There is a great deal of division in His Body, some of which is so petty that our authority is greatly diminished in affecting the world. This fuels the enemy's camp, empowering his strongholds and preventing us from making progress or shining light in the darkness.

That is why, as we enter this final phase in history before the Lord returns, we are often surprised that the world is getting darker, and sometimes we long for the way things used to be. However, Yeshua/Jesus foretold us of this time in the story of the wheat and tares (see Matthew 13:24–30). It is as if sin has to come into its fullness before it is finally harvested. So let's take courage that the light in us will become ever brighter as the darkness increases. This is our Father's will for His children.

GOD IS IN CONTROL

It is comforting to know that God is always in control. He will ultimately have His way through His Church and Body of believers as we respond to His call and His end-time plans. This is certain because all things are under God's dominion. As evil rises, so must righteousness. Each one of us is being called into a greater personal victory to shine that light from within the darkness, as the darkness increases.

We, His living temples, are to flow like fountains of spring waters, full of His love, peace, joy, liberty, freedom, faith, and power. Condemnation has been dealt its blow, and victory flows from within our hearts with the fruit of His Spirit and the aroma of Mashiach/Christ. My good friend, Brian Simmons, who has just completed his Passion translation of the Bible, speaks about this type of effervescence, and he lives it, too! Brian wrote the foreword to my book *The Ezekiel Generation.*

WHAT WILL IT TAKE?

So what will it actually take for the enemy to be dislodged from his place, and what are the final battles in God's timetable for us to contemplate? I believe that the enemy still needs to be dislodged from his heavenly place, that this has not happened yet, and that the Lord must take His seat on David's throne upon the Earth. This is at the heart of Messianic eschatology. In this light, Scripture tells us that there will be a great spiritual battle in the heavens: *"And there was war in heaven, Michael and his angels fought against the dragon, and the dragon and his angels fought back. But he was not strong enough*

> *So what will it actually take for the enemy to be dislodged from his place, and what are the final battles in God's timetable for us to contemplate?*

and they lost their place in heaven. The great dragon was hurled down to the earth, and his angels with him" (Rev. 12:7–9). Right after this text, a proclamation is made concerning Jesus's authority and the dominion He is about to take on the Earth. The devil is enraged, and there is a sense of urgency regarding what is about to take place.

WATCH AND PRAY

All timing is in the Father's Hands. Even Yeshua/Jesus Himself, while on the Earth, did not know the timing of His own return, but He did tell us to *watch* and be prepared. In Matthew chapters 24 and 25, He uses the word "watch" four times, and in Matthew 26:42, He tells us to *watch* and *pray* that we will not fall into temptation.

If I were to ask most believers today if we are actually living in the end times, nearly all would respond "Yes." The story of the ten virgins alone should beckon us to be ready (see Matthew 25:1–13). It is more important than ever during these days to look, pray, and be on guard because the hour draws near. Let us look with faith and not with fear, viewing it more with our personal involvement rather than from the sidelines, looking for our own prophetic beliefs to be fulfilled.

The reemerging Apostolic movement can be commended in this place because they are stirring the Church to challenge the main spheres of influence in the world through prayer, worship, and life-styles designed to honor the coming of Mashiach/Christ.

TWO MAJOR BATTLES

Beyond this significant focus to take back the land for the Kingdom, there are two major spiritual battles that are fundamental for His Body to be immersed in through supplication, witness, and evangelism. I believe that these end-time battles and their subsequent victories, which will be led by the Holy Spirit, will fulfill our mission to the nations and ultimately spark the enemy's confrontation in the heavenly realms. This end-time focus will help bring about the Lord's return. We must come to understand that Israel's spiritual awakening acts as the ticking time clock to the devil's demise.

The first major battle has to do with Israel's spiritual awakening, and the second relates to the last great Harvest of Souls. Both battles are intricately linked and might not have been seen as such up until now. The Holy Spirit's directive, which will include our involvement, will need our full attention.

The strongholds of the enemy still need to be severely impacted and crushed. The battle for the souls caught under Islam and other false religions, the influences of secular humanism over the western world, and many different ministries focuses that are in a much greater need of more effective prayer and intercession. The Holy Spirit will lead us to achieve these objectives, which we will learn more about in this book.

A NEW TYPE OF INTERCESSION

This is serious and will need a new and fresh perspective from God's children. *New battles* require *new strategies*, and none more than these. Heavenly battles require heavenly tools. Times are coming upon the Earth when each of us will need to have a far greater dependency on the Holy Spirit than we might need right now. We are being individually trained, without necessarily knowing it, to overcome the evil one in numerous daily battles within our minds and thoughts. This is necessary so that when the time actually comes, we will be ready, and His grace will be sufficient for us. We must always *shine* the light of Mashiach/Christ to the lost generations of the Earth.

> We must come to understand that Israel's spiritual awakening acts as the ticking time clock to the devil's demise.

This time will usher in the greatest harvest upon the Earth but will be preceded by a new type of fiery, Spirit-led intercession that will help fuel it and fill us with the overflowing power, love, authority, and victory of the Holy Spirit in our lives. Parts of the emerging prayer movement are already beginning to discover this. This will be a new day for the Body of Messiah/Christ upon the Earth and one we will truly need to prepare for. We discuss this prayer focus in greater detail in part four of the book in chapter 11.

TWO THOUSAND YEARS FOR JEWS AND TWO THOUSAND YEARS FOR GENTILES

In light of this timing and the fulfillment of God's Word and Covenants, the winds are blowing, and the Holy Spirit is shifting us into a new time and era that is different from the days that have preceded us. When it comes to the awakening and gathering of His spiritual family, from the times of Abraham to Yeshua/Jesus and to this present day, we have had two thousand years focused on His firstborn children—Israel—and then two thousand years focused on His children from the nations. For the most part, the two have remained separate from each other.

Here I would like to point out how equitable God has been with time spent on each family group. But these individual foci have now passed as God moves on to reunite His Body to fulfill His end-time plans on the Earth. And in God's end-time plan, neither can come into its spiritual inheritance without the other.

RUTH, NAOMI, AND BOAZ

There is a beautiful picture here of Ruth, the Moabitess, and her mother-in law that I believe the Lord is beckoning His Body into at this time. It represents a type of spiritual remarriage between Jew and Gentile that will truly help us to Reconnect as family in *TONM*. Ruth had an overwhelming dedication and commitment to her Jewish mother-in-law and then to her subsequent marriage to Boaz, the Kinsman Redeemer (the book of Ruth). You can read more about this in Robert Wolff's book on *Awakening The One New Man* and Sandra Teplinsky's chapter on the subject (chapter 7).

GOD'S GLORY PLAN

This is a divine plan that only our Heavenly Father could devise to finally unite His family and make us one as a means to achieve His end-time plans and purposes through us to prepare for His coming. This plan has been *hidden* from past generations but must now be revealed to us so our Father's Glory plan can be achieved to redeem the Earth through His Son.

As we draw close to the end, this second family mystery is beginning to unfold with Israel's spiritual awakening and its Restoration to the family of God. As Yeshua/Jesus foretold, *"The first would be last"* (see Matthew 20:16).

The Apostle Paul referred to this time as the gathering of the full number of the Gentiles, and all Israel will be saved (see Romans 11:25–30). Please note here how these two points are linked together in the same sentence. When we enter that time, it is not as if God will remove His focus from either Jew or Gentile; rather, He will bring us into their *fullness*. There is not necessarily a definite order here, either as in all Gentiles coming in and then Israel being awakened. Instead, both are beginning to happen at the same time as we enter this final era before the Lord returns, while Israel's mass awakening comes at the end.

This time will usher in the greatest harvest upon the Earth but will be preceded by a new type of fiery, Spirit-led intercession that will help fuel it and fill us with the overflowing power, love, authority, and victory of the Holy Spirit in our lives.

This is a mystery that He exhorted us not to be ignorant about, and it will require adjustment and change on the part of His Church, just like it did with the Jewish apostles and believers when the first mystery that had been hidden was being revealed, in how the Gentiles were coming to faith. In this Glory plan, we will ultimately come full circle, which is necessary to reunite His family. Just as Israel was used to bring the Gospel to the nations through the apostles and the Jewish believers of that day, now, to complete the family unit, God's children from the nations will release that same life back to the balance of Israel so that they can be properly restored into their inheritance. This will also bring the rest of us into our inheritance, for at that point, we will be very close to the Lord's return. They need us, but we also need them.

As a result, the time during which both Jew and Gentile have had God to themselves is over, and the Holy Spirit is now transitioning us into a new time of love and unity and togetherness between both parts of the family that we must properly prepare for at this time. This is a major revelation for us to grasp concerning our spiritual Reconnection to Israel, their regrafting into the vine, their Reconnection to us, and our Realignment to them. *I am not talking about going back to the law, but rather for the Church to fully bless the reemergence of the Jewish branch of the faith into its own identity and heritage, while maintaining its own with a connectedness to Israel as its commonwealth.*

The idea is that both groups will ultimately coexist from within the unity of *TONM,* much like they did at the beginning of the Church. Not to Judaize in any way, but this is a must for God's children from the nations to Reconnect to the fullness of their identity in and with Israel and for Jewish believers to fully embrace their Gentile family in Mashiach/Christ.

THE JEWISH BRANCHES REEMERGE

With great respect and love to my Gentile family, there is so much more for us to learn and understand about this time that is challenging because the Church has been disconnected from Israel for so long that it does not properly identify with it as it should. *The Church has identified as a separate child with a Gentile lens that mostly excludes any reassociation to Israel, or the significance of Israel's spiritual awakening and regrafting into the family to complete the Bride.*

I believe the revelation and full understanding of the *Israel Piece* is the final piece that will ignite the rest. It is not all that God is doing, obviously, *but it is central to it and at its very core. If we truly understood the significance of this transaction in us, and the Heart of the Father for His children as we Reconnect as brothers and sisters, we will run to it with all our strength and might.* This is because our refocus on Israel and its spiritual awakening is also intricately linked to the last great outpouring of the Holy Spirit upon the Earth and the fullness of the power therein.

It is the *resurrection* equation for His end-time Church and Body of believers.

You can't have one without the other (as most of the Church is attempting) because we do not yet fully comprehend the significance of Israel's Restoration and the love, unity, healing, and power it will bring to His Church and Messianic

> If we truly understood the significance of this transaction in us, and the Heart of the Father for His children as we Reconnect as brothers and sisters, we will run to it with all our strength and might.

bodies. Scripture tells us that their Restoration will bring *resurrection power!* (See Romans 11:15.) This is the power that most of the Church is yearning for but is still looking for in the wrong places.

A RENEWED PERSPECTIVE

Let's look at a Scripture that relates to God's Covenants, promises, and Israel's rebirth. Please understand that the current Church at large is greatly divided when it comes to Israel's spiritual Restoration; the majority don't believe in it at all. However, even the part of the Church that is beginning to understand this eschatology is in greater need of an increase in its revelation. Most people remain on separate paths because they still see no spiritual Reconnection happening before the Lord's return and because of all of the negative spiritual influences still at play.

In addition to which, the Church does not yet comprehend the significant role it is about to play to help the Lord bring God's *Glory Plan* to pass. Before the Lord can return to us, certain *promises* and *Covenants* must be fulfilled in regard to the people of Israel. These are vital to our understanding. We cannot overspiritualize these Scriptures, or else we will *nullify* a great deal of their future meaning and fulfillment. To think that the Church has fully replaced Israel, as otherwise, we would be in error.

These promises and Covenants relate *solely* to Israel's spiritual Restoration and to the seat of David, which beckons our Lord here on Earth. We must gain *fresh* understanding to embrace our family connection toward them through love and faith. We also must fulfill our most *strategic intercessory role* to cry out for the fulfillment of these Covenants and promises so that they will come to life, as the Word of God foretells.

A role that has been mostly hidden up until this time is revealed now to these generations: *"And His reason? To show to all the rulers in heaven how perfectly wise He is when all of His family—Jews and Gentiles alike—are seen to be joined together in His Church, in just the way He had always planned it through Messiah Yeshua/Jesus our Lord"* (Eph. 3:10–11 NLT). Wow!

GOD'S COVENANTS TO ISRAEL MUST BE FULFILLED

The key word in *God's Glory Plan* is "Covenant." It is through Israel's spiritual Restoration that this plan is revealed. Through the Prophet Ezekiel, we learn that Israel's spiritual awakening will bring Glory to His name: *"...I will be proved holy through you in the sight of the nations"* (Ezek. 20:41). Stated a second time, *"...Then the nations will know that I am the Lord, declares the Sovereign Lord, when I am proved holy through you before their eyes"* (Ezek. 36:23). I believe that these prophecies and promises relate to the end of history, when Israel is finally restored spiritually. It is not primarily for their sake, but rather for the sake of His *Holy Name* (see Ezekiel 36:22). Not to make lesser of the Jewish people, but whenever God Covenants and promises, He always keeps His Word, and none is greater than His Covenants and promises to restore His firstborn to Himself, just as He has kept His Covenants to His children from the nations.

ISRAEL BROUGHT BACK FIRST

Many Christians have had great difficulty with Israel's physical Restoration to the land because as of yet, most are still not saved or spiritually restored. However, with closer reflection, the Word of God states quite clearly that Israel will be brought back to the land *first* and *then* cleansed from sins.

When I teach about Israel and the Church, I often talk about the "And Then Sermon" because all major sections of Scripture reinforce this detail. In the Torah (five books of Moses), Moses prophesied to Israel that its people will be dispersed into the nations. In Deuteronomy 30:4, he states, *"Even if you have been banished to the most distant land under the heavens, from there the Lord your God will gather you and bring you back."* Then in verse 6, he states, *"The Lord your God will circumcise your hearts and the hearts of your descendants, so that you may love Him with all your hearts and all your soul, and live."* Moses foretells that Israel will be brought back *first*, after which time their hearts will then be circumcised.

However, with closer reflection, the Word of God states quite clearly that Israel will be brought back to the land first and then cleansed from sins.

In the books of the prophets, Ezekiel 36:4 says, *"For I will take you out of the nations; I will gather you from all the countries and bring you back into your own land."*

Verses 25 and 26 say, *"I will sprinkle clean water on you, and you will be clean; I will cleanse you from all your impurities and all your idols. I will give you a new heart and put a new spirit in you; I will remove from you a heart of stone and give you a heart of flesh."*

And verse 27 says, *"And I will put my Spirit in you and move you to follow my decrees and be careful to keep my laws."* Ezekiel declares *first* that Israel will be brought back to the land; *second*, that its people will be cleansed and brought into repentance; and *third*, that they will be filled with the Holy Spirit.

Then, in the New Covenant (New Testament), in the book of

Romans, the Apostle Paul reminds us of this Covenantal promise: *"And this is my Covenant with them when I take away their sins"* (Rom. 11:27).

Don't ask me why God decided to do it like this, but He obviously has given us the Word as a guide for us to contemplate and comprehend. Plus, half of these prophecies have already been fulfilled at this point. Little faith is

This is where the battle cry for His Body comes into play, and must now go up. At this time, the heavens are beckoning this type of intercession to help fuel what is about to take place.

even required when it comes to Israel being returned to the land because it is already happening.

However, it is quite different when we contemplate their spiritual Restoration because these prophecies are yet to be fulfilled in total. *This is where the battle cry for His Body comes into play, and must now go up.* At this time, the heavens are beckoning this type of intercession to help *fuel* what is about to take place.

As a result, we must be Realigned in our hearts and by His Spirit, so when we cry out, our prayers are not for a *foreign people*, as Israel is to us currently, but rather for our *spiritual family*, whom we will *rule* and *reign* with when Yeshua/Jesus returns. This is altogether different from what we've been taught, and there is a vital *spiritual transaction* that must take place from within to properly Reconnect us so that we can do this Kingdom's bidding.

DRY BONES COME TO LIFE

There is no clearer prophecy relating to Israel's Restoration than the prophecy of the "dry bones." But even here, the prophecies are split into the same divide (see Ezekiel 37:1–14). Restoration comes first *and then* their spiritual awakening. But please note that it is not God alone who does this bidding; rather, it is man, whom God commands to prophesy to the bones to hear the Word of the Lord.

This is a prophetic picture of the teamwork that God has set up to bring it to pass.

Ezekiel prophesied as he was commanded. As he was prophesying, there was a noise, a rattling sound, and the bones came together, bone to bone. He looked, and tendons and flesh appeared on the bones, and skin covered them, "but there was no *breath* in them" (Ezek. 37:1–8).

We must cry aloud with all our might and strength for the breath of God to be released from the heavens from the four winds, to enter into the Father's lost sons and daughters, that they might live (and be saved) and that our Father's holy words and Covenants to restore them would now be fulfilled.

This is part one of Ezekiel's prophecy; it relates to the other prophecies that indicate that Israel will be brought back to the land first. Part two is just beginning to take place. This is where our intercessory role in the current generation of believers comes into play. We must *stand in the gap* for our firstborn brother, Israel, who is to be restored to our family. *We must cry aloud with all our might and strength for the breath of God to be released from the heavens from the four winds, to enter into the Father's lost sons and daughters, that they might live (and be saved) and that our Father's holy words and Covenants to restore them would now be fulfilled.*

Please note in verse 5 that it was always God's intention to *breathe* the breath of God back into Israel (Holy Spirit). They are first restored physically and gathered back to the land, with the repentance and in-filling taking place after the fact. Here, along with the other prophecies and Covenants that are yet to be fulfilled, the cries of the saints must ascend into the heavens to both remind them of and proclaim their coming fulfillment through the Word of God. *This is heaven's call for us during this time and hour. Earth must agree with heaven in order for this to take place.*

TO THE JEW FIRST AND THEN THE NATIONS

Finally, as the Church Reconnects spiritually as family and Realigns itself to its heritage and roots with everything that goes along with this, including its fivefold ministry focus, which properly equips the saints for the works of the ministry (see Ephesians 4:11–12). The Church will quickly rediscover its Kingdom principle, *which is to the Jew first and then the Greek* (see Romans 1:16), and the additional *power* available to promote the Gospel to the nations as a result. The Kingdom of God never changed this position regarding the Gospel.

This was changed by the ancestral Church. However, as this gets corrected and the Church fully recognizes its connection and significance, the additional power it needs will be released. This coming revival and awakening is greatly dependent on this *Kingdom principle* and on the changes and adjustments we need to make in the Church to effectively move into these times. This includes the Church's role to help advance the Kingdom of God so that it can be established on the Earth for the millions upon millions of souls that will be awakened in this process.

Let us not forget the driving force behind *The Reconnection*. The *Heart of our Father and His Son* for His lost children is that none would perish and all will come to the knowledge of the truth before it is too late (see 2 Peter 3:9). And let's not forget the heart of Paul, who became all things to all people, that by all possible means, he might save some (see 1 Corinthians 9:20–23).

DO NOT REST UNTIL HE ESTABLISHES JERUSALEM

The same is true now regarding our refocus. We are not to *spiritualize* the Scriptures in Isaiah concerning Jerusalem toward the Church but to give God no rest until He makes it the praise of the Earth (see Isaiah 62:6–7). We must come to understand that the believing Body in the land (Jews and Arabs)—the Jerusalem Church—is on the *front lines* of the faith and is in great need of our love and support. The spiritual awakening of the Jewish people and the last great harvest of souls become center stage for the Church, for not only do they take place in the same era and time, but they will be the greatest battles ever fought and won for the Body of Messiah/Christ on the Earth to help bring Jerusalem forth.

SIN WILL BE JUDGED

In the story of the Passover, after the lamb has been slain, the angel of death enters Egypt and looks for blood protection. The angel destroys the places where there is no blood on the doorposts. This is a picture of the midnight hour before the Lord returns. He will come as a roaring Lion, for His time has come to establish His Kingdom upon the Earth. But whoever does not have the *Blood of the Lamb* on the doorposts of their hearts, who has not yielded their hearts and souls to Yeshua/Jesus, will face God's wrath and His final judgment against sin.

This is a major reality for the world to face. However, our greatest call during this hour is not necessarily to seek out our own protection, but rather to *save others from it*. This will be a most extraordinary time upon the face of the Earth, and although it will be extremely challenging, it will become the greatest hour for the Body of Messiah/Christ. As His *living temples*, we should overflow with the presence and power of God bearing the fruit of the Spirit at a most crucial time in our world's history.

With this background and depth in mind, we are now ready to better define exactly what *The Reconnection* is and the changes we will need to process through the Church and Messianic bodies for it to take place.

What an honor that God is bestowing on His end-time Ekklesia/ Church! To think that our prayers and supplications that are led by His Holy Spirit will actually *move these mountains* and cast them into the seas is incredible. We get to aid in the clearing of the spiritual skies so that God's will and our Father's plans to glorify His Kingdom upon the Earth through Yeshua/Jesus will actually come to pass. We can be the ones who are raptured into the skies to take up our inheritance on Earth. That is worth *fighting for*! (See Matthew 24:40; 1 Corinthians 15:52.)

PART II

THE ONE NEW MAN (TONM),
TOGETHER AGAIN

CHAPTER 5

IF WE WANT THE FIRE, WE HAVE TO RECONNECT THE WIRE!

THIS IS THE most exciting chapter of all! "What is *The Reconnection?*" And why is it so necessary for us in the Body of Messiah/ Christ to process at this time? First, let me define it, and then we will explore what it might actually look like in the Church and Messianic bodies.

WHAT IS THE RECONNECTION?

The Reconnection cannot be defined with one specific directive because it is multifaceted. Here are some key points about *The Reconnection*:

1. *The Reconnection* infuses greater love with the Father through Yeshua/Jesus, and with one another (John 17).

2. Foremost, *The Reconnection* is a spiritual transaction in the *Heart of the Father.* It is a spiritual reunion between Jew and Gentile in *TONM,* which is foundational to John 17 unity and the Heart cry of Yeshua/ Jesus for His family to be one.

3. *The Reconnection* restores the right relationship between the Gentile Church and the Remnant of

Israel (Jewish believers) through a Realignment to its apostolic roots, as it was when the Ekklesia/Church first began.

4. *The Reconnection* breaks off all past (and present) negative influences through the mercy of God so that we can regain this unity. Emotional, spiritual, and theological obstacles, especially antisemitism and Replacement Theology, are removed at the roots. This washes away all prior sins, judgments, misunderstandings, and generational bloodline issues on both sides of the family of God between Jew and Gentile, without condemnation.

5. *The Reconnection* honors and upholds the diversity that exists between both Christians and Messianic Jews within the love and unity of *TONM*.

6. *The Reconnection* corrects both theological and eschatological positions that have excluded *The Reconnection* and places the Body of Messiah/Christ into strategic positions for the following: Israel's spiritual awakening, the end-time harvest of souls, world revival, and the Preparation of the Bride for the Lord's return.

THE HEART OF THE RECONNECTION

There is a vital *spiritual transaction* that must take place in each of us, between Jew and Gentile, that is not only essential to *The Reconnection* but also fundamental to everything else. We must not miss this important piece!

The Reconnection opens our hearts to be Reconnected spiritually with our Jewish family and to the works of the Holy Spirit in this most significant place. As I have already stated, it is a type of remarriage between the two entities. This transaction in itself Reconnects us to the *Heart of the Father*, to *Yeshua/Jesus*, and each other, for His family to be *one* so that we can fully re-embrace one another in love, in the faith.

The Reconnection connects us in the Church to the Remnant of Israel, to our firstborn brothers and sisters, and to the spiritual roots of our faith. *The Reconnection rebonds* Jew and Gentile as family in *TONM*.

The Reconnection not only opens the door for our hearts to be washed and cleansed of all past influences through the Holy Spirit; it also *circumcises* our *hearts* with a *supernatural love* for Israel and the Jewish people in a way that *shifts* our hearts and our thinking.

> There is a vital spiritual transaction that must take place in each of us, between Jew and Gentile, that is not only essential to The Reconnection but also fundamental to everything else. We must not miss this important piece!

It is like a veil is being lifted from us, even as it was for the Jews when the Gentiles first started to come into the faith. Many Christians who have already experienced receiving the *Israel Piece* often describe it like this. This also helps the Gentile side of the family fulfill its role to release the *mercy* of God back toward the Jewish people, *provoking them to jealousy* to find intimacy with God (see Romans 11:11, 30-31).

GENTILE BRANCHES

Speaking from the Gentile side of the family, we must also understand that without this spiritual Reconnection, it is simply not possible for us to be able to carry out the role that God has for us during these days. It is only in the Father's love and Spirit that we will be able to achieve His plans to love Israel and the Jewish people as God does, so that His mercy flows through us to win them back to faith. We have already witnessed the works of our own humanity from the Church's past toward Israel, so nothing short of this will do.

MERCY TRANSACTION

As I have already written, *The Reconnection* is a merciful transaction into His plans and purposes for the end to come through
believing Jew and
believing Gentile. It is
the very fulfillment of
the end of the Apostle
Paul's dissertation in
Romans 11 about Israel
and the Church and how
His *mercy* will be poured
out on us all (see Romans 11:32).

*Speaking from the Gentile side of the
family, we must also understand that
without this spiritual Reconnection, it is
simply not possible for us to be able to
carry out the role that God has for us
during these days.*

Through *The Reconnection,* the full blessings and love flow
from the Gentile branches of the olive tree, not only to bless the
reemerging Jewish branches, but also to respect their identity and
various expressions of faith as Jewish believers. This will fully
strengthen and support the Jewish branches to help them flourish,
which, in turn, will release the greater blessing and power back
upon the Gentile branches so that the full olive tree bears great
fruit for the Kingdom of God.

The Apostle Paul fully understood this principle and greatly
encouraged the emerging Ekklesia/Church to give back to the
Remnant of Israel, which brought them spiritual life through
Yeshua/Jesus (see Romans 15:27).

JEWISH BRANCHES

The same is also true from the Jewish-believing perspective (the
Jewish Remnant). Where we fully spiritually embrace our Gentile-
believing brothers and sisters as our own family and respect their
identity and various expressions of faith. Both sides of the olive tree
can flow freely with the love and liberty we now have in Yeshua/
Jesus. This is to our *Father's Glory,* as the Messianic apostles did
before us. The goal is that even with all our differences as Jews and
Gentiles in the faith, we would truly become one in the Spirit of

God, just as the Father and Son are one with us. Amen! (See John 17:20–23.)

LIBERTY AND LOVE

This is the great challenge to both Jewish and Gentile believers during these last generations: that through His *love* and *mercy* we can lay down issues that keep us separate and apart as family. Romans 14 may help us here. Although most of this text deals with the issue of food and observance, the principle is identical in the sense that we *must be tolerant of our differing expressions* of the faith, especially when it comes to Jewish and Gentile practices. This also includes perfect theology and eschatology, which will come to us in its fullness only when Yeshua/Jesus returns (see 1 Corinthians 13:11–13). We must both honor and respect each believer's journey in how he or she personally expresses this newfound connectedness in *TONM*. Some might be more expressive, and some might be less, depending on the Holy Spirit's leading and calling in their lives as we move into it.

Please note that I am not downplaying our theological understanding, or its significance; rather, I am emphasizing that the *liberty* and *love* flowing between the branches of the family tree of God need to take priority. This is protective for us to keep us from division and from the enemy's traps.

> *In The Reconnection, we hold fast to the Word of God, but we learn how to apply it more effectively in love.*

Similarly, if you are a Jewish believer, or a Messianic Gentile, don't expect others to see things exactly from your perspective. What counts most is to Reconnect spiritually as family and to love and bless one another. We need to embrace our roles and callings so that we all can enter the fray that will beckon our Lord's return. *The Reconnection* must take priority to our expressions of faith, which is crucial to our understanding, because it is God's power source to the rest. In *The*

Reconnection, we hold fast to the Word of God, but we learn how to apply it more effectively in love.

THE WORD OF GOD

As we draw closer to the Lord's return, the prophecies about falling away from the faith are coming to pass. And there is an increasing division over the Word of God, with many caving to humanity's call over Scripture, as well as clear doctrines and understandings (see 2 Thessalonians 2:3; 1 Timothy 4:1; 2 Timothy 3:1–4 NKJV).

A wave of secular humanism has swept the mindset of the Western world, causing many to fall away and deny the Truth. This is also creating a liberalism in the Church that is reinterpreting the Word of God to lift up Man's will over our Creator's. It is a form of godliness but a denial of its power and source empowered by social justice (see 2 Timothy 3:5). *Who does that sound like to you?* The father of lies is fueling the furnace of these rebellions with his counterfeits, vilifying the very ones who are standing for love and Truth.

Perhaps the greatest challenge to this insurgency has come to the very core of our beings, giving liberty and support to the reinterpreting of our genders and the way in which we have been made, created, and formed by God in His image, both male and female alike (see Genesis 1:26–27). The absurdity of this slant truly demonstrates the level of deception and the closeness of the pending judgment of sin that will ensue as the battle for light and darkness come to a head in our age (see Matthew 13:24–30).

The apostle Paul was not ignorant to satan's devices, nor should we be, either (see 2 Corinthians 2:11 NKJV). During these times, we must learn to renavigate ourselves through our prayers for the Ekklesia/Church and the way in which we witness and present the Good News of Yeshua/Jesus. The Word of God must always be our source and our anchor, and humanity's frailties or sins should never compromise it. In our pursuit of love and unity in the family of God and to reach the lost, we do not challenge the authority and inerrancy of Scripture (see 2 Timothy 3:16). On the contrary, rather, we uphold the Truth, guarding it through our walks and lives with the King.

We must continue to stand up for what we believe and stand against the sins of humanity that beset our world against the *killing of the unborn, sexual immorality, homosexuality, greed, lasciviousness, and the like* (see Romans 1:18–32; Galatians 5:19–21). However, we must do this in a way that does not bring judgment to those caught under these influences. This is one of our greatest challenges, but we must overcome it! *"For our struggle is not against flesh and blood, but against the rulers, against the authorities, against the powers of this dark world and against the spiritual forces of evil in the heavenly realms"* (Eph. 6:12).

As we draw closer to the Lord's return, the prophecies about falling away from the faith are coming to pass. And there is an increasing division over the Word of God, with many caving to humanity's call over Scripture, as well as clear doctrines and understandings (see 2 Thessalonians 2:3; 1 Timothy 4:1; 2 Timothy 3:1–4 NKJV).

We need to learn to outsmart the devil in these places, with love leading the way, just as our Lord did. He spent time with sinful people, helping them find the Truth. Through *The Reconnection* teachings, and the message given to us through the "Two Hands of Nehemiah," we learn how to hold up Truth in love and to fight in the Spirit through prayer and intercession for change to come to the other parts of the family who do not properly recognize it yet. And we pray and contend for those parts of the Church and the world that have compromised or are without knowledge, that they will come into repentance before it is too late.

I believe this is one of the promises of the last great harvest and final outpouring of God's Spirit upon the Earth—that many more will come into a personal relationship with the King. (Please review these teachings in the *Romans 911 Study Guide* on the *Two Hands of Nehemiah* – Personal Focus – Session 3, Part A – Renewing our Minds.)

There is a delicate *balance* between love and Truth that we must lay hold of during these days that can help change and transform our witness and expression of faith as the Father rebuilds this love and unity in His family. If we lean too much to Truth without the balance of love, it more easily creates division and separation, not only with those we are trying to reach with *The Reconnection* message, but also with those still veiled to sin: *"He has made us competent as ministers of a new covenant—not of the letter but of the Spirit; for the letter kills, but the Spirit gives life"* (2 Corin. 3:6 NIV).

Let the Body be freed from this trap of upholding Truth over love and the division and separation it causes. First, among ourselves in the Ekklesia/Church, and second through our witness to the lost. Let's leave the conviction and correction to the Holy Spirit, guided through our intercession for those we are trying to reach. I'm not suggesting that we don't put Truth out there, *but we must let love lead the way*; this will ultimately open the doors to greater depths and understanding. But let everything we do and say in these days be tested by the Word of God. May we cling to the light of His Word and use the sharpness of its edges to proclaim life and Truth with great wisdom and authority. And let it all be clothed in the heart of love that always overcomes and never fails (see 1 Corinthians 13:1–13; Colossians 3:14).

THE RECONNECTION IS VITAL

Getting back to the heart of *The Reconnection* message, which is multi-faceted, without this relational connection and change, I have been emphasizing in *TONM we remain a separate entity*. This might have been okay while God was focused solely on gathering His other sheep from the nations (see John 10:16—the Gentiles), but it is not anymore, as He looks to reawaken Israel and reunite the two (see Romans 11:25–26). First, there needs to be a *personal relational* change between one another as believing Jews and Gentiles and second, a *corporate* change in how this is expressed between the Church and the Messianic Body (Israel's Remnant).

THE GENTILE BRANCHES REPRESENT ISRAEL'S COMMONWEALTH

This transaction is necessary not only to enable Christians to more effectively love, pray, and reach the Jewish people, but also to fulfill their role to prepare His Ekklesia/Church for a Messianic Kingdom here on Earth, when Yeshua/Jesus returns. Please remember, the Gentile part of the family represents Israel's commonwealth. As it is written, *"With your blood you purchased for God persons from every tribe and language and people and nation"* (see Revelation 5:9).

THE DEVIL WILL DO EVERYTHING IN HIS POWER TO RESIST

The devil will do everything in his power to keep us from the fullness of *The Reconnection* because he knows that when it happens, his time is drawing to a close. It is the beginning of the end for him because God's Ekklesia/Church is the chosen instrument to pour through for Israel's reawakening, which will bring about his ultimate demise. These are strong words, and they are true!

You see, the cleansing and purifying of our hearts is just the beginning of this process. However, we need to be willing to allow God to complete this transaction in us, which will take a great deal of humility on behalf of all family members because the devil will throw everything at us to continue to block it. The devil knows the theological, emotional, and spiritual barriers that continue to fuel our separation. Metaphorically speaking, these barriers prevent the source from flowing from the root of God's olive tree to the outer branches to produce the best of fruit (see Romans 11). This stops the fullness of *The Reconnection* from flowing from one side of the tree to the other to release the full blessing and power behind it. We need to give the Holy Spirit permission and full rights to do this work in us to Reconnect us to one another. The will of God for us during these days is to be one! As is demonstrated in the name of this chapter, *"If we want the fire, we must (fully) Reconnect the wire!"*

When I first wrote *The Ezekiel Generation*, which exposes satan's influence over the Gentile Church through generational antisemitism, I thought that influence was the main barrier that prevented us from connecting spiritually. Although it definitely is the foremost root in our hearts and is the beginning of the Restoration process in *TONM*, as we confess it and break off its influence, the enemy has many other barriers and obstacles in place. The devil is extremely crafty and will use anything he can to prevent us from finding the fullness of *The Reconnection*.

It might help us to compare receiving the fullness of *The Reconnection* to the seed that fell into the good soil in "The Parable of The Sower" that yielded thirty, sixty, and a hundred times what was sown, but many other obstacles were in place to prevent people from finding it (see Matthew 12:1–23). This is the case with our humanity with *The Reconnection*, where we can so easily hang our hats on some issue that will cause us to shut down and miss the mark.

I have personally witnessed this on several occasions with brothers and sisters on both sides of the family who hold tightly to what they believe or are so swayed by some kind of fear that there is no room left for this reunion unless it is fully on their terms. But who is in charge here? And what is His will, timing, and plans for us in order for the end to come?

This is the enemy's goal: to maintain control. I have personally witnessed this on several occasions with brothers and sisters on both sides of the family who hold tightly to what they believe or are so swayed by some kind of fear that there is no room left for this reunion unless it is fully on their terms. But who is in charge here? And what is His will, timing, and plans for us in order for the end to come?

A GOOD DEAL TO CONSIDER

There is a good deal for us to consider here, but it is not as complicated as we might think. We will explore this in greater depth so it can properly take root in us. Nothing that I am communicating here is revelation per se; everything has already been written in the Word of God. Rather, this is a *renewed* way of exploring the depth of the *Father's Heart* for His family to be united at this time.

For the sake of clarity, some of what I am writing here might repeat what we have already established. However, I think it is significant for us to try to define *The Reconnection* systematically and what it might look like. Nothing I have written is carved in stone, but we have to start somewhere with this Realignment in the family that will ultimately bring about huge blessings and much greater power than we have even witnessed or experienced in the Ekklesia/Church and on the Earth.

WHAT DOES THE RECONNECTION LOOK LIKE?

For the sake of clarity, some of what I am writing here repeats what we have already established. However, I think it is significant to try to define *The Reconnection* systematically and what it might look like. Here are seven key points to consider when visualizing what *The Reconnection* looks like and what it will produce in the Body of Messiah/Christ and the Ekklesia/Church.

1. *The Reconnection* reunites the family of God into *The Father's Heart* to love one another.

   A. **The Reconnection is a spiritual transaction in the**

Heart of the Father, **into a spiritual reunion.** It is a type of remarriage in the family of God between Jew and Gentile in the Church and Messianic bodies, reuniting us in the Holy Spirit as one Bride, one Body, and one family in *TONM. The Reconnection* helps both sides of the family find healing and Reconciliation for end-time purposes.

B. *The Reconnection* **breaks off all past negative influences through the** *mercy of God* **so we can regain this unity.** Emotional, spiritual, and theological obstacles, especially antisemitism and Replacement Theology, racism, and rejection, are cut away at the roots. This washes away all prior sins, judgments, misunderstandings, and bloodline differences on both sides of the family of God between Jew and Gentile, without condemnation (see Romans 11:32).

C. *The Reconnection* **moves the Gentile-believing Church into a full repentance of Replacement Theology,** along with all the influences that have fueled its separation in *TONM.* Through the power of the Holy Spirit, *The Reconnection* helps remove all critical and judgmental attitudes between the two groups. This reunites the Body in love for one another. Replacement Theology is replaced with "Restoration Theology," which renews the mindset of the Gentile Church.

D. *The Reconnection* **moves the Gentile-believing Church and Messianic bodies into and through** *identificational repentance.* It is designed to fully break off the past from any generational curses and demonic influences of antisemitism and to spiritually connect us as one family in God.

E. *The Reconnection* **empowers the Body of Messiah/Christ in the** *Heart of the Father* **to heal and reconcile all other racial and theological divides.** This will help us fulfill Yeshua/Jesus's Heart cry of John 17 love and unity in the family of God.

2. *The Reconnection* **is the final act of Reformation for the Body of Messiah/Christ between believing Jews and Gentiles and between Israel and the Church.** This final act properly Reconnects Christians to the Remnant of Israel and Jewish believers to the Gentile-believing Church in love, liberty, fellowship, and harmony. It celebrates diversity and freedom of expression between Jew and Gentile in the love and unity of *TONM*, acquiring greater depths in God through one another. *The Reconnection* also fully prepares us for God's end-time Glory plans on the Earth before Yeshua/Jesus returns.

3. *The Reconnection* **reunites the family of God.**

A. *The Reconnection* **Reconnects the Gentile-believing Church to its Jewish roots and heritage.** It fully embraces the re-emerging Jewish branches while continuing to maintain its own branches of the faith. The purpose is not to go back to the Mosaic Covenant but rather to restore the Ekklesia/Church to its apostolic foundations, which flowed out of its Jewish roots and heritage.

B. *The Reconnection* **Reconnects the Messianic Body to the Gentile-believing Church.** It fully embraces and honors the Gentile branches of the faith (expressions) while continuing to maintain its own branches. When this happens, both groups can bless each other, their unique identities, their diversity, and their roles through one faith—one Father, one Son, and one Spirit.

4. **Although *The Reconnection* requires great unity and love in the Spirit, it does not require Gentile believers to become like Jews or Jewish believers to become like Gentiles.** It blesses all branches of the olive tree, introducing greater love and liberty in the Spirit that enables both groups to bless one another and more freely flow from one side to the other.

5. ***The Reconnection* also recognizes certain Gentile believers who are called to serve their Jewish-believing family, otherwise known as Messianic Gentiles.**

6. ***The Reconnection* brings to light the huge theological significance of Israel's spiritual awakening.** And it prioritizes it in God's end-time plans without taking it out of context.

7. ***The Reconnection* restores the right relationship between the Gentile-believing Church and the Remnant of Israel through a Realignment.** It causes a shift in the heavens to release greater love and power on the Body of Messiah/Christ. *The Reconnection* restores the Ekklesia/Church to its apostolic roots, as it was when it first began in preparations for the Lord's return. *The Reconnection* reestablishes synergy and active cooperation between the two groups, both in Israel and in the nations.

The Realignment is lived out and experienced in in the following six ways:

1. **It Realigns the Church to the Kingdom principle of the Gospel**—*to the Jew first and then to the*

nations—fully recognizing how they are intrinsically linked together through love, power, prayer, intercession, and evangelism (see Romans 1:16).

2. **It helps the Church fully recognize its end-time role to become Israel's salvific agent.** It assists in Israel's spiritual awakening through love, prayer, intercession, personal lifestyle witness, and evangelism, and it takes on the Father's burden for His firstborn children as their own. It also fulfills its call to properly move Jewish people to jealousy through the mercy of God it has received and to help restore them (as Jewish believers in Yeshua) into their own branches of the olive tree (see Romans 11).

3. **It Realigns the Body of Messiah/Christ to fully embrace the fight that is preventing *The Reconnection* from taking place through Spirit-led prayer and intercession.**

    A. First, this will lead the Church and Messianic Bodies to address all the obstacles that are in the way of *The Reconnection.*

    B. Second, it will culminate in Israel's spiritual rebirth, which will come through the power of the Holy Spirit. *The Reconnection* helps the Church see the broken-off branches of Israel by faith as they will be through Scripture, not as they are currently. This will fuel the heavens for their spiritual awakening and help bring about the last great harvest of the Earth throughout the nations.

    C. Third, the Church will fully embrace these spiritual battles for Israel and the nations to be saved. The Body will cooperate with the Holy Spirit as led and engage in deeper prayer and intercession to encounter the enemy's strongholds over Israel, Islam, Hinduism, Buddhism, and the like.

4. **It Realigns the Church in the nations to help bless and strengthen the Remnant of Israel.** This will happen both in the land and in the diaspora (those Jewish believers in the nations).

5. **It Realigns the Church's eschatology regarding Israel and the Church into the unity of *TONM* between Jew and Gentile.** *The Reconnection* adjusts both theological and eschatological positions that have excluded *The Reconnection*. It places the Body of Messiah/Christ into a strategic position for the following: Israel's spiritual awakening, the end-time harvest of souls, world revival, and the Preparation of the Bride for the Lord's return.

6. **It Realigns the Ekklesia/Church in the nations to accurately represent Israel as its commonwealth upon the Earth when Yeshua/Jesus comes back to reign.** A holy Priesthood from every tribe and language and people and nation will reign with Yeshua/Jesus on the Earth (see Revelation 5:9–10).

BLESSING OUR IDENTITIES

Instead of wanting each group to become like each other, as we have done through most of our past in the family of God, may we, through the *Father's Heart*, celebrate our diversity and bless and *serve* each other into our callings and roles to glorify God from within the unity of *TONM*. I believe that as Jewish and Gentile believers, we are supposed to uphold our identities, fully representing Israel's monarch when the Lord returns (see Revelation 5:9–10).

In the New Covenant and *The Reconnection,* a divine *love* exists to honor one another as well as our differing traditions, feasts, and celebrations, so that we can participate and share with each other.

THE LIGHT OF THE WORLD THROUGH CHRISTMAS

As a Jewish believer who holds to the biblical calendar, can I not enjoy the beautiful celebrations of Christmas Eve with my Christian-believing family? When the Church is lit with a thousand lights, can I not honor the birth of the Jewish Messiah, our Lord, and Savior as the great light of the world (see John 9:5), the light that Yeshua/Jesus Himself foreshadowed through and around the Hanukkah feast? (See John 10:10–38.) Or when He is lifted up in such worship and adoration among His children from the nations, can I not share equally in the experience and vice versa? Or how about when the incense swings and fills the Church in Santiago de Compostela in Galicia, Spain, that honors the Apostle James, and the Lord is lifted up? After all, if my God has told me beforehand that He will be in the midst when two or three gather in His name, then why can't I do the same as He, without necessarily compromising my own practices? Isn't this how the apostles acted as the Gospel was being built and established throughout the nations?

> *The Reconnection introduces love and a liberty in the Spirit that enable both sides of the olive tree to freely flow from one side to the other.*

THE FEASTS OF THE LORD

Similarly, when Jewish believers celebrate and uphold the feasts of the Lord, why can't Christians do the same to enjoy the awesome presence of God that is available to all during these anointed days? I believe that an additional presence of God is available to us during the Lord's Feasts, when the portals of heaven are open wider for all His children to experience. Even on the Shabbat, there is a special anointing of *peace* that we can experience just by reflecting and breathing in the presence of God.

The Holy Spirit actually showed this to me while I was with a group of Christians at the Wailing Wall one Friday night in Jerusalem. The Shalom of God fell upon us in a most majestic manner as *we were connecting to the Shabbat in the Spirit.* Since that time, Shabbat has taken on a much deeper meaning and connection for me without getting religious about it. I receive rest on the Shabbat, and I worship on the Lord's Day, so I take in both, which is my own personal perspective on how to approach these differing expressions of the faith. However, I also hold great respect and love for those on both sides of the olive tree who might see this and experience these traditions differently than me. *Is it too much to ask that we bless one another despite our differences?*

The truth is, we have much to offer each other. As we move into this unity and Reconnection, we will discover a greater revelation of exactly what *TONM* is supposed to be while absorbing greater understanding and insights regarding both sides of the family.

PASSOVER AND THE RESURRECTION

I have one great personal desire regarding traditions and holidays in the Church as it embraces *The Reconnection:* that it would once again Reconnect its celebrations of the resurrection to the Feasts of Passover, Unleavened Bread, and First Fruits, which were a prophetic proclamation of the Gospel. It was through the Passover feast that Yeshua/Jesus took the very elements from the Seder table, the unleavened bread that is pierced, and the third cup of wine, representing our redemption making both of them eternal through His Body and blood (see Leviticus 23:4–8; Luke 22:13–20). On Passover, Yeshua/Jesus was sacrificed; on the Feast of Unleavened Bread, He was buried, and on First Fruits, He rose by becoming the firstborn from the dead (see Leviticus 23:4–14; 1 Corinthians 15:20).

There's no question in my mind that the Feasts of the Lord are a more effective tie-in to the resurrection than bunnies and eggs, which would also help our outreach to our Jewish friends and neighbors celebrating Yeshua/Jesus in the midst of these divine dates. I truly believe that when the ancestral Church broke away from its Jewish roots, many other aspects of our heritage were lost. My hope is that now they can be restored.

LIBERTY

The greatest factor in applying *The Reconnection* is *liberty*. During this time of spiritual Reconnection, we must show love, mutual respect, tolerance, and patience for one another in how we see and view *The Reconnection*. We will go about these changes in different ways to accommodate God's will.

The lifeblood here is the spiritual Reconnection between us through the *Father's Heart* and the *roles* that He will move us into to help save Israel and awaken the last great harvest. Pray to God that we never forget this! This is far more important than our exact theological understanding.

I don't want to downplay this, either, but our theological understanding must take second place to our love and patience for one another, as we so easily get distracted with it, while the enemy is looking to shut us down at every turn! This is often where we are most vulnerable and where the devil can quite easily divide us.

TWO MAIN FOCUSES

As I have stated, I think we will be quite surprised by what God is actually looking for in how we apply *The Reconnection* into our different bodies, Churches, and Congregations.

Within the context of believers in the unity of *TONM,* Jews are called to be Jews, and Gentiles are called to be Gentiles through our various traditions and in the way in which we express and practice our faith in God. However, because of the coming Kingdom, along with Israel's spiritual awakening, we are called to Reconnect and Realign the Church to its Jewish roots and heritage to help complete us and prepare us for the Lord's coming. The *Heart of the Father* is to finally unite us, which will ultimately establish an Israeli monarch upon the Earth of which God's children from the nations are grafted in to represent along with believing Israel (see Ephesians 2:19–20).

This is a major *shift* for us in the Church, as it was in the first century. But it is one we must be willing to face for His Body to find His will for this time.

To more easily understand this process, let us separate the Church into two main areas: the Church as a whole and those Churches located in more Jewish-populated areas. Concerning the whole Ekklesia/Church, fundamental adjustments need to be made at this time throughout the Body of Messiah/Christ (Jew and Gentile), which start in the Spirit before anything else. Then there are additional changes for Churches located in more Jewish-populated areas in their outreach and witness toward Jewish people. As well as becoming a lot more sensitive to drawing and attracting Jewish people through Church services, we must encourage them into their Jewish identities as believers, which we have outlined in the various points in this chapter.

The difference in *The Reconnection* is that Christians are spiritually Reconnected to Israel with its Remnant (Jewish believers), as God has willed it. As opposed to operating as a separate group or religion, the Church comes into a greater fullness, understanding, and revelation of its role in Israel's commonwealth, as well as to bestow blessings on its Jewish family into its priestly calling and identity, along with our own. The Remnant of Israel has also fully embraced its spiritual family from the nations equally, blessing them into their own priestly calling and identity, which ultimately unites us and makes us one. These priestly callings will also be realized in the Millennium, when we will receive our inheritance and rule and reign with Mashiach/Christ (see Isaiah 61:6; Revelation 5:9–10). This is the reward for all believers who lay down their lives for their King.

Let's take a look at these adjustments to better define how we can apply *The Reconnection* to our local Churches and Congregations. Some of the principles we have just detailed in this chapter are repeated with this focus; however, I believe the breakdown will be helpful to us.

MODIFICATIONS FOR THE CHURCH AS A WHOLE

1. **To Reconnect in the *Heart of the Father*:**

   A. For God's children from the nations to Reconnect spiritually to Israel and our Jewish family, the Remnant of Israel. God's children from the nations are grafted into Israel, not the other way around. This will begin to the change the way we think of ourselves and the way in which we present ourselves to the world.

   B. For Messianic Congregations and Jewish believers to reunite spiritually with the Church and with their Gentile-believing family.

   C. For Jewish and Gentile believers to enter a "reconciled diversity" that loves, honors, and respects our differences.

2. **Christians and Messianic believers will gain liberty in the process:**

   A. For Christians to be free to understand and experience the significance and relevance of *The Feasts of the Lord* with their Messianic family through a New Covenant context.

   B. For Messianic believers to be free to participate in the celebration of Christmas with their Gentile-believing family. Both will have the freedom to join in their celebrations and fulfillments through the God of Israel.

3. **Our prayer, intercession, evangelism, and theology should not just be for God's focus on the nations but for Israel and the nations; they are linked to one another.**

   A. We are called to one of the greatest fights for the Ekklesia/Church: for Israel's salvation and for the last great harvest of souls, to spiritually impact our communities, regions, and countries for the Kingdom of God. The greater Kingdom power will be unleashed on us as we Realign the Ekklesia/Church into this principle to reawaken the firstborn into the family.

   B. Churches everywhere should be involved, not just with prayers for Israel, but also for the Church to Realign into its connection and role to help them re-birth spiritually. If the Church is the chosen instrument and vessel to bring forth the mercy of God back to the Jewish people, then our prayer focus for Israel needs to be modified to include the awakening of the Church into this great role. Before the veil can be spiritually lifted from Israel, it first has to be lifted from the Church. We must not put the cart before the horse here; the two go hand in hand!

   C. Churches everywhere should embrace "Restoration Theology" to begin a fresh approach to study, to help renew the Gentile mindset to be personally Reconnected to our Jewish-believing family in *TONM*. These studies should also include all other reformations associated to the *Reconnection* and *Alignment* message.

   D. A greater prayer focus is necessary for all believers because we are all called to prayer: *"I have posted watchmen on your walls, Jerusalem; they will never be silent day or night. You who call on the* LORD, *give yourselves no rest, and give Him no rest till He establishes Jerusalem and makes her a praise of the earth"* (Isa. 62:6–7). Let us also recognize those who are called into *Harp & Bowl* and *Strategic Intercession* for God's plans and purposes. We must become effectively equipped in all areas of prayer to lead us into this fray!

4. **Israel's Remnant first:**

   A. The Church should help strengthen and support the Remnant of Israel before anything or anyone else (Jewish believers in the land and the nations). The first fruits of our offerings in the Church should go to Israel (Jewish-believing ministries), in line with the Gospel principal going to the Jews first and then the nations (see Romans 1:16). The Church needs to follow this principal. This happens through financial support and spiritual aid. The Remnant of Israel represents a tiny microcosm of the Body of Messiah/Christ. However, their spiritual strength and fortitude is a vital link to the fullness and well-being of the entire olive tree of Israel, which includes all believers in the Ekklesia/Church. Assisting our Father to bless the first-born in our family, will release greater blessings on all the other children.

   B. The Church and the prayer movement should offer its first fruits of worship and prayer to the land of Israel to help strengthen the Body there. Along with *The Reconnection* comes the spiritual understanding that all believers (Jews, Arabs, and Gentiles) in the land of Israel are on the front lines of the Ekklesia/Church, where the greatest end-time spiritual battles will ensue. They are in great need of our love and support. It all started in Israel, and it will all end there. Through a Reconnected mindset, we understand that the greater Body of Messiah/Christ must focus on lifting up the arms and hands of the Jerusalem Ekklesia/Church, now that she is awakening, to be able to win the more significant battle against the enemy (see Exodus 17:8–13). We need to send regular worship and prayer teams into the land to join with the Body there; to impact the spiritual skies over the land more effectively. We need to pray for greater unity and blessings among all believers in Israel, including Arab and Palestinian believers.

C. The Church and the prayer movement would more effectively cooperate with the Holy Spirit to engage the intercession needed to impact the strongholds over the lost, specifically over the Jews and the nations, and the hundreds of millions of souls caught under the spirit of Islam, Buddhism, Hinduism, and the like that need to be freed and released to connect with Mashiach/Christ.

5. **Embracing end-time reforms:**

A. Prayer must be re-prioritized as our number one objective in the Ekklesia/Church. Prayer provides the necessary fuel and directives for all ministry focuses. Leadership should lead by example in prayer.

B. For the Church and Messianic Bodies to embrace *all* the gifts of the Holy Spirit given to the founding Ekklesia/Church (see 1 Corinthians 12:1–31; Ephesians 4:11–13).

C. For the Church and Messianic Bodies to embrace the fivefold ministry gifts (apostles, prophets, evangelists, pastors, and teachers) in servant leadership (see John 13:12–17) to equip the saints for the works of the ministry for the Kingdom of God upon the Earth.

D. For the Body of Messiah/Christ to commit herself to the preparations of the Bride in line with Revelation 19:7. *"His bride has made herself ready."* For the Fear of the Lord to return to His Ekklesia/Church, and for His Bride to walk in greater intimacy, greater humility, and repentance; greater love, and servitude; greater authority, and greater victory. For His Bride to arise in light and power to overcome the world.

MISUNDERSTOOD

Up to this point, the Remnant of Israel has been greatly misunderstood by the Church and has been rejected by its own (unsaved Jewish people) for believing that Yeshua is the Messiah. As a result, the Messianic Body has operated in what I call *the squeeze zone* because most Congregations are struggling financially to survive. Who did God use to bring the Gospel of Yeshua/Jesus to the nations, if it wasn't the Remnant of Israel (see John 17:20)? We must now *return* the blessing back to them and help strengthen Jewish believers wherever they are.

This is a major shift for us in the Church, as it was in the first century. But it is one we must be willing to face for His Body to find His will for this time.

The Apostle Paul greatly understood this *principle* and did all he could to aid the Jerusalem Church—the former Remnant of Israel. *"They were pleased to do it, and indeed they owe it to them. For if the Gentiles have shared in the Jews' spiritual blessings, they owe it to the Jews to share with them their material blessings"* (Rom. 15:27).

This principle goes back to the verse in Genesis, *"I will bless those that bless you..."* (Gen. 12:3).

This is the last part of the Church's Realignment. The Church needs to support and strengthen its firstborn brothers and sisters as well as all the ministries that God has raised up to help awaken Israel spiritually.

Churches located in Jewish areas with low populations might not be involved in harvesting the Jewish people as much, unless they have enlisted in some kind of missions to the Jews. But they can still support the ministries that do. There is a *power equation* here spiritually, that as we release our blessings upon Israel, especially Jewish believers, God would multiply them as He releases them back to us. Although this should not be our motivation, it is right to apply this principle.

However, these finances need to be directed into the right hands and through trusted ministries that are properly connected to Israel's Remnant; otherwise they can be misplaced. This is fully in line with the Apostle Paul's teaching on unity in the Body through our many different functions and Body parts. If one part suffers, we all suffer! This is also true of believing Jews and Gentiles in this context, so please read the Scriptures in this light to gain this understanding (see 1 Corinthians 12:12–26).

BECOMING ISRAEL'S COMMONWEALTH

These actions in and of themselves through the love of God will properly Realign the Gentile-believing Church to represent Israel as its commonwealth and to receive the additional *authority* in the Spirit that goes along with this reassociation. This is the heart of *The Reconnection* and the fullness of the Kingdom of God for His family to be one. It is at the very *epicenter*, bringing its authority and resurrection power into the Church and Messianic bodies, along with its apostolic fivefold foundation. We must come to understand that the Church *loses* nothing in this reassociation, but rather *gains* the fullness of the Kingdom of God.

IT'S NOT THAT COMPLICATED

These are the major changes and adjustments for the Church as a whole in *The Reconnection* as they seek to Realign the family of God between Jew and Gentile, like they were when the Church began. Our greatest challenge to embracing *The Reconnection* will be in our hearts and minds. We must be able to accept the people of Israel as *coheirs*, just as the Father did with His lost son in the story of the prodigal. To be a coheir means that we share the reign with others who are called. Now that Israel has awakened, we will need to shift our focus back to Israel, as it states in His Word (see Ephesians 2:19; 3:6).

If we work to apply these principles in greater measure throughout the Church and Messianic bodies and allow the Father to Reconnect us to each other, this will have huge spiritual dividends as we are rooted once again in the right foundation of the family of God. Also, we will be on the *corrected pathway* to the end-time revival and fire of God that we are so hungry for in the Church. We will now be ready to place the *golden key* in the door to unlock its unquenchable power!

JEWISH AND GENTILE BRANCHES IN TONM

In *The Reconnection*, I do not believe that God wants the Gentile-believing Church to change the way it necessarily practices, through its worship or its schedule (calendar). It can if it wants, but more important is how it connects spiritually and re-embraces its Jewish family and its roles and calling during this hour. The Church continues to operate the Gentile branches as the other part of the olive tree, along with its traditions and practices that have also been established to honor the Lord so that the two can coexist and bless each other in the unity of *TONM*.

The council of apostles and prophets who met in Jerusalem were quite clear about these distinctions between Jew and Gentile in the faith that we read in Acts chapter 15. However, it is important to note that while no demands were put on Gentile believers concerning the following of Jewish practices in their associations to the Mosaic Covenant, the Church had a natural affiliation to Israel's heritage because it came out of it. However, these natural ties were lost when Rome nationalized the faith and disconnected the Church from its Jewish roots and God is now in the process of repairing and restoring this divide so the end can come.

THE FUNDAMENTALS TO A RECONNECTED CHURCH

In a Reconnected Church, we have all connected spiritually to Israel and its Remnant as family and have broken off past hurts, wounds, and generational bloodline influences. We have Realigned our ministry focus to the Jew first and then to the nations, fully understanding this principle in how they are linked together in the context of *TONM*.

In a Reconnected Church, we have corrected our theology and are actively praying and interceding with these principles, petitioning the Father to awaken and prepare the rest of the Church and Messianic bodies to enter the fray.

A Reconnected Church fully understands The Israel Equation and has Reconnected to it as its partner, co-heir, and commonwealth to fully embrace God's end-time plans to establish His throne upon the Earth.

A Reconnected Church is first fruiting its tithes and offerings toward the Jewish branches to aid in their strengthening, support, and well-being. It is also reaching out in any way it can into the local Jewish community, as small as it may be, so that God's mercy and blessings can flow through His Church to love their Jewish friends and neighbors, ultimately winning them to faith.

A Reconnected Church fully understands *The Israel Equation* and has Reconnected to it as its partner, co-heir, and commonwealth to fully embrace God's end-time plans to establish His throne upon the Earth.

CHURCHES LOCATED IN JEWISH POPULATED AREAS

These principles apply to all of us in the Church. Equally, Jewish believers are called to lay down their issues and differences that might be keeping us apart. However, those Churches that are situated in more heavily populated Jewish areas have a greater responsibility than the rest of the Church. It is here that more definite changes are required (in addition to the ones already stated) to more fully cooperate with the inclusion and gathering of Jewish people spiritually among us in the Body of Messiah/Christ.

So the $64 million question is, how can we create a healthy environment in The Reconnection through the Holy Spirit between believing Jews and believing Gentiles that encourages both to mingle and intertwine in love and unity, without anyone feeling like they are losing anything?

Now let's take a deeper look at this topic and some of the changes we can consider if you are a member of one of these Churches. First let's address the practical issues in their application and then some of the more delicate matters that might arise as a result of them. These changes are in addition to the *five* major principles I have already pointed out for the Church at large.

Keep in mind that, because *The Reconnection* is so new and there is currently so little material and teaching written about the subject for how to apply it into our Churches, there are already varying degrees of expression in how to achieve it. So the $64 million question is, how can we create a healthy environment in *The Reconnection* through the Holy Spirit between believing Jews and believing Gentiles that encourages both to mingle and intertwine in love and unity, without anyone feeling like they are losing anything? *The Reconnection* should bring us a greater blessing rather than leaving us feeling like anything is being taken away from us.

GENTILE LEADERS MUST TAKE THE BATON

We must also understand that for *The Reconnection* to fully take root in the Church, its leadership needs to embrace its principles. As Jewish leaders, we can sound the alarm and blow the shofar of *The Reconnection* into the heart of His Church, but until our Gentile leadership takes hold of this baton, its message, and its vision, it will not take root in us as it should. *The Body of Messiah/Christ needs to be properly shepherded into The Reconnection.*

MODIFICATIONS FOR CHURCHES LOCATED IN JEWISH POPULATED AREAS

Here are some guidelines for making modifications in Churches that are located in more-populated Jewish areas:

1. **Encourage and shepherd Jewish believers to experience the fullness of their identities and to live out Jewish lives within the context of the New Covenant.** Encourage them to be a light back to their own people, demonstrating that their connection to Yeshua is Jewish. This reassociation sends a powerful message back into the Jewish community that all founding apostles also expressed. This is not to encourage legalistic practice, but rather a newfound love for their heritage and traditions. There must be liberty and freedom to be led by the Holy Spirit. Associations to Shabbat and the Feasts of the Lord do not have to be religious, but rather spiritual. The Shabbat should be more about peace and rest than anything else.

2. **Connect the Church to some form of Messianic expression.** If there is none in the area, they can start their own. We encourage all Jewish believers in the Church to be a part of it, as well as those called out

from the nations of believers to serve their Messianic family (Messianic Gentiles).

3. **Introduce dual languages in Church services that will help Jewish believers feel more at home when worshipping with their Gentile-believing family.** As a Jewish believer, I use Messianic names first like Yeshua/Jesus. God's children from the nations can use English or Greek names first, like Jesus/Yeshua. If there is just one Jewish person in the room, or the Church, we need to show sensitivity to our Jewish family and help them to feel more included with the rest of us and present the Kingdom of God in a Reconnected manner.

4. **Encourage congregants to share in any local Messianic expression.** Lead them to actively support efforts to reach out to the Jewish community.

5. **Teach and equip Christians to effectively and actively bring the Gospel to their Jewish friends and neighbors.** In general, Christians need to learn a lot more about Jewish people so they know how to reach them more effectively with the love of Yeshua.

CONNECTING TO SOME KIND OF MESSIANIC WORK OR EXPRESSION

First, before a Church can Realign itself to work with the Jewish branches, it has to have some kind of association to the current Jewish ministry or ministries in its area. If one does not exist, they can start a work of their own to reach out to the Jewish community. This is, in fact, already happening; some Churches are establishing their own Messianic work for Jewish believers to connect further within the Church.

This also provides an outlet for those believers in the Church who want a deeper connection to their Jewish roots, as well as for those who are called to serve the Jewish Body. I will discuss how this can be achieved in five different ways:

1. Working beside local Messianic Congregations

2. Using dual expression in the Church

3. Using a parachurch Messianic ministry with the local Church

4. Merging Jewish and Gentile expression into one Body

5. Through Messianic Missional Communities

WITH LOCAL MESSIANIC CONGREGATIONS

There can be no doubt at this point that God has established *The Messianic Movement*, which is now at the forefront of Jewish ministry through the reemergence of the Jewish branches. In the United States today, there are more than three hundred Messianic Congregations, with many full-time and part-time leaders. Most of these Congregations are obviously located in more heavily Jewish populated areas that focus on shepherding the Jewish Remnant, as well as a good number of Gentile believers who feel called out to serve with their Jewish-believing family and other Christians who want to connect more to their Jewish roots and are not receiving this message from their home Churches.

That said, I do not believe that every Jewish believer is necessarily called to a Messianic Congregation, as there are many more Jewish believers participating in Church fellowship. And why should they leave, if they are being properly ministered to spiritually? Where they actually worship and serve should be between them and the personal guidance of the Holy Spirit.

The key for all Jewish believers is to fulfill their *identities* in Messiah as Jews. This can be achieved as long as the Church Body is openly encouraging them into some kind of association with Jewish expression so they can learn and grow into their identity.

If you have a Messianic Congregation in your area, pray to be connected with them, and start working more closely in Jewish ministry. It is really healthy for our communities when they can see both the Church and Messianic bodies working together. The truth is that we have much to learn from each other.

One of our board members, Barry Feinman, a Messianic Rabbi in the Albany, New York, area, has a wonderfully close relationship with Pastor Jay Francis from Rock Road Chapel in Berne, New York, who is a Gentile leader. These two brothers serve one another in love while fusing their ministries. The fruit of this partnership is a great blessing for all to see and receive.

THROUGH DUAL EXPRESSION IN THE CHURCH

"Dual expression" is a term used to define a Church that holds separate services for Jewish and Gentile believers. One service is on Sunday, and one is on Saturday for Jewish believers and those who feel called to a greater Jewish expression. These services recognize the Messianic observance of Torah and Shabbat, along with feast-day celebrations and introduce them to the local Church. So both the Messianic and Church services are encouraged through the Church and from within the unity between Jew and Gentile, and both can be enlightened from the teachings and traditions of the other. Leadership is needed to facilitate these meetings.

THROUGH PARACHURCH MESSIANIC MINISTRY WITH THE LOCAL CHURCH

This is somewhat similar to dual expression, but it has more of an evangelistic focus to reach Jewish people with the Gospel and to help Christians Reconnect to their Jewish roots and heritage. The Messiah's House ministry in Connecticut that I oversee functions in this manner. Rather than be Congregationally focused, it works with the local Churches in the area to foster Jewish ministry. This parachurch ministry focus also requires leadership for management purposes.

MERGING JEWISH AND GENTILE EXPRESSION INTO ONE BODY

Some Church bodies might be led to unite both expressions. We are beginning to see this type of expression emerge through *The Reconnection*, where Church bodies follow and observe the biblical calendar, as opposed to the one set by the Roman Church.

MESSIANIC MISSIONAL COMMUNITIES

I should also mention the Rudolph family, who carry a prophetic mantle in the Messianic Body of Messiah. David and Emma Rudolph were early pioneers in the Messianic movement and founded Gateway Beyond International (GBI) in Cyprus in 1999.

GBI is a family of Messianic missional communities and ministries committed to sharing a life of daily worship and prayer, discipleship, and world outreach. Their foremost desire is to help hasten the imminent return of the Lord. Their primary areas of ministry are Gateways Training School and internship, worship and prayer, Israel and the Jewish people worldwide, outreach and evangelism, ministry to the poor, and community and hospitality. Their physical and spiritual children are carrying this vision into the next generation with locations in Cyprus, Germany, France, and the United States. GBI is led by Matthew and Serah Rudolph, Chandy and Sarah Thomas, and Nehemiah and Shersti Rudolph.

HOW DO WE COEXIST?

The key here is for us to find the healthiest possible connection between the Church and the Messianic work to which it is associated. Then to interconnect them so we can share our differing expressions, which should be fully promoted to all congregants. For example, if a healthy connection between a Church and Messianic work has been established, in a

The key here is for us to find the healthiest possible connection between the Church and the Messianic work to which it is associated.

Reconnected Church that is located in a more heavily populated Jewish area, the Church has opened up to using a dual type of language where Jewish people and believers are made to feel more at home. In addition, the Church is actively encouraging its congregants, and especially Jewish believers, to associate with the Messianic expression. It can be offered and communicated like any other program that the Church may be offering.

SHEPHERDING GENTILE BELIEVERS INTO THE RECONNECTION

I think we must consider the potential discomfort of Gentile believers in this adjustment because the Church has been Gentile now for such a long period of time. However, we must also consider the needs of the Jewish believers, which up to this point have been overlooked.

At the beginning of this transition, the association *can feel quite foreign*. Most Christians will need a good deal of encouragement from their pastors and leadership, including good teaching, to help move their bodies in this direction. Here, a great deal of wisdom should be used in exactly how we introduce this transition in our Churches. This is similar to a Church Body moving into the gifts of the Holy Spirit for the first time. However, we should also be conscious not to give root to fear; there might be resistance in this area with certain congregants who might reject its teachings.

Moving a Church into The Reconnection can be compared to moving a Church into the gifts of the Holy Spirit for the first time.

We might also be afraid of what *The Reconnection* can produce in us by taking us away from what we are most comfortable with. This is because of a lack of understanding, and it can hold us back, shut us down, and prevent us from finding its fullness, which is always the devil's goal. As a result, a great deal of prayer is required to bring this to a healthy fruition.

HEALING FIRST

Before any of this can be achieved, the Church leadership needs to move its Body into spiritual healing and identificational repentance between Jew and Gentile to break off all past influences. This is the first step needed before any other progress can be made. There also needs to be a complete understanding in the leadership between the two groups (the Church and the Messianic association) in how they function together. Although we might operate as two distinct organizations, there needs to be a marriage of sorts to achieve love, flow, and unity.

LET PRAYER FUEL THE WAY

Most importantly, a greater prayer focus needs to be introduced for *Israel and the nations* in the Church and Messianic Body to mobilize us into the fray. We must encourage all believers to study the greater revelation of *The Reconnection* in *TONM* and to enter into the prayer focus that the Holy Spirit is beckoning us into for these end-time battles to be fought and won.

This will release the greater Body into the works of outreach and evangelism toward our Jewish friends and neighbors with more focused teaching and help us more effectively draw Jewish people to jealousy to win them back into their own Covenant. Our efforts to share the Gospel will be transformed as we create bridges that reveal the fact that belief in Yeshua is very Jewish. This will restore our witness to the way it was when the Church first began and for the first several centuries.

WHAT CAN WE EXPECT?

It is not possible for us to anticipate every possible scenario in *The Reconnection*, but we can provide certain guidelines to help the Body of Messiah/Christ move into it. This Reconnection in the Spirit between Jew and Gentile will bring great pleasure to our *Father's Heart* and to Yeshua/Jesus. They have longed for this unity to see their family working together.

REVIVAL

The Reconnection will release greater power, authority, and blessing over us to reach the lost, but this also means that there will be greater resistance. Until the enemy is defeated, these two go hand in hand. The closer we get to our Father's will, the more the enemy will rise against us.

I believe that *The Reconnection* is at the heart of the world revival we are so hungry and thirsty for in the Church, but up to this point, we have been looking for it in the wrong places. This final awakening and outpouring will not come as it did in the past during the time of the Gentiles, or through an old wineskin, but rather through a Reconnected Body of believers living out

> I believe that The Reconnection is at the heart of the world revival we are so hungry and thirsty for in the Church, but up to this point, we have been looking for it in the wrong places.

John 17 love and unity, that is fully associated with its fivefold apostolic roots. *As we Reconnect the wire, we will receive the fire!*

THE FINAL LINK

The Reconnection is the final link to be connected in the chain, especially with the new *prayer* and *intercessory* focus that is so absolutely necessary to help get us there. Without the Holy Spirit's leading, we will not even be able to enter this fight.

IT IS GOD'S WAY

For a moment, think back to Israel's experience and David's struggle to bring the ark to Jerusalem with the loss of Uzzah's life for not following the correct procedure to handle the ark (see 1 Chronicles 15; 2 Samuel 6). As soon as he discovered that the ark could be handled only by the Levites, as God had ordained it, the blessing was released. Even the preciseness of the cross and the resurrection of Yeshua/Jesus occurred through the exact timing of the feasts. God has ordained times and plans for us to follow.

The same is true for *The Reconnection*. As we Realign ourselves with the plans and instructions of God regarding our Reconnection to Israel's Remnant that has been planned for us since before time began, greater blessings and power will be released on us. This is why we call

> In wanting to bring the balance in the message of The Reconnection, it is not as if our total focus has to be on it. However, we have to shift our priorities in applying the principles of the Kingdom of God, which are to the Jew first and then to the nations, so the fullness can flow from the source to the outer parts. This is the most strategic approach to the battles we are about to commence.

the *Israel Piece* the "golden key"!

ISRAEL IS NOT GOD'S ONLY FOCUS

As I stated, Israel is not the only piece of the puzzle. In wanting to bring the balance in the message of *The Reconnection*, it is not as if our total focus has to be on it. However, we have to shift our priorities in applying the principles of the Kingdom of God, which are to the Jew first and then to the nations, so the fullness can flow from the source to the outer parts. This is the most strategic approach to the battles we are about to commence.

There are many battles to fight and many issues that are gravely affecting us in the Church. Millions and millions of souls are caught under the spirit of *Islam, secular humanism, false religion, abortion, immorality, homosexuality, and wrongful understandings of science*. However, the Church's spiritual Realignment to Israel sets a Kingdom pathway and connects us to a greater level of authority and power from the God of Israel to address these issues to help save the multitude of souls from their influences.

Whatever happens in our world leading up to the Lord's return, the end-time Ekklesia/Church is truly a victorious one. God's presence will flow out of His *holy temples* to reach and impact a lost and dying world. This is the *Heart of the Father*: that none would be lost!

PRAYER FOR THE RECONNECTION

If you are in agreement concerning *The Reconnection*, please pray this prayer:

Dear Father in Heaven, the God of Abraham, Isaac and Israel:

I thank you that Your Heart is for Your family to be one and to be restored between Jew and Gentile. God, I thank you that through Yeshua/Jesus You have made God's children from Israel and God's children from the nations as one. I thank You that we are now coheirs together with Mashiach/Christ and are to be a nation of priests before You, representing Your Kingdom on the Earth, both in Israel and throughout the nations.

Lord, I thank you for this chapter in Romans 911 putting legs and a face to this Restoration in Your family. Father, help me contemplate these changes, modifications, and adjustments that You are now bringing to our hearts and Your Ekklesia/Church. Not only to understand them but also to fully embrace them. Lord, please give us wisdom and discernment, especially to our leaders, in how to apply them into our Churches and Congregations. Please lead us by Your Holy Spirit, and help us to outsmart the enemy here who wants to keep us divided and apart from one another. Father, let Your love melt our hearts for each other and melt away all of the obstacles standing in Your way.

Lord, we are not ashamed of the Gospel because it is the power of God that brings salvation to everyone who believes—first to the Jew, then to the Gentile. Thank You that we are now fulfilling Israel's great mission through Your Church and Messianic bodies as we bring Your light and

145

truth to the ends of the Earth through TONM in Yeshua/ Jesus.

Lord, in this light, we bring before You the current separation in your family between Jew and Gentile. We bring before you the divisions in Your Church and Messianic bodies, which the enemy has also fueled. We ask for a move of Your Holy Spirit and Your love; for a move of Your peace and of Your joy. Please bring forth Reconciliation, healing, and new life among us so that this spiritual Reconnection in Your family and all it produces, which has not been revealed to prior generations, would now be fully made known to us. Lord, we ask that You would fully reestablish Your fivefold gifts in Your Ekklesia/ Church to equip the saints for the works of the ministry. And we pray that You would raise up an end-time focus on prayer, intercession, and evangelism to stand in the gap for these changes to come to pass as a unit so that we can proclaim the authority of God through the power of the Holy Spirit to reach the lost. We also pray that You would make this Reconnection and Realignment message known to the rulers and authorities in the heavenly realms according to Your eternal purposes through Mashiach/Christ; that Your will and plan to restore the Earth to Your Sonship and His Kingdom would be established. Father, we pray these prayers in Your most precious Son's name, Yeshua/Jesus. Amen.

CHAPTER 6

TWO BRANCHES, ONE OLIVE TREE

IN THIS CHAPTER, I focus on the family of God. Both His Jewish children and His children from the nations. We will begin with the reflection of the image of an olive tree that the Holy Spirit gave to the Apostle Paul for this very purpose (see Romans 11:16–24). I will personally embellish on this image to reflect the family of God from its beginning to the present to help us gain a clearer picture of God's family.

The shape and form of an olive tree is a perfect image for these illustrations because it wonderfully portrays a picture of God's family between Jew and Gentile, including how they were born, how they came together, how they broke away, and how they will come together again. However, our main focus here is to show what the olive tree looks like now, as the Jewish branches are reemerging in the faith, taking new shape in the Body of Messiah/Christ.

Before we can explore that topic, let us go on a four-thousand-year-old journey in the family of God to view these differing images of the olive tree through the various stages in the development in God's family.

As the old slogan goes, "A picture is worth a thousand words." No image is more vivid than that of the olive tree that God used in Romans 11:16–24. The olive tree image represents His family and the greater significance of our unity. In this unity, we receive blessings and power as we experience its fullness.

When I preach on the olive tree imagery, I always ask people to close their eyes to help activate their imaginations. I hope that what follows will help you visualize each stage of the olive tree's transformation.

THE OLIVE TREE OF ISRAEL

First, I want to present some theology to help you understand the olive tree imagery and the purposes of this illustration. This is not meant to be an exact exegesis of the text, but rather an analogy of the olive tree between the two apostolic streams of the family between Jew and Gentile.

The end result of the *olive tree of Israel* image that the Apostle Paul uses does not merely present a picture of *TONM* between Jew and Gentile; rather, it presents an image of the family of God. It is significant for us to grasp the difference here because God's purpose is to unite us by explaining this great complexity to us. This is the heart of Paul's message in Romans 11. The family of God is not complete until the Jewish branches are fully restored. This Restoration concludes with the fulfillment of God's unconditional Covenant to restore physical Israel by taking away its sins (see Romans 11:25–27). Until that time, Paul asks the Ekklesia/Church to love them and goes on to explain how we are, in fact, the vessels of His mercy to be used to help bring them back to life (see Romans 11:28–32).

> As the old slogan goes, "A picture is worth a thousand words." No image is more vivid than that of the olive tree that God used in Romans, chapter 11. The olive tree image represents His family and the greater significance of our unity. In this unity, we receive blessings and power as we experience its fullness.

The olive tree represents spiritual Israel, which consists of two sections with numerous branches. One section is natural, represented by the Remnant of Israel (Jews who follow Yeshua), and the other section is the one grafted in representing God's believing children from the nations (Christians who follow Jesus).

"Fellow citizens with (believing) Israel; members of His household, built on the foundations of the (Jewish) Apostles and prophets, with Mashiach/Christ Yeshua/Jesus Himself, as the chief cornerstone" (from Ephesians 2:19–20, paraphrased).

This is the identity of spiritual Israel. The root is the Godhead: the Father, Son, and Holy Spirit who provide the life and sustenance to its branches (see Romans 11:17–18) and who established the adoption and Covenants through the patriarchs: Abraham, Isaac, Israel, and Moses. The olive tree is rich in the Word of God (Genesis to Revelation), Israel's heritage, promises, and prophecies.

"And from them is traced the human ancestry of the Messiah, who is God over all, forever praised! Amen" (Rom. 9:5). It is clear that the olive tree is Israel.

To begin with, let's imagine the olive tree when Abraham was called into the family. Through faith, Abraham was chosen and given the Covenants. He was the first Jew, and from him came Isaac and Jacob, the other patriarchs of Israel. Through Jacob's struggle, a nation was born, and Israel multiplied into many branches from this tree. Israel went into slavery in Egypt and began to cry out to the God of their Fathers. Moses was sent to deliver them, and God chose this little nation to receive and embrace His law, which would bring sin into account for all humankind. Then Yeshua/Jesus could be sent into the world to deliver us from its curse, to set us free spiritually through the cross and resurrection, and to introduce His New Covenant for all family members, both Jew and Gentile alike, to ultimately restore us to Himself.

THE NATURAL OLIVE TREE

Let's now begin to picture the olive tree of Israel emerging with branches, green and silver leaves, and fruit. The tree is formed with its trunk and roots.

At this point, the olive tree, its branches, and its fruit are at their height when Israel marches into the Promised Land. But it doesn't take long for humankind's flesh and struggle to arise in the next generation of Israeli's after they enter the land, which can be seen in the book of Judges.

However, the tree maintains a fair amount of its strength and color up until the time of King David and King Solomon, some 440 years later, after which time Israel gets divided into two Kingdoms. It is important to note that there was a good deal of faith and prosperity during this time for most of Israel. However, before long, through backsliding and mass idolatry, both Israel and Judah face discipline and judgment from God. It is here that the first dispersion occurs as a great percentage of Israel is scattered throughout the nations through the Assyrian invasion in 722 BC, never to return. And later, the remaining Remnant of Israel living in Judah is dispersed through the Babylonian conquests in 597 and 586 BC, with only a smaller Remnant of Israel returning after the 70 years that was decreed by God (see Jeremiah 25:1–14).

Without a doubt, the branches of the olive tree were now weakened, and many were broken off. Yet God saw to it that a Remnant of Israel would remain, who again, for a time through Nehemiah and Ezra's leadership, recommitted themselves to the core principles of God, justice, mercy, and faithfulness through the practice of the Mosaic Law.

From that time forward to the time of Mashiach/Christ, Israel was sufficiently weakened, controlled by some kind of foreign entity. And except for the time of the Maccabean uprising (167 BC), which witnessed and experienced the miracle of Hanukkah, very little has been written about this period, especially in the Bible.

It is important to note, in light of the Pharisaical behavior during the time of Yeshua/Jesus, that at some point over this period of Israel's history, or even before, a religious legalism set in over its leaders, and they used the law to control the people, rather than using it to draw closer to God.

In this light, numerous branches of the olive tree had faded, and its leaves began to dry out. Some fell away, and very little fruit materialized on them. This is similar to Jesus's observations of the fig tree, which he ultimately cursed (see Mark 11:12–14). This was the state of the olive tree when Yeshua/Jesus was born into the world.

It is important to point out that most of the Jewish people living in the land at that time were doing their best to keep the law and follow the Jewish customs, as they were directed by their religious leaders.

We learn this in the New Testament from the Apostle Peter himself, in his prayer to God in the vision he received when approaching Caesarea (see Acts 10). Although the Jews of Jerusalem and Judah looked down on him and Yeshua, through their religious snobbery, because they came from the Galilee, many Jews still tried their best to be obedient to the commands. *"I have never eaten anything impure or unclean!"* Peter exhorted (see Acts 10:14).

THE OLIVE TREE IS REBORN

It is at this point that the olive tree is about to be shocked and transformed. And once again, an even smaller Remnant is chosen from Israel.

> *"See, I lay a stone in Zion, a chosen and precious cornerstone, and the one who trusts in him will never be put to shame. Now to you who believe, this stone is precious. But to those who do not believe, 'The stone the builders rejected has become the cornerstone...A stone that causes people to stumble and a rock that makes them fall'"* (Is. 28:16; Psa. 118:22; Is. 8:14; 1 Pet. 2:6–8).

Suddenly, through the life, witness, and mission of Yeshua/Jesus, through His cross and resurrection, the olive tree is about to be reborn. Here in the midst of some very dry and fruitless leaves and branches, a tiny Remnant is chosen—entirely bewildered by what had just transpired.

Yeshua/Jesus then appears to His disciples. He strengthens them and opens their eyes and minds so they can understand the directives of the Scriptures. He commands them to wait in the city until they have been clothed with power from on high (see Luke 24:44–49; Acts 1:4–5).

Suddenly, *"ka-boom!"* A great fire hits the apostles and the 120 in the Upper Room. This little branch that is remaining among the natural branches of the olive tree is suddenly ignited with flames of fire and the power of the Holy Spirit.

The part of the Spirit of God that had been hovering over the Ark of the Covenant between its Cherubim under the Mosaic Law and reserved for the hearts of mankind had been released through Yeshua/Jesus's obedience to death and sacrifice on the cross

> *Suddenly, "ka-boom!" A great fire hits the apostles and the 120 in the Upper Room. This little branch that is remaining among the natural branches of the olive tree is suddenly ignited with flames of fire and the power of the Holy Spirit.*

to pay the price for humanity's sins. The curtain was now torn in the holy place and opened the way for the New Covenant to be released—not just now for the Jews, but for all humankind (see Jeremiah 31:31–34).

This little branch of followers, specifically the apostles and prophets, would become the new foundation for Israel's authority, of which Yeshua/Jesus was its cornerstone (see Ephesians 2:20). The Spirit of God went before them to fully awaken Israel's Remnant, with thousands upon thousands of Jews being born again into the Kingdom of God.

The branches of the olive tree were being reformed and made new, and this new life began to spread like wildfire. This is still happening on the natural part of the tree, except now amid the dry and lifeless branches of the olive tree, a new branch had appeared, igniting many of the other branches. Its leaves were aglow and once again full of life, with the flowering of the spring and its developing fruit. The Jewish *Ekklesia* (meaning assembly or Church) had been born and was emerging.

"Our God is merciful and gracious, slow to anger and abounding in loving kindness and truth" (Psa. 86:15). Although the balance of Israel was heading for judgment because its leaders rejected Messiah, the apostles, prophets, and initial Jewish followers were given a whole generation (forty years) to sow the seed of the Gospel and get the word out so that many would hear and receive its message.

Many thousands of Jewish people received Yeshua during those days and helped found and build the Ekklesia/Church wherever they were living, whether in Israel or throughout the nations.[6] However, the balance of Israel continued in their blindness and faced the horrible judgment that befell them when Rome destroyed Jerusalem in 70 AD. Yeshua/Jesus had foretold of these events to His disciples in the Gospels (see Matthew 24:2).

Imagine now that the olive tree is still completely natural, but with new branches with leaves and fruit coming to life, while the dry and brittle branches were beginning to fall away through unbelief. This was Paul's understanding of what happened to Jewish people who did not fully embrace Yeshua/Jesus (see Romans 11:7–10, 17–21).

THE GENTILE BRANCHES EMERGE

It is now several years later as the Jewish Church has been emerging. In reality, this is the only true and proper extension of Judaism through Messiah. The door is now opened to God's other children from the nations to come in; the mystery to awaken the Gentiles to faith was now upon the Church (see Isaiah 42:6; Acts 10; Ephesians 2:11–3:13).

Many Bible scholars believe that Cornelius[7] was the first fruit of the Gentile world to Mashiach/Christ. He and his family were baptized and admitted into the early Jewish Church. Cornelius was a centurion whose history is narrated in Acts 10. He was a "devout man" and, like the centurion of Capernaum, believed in the God of

Israel. His residence at Caesarea probably brought him into contact with Jewish people who communicated to Him their expectations regarding the Messiah. For that reason, Cornelius was prepared to welcome the message Peter brought him. However, Cornelius might have not been the very first Gentile convert to the faith because Yeshua/Jesus ministered directly to a number of Gentiles we know about whose lives were sovereignly changed in His presence.

A few at Pentecost were Gentile converts to Judaism. And what of the Samaritan woman in John chapter 4, or the man who the legion of demons were cast out of whom Yeshua/Jesus commanded to return home and to tell how much God had done for him? (See Luke 8:38–39.) And who actually knows how Paul's witness was developing among the Gentiles at that time in light of his call and gifting, as well as many of the other apostles' and disciples' day-to-day experiences with the people all around them. However, Cornelius's conversion experience became the official commence-ment of the gathering of the Gentiles, which was always in God's plans to reach both Jew and Gentile alike (see Isaiah 42:6; 49:6; 52:10; John 10:16).

It is at this time, from the perspective of the olive tree image, that a wild olive shoot is grafted into the tree of Israel, with Gentile followers of Yeshua/Jesus beginning to come to faith. Once again, the olive tree is shocked, and a whole new section of the tree forms. The fire of the Holy Spirit sweeps over the Gentiles, and God begins to gather His children from the nations. The mystery that had been hidden is now revealed and proclaimed. The Gentile branches begin to take root in the tree and flourish (see Ephesians 3:2–10).

THE OLIVE TREE TAKES SHAPE

Imagine the full shape of an olive tree with two main sections. The tree is now in full bloom, and its fruit are the very best olives you've tasted in your life; their oil is the finest and sweetest there could ever be. From its roots flow love, freedom, and power to energize all the branches. Great joy and liberty freely flow from one side to the other. The left section (Gentile believers) of the tree is so glad to be joined to the right section (Jewish believers), while the right section is so happy they have come in. In this beautiful picture, God has created *One New Man* that dwells together in unity and love, despite differing characteristics.

THE OLIVE TREE THAT CHANGES THE WORLD

It is this olive tree image that changes and transforms the world. The Word is preached, and the Holy Spirit is released through the power of God with signs and wonders following. Its servitudel government is formed through the fivefold, and the world is forever changed.

For the next couple of centuries, the Church explodes and flourishes, despite Rome's opposition, reaching a good deal of the more heavily populated areas in the world at that time. And even though many of its initial Jewish believers and followers had passed on, the Church continues to grow from within this footprint and framework that was established by the Jewish apostles and leaders of the founding Church.

> It is this olive tree image that changes and transforms the world. The Word is preached, and the Holy Spirit is released through the power of God with signs and wonders following. Its servitudel government is formed through the fivefold, and the world is forever changed.

However, throughout this time, opposition continues against the Church from the broken-off branches of Israel (traditional Jews who did not believe in Yeshua) and antisemitism begins to grow among the Church's ranks so that by the fourth century, when Rome united itself with the Church, the spirit of antisemitism had taken full root.

THE JEWISH BRANCHES ARE CUT OFF

For whatever reason, the Church, which had already witnessed Israel's judgment and dispersion, did not properly comprehend Israel's Restoration nor the blindness that would continue to come upon them until the appointed time for it to be removed. The Apostle Paul did his best to explain this to the Church through the Holy Spirit in his dissertation in Romans 9–11.

As a result, the enemy was able to deceive the Church in this area. In fact, the very vessels that God had called to release His mercy back toward Israel to draw them to jealousy (because they were now living and operating in their Covenant), were now being used to vilify and judge them instead. It was a most despicable plan, but the ancestral Church fell for it!

This led to a great misunderstanding regarding the plight of the Jewish people. The Church then began to force itself upon them and instead of loving them, even persecuted and killed them for not converting to the faith. Plus, whenever one of the Remnant Jewish believers Paul spoke of in Romans 11:1–6 would come to the Lord, they had no choice but to be grafted in through the Gentile branches and become like one of them. As a result, they had to follow Gentile Church traditions rather than the ones the Lord had established for them through their heritage.

The ancestral Church then began to outlaw any association with its Jewish branches, not only cutting them away, but also persecuting both Jewish and Gentile believers for wanting to hold on to their roots in the faith. This occurred throughout the fourth and fifth centuries and beyond until the Church was fully rid of any Jewish influence.[8]

Imagine now the right section of the tree (the Jews) going dormant but the rest of the tree being impacted and affected by this loss of life and sustenance; its leaves are now sullen. Shortly after that, the Church goes into its dark ages into a slumber, and Islam is born. The olive tree returned to the way it was before, when religion and overbearing government overwhelmed it. Its branches and leaves were dry, and its fruit was sparse. Indeed, the mirror images that exist in our humanity between both groups, symbolizing how we have acted, is somewhat uncanny.

This is pretty much how the olive tree continued until the Reformation. Of course there were always pockets and Remnants of life from within the tree with believers who discovered the greater depths of the faith, even in the ancestral Church. God would always have a witness to His life throughout the ages, just as He did with Israel and the prophets of old.

In Robert Heidler's writings, the Reformation begins in the sixteenth century as Luther challenges the establishment and the Word of God becomes accessible to the masses. Salvation is taught, and people are saved. In the eighteenth century, the Church responds to a holiness movement, and by the twentieth century, the gifts of the Holy Spirit are poured out and restored.

Yet during the times of the Gentiles, the Jewish section is still dormant in the tree, and the Christians are still separate from their Jewish roots. Imagine the mainly Gentile branches of the tree, which had become dry and brittle like the Jewish ones before Yeshua/Jesus, coming to new life with new fruit. Think of the very center of those branches becoming lit and beginning to spread throughout the others, while others are being severed on account of unbelief. The olive tree, in this regard, is always active with some kind of life or death.

In 1948, Israel is reborn as a nation, and God's Covenants and promises to restore it commences. In 1967, Israel takes back Jerusalem, and there is a reaction in the heavens as Israel's spiritual Restoration begins with many thousands of Jews coming to Yeshua out of the Jesus Movement.

MADE ALIVE AGAIN

In 1948, Israel is reborn as a nation, and God's Covenants and promises to restore it commences. In 1967, Israel takes back Jerusalem, and there is a reaction in the heavens as Israel's spiritual Restoration begins with many thousands of Jews coming to Yeshua out of the Jesus Movement.[9]

Ka-boom! Suddenly, the dormant section in the olive tree is lit and once again the tiny branches are awakened to new life in Messiah. However, these branches quickly become very isolated from within the tree. They are totally rejected by the dormant branches (unsaved Jewish people): "You can't be Jewish and believe in Jesus!" And they are rebuffed by the Gentile branches in the other section of the tree: "You can't do that Jewish stuff anymore!" So for the last fifty years, the *Remnant* branches have been growing yet have very little connection to the rest of the tree.

I would like to present two additional images and the difference between them: the olive tree as it looks now and then the olive tree that Abba wants for His family.

THE OLIVE TREE NOW

Imagine the olive tree again with two sections: the Gentile section on the left, which has life, and the right side, which is still mainly dormant. Except in the very center of the dormant side are renewed branches, in shape and form much like the Gentile branches I just described. Life and sustenance are now going to all the branches that are living. Yet from within this picture and image, you cannot only see the separateness of Israel's Remnant, which is totally apparent; you can feel it as well. There are also some Jewish leaves on the Gentile branches (Jewish believers in the Church), but these are made to look Gentile, even though they are still Jewish. This is the present state of the Body of Messiah/Christ between Jew and Gentile.

ABBA'S OLIVE TREE

Now, for a moment think of Abba's olive tree. A Reconnection has taken place between some of the branches of Israel's Remnant and some of the Gentile branches. The healing of the Holy Spirit has washed away the sins and wounds of the past, and the devil's influence over the family of God has been broken off. The divisions that once existed have been washed by the Blood of the Lamb into the sea of forgetfulness.

There is now a lifeline between the two sections, and love and liberty freely flow from one to the other. The branches, their leaves, and their fruit are suddenly reenergized, and these leaves and branches stand out from the rest of the branches, even the ones that are alive. These Gentiles' branches have been rejoined to Israel and are experiencing greater health, greater blessing, and most importantly, greater harvest from all around them. The power of God and the anointing on them have increased, and they are beginning to affect the rest of the Gentile branches. Their leaves and fruit are once again the strongest, the brightest, and the tastiest they could be, even more so than before. Signs and wonders of the Kingdom and power of God are freely flowing all around them. They have been blessed by an increase in revelation for the Kingdom of God by reuniting with their Jewish brothers and sisters.

Now, for a moment think of Abba's olive tree. A Reconnection has taken place between some of the branches of Israel's Remnant and some of the Gentile branches. The healing of the Holy Spirit has washed away the sins and wounds of the past, and the devil's influence over the family of God has been broken off. The divisions that once existed have been washed by the Blood of the Lamb into the sea of forgetfulness.

The Jewish branches that have Reconnected have also experienced the same new life from within them through the power of the Holy Spirit. They are now helping their Gentile family connect to their Jewish roots and heritage. Their Gentile family has also helped to strengthen them in *TONM*.

The Jewish branches have received greater spiritual healing and are now moving more effectively in the gifts of the Holy Spirit. These branches are now aglow, and they are beginning to light up the branches from within their section that have been dormant (the broken-off branches of Israel). Now some of the Jewish leaves on the Gentile side have refound their characteristic (Jewish believers in the Church). The same is also true of the Gentile leaves on the Jewish side (Messianic Gentiles), who have found greater clarity and understanding to their calling to assist and serve the Jewish branches. The confusion that once existed in both sections is gone as the fullness of the revelation in *TONM* has been released from the Father to His children.

A new *dunamis* (power, might, strength, ability) has been given from heaven into the hearts of those who have Reconnected. People are gleaning new insights and understanding from each other into a greater unity and understanding of the *Father's Heart* and His love and desire for us to be one with Him and each other.

> A new dunamis (power, might, strength, ability) has been given from heaven into the hearts of those who have Reconnected. People are gleaning new insights and understanding from each other into a greater unity and understanding of the Father's Heart and His love and desire for us to be one with Him and each other.

The ornaments of our traditions and feasts hang all around the tree. Sparkling emblems of glass and crystal, gold and silver, jasper and ruby clasp the branches, freely dangling for all to see and touch. They represent Christmas, Resurrection/Passover, Shavuot/Pentecost, Rosh Hashanah, Yom Kippur, Sukkot/Tabernacles, and Hanukkah.

Finally, as the veil lifts among the dormant branches and they begin to come back to life to complete the olive tree, there is an incredible growth of new branches, new leaves, and fruit in the Gentile section of the tree. The growth is almost uncontrollable. Through Spirit-led prayer, worship, and supplication, the barriers and obstacles have been broken off from both sides of the tree, and there is a new joy in the family of God. Finally the balance of the veil is broken off, and Israel is restored. Not only is the olive tree now complete, but it is truly readied to be harvested.

"This is to my Father's Glory, that you bear much fruit showing yourselves to be my disciples" (John 15:8).

What a grand picture and image of new life and the power of God and blessings upon the Body of Messiah/Christ! It is time for us to arise in the power and authority of the Holy Spirit and shine forth His light in a darkened world that is so desperate for salvation, love, and light.

This is a picture of God's end-time Church and all He wants us to be: a Body that is true to His Word and personally victorious in each of our own lives so that His Glory and love will shine through us to the rest of humanity. Through *TONM*, the people of the world will know that Yeshua/Jesus has been sent (see John 13:34–35; 17:22–23).

I believe God's perfect will for us is to come into the fullness of His Kingdom, which will enable His end-time plans to work through us to redeem Israel and the last great harvest of souls.

This is a picture of God's end-time Church and all He wants us to be: a Body that is true to His Word and personally victorious in each of our own lives so that His Glory and love will shine through us to the rest of humanity. Through TONM, the people of the world will know that Yeshua/Jesus has been sent (see John 13:34–35; 17:22–23).

In this light, there is much to be done; our next step is to be able to fully embrace our Jewish-believing family and their varied expressions of faith. This also means that Jewish believers need to accept and embrace their Gentile-believing family. Please remember that the key here in the Kingdom of God is in our diversity, unity, and the love we have for one another.

Now let's see what God has established among these Jewish branches of the faith and how they are developing at present.

MESSIANIC EXPRESSIONS

It is quite apparent to us that in both sections of the olive tree between Jew and Gentile, there are varying degrees of expressions of faith, ranging from charismatic to liturgical. However, if we could become more open to one another and less divisive, we might find that we can learn from each other and find a greater fullness in Mashiach/Christ.

Although each of us might have our own personal views and likes in this regard, as long as Yeshua/Jesus is lifted up and His Word is not compromised, we can show mutual respect to one another with regard to our varying expressions of faith.

I believe the word expression is very descriptive for the varying expressions of faith that are reemerging among the Jewish branches of the olive tree, from Congregational foci to parachurch ministries. It can help us better grasp and understand what Abba and Yeshua/Jesus are doing among our Remnant Jewish family.

This might be more evident to most through the Church and its denominations, but these varying degrees of expression are also found in the Messianic community. With Jewish believers, though, the liturgical side adheres to more conservative associations with Torah, while charismatic expressions lean more fully to *TONM* between Jew and Gentile. Then there are a good number who hold to both with a greater balance.

The key for us is *love* and *tolerance* for one another, assuming our understanding of salvation can come only through Mashiach/Christ. We must not legally bind ourselves to a spirit of religion, which would steal away the liberty we now have in the New Covenant through Yeshua/Jesus.

I believe the word *expression* is very descriptive for the varying expressions of faith that are reemerging among the Jewish branches of the olive tree, from Congregational foci to parachurch ministries. It can help us better grasp and understand what Abba and Yeshua/Jesus are doing among our Remnant Jewish family.

To help us better understand Jewish identity and these varying expressions, I have listed some of them below. Please note that while there were a few Jewish-focused ministries before 1967, when Israel took back authority and control over the city of Jerusalem, this movement really started to emerge after that date, as I have mentioned.

Was it a coincidence or a divine response that at nearly the same time, out of *the Jesus Movement* (1960s and 1970s), ten thousand to fifteen thousand hippie Jews got saved? Some of them now represent the senior Jewish leadership in the Body of Messiah.

This movement is known today as *the Messianic Movement*, and out of it emerged a Congregational focus and parachurch ministries like Jews for Jesus and Chosen People Ministries, which is one of the oldest Messianic ministries.

Let's take a look at Jewish identity and the various expressions of faith in the Messianic Movement emerging from the Jewish branches of the olive tree.

MESSIANIC JUDAISM

Simply put, Messianic Judaism is a movement of Jews who believe that Yeshua/Jesus is the Jewish Messiah; who have received the Holy Spirit, and who are called to live and reflect a Jewish life through their heritage and traditions.

In light of the New Covenant through Yeshua/Jesus, there are varying degrees for how this is expressed. They form Messianic Congregations, as well as other types of Messianic expressions for Jewish and Gentile believers who are called to serve together. All Messianic ministries are focused on reaching the Jewish people.

JEWISH IDENTITY IN MASHIACH/CHRIST

Similarly, Jewish identity in Messiah is defined as one who has been born Jewish into the generational bloodline of Israel—the traditions and heritage of Judaism and through the promises and Covenants of the patriarchs: Abraham, Isaac, and Israel.

This identification can express itself in a number of ways: through Shabbat and through traditions such as holidays, food, and connection to the state of Israel, or through religious expression.

This distinction between religion, tradition, and heritage is seen quite clearly through traditional Jews who do not yet know Messiah. They are separated into two parts, religious and secular. Secular Jews are far less religious and will focus much more on the traditions of the faith through certain Jewish holidays such as Passover, Rosh Hashanah, and Yom Kippur, while Orthodox Jews will focus on both traditions and religious practices.

Although Messianic Jews are no longer under the law through Mashiach/Christ, there are varying degrees to how Jewish believers will connect to their heritage regarding how they associate with the Torah and its commands. All of them, however, will still connect to the Feasts of the Lord (Jewish holidays) as well as the Jewish calendar, based on lunar cycles, as opposed to the Gregorian calendar, based on solar cycles. Messianic Jews connect the remaining truths of the Torah to the New Covenant; they do not separate the two.

For example, most Messianic Jews no longer keep the dietary laws that were established through Moses. However, many will remain "biblically Kosher," which means that they will not eat pork or shellfish because Torah states not to eat these types of food (see Leviticus 11).

Jewish identity is less of an issue for Israeli believers. I will discuss this further in chapter 8. However, all Jewish believers are called to uphold and maintain their identity, which is found in the Holy Spirit, to be a light back to their own people.

It is my belief that Jewish believers who have converted to

Christianity in the Church, without any association to their heritage and traditions, will need to regain their roots and heritage and allow the Holy Spirit to restore the fullness of their identity. This is especially important in the last days we find ourselves living in so that we can be a light back to our own people and win them to the faith. This is significant for Jewish believers who find themselves in the Church who do not have to become religious to fulfill their Jewish identity or leave the Church.

MESSIANIC CONGREGATIONS

Today there are more than three hundred *Messianic Congregations* in the United States, more than one hundred in Israel, and more worldwide. Nearly all these Congregations celebrate on the Hebrew Shabbat, either Friday night or Saturday morning, or hold to some form of Torah service and Messianic-style worship. Plus, Messianic worship has emerged in the local Church through such notables as Paul Wilbur, Marty Goetz, and Jonathan Settel. More are emerging in the next generation of believers, such as Joshua Aaron, Sarah Lieberman, Greg Silverman, and Misha Goetz.

Up to this point, most in the Church have not yet understood the call of the Jewish believer. Yet some Christians have recognized it and have wanted to find a greater connection for themselves. As a result, they have been drawn into the movement. Most Christians are surprised to hear, however, that there are far more Gentile believers in a Messianic Congregation than Jewish believers. This is because there are still so few Jews who believe in Yeshua/Jesus. This is obviously not the case with Israeli Messianic Congregations.

Connecting to Jewish roots is good, but sometimes it can get out of hand. I also believe there is a call on some Gentile believers to serve the Messianic community. These people are called *Messianic Gentiles.* This calling should always be an inward transaction of the heart first, not necessarily an outward religious expression of wearing Jewish religious garb.

Although we should have liberty, and there can be special times to wear *tallit* (prayer shawls), I do not think it is necessarily a good witness into the Jewish community when they see Gentiles dressing up like religious Jews all the time. Jewish people think this is strange.

MESSIANIC SERVICES

Most Messianic services follow the outline of the traditional synagogue service, reading weekly Torah passages, except with strong Messianic overtones (belief in Yeshua as Messiah). In a Torah service, worship will be sung, and during it some might begin Messianic dance, which has its roots from Miriam's dance (Moses's sister) after Israel was delivered out of Egypt. A *drash* can be read, and then it is usually explained. *Drash* is a Hebrew word that describes the different readings from the Torah (five books of Moses), the Haftorah (prophets), and then in Messianic Congregations, a reading from the Brit Chadasha New Covenant Scriptures will occur.

In a Messianic service, worship will be sung, and during it some might begin Messianic dance, which has its roots from Miriam's dance (Moses's sister) after Israel was delivered out of Egypt. A drash can be read, and then it is usually explained. Drash is a Hebrew word that describes the different readings from the Torah (five books of Moses), the Haftorah (prophets), and then in Messianic Congregations, a reading from the Brit Chadasha New Covenant Scriptures will occur.

The Torah is read through a 48-week cycle throughout the year. And then the Torah scroll is lifted up and walked around the Congregation, where all may show honor to it. This is similar to how the Gospels are lifted up and honored in an Anglican Church service. Several prayers can also be prayed from a *Messianic Siddur*, which is a book of Jewish prayers and liturgy. It has been updated to include belief in Yeshua as Messiah and Lord.

Sometimes to start the service, the Shabbat candles are lit and at the end of a service, prayers can be prayed for the bread and the wine. An *Oneg*[10] will also be served with some type of food and refreshment. Communion will be shared among the Congregation about once a month, as is done in most Protestant Churches.

EVANGELISTIC JEWISH MINISTRIES

The most well-known ministries for Jewish evangelism are Jews for Jesus and Chosen People Ministries. Both of these ministries have missionaries or evangelists in many of the more Jewish populated areas across the United States. Both have an international presence and also are in Israel.

MESSIANIC ORGANIZATIONS

Four major organizations exist in the Messianic movement to help coordinate and manage it, and one has started more recently by both Jewish and Gentile leadership to help facilitate communication between the Messianic Body and the Gentile Church. These organizations are listed below.

- **Messianic Jewish Alliance of America (MJAA)—** Founded in 1915, it is the oldest organization of Jewish-focused ministries and the most well-known for its management and organization of the Messianic community. Marty Brotman was one of the first proponents of Messianic Judaism in the Hebrew Christian Alliance, which was later named the MJAA. This organization really took off in 1970s as the Messianic movement exploded onto the scene. It was aided by one of the movement's spiritual fathers, Marty Chernoff, who founded Beth Messiah Congregation in Cincinnati. His two sons, Joel and David, are still serving on its ministry board. The MJAA has also founded The Joseph Project, which has become the number one humanitarian aid group in Israel.

- **The Union of Messianic Jewish Congregations (UMJC)**—With the initial influence of Marty Brotman, the UMJC was founded in 1979 by two Messianic Congregations from Chicago, Adat HaTikvah and B'nai Maccabim. Dr. Daniel Juster was its founding president. The UMJC is smaller than the MJAA, but it is has also become a voice for Messianic Judaism worldwide, with a strong focus on training up Messianic leaders and aiding Jewish causes.

- **Tikkun America and Tikkun Global**—These organizations were also founded by Dr. Daniel Juster, Asher Intrater, Eitan Shiskoff, and Moshe Morrison. Tikkun Ministries is committed to a fivefold ministry focus to aid and strengthen the Messianic community in the things of the Holy Spirit. It is the first of its kind to work within this most crucial area. All three named leaders have moved to Israel, where they have established and planted new Congregations and a ministry focus of apostolic leadership in Israel, which is connected to the nations. It is significant to have these spiritual leaders living back in the land. In the past few years, Tikkun Ministries is experiencing significant growth in the United States, Israel, and in other countries.

- **Jewish Voice Ministries International**—This organization was founded by Louis Kaplan in 1967 with a focus on Jewish evangelism through media. This ministry is now led by Rabbi Jonathan Bernis, who founded Hear O Israel Ministries, which helped to awaken the Russian-Jewish community in the 1990s after the Berlin Wall came down. Jewish Voice

Ministries airs a very popular TV show hosted by Jonathan Bernis. Through Jonathan's vision, Jewish Voice Ministries is now also involved in helping organize, strengthen, and mobilize the Messianic community. It has held an annual meeting in Arizona specifically for Messianic leaders to be renewed and strengthened in their mission with a greater percentage of messianic leadership attending. This conference is called the Messianic Leaders Roundtable (MLR).

- **Toward Jerusalem Council 2 (TJC2)**—This organization was formed especially for dialogue between Israel and the Church. A group of Jewish and Gentile leaders established the organization with the vision of love and Reconciliation between the two groups. Rabbi Marty Waldman, the original visionary, provides leadership as general executive secretary. John Dawson, former head of Youth with a Mission; Dr. Wayne Wilks of Gateway Church; and Dr. Daniel Juster of Tikkun provide leadership as cochairmen.

DUAL-EXPRESSION CONGREGATIONS AND CHURCHES

A dual-expression Congregation is one that coexists with a local Church. There are separate services on Shabbat for Jewish believers and those Gentiles called to serve the Jewish community, much like the focus for a Messianic Congregation. Meanwhile, the Church continues to maintain its usual Sunday services for

A dual-expression Congregation is one that coexists with a local Church. There are separate services on Shabbat for Jewish believers and those Gentiles called to serve the Jewish community, much like the focus for a Messianic Congregation. Meanwhile, the Church continues to maintain its usual Sunday services for everyone else. Plus, congregants in both groups are free to mingle with one another to experience the best of both worlds.

everyone else. Plus, congregants in both groups are free to mingle with one another to experience the best of both worlds.

The dual-expression concept is relatively new and is now beginning to emerge in a number of Churches across the country, especially in more heavily Jewish populated areas. Gateway Church, pastored by Robert Morris in Dallas, Texas, is leading the way with this dual-expression focus.

PARACHURCH MESSIANIC MINISTRIES

The ParaChurch Messianic ministry focus is also relatively new from within the Church community. It offers a number of advantages to a Church community that is looking to reach out to the Jewish people. There are three main foci with this type of ministry: 1) To help Jewish believers in the Church find the fullness of their identities, 2) to help Christians Reconnect to their Jewish roots and to equip them for Jewish ministry, and 3) to hold evangelistic outreach where Christians can bring their Jewish friends to hear the Gospel. They also usually practice the Feasts of the Lord, which are wonderful for Christians to be able to share and experience and to extend an invitation to their Jewish friends.

ONE NEW MAN CHURCHES AND CONGREGATIONS

New groups are emerging from within the Church community who are wanting to find a greater expression of *TONM* by aligning themselves to the biblical calendar and moving away from Gentile traditions and practices.

The key for us is how can we work together to achieve God's aim and plans through us. We must follow His guidance to become more effective in TONM and with Jewish ministry. Whatever we do should be birthed and led by the Holy Spirit.

One of the founders of this movement is a pastor named Mark Biltz, who wrote a book titled *Blood Moons: Decoding the Imminent Heavenly Signs.* He and his ministry team are building a vibrant Congregation that is very well-attended in the Seattle area, with a huge following through the internet from all over the world. This response alone is an indicator of the interest that is emerging from within the Church for us to Reconnect to our Jewish roots.

CHURCHES CONNECTING TO THEIR JEWISH ROOTS

Then there are also Churches wanting to find a greater connection to their Jewish roots without losing their Gentile expression by associating with the biblical calendar and the feasts of the Lord. Chuck Pierce and Robert Heidler are leading this charge, along with a number of other lesser known Christian leaders in the Church.

THE KEY

The key for us is how can we work together to achieve God's aim and plans through us. We must follow His guidance to become more effective in *TONM* and with Jewish ministry. Whatever we do should be birthed and led by the Holy Spirit.

MESSIANIC TV

There are three main television shows in the United States and a number of other smaller ones on cable TV. Jonathan Bernis's *Jewish Voice Ministries*, Sid Roth's *It's Supernatural*, and Rabbi Kirt Schneider's *Discovering the Jewish Jesus* are the most well-known. In Israel, *Yeshua Israel* has been on the air since 2004, hosted by Kobi and Shani Ferguson. More recently, Ron Cantor hosts Out of Zion on God TV. Ron is also a senior leader of Tikkun Global Ministries and is quickly becoming a major leader in the Messianic Movement.

MEDIA MINISTRIES

With the advancement of the internet, new high-tech evangelistic ministries are emerging. One such Messianic ministry is *One for*

Israel, which uses Facebook, YouTube, and other internet outlets to share Jewish testimonies through film and video posting.

BIBLE TRANSLATIONS

Two major versions of the Bible have been translated with a Messianic perspective. The first was the *Complete Jewish Bible*, which was translated by Messianic scholar David H. Stern. The second one, *The Tree of Life Version,* founded by Daniah Greenberg, was translated by both Jewish and Gentile scholars with the aim of creating a translation that is truer to the Jewish roots of the faith.

JEWISH BELIEVERS IN THE LOCAL CHURCH

I would be remiss to finish this section without mentioning the fact that there are far more Jewish believers in the local Church than anywhere else. There are as many as 250,000 Jewish believers in the United States, 15,000 to 20,000 in Israel, and as many as 350,000 worldwide.[11]

Rabbi Jonathan Bernis, who heads *Jewish Voice Ministries,* has done a personal study on the Jewish population in the Messianic Body in the United States. He estimates that there are approximately fifteen thousand Jewish believers in Messianic Congregations. This means the vast majority are in the Church. However, a good number of Jewish believers in the Church are not yet properly Reconnected with their identity, as they should be, because most have converted to Christianity without returning to their own roots and heritage.

I was one of the blessed ones because my first pastor was half Jewish and fully encouraged me into my Jewish identity in Messiah. In fact, I was so comfortable in my Jewishness in the Holy Spirit that I did not necessarily need to follow synagogue practices to feel more connected to my roots and heritage. When I accepted Yeshua (my testimony is recorded in my first book, *The New Covenant Prophecy*), I found the God of Abraham for the first time in my life, and I couldn't be more Jewish if I tried.

However, this has not been the experience for a lot of other Jewish people coming to Jesus in the Church. It was almost as if they had to sever their previous connections to convert to Christianity. This was Hali's experience in her first Church before she discovered her own Jewish roots.

In reality, Jews do not *convert* when coming to Yeshua; rather, they *return* because God has already made a Covenant with them. In fact, it is quite common for Gentile Christians to comment, when hearing a Jewish person's testimony, that he or she is no longer Jewish when believing in Jesus. But this could not be further from the truth. When Jewish people accept Yeshua, they have now come home and are indeed fulfilled in their calling.

This has come about mainly because of the Church's misunderstanding toward the calling and role of Israel's Remnant (see Romans 11:1–6)—Jewish believers who are naturally a part of spiritual Israel when they believe. This is a problem and is in great need of correction. This transition has been painful for many Jewish believers in the Church, to say the least. Many have to leave loved ones or are shunned by them and become disconnected from their heritage. After making this journey, some of them want nothing to do with their Jewish roots and heritage anymore and are now comfortable being Christian, like everyone else.

> It is my sincere hope and prayer as this Reconnection takes full root in us that these Jewish believers in the Church will be awakened to their calling and identity.

They have crossed over once, so why should they return now? This is how some may feel at this point. However, Jewish believers have a call to be a light back to their own people. In fact, they typically need a great deal of encouragement from their Gentile pastors and Christian family to properly reflect Yeshua back to their own people as a Jewish faith. This will ultimately help other Jewish people more easily recognize belief in Yeshua as Jewish.

It is my sincere hope and prayer as this Reconnection takes full root in us that these Jewish believers in the Church will be awakened to their calling and identity. I pray that they will be greatly encouraged by their Gentile-believing family to properly Reconnect to their roots and heritage, however that manifests in the differing expressions I have already described, and to fulfill their calling as Jewish believers in the family of God.

PART III

OBSTACLES TO THE ONE NEW MAN

CHAPTER 7

THE CHRISTIAN LENS

SECTION 1
EXPOSING REPLACEMENT THEOLOGY

IN CHAPTER 2, we focused on the "heart" obstacles that need to be addressed through the generational bloodline—namely, the influences of antisemitism and all other humanistic obstacles. But for our *freedom* to be complete, we must also be willing to address the *obstacles* that exist in our *mindsets* and our thinking. This is in reference to our theology and eschatology.

Receiving *The Reconnection* revelation is a spiritual transaction that comes to us only through the power of God's Holy Spirit. Therefore, we must show love and restraint—not to judge those who are not presently seeing this final piece the way it needs to be fully recognized but rather to stand in the gap and intercede for them according to God's plans and purposes for the rest of the Body of Messiah/Christ to receive it.

At this time, God wants to wash us clean from all past influences so we can be prepared for what is to come. This is Abba's Heart for all of us in His Church and Messianic bodies. This is not negative per se, even though we must be open to looking back. But for us to receive this cleansing, we have to be able to recognize the error first and see exactly how our *hearts and minds* have been influenced in this area, as well as how it still affects our thinking as Gentile followers of the King of Israel. This applies to the whole Church, not just the part that still believes it has fully replaced Israel. Whenever

God brings correction, it always begins first in His House—but it never ends there.

RENEWED ESCHATOLOGY

It is for this reason, now more than ever, that we need to be willing to lay all of our theological and eschatological views on the altar of understanding. This is not so we will see everything exactly the same way but rather so that we can become open to the Jewish-believing mindset that is part of our Restoration in *TONM* and His end-time plans to work through us to bring it to pass. We must be willing to enter a new place of dialogue, love, and respect where we can openly share our views without causing any anger, dissension, or division. This has been one of the Church's missing elements up to this point in time.

As already discussed, how could we expect God to give us fullness of revelation and understanding toward Israel and the Church when the Church has moved in the opposite direction of the mandate it was given to love Israel? (See Romans 11.)

With all due respect and with a great amount of humility and deference to my Gentile family and the many brilliant minds and theologians, the Church's separation from Israel has led to the development of numerous theological and eschatological positions from a Gentile-believing perspective that are in need of correction. *TONM* is not Gentile alone; it is both Jewish and Gentile. We reign together with Israel, as the Scripture says, especially now that Israel is awakening (see Ephesians 3:6).

As already discussed, how could we expect God to give us fullness of revelation and understanding toward Israel and the Church when the Church has moved in the opposite direction of the mandate it was given to love Israel? (See Romans 11.) Through the ancestral Church's misconception of Israel's plight and journey regarding their ultimate spiritual Restoration, coupled with antisemitism and jealousy, they opened up the Church to one of its greatest deceptions from the devil known as *supersessionism,* which is known today as *replacement* or *Fulfillment Theology.*[12] (See Appendix for books on Replacement Theology.)

Simply put, Replacement Theology is the belief that the Church has replaced Israel and that none of the promises and Covenants to Israel apply exclusively to them, but rather to the Church. I address this more extensively in *The Ezekiel Generation* (page 71, first and second editions).

This teaching not only transformed the Church's theology; it also infiltrated the Gentile side of the family with a separatist mentality that moved the Church away from its proper connection to Israel and the Jewish roots and heritage of the faith through Yeshua/Jesus.

These teachings have fueled a disconnection in the family of God, created by Yeshua/Jesus at the cross and resurrection. Through supersessionism, the Church inherited a false identity away from Israel that has remained until now.

Please understand that my intent here is not to lay blame in any way, but rather for us to fully recognize the *severity* of the influence that Replacement Theology has had on us in the Gentile Church and to fully recognize its *lingering effects.* As I am writing this, I feel like a doctor composing his diagnosis so that we can understand and be aware of the symptoms and get totally free.

Please tarry with me, your Jewish brother, because there is no other way for me to say this. For us to get there, we must be willing to rid ourselves of *all* past negative influences, not just generational bloodline issues that affect our hearts. We must also consider theological issues that affect our minds and the way we think. These are the greatest *obstacles* to *The Reconnection* for God's Gentile family. We must not remain separate anymore!

This cleansing in us must be total and complete, as nothing short of this will do. *Any yeast leftover in this place will still affect and influence the dough; it must be removed!* (See Galatians 5:9.)

The Lord is calling for a *complete cleansing* to put the ax to the root of all issues on both sides of the tree that stand in the way of this Reconnection. We need to put away all our differences that have fueled a separation—the hurts, the wounds, the sin, and the affected theology under the blood—so we can be set free. Afterward, we must never look back at what once was but rather come into a glorious new union that will again *set the world on fire* with His love and His power. These are the full fruits of a Reconnected family in the *Father's Heart* in the Israel of God that will change the world forever!

REPLACEMENT THEOLOGY

I cannot mince words here: we must fully come to terms with the grave error of Replacement Theology and its *entire* influence on

I cannot mince words here: we must fully come to terms with the grave error of Replacement Theology and its entire influence on the Body of Messiah/Christ if we want to be free from all its effects.

the Body of Messiah/Christ if we want to be free from all its effects. It has fueled our separateness and thinking in the Church, which is one of the main lingering effects. Not only does it still grasp a greater percentage of the Church that believes it has entirely replaced Israel. But without even knowing it, its residual effects from the past 1700 years are still affecting the balance of the Christian Church that wants to bless and love Israel. This is the mindset spiritually and emotionally and its theological viewpoints concerning Israel, which are still coming from a Gentile perspective rather than from the fullness of *TONM*. This perspective and separation affect the way Christians relate to the Jewish people. It has caused us to be indifferent and numb in the heart.

This is why there is so much confusion and so many differing viewpoints in our eschatology: amillennialism, postmillennialism, premillennialism, pre-tribulation rapture, mid-tribulation rapture, post-tribulation rapture, preterism, partial preterism, dispensationalism, futurist, historic, Kingdom now, dual-Covenant theology, and all sorts of groups thinking and believing they are the new

Israel. Oh my God, what a mess! And I'm not just saying this for us to come into perfect agreement regarding our eschatology, but rather for us to recognize the *separateness* and *divisiveness* that it brings and how the enemy uses it to keep us apart.

The recognition of this wrong is just the beginning of the process toward healing and repentance. However, just to think of recognizing and confessing it without much *deeper reflection* would be a deception to the depths of just how much it has influenced the Gentile side of the family in its psyche and theological perspective concerning Israel and the Church.

The roots of these teachings not only created a separateness between Gentile and Jew, but without us even knowing it, they continue to fuel the very separateness between us that God is wanting to heal and restore in *TONM*.

This might be a hard pill for us to swallow, but it is most necessary if we are to pull out all these roots, once and for all! As discussed in chapter 2, we must break off all generational influences

The roots of these teachings not only created a separateness between Gentile and Jew, but without us even knowing it, they continue to fuel the very separateness between us that God is wanting to heal and restore in TONM.

relating to the generational bloodline. This is an essential process for every Church and every Christian; no Church group has been unstained by this influence. We must also fully reflect on how much these misguided teachings have affected and influenced our theology and the way we think, as well as our perception of *TONM*. This is the *second major process* in this Restoration for us to consider and address. If we confess this and afterward still remain in a separate mode from Israel and its Remnant, then we have missed something extremely significant that will enable us to move into the full process of repentance.

Simply put, on behalf of His Gentile Church, if we haven't repudiated Replacement Theology in its entirety, then we have missed the mark. Until we can fully embrace that our Jewish-believing family is called to a Covenant loyalty to being Jewish (fully encouraging them to find their identities as Jews), something is still missing from us. This is a pillar in *The Reconnection* for the entire Church to recognize and help shepherd Jewish believers into this place in the Church.

Full repentance means to embrace the Jewish branch of the olive tree and the Covenants and election of the people of Israel, along with our own: "One New Man does not mean one less Jew!" Without this, we remain incomplete in this area, giving play to the enemy's divide and influence in our theological views that continues to fuel a separation between believing Jew and Gentile.

Full repentance means to embrace the Jewish branch of the olive tree and the Covenants and election of the people of Israel, along with our own: "*One New Man* does not mean one less Jew!" Without this, we remain incomplete in this area, giving play to the enemy's divide and influence in our theological views that continues to fuel a separation between believing Jew and Gentile. This shuts us down from walking the path and role Abba is calling us into to help awaken the balance of Israel spiritually to win them back to faith.

OUR OWN HUMANITY WILL NOT DO

A good example of the power and effect of this human influence related to Replacement Theology is the Church after World War II, when a decent number of Church bodies, including Catholics (Vatican II), repudiated Replacement Theology in light of the Holocaust experience. They recognized that it was connected to an antisemitic orientation, so they all adopted clauses that the Jews were God's elect people.

However, what is done out of our own humanistic efforts will never be enough to sustain us through this transaction. *Only through a circumcised heart full of the Father's love for each other can we be connected spiritually together to fully restore Israel.* This bond between us must also include an undying commitment to the word of truth related to God's Covenants to awaken His firstborn children.

Fast-forward one or two generations to the plight of the Palestinians and Israel's right to defend itself; conflicts have obviously arisen. Yet at the same time, many of the Churches that denounced Replacement Theology have once again picked it up in light of the humanistic issues involved here. Its influences have also affected some of the charismatic and evangelical communities.

Is this purely a coincidence? I think not. If the heart has not been fully cleansed and transformed in this area, the generational bloodline influences can so easily be resurrected by the enemy affecting the way we think. For this reason, we must be willing to look back at this issue so that we can see it from our Father's perspective through a transformed heart and mind in His Word, not from our own humanistic mindset (see Romans 12:2). And nothing less will do here!

ISRAELI/PALESTINIAN ISSUES

These are challenging issues for sure, and I am not necessarily condoning or accepting everything Israel does as righteous, as I have already pointed out. However, for certain this land belongs to God and His purposes before anyone or anything else. And any attempts that

Only through a circumcised heart full of the Father's love for each other can we be connected spiritually together to fully restore Israel.

are made by humankind to divide or separate the land away from Israel and the Covenants are met with some kind of judgment and disaster. A great book on this subject is *Eye to Eye* by William R. Koenig, a fascinating read.

This is a most perplexing situation that I believe will not get fully resolved until our Lord returns and all things are brought under

His sovereignty. However, it does not help when the Palestinian authorities will not even recognize Israel's right to exist, and its terror groups will not settle for anything less than Israel's complete and utter destruction. How can you negotiate with that? Can you imagine if this conflict was in your own backyard? Nor does it help though, when Jews or Jewish believers totally reject Palestinians. In particular, can we please pray for peace and Reconciliation between Jewish and Palestinian believers that God would raise up a standard in us of love and Reconnection in Yeshua/Jesus between the two groups. This would be special and could serve to be a light to the rest. The Ekklesia should always lead the way!

It is not my intention to get into a debate about the Israeli/Palestinian conflict or to offer a solution. Nor will I attempt to address the rights and wrongs because wherever humankind is involved, there will be error in some form or another. It is my intent, however, to emphasize the significance of the understanding of the Word of God and His Covenants to the people of Israel. These are in process now for a complete Restoration.

So where do the Palestinians and the 1.6 billion souls that are caught under the spirit of Islam fit here? Keep in mind that Islam is the ultimate replacement religion for Israel! At the Dome of the Rock (the Golden Mosque in Jerusalem), where Isaac was offered up to God, they say it was Ishmael instead. And where it is written on its very walls, it states that God has no Son!

What will be their plight, and how should we respond? First, we need to understand the consequences for all those who do not believe in Yeshua/Jesus, and then we must pray mercifully and without ceasing for their salvation and Restoration. I believe this spiritual battle against Islam will be one of the greatest ever fought in the Ekklesia/Church. It must be evermore on our prayer radar, beside Israel's awakening and the last great harvest of souls. In the natural we love, but in the Spirit we must contend.

Just between the time of *Romans 911*'s first launch on Shavuot/Pentecost 2018 and this second edition in 2021, an awakening of those caught under Islam's influence has begun. Many thousands upon thousands of souls are coming to know the Lord in the Middle-East and beyond. We are hearing of underground revivals and numerous testimonies where Yeshua/Jesus is appearing to them in dreams and visions. It is wonderful to hear of these stories, but I think it is only the beginning of what we are going to see as more and more Muslims come to Mashiach/Christ.

The Word of God is encouraging in this light and offers good insight for prayer and future change among Abraham's physical descendants. Isaiah 19:23–25 tells us of a highway from Egypt to Assyria: *"In that day Israel will be the third, along with Egypt and Assyria, a blessing on the earth. The Lord Almighty will bless them, saying, 'Blessed be Egypt my people, Assyria my handiwork, and Israel my inheritance.'"*

This Scripture, which has not yet been fulfilled, speaks of a unity and love between these peoples, of an order, a cooperation, and submission to God.

I have a Jewish-believing friend in Israel whose name I cannot mention for the sake of his own protection. He is looking to build bridges of healing and Restoration between Arabs and Jews through humanitarian efforts, which is the very beginning of the fulfillment of this prophecy. Similarly, many Messianic believers who carry Yeshua's Heart and burden in the land have the same focus, reaching out to the Arab communities with the love of Yeshua/Jesus.

The leaders of the Toward Jerusalem Council 2 (TJC2) met recently in an act of repentance and intercession for this very purpose. The Spirit of God is making preparations for what is coming.

James Goll has also been used of God in this place of intercession, as well as a good number of unnamed saints the Lord continues to touch to help break up this ground in the Spirit, so that this Reconciliation can break forth in the natural. However, we have only just begun to touch the hem of the garment in this area. Far *more* intercession is needed in the land to help strengthen the

Body there. This is one of the main purposes of our annual Worship & Watchmen Mission to Israel, where we visit both Messianic and Arab prayer houses to lift up their arms and pray for the Ekklesia in Israel.

In addition, look at how God instructed Moses in the Passover related to foreigners among them in the old Covenant. As they were circumcised, they could partake like one born in the land, and there was to be no distinction between them; the same is true now (see Exodus 12:48–49). This is the Heart of God; He wants us to be one with Him, but God still has an order that must be followed.

> *"My command is this: Love each other as I have loved you. Greater love has no one than this: to lay down one's life for one's friends. You are my friends if you do what I command"* (John 15:12–14).

This is the type of love that will truly transform us. We need to embrace the *Father's Heart* for each other as family and love one another as we love ourselves.

And what of the Palestinian Christians immersed in this conflict? Are we so one-sided in our beliefs and support of Israel that we are steamrolling our very own brothers and sisters? Or can the love of the Father reach out to cross these barriers and help melt away these wounds that divide us? I say a hearty "Yes!" and "Amen!" to this statement.

This is the love and the power of *The Reconnection* in the *Heart of the Father* to love one another before anything else. This is Jewish and Gentile believers living in the land on both sides of this conflict, finding peace and Reconciliation. In fact, what a testimony it would be for both Jewish and Palestinian believers to be able to lay down their lives for one another.

Believe it or not, this initiative has already begun with two such believers: Lisa Loden, a Messianic matriarch in the land; and Salim J. Munayer, a Christian Palestinian leader. They have written a book on this very issue, *Through My Enemy's Eyes*. They also are meeting regularly for prayer and dialogue in this most crucial area of Reconciliation. These believers are in desperate need of our prayers and support for their causes.

GOD WILL HAVE HIS WAY

God will have His way through us in all areas of *The Reconnection* as we move over and allow Him to fully take the reins in this area. However, we must be willing to open up so that we can see some of the mistakes we have made along the way and allow Him to guide us to finish the job.

Recently, in one of our *Pure Intercession* prayer meetings for *The Reconnection*, the Holy Spirit gave us some very interesting insight specifically on this subject that I would like to share with you. Here is the email that was sent out after the meeting, which took place in the fall of 2016:

> After seeking out the Lord about issues to pray on in *TONM* for last night, I have been particularly burdened recently, as I have been writing a new section in the book about the influences of Replacement Theology in the Church. And I do not mean just the part of the Church that still believes in this deception, but also how it is still affecting the part of the Church that is moving toward Israel, in our thinking and our theology.
>
> In this light, I shared it with the group, and after Communion and brief worship, the Holy Spirit led us into the greater depths of this issue. Several people in the group shared their hearts, and John Maclean confirmed this sense in his spirit. There was a focus on prayer and prophecy for Grant in this area as he is writing the book, with much encouragement, but also specific direction and clarity. They are recorded.
>
> There was a deeper understanding given by the Spirit of the depths of this deception and its lingering effect on

the Church. And a root of jealousy was exposed by the Spirit for us to pray on.

The Spirit fell on Grant as the group was praying for him, who went into a deep cry and weeping, as he felt and experienced Joseph's heart, as his brothers sold him into slavery. The weeping was intense, as in travail, and continued for a while with a sense and connection to Joseph as the Jew and the brothers as the Gentile believers in the Church. What a picture!

Prayers were then offered for repentance in the Body, as the rest of the group felt this burden in their hearts; and for the Lord to take us deeper into this issue.

THE VISION OF A PIECE OF FABRIC

Susan Torregrossa, a member of the meeting, had a significant vision about this. Here are her thoughts:

As Sheryl was talking, the Lord showed me a piece of fabric. I was reminded of a video I had seen regarding the shroud of Turin.[13] I could see the fabric as a whole cloth at first; then I could see individual strands of thread in the fabric, and it became magnified. The Lord showed me that what seemed to the naked eye to be a homogeneous piece of cloth was in fact made up of two different materials. He didn't specify what the materials were, but I will use the example of the shroud because I believe it is significant. It was found during inspection of the shroud that the original cloth was made up of linen, which comes from flax. In one corner where an expert "repair" had been made, cotton had been interwoven into the strands of the fabric. It was nearly imperceptible except under extreme magnification. The strands were slightly different colors and reacted differently to testing.

Grant mentioned that while some Churches have

moved on past Replacement Theology, most are still being held back by the residue of its influences.

I feel that what the Lord is showing me is that some of the old lies of Replacement Theology are still affecting the Church because they are the counterfeits of the truth and are interwoven into their fabric. They are imperceptible to the naked eye and can only be exposed through spiritual discernment.

It reminded me of what Pastor Glenn Harvison always says about the leaven: once you mix the yeast into the dough, only God can identify and remove it supernaturally.

We need to ask the Lord to remove it. We need to ask Him to unravel the strands of the fabric, to expose the counterfeit cotton portions and unravel them from the original linen.

> *We need to ask the Lord to remove it. We need to ask Him to unravel the strands of the fabric, to expose the counterfeit cotton portions and unravel them from the original linen. — Susan Torregrossa*

I didn't mention this last night, but I believe that I was seeing the linen/cotton combination because the garment of a high priest was always made of pure linen, representing purity. Just as His priests were called to wear the *linen ephod*, so we are called to do the same, and so the linen represents this (see appendix for link to video).

When you watch it, you will see the close-up magnification of the strands—that is the detail of what the Lord was showing me last night. Down to the very fiber of the core of the Church, I believe there are counterfeit ideas and beliefs, many that are so close to the truth that people feel that they are harmless and don't recognize them. But the Lord is saying that these things must be exposed, unraveled, and removed from the truth so His Church can move forward, unhindered.

When you watch the video, you will see how easy it would have been for the scientists to overlook those cotton fibers if they had not been accidentally torn and exposed.

That is what God wants to do now in the Church. There may be a bit of collateral damage, but in the end, there will be a course correction that is needed in the Church for this time we are living in.

This is a significant vision from the Holy Spirit to get us to understand that we must be willing to go deeper into the lingering effects of this issue in all parts of the Church—not just to repent and renounce Replacement Theology but to understand how it has affected and influenced us in the Church. This will allow us to break off *all* of its influences and restore us fully into *TONM* between Jew and Gentile.

Hali, my wife, was also in the meeting. She had further insight about Susan's vision of the fabric. She explained that when you wash this fabric with the two different materials, one might appear to be cleaner than the other. If you continue to wash them, they will look different. The good fabric will wash well, but the bad fabric will shrink and become wrinkled and shriveled.

I believe that as the Lord continues to cleanse in this area, more will be exposed, and the counterfeit will be revealed.

WHAT DO WE DO WITH THIS INFORMATION?

The replacement teachings became so predominant in His Church that the separateness it produced is closely interwoven, making it almost impossible for us to see our own disconnection.

From the Church's perspective, just how much cotton is still present within us from past influences that continue to prevent us from seeing the fullness of God's plans for us? And to what extent is that blindness still over our eyes through Replacement Theology, either directly or indirectly?

This vision and insight of the Holy Spirit fits fully within the context of *The Reconnection*. Let us pray for the Lord to wash away all past influences so that we can put on that pure linen garment and become His priestly vessels in *TONM*—ready and able to fully embrace our end-time roles. However, first we need to recognize where we went wrong and look to fully correct it.

As a Jewish believer in the Church, it is easy for me to see these roles in Scripture; it is all written there. Yet my Christian family has embraced certain misguided doctrines that are not of the Father, His Son, or His founding apostles, and they have blinded us and clouded our perspective.

The replacement teachings became so predominant in His Church that the separateness it produced is closely interwoven, making it almost impossible for us to see our own disconnection. *But now is the time* God has chosen to clear up the confusion and break it off so that we can properly see Israel's Restoration and understand its significance to the whole.

In this light, it should be clear to us now that we need to fully rid ourselves of Replacement Theology, along with all its influences, including the way in which it has affected the Christian Church in its eschatology. We must rid ourselves of this burden first to correct the path of the Church that still believes in it and second to help the balance of the Church already moving toward Israel so that they can break off any residual influences keeping them from finding the mark and the fullness of *TONM*.

It is possible to believe in Replacement Theology and not be antisemitic. However, as I also point out in *The Ezekiel Generation*, one does not need to be antisemitic to be affected by generational antisemitism and feel a great indifference within his or her heart. In this case, the two are usually intertwined. One can love and support Israel, as it does any other people or nation, while still believing that the Church has replaced it. A good number of loving

Christians live in this place, so we should try to reach out to help bring them to this new knowledge and understanding.

Let us also not be judgmental here because we have just discovered that we all need repentance and change in this area. Let us extend a hand of love and a heart of prayer for all those in the Church to come into a full repentance in this place.

THE COVENANTS

Christians who still uphold replacement/Fulfillment Theology see in a different light the part of the Covenants made exclusively to the people of Israel concerning their unveiling and their Restoration. They do so either through believing Jew and believing Gentile replacing Israel and/or through Jesus Himself fulfilling the Covenants, so that they no longer apply to the people of Israel.

Elect Israel is now the Church. Ethnic Israel is no longer a people of God with any additional spiritual significance, and the promises and Covenants apply solely to the Church—hence the word "replacement." They believe that the people of Israel now are like any other nation and that when Jews believe, they become Christians (believing Jews and Gentiles), which fulfills the Israel of God. But since there is no Jew or Gentile anymore (an incorrect understanding of Galatians 3:28), their identity is nullified. This happens without ethnic Israel's ultimate Restoration and is obviously the missing piece of the puzzle (see Romans 11:15).

Forgive my play on words, but we must "replace this theology" and Reconnect spiritually toward Israel, as we did before this happened.

The Church's confession of faith that follows this doctrine does not include the Restoration of Israel, which ultimately leads to the Restoration of the nations. As such, there is a gap from the Garden of Eden, or God's Covenant to Abraham, to the birth of Jesus, which omits a great deal of the depth, background, and history of Israel and the Church. In most cases, it causes them to nullify much of the Old Testament or consider it irrelevant, specifically its connectedness to the Jewish people.

This also led the Church to believe that the New Covenant made everything totally new rather than the old being transformed through Mashiach/Christ. This led us to make the Church Gentile and break away from our roots, thus departing from our heritage and our connection to Israel.

Gerald R. McDermott's book *The New Christian Zionism* addresses this subject extensively with fresh theological perspectives for the Church. McDermott points to Craig Blaisings's essay on Hermeneutics, which shows that Israel has an ongoing presence in the New Testament: "Nothing about the presentation of Jesus the Messiah as the center of the New Testament message needs to exclude God's commitment to Israel as a people or nation. The Christification of the promise does not mean the nullification of hope for Israel. Promises of Restoration after proclamations of judgment are rooted in God's speech acts in the Torah and in the New Testament" (McDermott, 306).

Because most of us have yet to rid ourselves of past theological influences in the Church, some of the old cotton that is intertwined into the linen is still having its effect on us, without us even being aware of it, or knowing. This prevents us from either seeing or fully recognizing the mark, which the Lord wants to correct to break off these negative influences in His family.

In *The God of Israel and Christian Theology*, author R. Kendal Soulen argues that our whole understanding of God has been compromised because of the influence of Replacement Theology.

Forgive my play on words, but we must "replace this theology" and Reconnect spiritually toward Israel, as we did before this happened.

In a Reconnected environment, *The Covenants* toward Israel are just that, and they relate solely to Israel's physical and spiritual

Restoration to complete the family of God. This is inclusive of Israel's Remnant and the broken-off branches that are yet to be Reconnected.

This is fundamental to our understanding and should be enough of a compelling argument for us to want to see Israel spiritually reborn to make us whole. In this time of Reconnection, our refocus on the *Israel Piece* is the epicenter to the rest!

However, because most of us have yet to rid ourselves of past theological influences in the Church, some of the old cotton that is intertwined into the linen is still having its effect on us, without us even being aware of it, or knowing. This prevents us from either seeing or fully recognizing the mark, which the Lord wants to correct to break off these negative influences in His family.

REMOVING THE COTTON FROM THE FABRIC

This manifests itself in numerous ways in our theological and eschatological thinking in the Gentile part of the family. But it is not my goal or plan here to lay out an exact eschatological viewpoint; I already stated my thoughts concerning our understanding of prophetic Scriptures in chapter 4. Many of us have differing views, and when prophecy is fulfilled, we will be able to look back and see how perfectly every aspect of Scripture tied into its fulfillment; without taking any of it out of context. But beforehand, this is simply not possible with every Scripture.

If Israel's redemption and Restoration are not a part of our eschatology, and it is not the Church's role to help bring it about, then I can tell you quite plainly that our viewpoint is in need of adaptation to the Father's plans to glorify His Son upon the Earth through the regathering and reawakening of Israel.

Isn't it interesting that no one recognized the fact that John the Baptist was the Elijah to come? And look how diplomatically Yeshua/Jesus introduced that thought to the disciples:

"And if you are willing to accept it, he is the Elijah who was to come" (Matt. 11:14).

When you think of the Jewish Body before His coming, its eschatology for almost two thousand years was mainly focused on Yeshua's second coming and as such, totally missed the first. Also, most of the Church for the past eighteen hundred years did not believe in Israel's Restoration to the land. So for us to think that we have it all perfectly laid out could be a deception to the ultimate truth of God's plan.

The Restoration of Israel, in this light, is no longer prophecy but rather a complete fulfillment of God's Covenants toward the Jewish people. This cannot be ignored or pushed aside anymore, or spiritualized. This is true both in the Restoration of the land and in their spiritual awakening, which is proof enough for us to reexamine what we believe and to fulfill our most crucial role to help bring it to pass.

We must not hold on to our viewpoint so tightly to the exclusion of anything else or these realities that have come to pass during our own era. Or are we still trying to work them into our belief system rather than using them to change or adjust our perspectives?

NEXT STEPS

So what do we do with this understanding now? If Israel's redemption and Restoration are not a part of our eschatology, and it is not the Church's role to help bring it about, then I can tell you quite plainly that our viewpoint is in need of adaptation to the Father's plans to glorify His Son upon the Earth through the regathering and reawakening of Israel.

Plus, if it does not take center stage in importance with first fruits, we will still be missing the mark, which is significant to point out. Upon beginning to receive this revelation, many moving toward the *Israel Piece* mistakenly look to slot it into a place with all the other ministry issues that need to be addressed in the Kingdom. They also mix it with their own eschatological view without understanding that it is the most central piece to the equation and to the *Father's Heart* or that everything else flows from this place—from the core, as I have described in other chapters. *The Reconnection* Realigns His family to the Jew first, back to this Kingdom principle, which never changed!

Israel is obviously not everything God is doing on Earth, but it is at the very heart of it right now. *Everything and everyone else is just as important to God, but all other issues are not equal to it; it is a corrected power source from God for everything else.*

How will we be able to fulfill our role with the spiritual rebirth of Israel through prayer, intercession, and evangelism if we have not fully reattached ourselves to Israel, taking on its plight as our very own flesh? This is all part of the enemy's tactic and strategy against God's Church—to use our eschatology to somehow keep us apart or separate and detach us from the heart of the goal. We must come together so that satan will be fully exposed, which requires a great deal of humility on our part.

Israel is obviously not everything God is doing on Earth, but it is at the very heart of it right now. Everything and everyone else is just as important to God, but all other issues are not equal to it; it is a corrected power source from God for everything else.

Isn't it interesting that in this light and up to this point in time that all current eschatology in the Church excludes this most vital spiritual transaction between us, or our role to aid in Israel's final Restoration? This is one of the main reasons, even among our apostolic movement in the Gentile-believing Church, that the gift of apostolic evangelism back toward the Jewish people is still missing.

The spiritual depths of this transaction in us cannot necessarily be put into words. But it is the exact position that the Father and Son are beckoning us into to reunite us in the Spirit so that the end can come. It is in this heart of love for one another, and of John 17 unity, that the Holy Spirit will Realign us into our greatest-ever role to ensure the intercession for the balance of souls on the Earth to come forth. These are the end-time battles for the Kingdom of God. The Church must take *spiritual dominion* wherever it *lives* and *operates* so that the enemy's strongholds will be *crushed* under the Lord's feet.

> *"You who call on the LORD, give yourselves no rest, and give Him no rest till He establishes Jerusalem and makes her a praise in all of the earth"* (Is. 62:6–7).

We would be mistaken if we spiritualize this Scripture. Our focus for the Kingdom needs to be on this great battle, physically and spiritually, for Jerusalem and Israel to come forth, for the Lord to take dominion, and for the veil to be lifted from our Jewish family so we can be complete and ready for His coming!

We don't know exactly how or when the Jewish people will be restored, even though Zechariah hints to a mass national repentance (see Zechariah 12:10). But one thing is for sure: when we go after their spiritual awakening and salvation, the *cries of the saints* will

This is the heart of the spiritual Realignment, as I have mentioned. Like David moving the ark back to Jerusalem, I believe God's hand and blessing will be upon it. The Father's plan is for us to take on our Jewish family's plight as our very own and to fight for them to be born again! Hallelujah!

go up to the heavens, and *thunder* will shake their very core. The rebirth of Israel will naturally increase, as well as the souls and the harvest from the nations, as they are supernaturally linked and connected in the end-time revival. *Church, can you see this now?!*

This is the heart of the spiritual Realignment, as I have mentioned. Like David moving the ark back to Jerusalem, I believe God's hand and blessing will be upon it. The Father's plan is for us to take on our Jewish family's plight as our very own and to fight for them to be born again! Hallelujah!

However, I would not want to be one of those who is still against Israel before the Lord returns to us. It is here that we must continue to show love and restraint for all those who do not agree with us. Our job is to continue to pray and contend for them in the Spirit to bring the breakthrough. This is love in action!

That's why it is so important for us at this point to refocus our efforts on awakening the Church, especially our intercession and to lift all of the effects that Replacement Theology and antisemitism have had on us. For certain, we are all in a season of His mercy (believing Jews and Gentiles), for His family to be fully and properly reconciled in *TONM*, and none of us is excluded here. This is His end-time plan to make us one!

SECTION 2
RIDDING US OF ITS INFLUENCES

DILUTION OF THE GOAL

In the balance of this chapter, I would like to raise issues and questions in the part of the Church that is moving toward Israel in our differing eschatological views that are somehow diluting us from this goal that we may want to reconsider.

The greatest theological misunderstanding and barrier to The Reconnection, on account of Replacement Theology, is that there is no longer any difference between Jew and Gentile.

As we enter more fully into *The Reconnection* in *TONM,* more will be revealed to us. Plus, I would like to suggest a Messianic eschatological approach that can be intertwined with certain Christian theology in how we see all of this transpiring. In no way do I wish to be critical of a particular viewpoint, but rather bring into question certain end-time views that might exclude the *Israel Piece* in its fullness or that might cause Christians to harbor views that keep us from this spiritual Reconnection.

MOST COMMON MISUNDERSTANDING

The greatest theological misunderstanding and barrier to *The Reconnection,* on account of Replacement Theology, *is that there is no longer any difference between Jew and Gentile.*

This understanding nullifies the call and Covenants to the people of Israel, reducing them to the status of all other peoples and nations that need to be saved. This eliminates their call and the Covenants toward them as being distinctive to Israel alone and applies them to both believing Jew and believing Gentile, as many in the Church currently believe. How often do we hear in the Church that there is no difference between Jew and Gentile?

Without necessarily knowing it, those who follow this belief take certain New Testament Scriptures out of context, often ignoring the Hebrew Scriptures and Romans 11, which speak of Israel's ultimate Restoration. However, even in this case, there is no greater significance to Israel's awakening and Restoration than to any other soul coming into the Kingdom.

This differing mindset has opened the Church to all kinds of confusion in our theological and eschatological positions. In studying this eschatology, I have found in almost every case that our theology ends up supporting our views, rather than the other way around. If we are most honest with ourselves, at some point in our theological dissertations, we end up overspiritualizing the word for it to tie into our beliefs.

In a sense, the Church divorced itself from the very people who brought it in and helped bring it to life. Recognizing this can help us process that a new marriage is needed at this point in time. We easily relate to Abraham, the patriarchs, and the prophets of old from a Christian perspective, but we still seem to skip the children and people of Israel, who are still a part of the Covenants.

In Rabbi Bob Wolff's book *Awakening the One New Man,* there is a chapter written by Jane Hansen Hoyt from Aglow International. It reflects beautifully on the unity of Adam and Eve in *TONM* between Jew and Gentile, eliminating the separateness between both groups.

It's best to look at this in the way of an analogy. This is obviously not a marriage between a man and a woman. However, there was something very special in the *oneness* that Yeshua/Jesus created at the cross and resurrection between Jews and Gentiles that is most unique. It is definitely something we must get back to, to restore the unity in God's family now that Israel's awakening has commenced, that enables us to move forward into our Father's end-time plans to redeem the Earth to Yeshua/Jesus (see John 17; Ephesians 2:11–22). This Reconnection to one another is most *central* and *foundational* to the Preparation of the Bride, who has made herself ready for the Groom, Yeshua/Jesus (see Revelation 19:7).

Not all in the Church have this understanding. However, this thinking still has its effects and plays a significant role in misguiding many of us toward the end of days. Repentance is needed here.

THE CHURCH'S ESCHATOLOGY

This mindset has also opened up the Church to differing views regarding when the Lord will return. Amillennialism, postmillennialism, preterism, and Kingdom-now theology say that Jesus comes again only at the end of the age to judge the world and set up the new Heaven and Earth. If this is the case, *the refocus on Israel is greatly reduced,* and *The Reconnection* cannot be fulfilled. In my perspective, there is just too much Scripture written that hasn't happened yet and seems to be in conflict with these beliefs concerning the thousand-year millennial reign of our Lord (see Revelation 20:12–15).

PARTIAL PRETERISM

There is another old Church view that has been catching on in the past few years known as "partial preterism." Harold Eberle's and Martin Trench's book on victorious eschatology makes a strong argument for the Scriptures that Yeshua/Jesus spoke about in the Gospels concerning the last days (see Matthew 24; Mark 13; Luke 21). They believe these Scriptures were fulfilled within the context of Israel's judgment and dispersion in the first and second centuries.

Preterists believe that Matthew 24 and the book of Revelation have already been fulfilled. Partial preterism opens the doors to some of these prophetic Scriptures being fulfilled in the future. And futurists and dispensationalists hold solely to a future viewpoint of these Scriptures.

Some partial preterists also believe in a final Restoration for the people of Israel; they believe it will bring a greater unity between Jew and Gentile, as noted in the end of Eberle's book. However, this viewpoint sees the final outflow of the Gospel to the nations as a means to help awaken Israel, rather than the other way around. This is crucial to our understanding and is in need of correction.

This viewpoint is currently justified because of its separation and connection to Israel, following the idea that we focus first on fulfilling the Church's call to the nations, and if we do so, Israel will be awakened. However, this is not what God established for His Kingdom and the Gospel. Therefore, it is not the way or path for us to be able to move the ark back to Jerusalem, speaking metaphorically.

The fullness of the Gentiles and Israel's spiritual awakening are not necessarily in a progressive order (see Romans 11:25–26), but rather a happenstance of both existing in the same era. As we come into the full number of the Gentiles, *in this way*, all Israel will be saved. Israel's calling was always to the nations as is now the Church's calling, but it was never to be exclusive of its own salvation! (See Isaiah 49:6.)

DISPENSATIONALISM

Dispensationalists, who have staunchly defended the Restoration of Israel, see a distinct separation between Israel and the Church, and their ultimate Restoration happens after Jesus returns. Although Israel is center in God's end-time plan to restore Yeshua to the Earth, both the Church and the broken-off branches of Israel play totally separate roles, without any spiritual Reconnection for the end to come. The Church gets removed at the beginning of the tribulation period, which most dispensationalists hold rigidly to, thus leaving God alone to awaken the Jews during this period.

This can cause Christians to become indifferent to Israel's spiritual Restoration and can fuel a continued separation between the two groups. In this light, I suggest that certain Christian Zionists can lack a genuine desire to see Israel spiritually restored, but rather for Israel to be central in their own eschatological perspective. This will hasten the world toward the tribulation period and then to Armageddon, which from their viewpoint will bring Christ back.

Some dispensationalists also believe in what is known as *Dual Covenant Theology*. This is a belief that because the Jewish people have their own Covenants with God, they don't necessarily need to come to the Lord through Jesus. This message of the Gospel is just for Gentiles until He returns.

This subsequently fuels the belief that all we need to do in the Church is bless the Jewish people without ultimately bringing the Gospel to them. Speaking from the Gentile perspective, this separates us from the very call and blessing God gave us to draw the Jewish people to jealousy and to release God's mercy back to them. Instead, we need to bless and support the Remnant of Israel first (Jewish believers), who are parts of the Body, along with its differing pieces (see 1 Corinthians 12:12–26).

With all due respect, this well-intentioned humanistic approach does not stand up to Scripture: First, the New Covenant through Yeshua/Jesus was given to Israel first, and Israel took it out to the world. Second, the Apostle Paul would have considered himself accursed for the sake of His own people coming to Yeshua/Jesus. Need I say more here?

If we hold to these understandings without *The Reconnection*, Christians can be void and separate of any direct participation or obligation in helping bring about Israel's personal salvation experience, as is currently the situation in the Gentile Church, except for viewing the fulfillment of end-time events relating to the land and the people of Israel actually taking place.

Second, if we are not here with the people of Israel when it goes through this period, will they be left to those who suddenly come alive to Mashiach/Christ during the tribulation? And how would younger believers have this kind of knowledge and depth of Spirit to properly bring Israel home when the time has finally come? Could it be that God will actually use this time to bring Jew and Christian together like never before, so His Holy Temple through us will be felt and experienced by the broken-off branches and help restore them to the faith? Will there be a *cost* and a *price* to pay for us to consider in this process?

THE MISSING LINK

What has become apparent to me as I studied many of these end-time views is that they are *missing the most significant link:* spiritual Reconnection as family and our most vital role in helping bring Israel back to life, which is at the heart of it all! From the devil's perspective, this would make sense because it is this exact connection and role that has been *hidden* from us. It is the

> What has become apparent to me as I studied many of these end-time views is that they are missing the most significant link: spiritual Reconnection as family and our most vital role in helping bring Israel back to life, which is at the heart of it all!

one that will fully expose the enemy and begin to move him toward his final judgment. When we really get this spiritual understanding deep down in our beings, the devil is close to being finished, and the Lord soon to return!

Dr. Patrick Zukeran of the Bible Institute of Hawaii wrote an excellent piece on the differing views of eschatology in the Church. It is titled "Idealist—Preterist—Historicist—Futurist." His text lists pros and cons of each view and leaves them open for debate. I recommend reading this piece and considering further discussion in regard to these issues. *(Please see appendix for further information about Dr. Zukeran and his writings and beliefs.)*

IT IS A PROCESS

Many Christians who hold to the dispensationalist view, or other eschatological views, have experienced some form of a spiritual enlightenment toward Israel and the Jewish people. However, as discussed in this chapter, more is needed to Realign us fully to *this* Reconnection message.

We could have dealt with the generational bloodline issues and other emotional barriers in *TONM* and have a right heart toward Israel, but then when it comes to our understanding in Scripture, our hats are hung so tightly to our Christian lens and perspective that we can easily tune out the rest.

Similarly, I have watched many believers coming into the *Israel Piece* and then try to fit it in succinctly to what they believe. They end up getting stuck on one issue or another and subsequently end up missing the mark.

We need to be careful here of the enemy's trickery not to get caught up in it, but to stay as open-minded as possible and allow the Holy Spirit to guide us into the fullness of *The Reconnection* message.

A MESSIANIC VIEW

What's interesting here is that the Messianic eschatological view is somewhat incorporative of a number of these differing

Christian views. Jokingly, I often refer to Messianic Eschatology as "Meschatology." It was actually my good friend Jonathan Friz from 10 Days of Prayer, who coined this term when we were immersed in a conversation about this Messianic perspective. It's funny, but it does help to bring emphasis to the Messianic perspective on these issues.

To explain and discuss these views, it makes sense to divide the Church into two main groups: those who believe in a literal millennial reign and those who do not.

First, regarding eschatology, most Messianics have a similar understanding of the Second Coming, as the Jews did before Yeshua/Jesus came. They were focused on interpreting prophetic Scriptures relating to the Messiah's coming through the Lion's viewpoint. As believers in Yeshua/Jesus, we know He came first as the Lamb, and we obviously discount this, but we do not necessarily throw the baby out with the bath water, regarding study or interpretation. This is because much of their understanding, when they carried the mantle of God concerning Mashiach's coming as the Lion, was correct.

For example, they believed that the Messiah must bring total peace to the world, that the exiles would be gathered from the nations, that there would be an end to wickedness and sin, that Jerusalem would be rebuilt, and that David's throne would be reestablished on the Earth. All of this is substantiated in Scripture.

While we know all authority in Heaven and Earth has been given to our Lord, most Jewish believers believe there is still something very strategic to take place when Yeshua/Jesus sits on David's throne on the Earth. Jerusalem and the Covenants to the firstborn in the family will play out a most strategic role in this process to help bring it to pass.

Asher Intrater, the leader of the Tikkun Apostolic Network in Israel, writes,

In the Siddur (Jewish prayer book), there is a prayer to restore the throne of David, and it comes right before the prayer for the coming of the Messiah. That is an amazing thought. That there is a throne—a place of government—to be restored that is less than the Messiah, but it must be set up to allow the Messiah to come sit on it. That goes along with the biblical pattern that a Covenant was made with David for authority on planet Earth. That position is set up so that Yeshua can fill it. David failed, as did all the earthly kings. Yeshua filled it morally and spiritually, but not yet in external government. (See "Revive Israel" in the Appendix.)

I do see the head of the government of Israel as a Restoration, at least to some degree, of David's throne. It would have to be in place for Yeshua to return and take that position. Yeshua is not only King of Israel (see John 12); He is also head of the *Ekklesia* (see Ephesians 1) and King of Kings. He has many crowns (see Revelation 19). Ultimately, He will take all the positions of earthly authority, like a combined UN secretary, pope, chief rabbi, president, or prime minister. Those who have true spiritual leadership in the *Ekklesia* will have positions of authority under Him. It will likely start with twelve senior apostle elders.

The fact that David and his sons were sinful did not mean that their place of authority was not legitimate as a position for the Messiah to fulfill. Yeshua will reign in both heaven and Earth. He reigns in heaven now as Son of God and will return to reign on Earth as son of David and son of Adam.

In heaven now, He is already "over" the governments of this world (see Ephesians 1), but He has not yet taken over active earthly authority. This should take place at the beginning of the Millennium, as prophesied by the seventh trumpet (see Revelation 11:15).

When the people tried to crown Yeshua as King, He fled (see John 6). The Church cannot have Yeshua as King of Kings without first having Him as King of Israel!

Hebrew Tidbits

The following are Hebrew facts you might find interesting quoted by Asher Intrater.

The word for president in Hebrew is *nasi*. It means one lifted up and is the word used in Ezekiel 40–48, usually called "the prince" in English. It is a play on words for "lifted up" on the cross (see Isaiah 53) and "lifted up" in Glory (see Isaiah 6). The word for "prime minister" in Hebrew is *rosh hamemshalah*, meaning head of government. This is a biblically oriented term. The Hebrew word *hamlacha*, is the causative form of *melech*, or King. *Hamlacha* means "to make someone king." There is no word in English for it.

So the *Baruch Haba* cry (*Blessed is He*—see Matthew 23:39) is not only an invitation; it is also a *hamlacha*. That is a mind-blowing thought!

David was anointed to be king many years before the elders of Israel appointed him as king. Yeshua is already anointed as King. There must be an appointment by the elders of the tribe of Judah for that to happen.

In Matthew 19, Yeshua says that His twelve apostles will reign with Him. Luke 19 says there are many other places of authority to be filled (the Parable of the Minas). The spiritual authority within the *Ekklesia* is converted to government authority at the Second Coming. The disciples tried to do a *hamlacha* to make Yeshua King at the "triumphal entrance," but the conditions were not right yet, obviously (see Matthew 21; John 12).

Hamlacha

On the Lubavitch (sect of orthodox Jews) campaign in Israel, they say, "Baruch haba" and then add "Melech hamashiah." This combines several concepts. One is that he is the Messiah, *bechezkat*. Their campaign is semipolitical in the sense that they believe that if they can get enough Jews to believe in Menachem Mendel Schneerson and thus "vote" for or "invite" him to be the Messiah, then it will happen. (Schneerson was an ultra-orthodox rabbi whom his followers claimed to be the Messiah.) Much of what they say is wrong, but the idea of declaring him king is very similar to what Yeshua taught about Himself.

It is not so much an issue of anointing as it is Covenant order. Messiah had to come through Isaac, not Ishmael, because of Abraham's marriage to Sarah. It was not a negative statement about Ishmael but an affirmation of marriage Covenant. The same is true for Leah. Judah was her child. Leah married Jacob before Rachel. Messiah comes through her line.

Also, just as Miriam (Mary) had to be of the tribe of Judah because of the biblical promises, so does the tribe of Judah have to be involved in the Second Coming.

This is an issue of God's Covenant with David. David and his seed is Yeshua and the physical descendants of David who believe in Yeshua. How can Yeshua return to sit on David's throne if some of the children of David are not there to affirm it? (See "Revive Israel" in the Appendix.)

ESCHATOLOGY THROUGH THE PASSOVER

Messianic eschatology suggests that both of the Lord's comings to the Earth are seen through the Passover story through the *Lamb* and the *Lion*, and judgments of God are tied into both. Israel was judged after Yeshua's first coming, through Rome's attack on Jerusalem in 70 AD and then again in 132

Messianic eschatology suggests that both of the Lord's comings to the Earth are seen through the Passover story through the Lamb and the Lion, and judgments of God are tied into both.

BC, in the Bar Kokhba revolt. The world will also be judged before Jesus returns for the second time.

THE LAMB

In the 1990s after the Berlin Wall came down, I took several missionary trips to the former Soviet Union with a group I cofounded called *Abraham's Promise*.

We brought the Passover story to a stage format in music and dance and helped reeducate the Russian and Belarusian Jews toward their heritage, which had been wiped out by communism. We explained the fulfillment of their heritage through Yeshua/Jesus as the Lamb of God and saw thousands of Jewish souls come to faith. You can view one of these outreach performances in our media section on the Reconnecting Ministries website (The Passover Story).

THE LION

Similarly, Dr. Daniel Juster has written a wonderful book on this subject called *Passover: The Key That Unlocks the Book of Revelation*.

These *two aspects of judgment* also fall directly in line with the principle of the Kingdom, which are first for the Jew, then for the Gentile. This does not only apply to blessings, but also to the judgments. *"But to those who are self-seeking and who reject the truth and follow evil, there will be wrath and anger. There will be trouble and distress for every human being who does evil; first for the Jew, then for the Gentile; but Glory, honor and peace for everyone who does good; first for the Jew, then for the Gentile. For God does not show favoritism"* (Rom. 2:8–11).

Is it possible for the Remnant of Israel to help God's Church find mutual ground in our eschatological views? What a blessing that would be!

I find it interesting that both partial preterists and dispensationalists or futurists have such strong views concerning Jesus's prophetic dissertations in Matthew 24, Mark 13, and Luke 21. Partial preterists believe that these Scriptures were fulfilled with the judgments on the Jewish people. Dispensationalists and futurists believe that these Scriptures are yet to take place before the Lord returns. While in a Messianic eschatological view, we can see both viewpoints in Yeshua/Jesus's words and in both comings of the Lord—both the judgment on Israel and the judgment yet to come upon the world.

Is it possible for the Remnant of Israel to help God's Church find mutual ground in our eschatological views? What a blessing that would be!

REPENTANCE

What is God saying to us in this chapter on the Gentile Christian lens? Is it possible that the *residual influences* of Replacement Theology have clouded our thinking and perspective so much that we are not seeing the end as we should? If we bought the lie in the ancestral Church and embraced the deception, that then became the foundation to our thinking in the Christian Church. It makes sense that it has separated us from our *true identity as coheirs in and with Israel* and ultimately to represent its *commonwealth* throughout the nations when the Lord returns. This is especially true now, as God is not only restoring Israel but also beginning to prepare us both for

Yeshua/Jesus's return. And to receive our inheritance to rule and reign with Mashiach/Christ (see Revelation 5:9-10).

In this case, not only are spiritual and emotional healing required to unite the family, but a theological repentance is needed to Reconnect us with the origins of our apostolic roots and heritage.

THE AX HEAD

So often in the Church, I have heard wonderful teachings and sermons on Elisha and the ax head (see 2 Kings 6:1–7) informing us that when going astray or recognizing we were off in some area of our lives, we should return to the place where the ax was the sharpest. This is the message I believe the Lord is sending to us at this time regarding our eschatology. We should return to the Church's original apostolic thinking regarding our coheirship with Mashiach/Christ and our connection to Israel in the unity of *TONM*.

SPIRIT AND TRUTH

Did not Yeshua/Jesus teach us about the balance of Spirit and Truth? In this case, the generational bloodline issues along with emotional ones in our hearts related to our firstborn family are spiritual matters of heart that we need to address and correct concerning this Reconnection. While the influences of replacement theology in our minds, in our beliefs and thinking also require correction.

Don't ask me why God has waited all this time to make this known to us. Perhaps it wasn't necessary in the times of the Gentiles. And look how the Jews had it wrong, too, before Yeshua/Jesus came!

The answer is that we will never see this place in our own humanity, in our own strength, or as a brother or sister, but only through our *Father's eyes* and through His most wonderful Heart. His wellspring of *mercy* and *love* will rise up in us and have its way upon the Earth! This is His plan for us now!

From a Messianic perspective, with great respect and love for the balance of God's family from the nations in His Church, there is a good amount of truth in many of the Church's differing eschatological views, especially if some of them can be combined. But up to this point, it is apparent that it is missing its most *vital link* and *role* to help aid and expedite what is to come; we must now get on track.

I speak the truth in love as your Jewish brother so that it might provoke your thinking to fully consider what is written. Much is at stake for His Body to come into one of its greatest-ever roles to help Israel be reborn in the end-time harvest of souls.

I am not suggesting either that the Messianic viewpoint is perfect. But we should comprehend that this spiritual Reconnection between us is His *perfect plan* of *love* and *unity* to help bring about the rest. The details will play out in God's time and according to His perfect will. We stand a far greater chance of seeing the end as He does after this transaction has taken place through us in the heart of *TONM* and in our unity and love for one another.

COULD HEALING THIS BREACH BE A PATHWAY TO THE REST?

In addition, could this healing and Reconciliation in *TONM* be a pathway to healing other divisions and breaches in the Body? And did this first breach and division in the Church open up and empower the enemy to bring other divisions among us? I believe both to be true.

In addition, could this healing and Reconciliation in TONM be a pathway to healing other divisions and breaches in the Body? And did this first breach and division in the Church open up and empower the enemy to bring other divisions among us? I believe both to be true.

MOVING A MOUNTAIN INTO THE SEA

This not only requires a complete and total response from the Christian community at large, but also an honest quest in the

Church to reexamine itself and return to its spiritual apostolic roots connected to Israel.

This is like moving a mountain into the sea. We must bring the necessary correction to His Church and cause it to turn about. We need to *pull up the roots* of this departing theology that took His Body away from its original Hebraic mindset in *TONM* through the apostles. This is no easy task! It also means we have to cut the supersessional theological ties from the Justin Martyrs, Irenaeuses, and early Church fathers who helped perpetuate these replacement teachings in the Church. I am not suggesting that these men of God and fathers of the Church be dishonored in any way; I am proposing that we break away from the replacement teachings they promoted and the subsequent influences and understanding that it produced in the Church.

This is similar to Martin Luther. Do I nullify the great revelation and understanding of grace that was given to him by God, in light of how he fell prey to antisemitism? Rather, I uphold and honor truth and separate myself from anything else that does not stand up to the Word of God. There is only one perfect Man Yeshua/Jesus, and He is God!

God does not want to make Gentiles Jews in this spiritual equation, as some new movements espouse. Rather, He wants to uphold our *unique expressions* and *traditions* on both sides of the olive tree (Jewish and Gentile). We need to come to a place of healing, cleansing, and Reconciliation, *fully breaking off* the separation in the Spirit that replacement teachings brought about, so both groups can be properly Reconnected as *one* family in God.

TRUE REPENTANCE

The word "repentance" does not only mean to feel sorrow for past actions but also to right what was wrong and work toward it through faith. The Apostle Paul taught us to *demonstrate* our repentance through our deeds (see Acts 26:20). In this case, what will a full repentance look like in His Church when all these influences are broken off spiritually?

I believe an amazing new connection will be established within His Church and Messianic bodies that will cause His olive tree to blossom and flourish like never before. *The Reconnection* will enhance everything else He has already made known to us, making it ever richer through our own Reconnected heritage in Israel.

This is going to be an amazing time and experience in His Church as we receive and embrace this revelation. The Word of God will be opened up to us like never before. How refreshing it will be, just like a river flowing in springtime.

My dear brother and good friend, Dominick Crincoli, who is from a Gentile background and was our worship leader for many years at Messiah's House says, "The root system of Jewish Covenants and promises must be rewoven into the fabric and foundation of the Christian Church. It cannot be something ancillary. Similar to the way that we, as Gentiles, were grafted in as wild olive shoots into the olive tree with its natural Jewish branches, the root system of our Jewish connection and ancestry needs to inform our Gentile Christian expression at the deepest, root level. This must flow from a natural debt of gratitude we have as Gentiles for everything we possess in the Jewish Messiah, Yeshua."

What an amazing comparison and analogy! Although the initial grafting in of God's children from the nations was abnormal to the rest, it is now completely natural. This is going to be an amazing time and experience in His Church as we receive and embrace this revelation. The Word of God will be opened up to us like never before. How refreshing it will be, just like a river flowing in springtime.

JOSEPH AND HIS BROTHERS RESTORED

Although we felt the anguish of Joseph's heart as his brothers sold him into slavery, we are reminded of the great forgiveness and

Reconciliation that transpired as the brothers were Reconnected: *"Then Joseph could no longer control himself before all his attendants, and he cried out, 'Have everyone leave my presence!' So there was no one with Joseph when he made himself known to his brothers. And he wept so loudly that the Egyptians heard him, and Pharaoh's household heard about it"* (Gen. 45:1–2).

I can tell you personally, because I have gone through identificational repentance with certain Gentile brethren leaders, that the weeping and the cries have been deep. This is an amazing picture of the healing and Reconciliation that is coming between us in the family of God.

THE SHEPHERDS OF GOD

However, this will not begin to take place in any fullness until the shepherds of God's House fully own this Reconnection message and begin to lead their flocks into this place of healing and Reconciliation in *TONM*. Our spiritual leaders, Bible scholars, and theologians need to properly consider all that it is in this book to help move the Body of Messiah/Christ in this direction.

The Reconnection will not begin to take place in any fullness until the shepherds of God's House fully own this Reconnection message and begin to lead their flocks into this place of healing and Reconciliation in TONM.

As Jewish believers, Dan and I can blow the trumpet and sound the alarm. We can hold up *The Reconnection* baton and the Covenant banner of Israel, as Derek Prince liked to say. But until Church and Messianic leadership fully grasps it, this movement will not take root in us.

This is not just about saying a prayer and breaking off from the past; instead, it is a beginning to something rather new and special among us. When something is broken off us, *what is it replaced with?* We need a renewed spirit and mindset in this area of family that will not only restore our full identity with Israel but open the door to the greater powers of the Holy Spirit to flow through us, with all the authority of the Kingdom of God that is awaiting it. This will help lay the correct foundation for the end-time revival and awakening. The *Israel Piece* is the golden key!

For a moment, reflect on Abba's olive tree that I described in chapter 6, with His Church Reconnecting to the root system that Dominick described. And just imagine the wellspring of life that will burst forth as we make this connection in the family of God with a renewed knowledge and depth of insight, along with everything else He has already made known to us in His Word. Wow!

In light of this great need for *The Reconnection*, we are asking God's leaders and teachers to come into a deeper place of reflection with this message and to fully examine it. We ask them to enter greater dialogue and understanding, which is where these things have their beginnings. As I always state, the changes that *The Reconnection* produces in us are not that complex; however, everything leading into and

As His shepherds, how can we be expected to lead the rest of the sheep into this new place if we have not fully understood and recognized it ourselves?

up to them are because of all the human elements involved. Also, as we have discovered, some of the deceptions are quite *subtle* and need to be *recognized* as such, and *exposed*. The enemy continues to keep us apart through our differences and creates fear in us, even as we step into this path of Restoration, to keep us shut down or away from the mark. We must not be ignorant of the enemy's devices here, as the forces of darkness know what is at stake, and so must we.

As His shepherds, how can we be expected to lead the rest of the sheep into this new place if we have not fully understood and recognized it ourselves? Up to this point, most of the Gentile and Jewish flocks have never known this place in *TONM*, so nearly everything is new to us. Much needs to be taught on *The Reconnection*.

RESTORATION THEOLOGY

Once we have fully dealt with the obstacles in the way of this message, we must give it time. 1,700 years of replacement thinking will not go away overnight. It will require commitment, dedication, and discipline on behalf of the Body of Messiah/ Christ and the Church. But let it be said unequivocally that all types of antisemitism, Replacement, and Fulfillment Theology must be replaced

> But let it be said unequivocally that all types of antisemitism, Replacement, and Fulfillment Theology must be replaced with "Restoration Theology."

with "Restoration Theology." Simply put, *Restoration Theology* is the full study and application of this Reconnection message with the relational piece in Yeshua/Jesus and *TONM* being central to this transformation.

ONE NEW MAN ORGANIZATIONS TO CONNECT WITH IN TONM

On this note, aside from our own ministry focus in Reconnecting Ministries to help the Body Reconnect, God has been raising up and preparing other ministries, many of which Dr. Daniel Juster is personally involved in.

As mentioned, the TJC2 (Toward Jerusalem Council 2) is a relatively new committee of both Jewish and Gentile leadership in the USA and globally. The Lord has established it as an ambassadorship of hierarchy for this Reconnection to take place between the Church and Messianic governments.

Similarly, the Messianic Bible Institute is a mix of both Jewish and Gentile leadership that is teaching and equipping leaders to move the Body into *The Reconnection* in *TONM*, honoring both Jewish and Gentile expressions in the tree.

Caleb Global also has a similar training focus.

FIRM (Fellowship of Israel Related Ministries) is a globally focused ministry in Israel to help believers and Churches around the world connect with the Body of Messiah/Christ in the land.

Tikkun Global Ministries is the first fivefold ministry on the Messianic side looking to unite with fivefold ministries on the Gentile side of the Church. They want to find unity through dual expression throughout the nations.

Watchmen for the Nations, overseen by David Demian, is an intercessory focused ministry centered on Reconciliation in the family of God, between Jew and Gentile, all races and peoples.

THE LORD IS SETTING THE PATH

God is setting the path for His Body to move into *The Reconnection* to assist the Lord with His plans to establish His Kingdom on the Earth. Glory be to God in the highest!

> *"Therefore, since we are surrounded by such a great cloud of witnesses, let us throw off everything that hinders and the sin that so easily entangles. And let us run with perseverance the race marked out for us, fixing our eyes on Yeshua/Jesus, the pioneer and perfecter of faith. For the joy set before Him He endured the cross, scorning its shame, and sat down at the right hand of the throne of God. Consider Him who endured such opposition from sinners, so that you will not grow weary and lose heart"* (Heb. 12:1–3).

SECTION 3—RESTORATIVE PRAYER

The following prayers have been written for all of us in the Church for confession, renouncement, and repentance so that the Holy Spirit can fully cleanse our hearts and minds from anything negative toward the Jewish people, Jewish believers, and the nation of

Israel. These prayers are not just for us; they are also for our generational bloodline and our ancestry.

For the sake of the Church at large and all of us in it, let us read through these prayers with open hearts. As you do, pay attention to any sensitivities the Holy Spirit might touch within you. Ask Him to shed more light on them for additional confession, renouncement, and repentance.

Please do not rush through this. Create the right environment between you and God, in stillness and quietness, to say these prayers, so

This is not just about saying a prayer and breaking off from the past; instead, it is a beginning to something rather new and special among us. When something is broken off us, what is it replaced with?

you can address this issue properly. You might also want to pray these prayers with others, or even in Church if the pastor or elders are leading.

In some parts you might feel conviction, and in others you might feel nothing at all. Please complete the prayers fully, allowing the presence of the Holy Spirit to work through you as you pray. As you start to pray, you might feel emotional, and I encourage you to let the emotions flow. This is the presence of God cleansing and purifying your heart. Not all of us react in this manner, and that is completely okay.

PRAYERS FOR BELIEVERS

The key for us is to fully confess, renounce, and repent of anything that has come against our firstborn brothers and sisters and *TONM* union, whether through us or through our family line. In doing so, the enemy's influence can be fully broken off us, freeing our spirits and our minds to receive the *Father's Heart* for Israel. In addition, we need to be careful of distractions because neither the devil nor his demonic forces are happy about these prayers.

PRAYER OF CONFESSION

Dear Heavenly Father, God of Abraham, Isaac and Israel, I come to You in the precious name of Jesus, the Jewish Messiah. Lord, I ask You to forgive me personally of any antisemitism against Jewish people, whether through words spoken, thoughts, or words received through any of my family members, any of my friends, or any other person who might have spoken negative words against the Jewish people that may have affected my heart. Lord, I confess all these words and thoughts to You, and I ask You to forgive me for all of them.

Lord, I confess any jealousy or envy in my heart toward them and ask that You would forgive me for it. Lord, I confess any anger or hatred that I have in my heart toward the Jewish people, and I ask You to forgive me for it. Lord, I confess any indifference in my heart toward the Jewish people for not caring about them the way You do. I ask You to forgive me for it. Lord, I confess any insecurity in my heart toward the Jewish people or thinking that I may be less than them. And I thank You that You have made me equal with them as Your coheirs in the Kingdom of God.

Lord, I ask You to forgive me for buying into any of the lies that I've been exposed to in my lifetime about the Jewish people and the nation of Israel. Lord, I confess any ignorance in my heart about Israel and the Church in light of the Apostle Paul's teachings in Romans 11. For not understanding their significance in the Kingdom of God and in Your overall plans, I ask You to forgive me. Lord, please show me and teach me Your ways for Israel and the Church in these last days. I confess that in my humanity I have not been able to love the Jewish people the way You love them, and I ask You to change my heart.

Lord, I confess the sins of my fathers and mothers toward the Jewish people and anything in my generational bloodline from my family tree through the generations who may have operated in antisemitism against the Jewish people. I ask You to forgive them for any acts against them, and as a qualified heir, I repent on their behalf.

I confess my indifference in wanting to share You with my Jewish friends and neighbors, as well as the indifference in the Church to move into our role to help win them back to the faith. Lord, please forgive us for this, and help us correct it.

Lord, I confess the sins of the Church against the Jewish people. Any antisemitism, judgment, hatred, jealousy, envy, covetousness, anger, indifference, lies, persecution, torture, murder, and false teachings—I ask You to forgive the Church for misunderstanding your words of forgiveness and Restoration toward Israel and the Jewish people and for operating in any deception against them and not being able to love them in our own humanity, despite Your call and direction to us in Romans 11. Help us to love them on account of the patriarchs, to draw them to jealousy, and not to be arrogant in any way, thinking that we or the Church has replaced them.

Lord, I ask You to forgive the Church and all its leaders throughout the centuries—its fathers, apostles, prophets, theologians, Bible teachers, pastors, and evangelists who have helped to promote any antisemitic doctrine, words, or teachings that have brought division, separation, and persecution to the Jewish people.

Lord, I ask You to forgive the Church, my ancestry, and me for embracing any of the teachings of replacement or Fulfillment Theology that states that the Church has replaced Israel in any way or that Jesus fulfilled the Covenants and promises to Israel so they no longer apply to Israel and the Jewish people. Lord, also please forgive us for any residual influences that Replacement Theology doctrines and teachings have produced over the past 1,850 years in the Christian Church and how it caused us as believers to become separated from the roots of our faith and the Remnant of Israel with whom we are now coheirs in your Kingdom.

Lord, we confess the sin of separation as Gentile believers from our Jewish roots and heritage, and we ask You to forgive us for it and to Reconnect us spiritually, as the Church was when it first started. Lord, please restore us and Reconnect us by the power of Your Holy Spirit.

In this light, we ask You to Reconnect us spiritually to our Jewish family, the Remnant of Israel, and to our roots and heritage in Israel. Lord, we ask you to restore and freshen our theology in this new place of Reconnection and to open our eyes to the fullness of TONM between Jew and Gentile in the Christian Church and Messianic community.

Lord, while I know Your Word tells us that both Jew and Gentile are one in the Spirit, I now fully accept and embrace the unique roles that You have for Israel and the Church during these times. I pledge my allegiance to You and Your plans for us so that You will ultimately be glorified throughout the Earth. And I say, "Come, Lord Yeshua/Jesus, and have Your way among us."

Lord, I ask You to help me forgive my Jewish brothers and sisters for their past and current rejection of Yeshua/ Jesus, as well as their indifference to the Gospel. I entrust them totally to You in the lifting of the spiritual veil that is upon them. I invite You to use me in any way to help bring this about through prayer, intercession, lifestyle witness, and evangelism, according to Your will and the direction of the Holy Spirit; that they may see Your love and life through me.

Lord, I ask You to forgive the balance of the Jewish people who have rejected Yeshua, their Messiah (the broken-off branches), and I ask You to lift the veil from their eyes and the deafness from their ears, as You have done for us in accordance with Your Words and promises to them so that we can all love You together as one spiritual family. Lord, I pray that You would prepare the Bride for His coming. Please release this burden to us from Your Heart for Your firstborn sons and daughters to help win them back to faith.

PRAYER OF RENOUNCEMENT

Dear Heavenly Father, God of Abraham, Isaac and Israel, I come to You in the precious name of Jesus, the Jewish Messiah. Lord, I formally renounce all these sins that I have prayed: all antisemitism in my own heart and any antisemitism from any other influence, through family members, friends, or anyone in my generational bloodline and ancestral past, and any teachings or influences from Replacement Theology from my mind, spirit, and soul.

Lord, in the most powerful cleansing name of Jesus the Jewish Messiah, I come into agreement with You and break any form of generational antisemitism or Replacement Theology that has either affected or influenced me or anyone else in my family. I take authority over it in Jesus's name, rendering it powerless over me and my family.

Lord, I also renounce and break agreement with any spirit that might have influenced either me or my family and generational bloodline in this place. I renounce and break off all vows and Covenants, all soul ties and generational ties, all hexes, vexes, and curses that would bind me to these generational bloodline issues and false

223

teachings against the people of Israel. Lord, I choose to love the Jewish people the way You do and ask for Your Heart, Your grace, and Your mercy to flow through me toward them. I formally renounce every spirit that is connected to these thoughts and attitudes and in the power of the name of Jesus, the Jewish Messiah, I take authority over it and render it powerless over me and my family, releasing it all to Jesus to break its hold. Amen.

PRAYER OF REPENTANCE

Dear Heavenly Father, God of Abraham Isaac and Israel, I come to You in the precious name of Jesus, the Jewish Messiah. Lord, I truly ask You to help me to repent of all of these things that I have just prayed about. I ask You to teach me Your ways and to give me Your Heart for Your family, both Jew and Gentile alike. Empower me to be in agreement with Your Word so You will be fully glorified through both Israel and the Church during these days.

Lord, help me to understand this is not a quick fix and requires commitment and discipline to study so You can renew my mind and thinking regarding Israel, the Church, and the family of God. Lord, would You now replace "Replacement" with "Restoration Theology" and restore my heart and mind with Your Spirit concerning all that is about to take place for Your Kingdom to come upon the Earth.

Lord, please restore us to our roots in Israel and refresh our theology, as well as our understanding of the end of days, so that we can more fully participate with You and Your plans to glorify Your Son on this Earth and to establish your Kingdom among us. Lord, I pledge my allegiance to You and offer You my full support between Israel and the Church and in the unity of TONM.

> *Lord, God of Israel, I offer myself up as a witness to fulfill my calling as a Christian to help draw my Jewish friends and neighbors to the jealousy you talk about in Romans 11. Not only will I pray for them but also love them unconditionally and shine your light and mercy back toward them to help win them to Messiah. Father, by Your Holy Spirit, please lead me into new relationships with my Jewish neighbors and/or coworkers so that they can see Messiah through me in my love and commitment toward them. Lord, I also ask you to raise up evangelists in the Church who will have a greater passion to help reach the lost sheep of Israel. In Jesus's precious name I pray. Amen.*

PRAYER FOR PASTORS AND LEADERS

Pastors and leaders have a greater responsibility to pray for and renounce any antisemitic thoughts and replacement teachings in light of the influence they have over God's flock. We have a responsibility to disavow any connection to replacement or Fulfillment Theology and any of its residual influences over us that might have been learned in past educational experiences.

Pastors and leaders have a greater responsibility to pray for and renounce any antisemitic thoughts and replacement teachings in light of the influence they have over God's flock.

If you are a leader in any of the denominations in the Body of Messiah/Christ—Roman Catholic, Greek Orthodox, Anglican, Protestant, Episcopalian, Presbyterian, Pentecostal, Charismatic, Baptist, Lutheran, Methodist, Church of Christ, Faith/Prosperity Churches, or any other denominational or nondenominational Church group—and you are in agreement with these prayers, please pray the following:

Dear Heavenly Father, I come to You in the precious name of Jesus, the Jewish Messiah, as one of Your shepherds and leaders. Lord, I ask You to forgive me of any connection and association to the teachings of Replacement Theology, or any other teachings about Israel that are or might be in contradiction with Your Word, through what I was taught in the past.

Lord, I formally renounce them and ask that You will fill my mind and heart with the truth of Your Word concerning Israel, the Jewish people, and their Restoration in the last days. I ask that You would reveal to me any role that the Church will need me to play to fulfill and help You achieve Your plans here in the world so that You will be glorified in all the Earth.

Lord, I pledge my allegiance as one of Your shepherds to uphold this Reconnection in Your spiritual family and give it my full support. Lord, I take The Reconnection baton from You to study it in depth. I seek to be able to articulate and teach it to my ministry board, my flock, and to help move our Church Body into The Reconnection in our Church area and community. I will seek the Holy Spirit's guidance as to how we should implement it and connect to the Remnant Body of Israel in our immediate area. Lord, I also ask You to help me share it with other leaders to help them to find this truth during these days. I pray all these prayers in Jesus's most holy name. Amen.

RECEIVING THE FATHER'S HEART—MY PERSONAL PRAYER

Now, Lord, please fill Your loving child with the fullness of Your Heart for Israel and the Jewish people, in the precious name of Yeshua. Amen.

Congratulations! You have just received the *Father's Heart* for the Jewish people and for Israel and the Church. From now on, expect to see things differently in this regard—not only in your understanding of the Word of God as it relates to Israel and the Church, but also in the way you feel or act toward the Jewish people. Please understand this is not a one-time event, but rather the beginning of a new process through the *Heart of the Father*, of enlightenment back toward Israel and the Jewish people. It will promote the overall transformation of your heart and mind for His family to be one through Israel.

FROM THE GENTILE TO THE JEWISH BRANCHES

Although this chapter has been focused on the Gentile side of the family, they are not the only ones who need to Reconnect spiritually. The same is also true for our Jewish-believing brothers and sisters; however, the issues that have separated us or keep us apart are quite different. We will explore these in the next chapter on the Messianic lens.

CHAPTER 8

THE MESSIANIC LENS

SECTION 1
OBSTACLES AND HINDRANCES

IN THIS BOOK, I have reintroduced the Remnant of Israel to the Church and the significant role that it will play with the rest of the Body in God's end-time plans to help redeem the balance of Israel and the end-time harvest of souls. In a sense, their spiritual health and strength set a pathway to the balance of Israel's Restoration. It is crucial for us to recognize this in the family of God at this time.

For the two-thirds of the book we have covered so far, we have focused mainly on the Gentile side of the family—God's children from the nations coming into *The Reconnection*. But there must also be an equal and opposite reaction on the Jewish side of the family for it to properly take root among us. Both sides must be committed to *TONM* so that the Remnant of Israel can Reconnect spiritually with its Christian family and love and embrace them as brothers and sisters and coheirs in the Kingdom of God. The Jewish side of the family needs to also accept and bless the Gentile-believing Church, along with its own expressions of faith, its heritage, and its traditions. This must happen for both sides of the olive tree to coexist in love, liberty, and harmony.

Although *The Reconnection* requires repentance of wrongful thinking and attitudes on both sides of the family, spiritually and mentally, it does not look to wipe away the heritage of either Israel or the Church. Rather, it respects both paths and upholds what is good and lovely in God's sight. Simply put, it is God's will for us to be one.

The Church needs to fully embrace Israel's Remnant, and the Remnant of Israel needs to fully embrace the Gentile-believing Church by loving, honoring, and respecting them.

As a Jewish believer reading this book, you might be thinking, "Wow! Yes, it's about time someone made this message clear to our Gentile brothers and sisters, but what about us? Where are we when it comes to walking in *love and unity* with the rest of our family?" You see, honestly, it's so easy for any of us to point the finger, but the *Heart of God* says to forgive and to love with no exceptions (see Matthew 6:14).

Although The Reconnection requires repentance of wrongful thinking and attitudes on both sides of the family, spiritually and mentally, it does not look to wipe away the heritage of either Israel or the Church. Rather, it respects both paths and upholds what is good and lovely in God's sight. Simply put, it is God's will for us to be one.

The key to our unity in *TONM* is not necessarily to be the same, but rather to fully accept the unique expressions that God has established on both sides of the tree, which has obviously been a challenge to our souls. In the Spirit, there is no difference between us, and love should have no boundaries; but in the natural realm, our paths and roles are uniquely different. The key for us is to embrace our differences and allow the Holy Spirit to once again create His harmony between us.

Isn't this also evident in the book of Acts? And isn't it evident now today, through both Church and Messianic expressions, that there are differences between us? God did not require Gentile believers to follow all the Jewish traditions, yet Jewish believers continued to observe them, removing any focus on the law for salvation, which can only come through Yeshua/Jesus. Therefore, can we not assume that God made and established both paths and that they are inclusive of *TONM*?

WE ALL NEED HEALING

Some might be surprised to read that our Jewish-believing family have their own set of issues and resistances when it comes to *The Reconnection* in *TONM*. I think it is fair to say that the need and understanding for *The Reconnection* is relatively new to all of us, both Jew and Gentile alike, which interestingly puts all of us in the same boat. In this light, both groups must be willing to move toward one another for God's love and will to be done between us. Isn't our God so masterful to design this reunion and Reconnection for such a time as this?

In reality, this is neither a Gentile nor Jewish issue when it comes to addressing our own resistance to *The Reconnection* but rather issues of our hearts and humanity that the enemy continues to play on both sides to keep us separate and divided. If it continues, we will miss the very mark of love and unity that the Father is beckoning us into. He wants us to be one so that the world will know Yeshua/Jesus (see John 17:20–23). And if you don't think that there is tremendous resistance to all of us finding this, then you would be deceived in this area.

With all due respect and with a great amount of humility and deference to my Messianic family and the brilliant minds and theologians who exist among the Messianic branches, we will never see the fullness of *TONM* and God's end-time plans just through a Jewish or Messianic lens. Nor will we see it solely through a Gentile lens, as I have already stated to our Gentile family in the previous chapters. But rather, we will see His fullness through the *Heart of the Father* for His family to be one and through a renewed unity and love for one another. This is a most essential *bond* for us all in God's family to see and the subsequent blessings and powers that will be released as a result of it.

We must understand and recognize that we have our own issues to deal with on the Messianic side. The enemy might also be stirring these up to keep us sidetracked and isolated from the rest of God's Body. Please understand that my intent here is not to lay blame in any way, but rather for us to fully recognize these areas and bring them back to God in prayer and repentance. I have been asking our Gentile-believing family to do the same.

In reality, this is neither a Gentile nor Jewish issue when it comes to addressing our own resistance to The Reconnection but rather issues of our hearts and humanity that the enemy continues to play on both sides to keep us separate and divided.

As a Jewish believer myself, I hope I have the liberty to speak more openly to my Messianic brothers and sisters. Please know that my words are written in love and in the hope that we would not be led astray. Yet among some of the Messianic branches of the faith exists a judgmental and critical spirit when it comes to the Church that is most grievous to the *Heart of the Father*, to *Yeshua*, and to the *Holy Spirit*. This creates division instead of *fueling* love.

WHERE WOULD WE BE WITHOUT THE CHURCH?

Dr. Daniel Juster[14] said this about the importance of the Church:

> I think it is important for Messianic Jews to realize that without the Reformation we would probably not exist and Israel would probably not exist, at least as we see the working of God in history through the Church. Why? The Reformation restored the central place of the Bible and education so that all could read it for themselves. Though Calvin did not see very much on Israel's election (he did see a promise for the later conversion of the Jews to Christianity), his later Puritan followers would come to much more understanding on God's love for the Jewish people, and some even to their Restoration to the Land. This influenced the Lutheran Pietists, the Moravians, the Methodists and many Anglicans. It

was this influence that brought Britain to make it their national policy to restore the Jewish people to their land. Christian Zionism was the fruition of this long process. Arthur John Balfour, the former prime minister and then foreign secretary, who had strong Christian Zionist family roots, affirmed Israel as the homeland of the Jewish people, and wrote the British Balfour Declaration itself.

WOUNDS

I would like to address this issue from two sides—first, from the hearts of Jewish believers and second, from the hearts of Gentile believers who have left the Church in search of their Jewish roots and now cohabitate among the Messianic branches of the faith.

JEWISH BELIEVERS' HEART ISSUES

Up to this point, it has been apparent that a great deal of the Gentile Church have not yet properly understood us (the Remnant) and have mostly rejected our calling as Jewish believers. But this does not give us any place to judge them in return. This would be a human response, rather than the godly one we are all called toward. Yet because of our humanity, these issues of *rejection* have affected many of us in the Messianic Movement. As a result, certain wounds might have occurred that have given the enemy the opportunity to play on this weakness and the way we view the Church.

Before I address this

The key for us is to embrace our differences and allow the Holy Spirit to once again create His harmony between us.

more fully, I need to remind you of the isolation that most of the Messianic movement has emerged and grown up in, in addition to the *thousands of years of rejection* that Jews have suffered in the world. These have been built up in our collective psyche through our own natural association and connection to the God of Israel and to the subsequent persecution it caused. This can never be discounted in the way we relate and respond to others.

In this light, most Jewish people, especially males, are driven to succeed and prove themselves as a means to justify their existence. Also playing into this dynamic is Jewish people's natural leadership and innovative gifts, which are irrevocable from the Lord, as in Romans 11:29. These issues run deep in the generational bloodline of all Jewish souls, who for the past several thousand years, in numerous periods, have had to fight with every breath to maintain their existence.

Going back to the olive-tree example to reemphasize the isolation of Messianic believers, the Remnant has been rejected by their own: "You can't believe in Yeshua/Jesus and still be Jewish!" But they have also been separate, apart from, and rejected by many of the Gentile branches: "You can't do that Jewish stuff anymore; there's no difference between Jew and Gentile!"

Going back to the olive-tree example to reemphasize the isolation of Messianic believers, the Remnant has been rejected by their own: "You can't believe in Yeshua/Jesus and still be Jewish!" But they have also been separate, apart from, and rejected by many of the Gentile branches: "You can't do that Jewish stuff anymore; there's no difference between Jew and Gentile!" Often, Jewish believers are expected to conform to the identity of the Gentile Church.

As a result, Jewish believers might have experienced certain frailties and insecurities from the outpost of faith that have caused the Messianic Movement to become somewhat compromised and quite defensive in its posture—both toward the Jewish community fighting to justify its existence and toward the Church looking to find acceptance in our calling. In certain cases, this can cause some of us to become defensive in the way we deal with or react to it, and this can lead to pride and arrogance.

This is the background to some of the main heart issues of most Jewish souls. It is important for us as Jewish believers to recognize them in the hope of receiving greater healing and deliverance in these areas, which is always available to us through the Holy Spirit.

I recognize this fully as one of the most common struggles in the Jewish-believing heart and mindset and how it has affected many of us, especially those in ministry. I am aware of it in my own heart with my ministry focus as a bridge between the family groups and how regularly I have to bring my heart toward the Lord in this area. I pray that the *mercy* of the Father would flow out of a heart of love and servitude, which is His will and plan for us all, as the flesh gets broken off.

It is like a very *deep root in our hearts* with many smaller roots coming from it that can and do affect us, sometimes without us even knowing it. If you are a Jewish believer, especially a leader on the front lines of ministry, please pray on this issue in your own heart, and ask the Holy Spirit to reveal it to you.

I think it is also true that nearly all Jewish believers have somehow been affected by this, whether in the Messianic Body or the Church. We need to address these root issues in prayer and become more secure in who God has made us, to help us move us into a more positive, bolder zone with our Jewish friends and neighbors as well as with our Christian family. This can make a huge difference to everyone around us. Then we will be able to reach out to the splinter groups among us that have gotten off track to help bring correction in us as a Body, if they are also willing to recognize their own flaws. But what about those who have allowed these wounds to *fester*; what *other influences* have we opened up to, and how are they affecting the Messianic Body of believers?

Aside from this deep root of rejection, there can also be anger. I experienced this when I first came to faith. I wasn't angry with my people, but I was mad at Jewish leadership. How could they have withheld Yeshua from us and the lies that were perpetuated about Him. But it was this very emotion in my heart that the Lord used to change me through the process of sanctification and give me a supernatural heart of love for all Jewish people. And this is how the Lord led me into deeper prayer for my people.

But we can also be angry at the Church for rejecting us and not understanding our call. As a Jewish believer, if you are reading this and still experience anger toward your Gentile family and to the Church, I want to encourage you to let this go. But this anger can also exist among Gentile believers who have been angry at the Church for not reembracing its Jewish roots and heritage.

GENTILE BELIEVERS AND ISSUES OF THE HEART

Unknown to most of us, some of the Gentile believers who have left the Church for the Messianic side have their own heart issues to deal with. As I have briefly mentioned, aside from mixed marriages to Jewish believers, Gentiles have left the Church for two main reasons: first, because of a calling or a leading to serve their Jewish-believing family and second, because they have had issues with the Church not wanting to embrace the Messianic side and our Jewish roots. In this light, a *critical* or *judgmental* heart can exist between the two groups if they have taken a position against the Church for not moving in this direction.

The blindness and the separation of the Gentile Church to the Messianic branches is obviously an issue for Jewish believers and Messianic Gentiles. However, in *The Reconnection,* timing is all within God's mercy plan to help reunite us (Jew and Gentile) as a family. And we must have hearts full of love, grace, forgiveness, and mercy. Otherwise, we run the risk of entering judgment and receiving a just measure in return (see Matthew 7:1–2). This is exactly what is happening to some of the groups on the Messianic side who have become more extreme in their ideas and their differing understandings of the fullness of Israel's identity. This has even caused them to break away from the Messianic Body to form their own groups if that can be believed—God help us!

It has become more and more evident to me, as the Lord has been taking me deeper into these heart and mind issues that exist on the Messianic side, that a great move of healing and Reconciliation is needed here, just as much as it is on the Gentile branches of the tree.

TIME OF HEALING

We are in that time like the hour before the wedding, when so much is going wrong, but we must be willing to focus on it, calling upon the love and mercy of God to get it resolved so we can prepare the Bride for the Bridegroom. For this to happen, we need to recognize these issues first in ourselves, which will take humility on our part to properly see these things and address them. But how can we properly expose extreme teachings among us when we are not yet fully clear of who we are ourselves? Perhaps we need

I believe we stand a far better chance of strengthening the Messianic Movement when we can be honest with ourselves and about our weaknesses as Jewish believers. Isn't our strength in Yeshua/Jesus made perfect through such struggles, and doesn't judgment begin in the House of God? (See 2 Corinthians 12:9.)

to address the issues that are holding us back first, as well as the divisions among us, so that we can see more clearly to help clean up the rest. Scripture says, *"First clean up the plank in your own eye and then you will see clearly to remove the speck from your brother's eye"* (Matt. 7:5).

I believe we stand a far better chance of strengthening the Messianic Movement when we can be honest with ourselves and about our weaknesses as Jewish believers. Isn't our strength in Yeshua/Jesus made perfect through such struggles, and doesn't judgment begin in the House of God? (See 2 Corinthians 12:9.)

Scripture could not be clearer to us in the Body of Messiah/Christ that Gentile followers were not required to follow all Jewish laws and traditions, as commissioned by our founding Jewish apostles (see Acts 15). *Any deviation from this mandate is simply not scriptural or accurate.* Yet, even amid the initial growth of the Church, there was a Judaizing spirit among certain followers that challenged this edict. It continued even as the Apostle Paul was spreading the Word throughout the world and establishing the Church with the other apostles.

Yeshua/Jesus warned us about this when He told us to beware of the yeast of the Pharisees and Sadducees (see Matthew 16:6). In other words, He warned that both religious and worldly spirits would lure us away from the liberty we have in Mashiach/Christ. This is something Jewish believers should always be cautious of when wanting to associate with the Torah (five books of Moses) and our heritage. This is why our reliance on the Holy Spirit should be even greater when we want to go down this path, so we can avoid the snares of legalism.

LEGALISTIC OR RELIGIOUS SPIRITS

Regretfully, this same spirit has reemerged on the Messianic side and penetrated parts of the Jewish Body of believers, much like a legalistic spirit can penetrate the Church. Similarly, those Gentiles who have left the Church in a judgmental or critical way would be vulnerable to these negative influences, with both groups becoming extreme in their thinking and adopting viewpoints that their own Messianic beliefs should replace the Church in its entirety. They look to fully identify *TONM* among the Jewish branches that the rest of the Church should follow. These splinter groups have three specific parts: the *Jewish Roots Movement,* the *One Law Movement,* and the *Ephraimite Movement.* We will discuss these in more detail.

A HEALTHY BALANCE

Christians need to gain a deeper understanding that Jewish believers do have the liberty to associate to their own laws and traditions, as the apostles did in the Jerusalem Church, as long as there is no emphasis on it for salvation (see Acts 21:20–25). However, it should not isolate them from any associations to their Gentile-believing family in the Church because many are still separate.

I want to empha-size that some in the Messianic Body are called to this under-standing with a greater emphasis and associa-tion to Jewish liturgy. And the rest of us in the Body need to be able to bless them into it, as long as they operate in it with a good balance from the Holy Spirit.

Christians need to gain a deeper understanding that Jewish believers do have the liberty to associate to their own laws and traditions, as the apostles did in the Jerusalem Church, as long as there is no emphasis on it for salvation (see Acts 21:20–25). However, it should not isolate them from any associations to their Gentile-believing family in the Church because many are still separate.

A CALL TO THE ORTHODOX

Who will be able to reach those still under rabbinical Judaism in the differing orthodox sects? This is much like the Apostle Paul's experience when he went back to Jerusalem (see Acts 21:20–29; 1 Corinthians 9:2–23). I must point out that the Judaism of then is quite different from the Judaism of today. Most orthodox sects of Judaism have adapted many of their practices from Rabinnical Judaism, whch began to form in the first century after the Temple was destroyed. Ultra orthodox Judaism was also revived in the eigh-teenth century and is best known now today as Hasidic Judaism. How do we address these needs of witness and evangelism in our modern day, and who will respond to this call?

It is important to point out that in any attempt to follow certain Jewish laws and customs, there is always the chance of being influ-enced or seduced by a legalistic or religious mindset. It is not diffi-cult to fall prey to this kind of spirit. We only have to look at those Jewish brothers when the Church first started to know what a battle this was, or look at the more religious institutions in Christianity to see how legalism is rampant in many parts of the Church.

For certain, whoever is called among the Messianic branches to reach the more religious Jews with the love of Yeshua has to have an even greater emphasis and dependency on the Holy Spirit to be able to go under the influences of Jewish orthodoxy without its control, for we are now under Mashiach/Christ (see 1 Corinthians 9:21).

Please also understand that there are varying degrees of expression within Messianic Judaism. We can compare these to liturgical expressions from within a Church context, where some can fall prey to legalism. However, it is important to note the vulnerabilities in this case and to pray and intercede for those of us who might be called in this area so that these influences would have no effects. Let us stand in the gap for our brothers and sisters to always have freedom and to know a healthy balance between the Holy Spirit and liturgy.

Much of what I am discussing here can be confusing to outsiders, especially for Christians to differentiate between good and solid Messianic teachings. When these groups become extreme, they need repentance and adjustment when it comes to contradicting the apostles' code concerning Gentile observance, their unity with them, and their apparent disdain for the Church. What is most challenging is that the majority of these leaders from the splinter movements in Messianic Judaism are not even Jewish; rather, they have a Gentile background, if you can believe that!

In fact, one of the Jewish leaders who began to perpetuate these teachings several years ago has already come into repentance on this issue. We must encourage all the others to do the same.

HEALTHY JEWISH ROOTS

It is important for us to have a good understanding of what is true and proper on the Messianic side of the tree, especially as the Remnant strengthens among us. This is why we need a greater emphasis on prayer and intercession to break up this ground and the confusion that exists currently, for the Messianic Body to be able to enter a deeper dialogue on these issues to find greater unity.

There is definitely a balance and a healthy understanding and association to our Jewish roots and heritage through a variety of Messianic expressions. Some are more liturgical, and some are more charismatic. These boundaries need to be more clearly defined. This will help the Church more readily embrace the Messianic Movement.

Dr. Michael Brown's book, *The Real Kosher Jesus*, is a good start on this topic. Dr. Daniel Juster's revised edition of *Jewish Roots* also speaks to this healthy balance. He writes and comments on these aberrations in chapter 11 and exposes the movements I described earlier.

ABERRATIONS AND COUNTERFEITS

To address these splinter groups, parts of the *Jewish Roots Movement* looks to replace the Church, both for Jew and Gentile, without giving any credence to what the Church has become, but rather condemning it for moving away from the biblical calendar and embracing paganism to incorporate its celebrations. Although the Jewish Roots Movement does focus on salvation through Yeshua/Jesus, some in this movement argue for a full observance of the law for both Jew and Gentile, excluding circumcision.

> There is definitely a balance and a healthy understanding and association to our Jewish roots and heritage through a variety of Messianic expressions. Some are more liturgical, and some are more charismatic. These boundaries need to be more clearly defined. This will help the Church more readily embrace the Messianic Movement.

The *One Law Movement* has become an offshoot of the Jewish Roots Movement, which teaches that the Gentiles and Jews in Yeshua/Jesus have the same responsibility to the whole Torah and that there is no difference. It upholds these laws as if it has become a replacement for the present Church in its practices. It also replaces Israel because these devotees now say there is no calling to Jews and Gentiles. *It is like Replacement Theology in reverse.*

Meanwhile, the *Ephraimites* are claiming that most believers from the nations are part of the lost tribes of Israel, from the tribe of Ephraim, and therefore need to follow and observe the law as Jewish believers are called toward.

In addition, many of these groups attempt to infiltrate more traditional Messianic Congregations, often attempting to challenge and divide them. This has become a real problem for the Messianic movement as a whole. However, in the long run, this will help the Messianic Movement to better define itself and exactly how it coexists with the Church at large.

Plus, the very Jewish or Biblical calendars that these movements so firmly attest to are questionable regarding the exact dates of all the feasts. Dr. Daniel Juster puts it best:

> No one really knows for sure the exact days of the biblical feasts. Judaism well knows and teaches that the Sabbath was set by God and is consistent and sure, but the feasts are set by man, because there is no biblical directive on how to reconcile the solar years with the lunar months. It is a legalistic mistake to think we have to have the exact day right. Some are so extreme that they think both the rabbinic and Church calendars must be rejected. They claim to have returned to the real biblical calendar.

We need to earnestly pray for these brothers and sisters to find the *liberty* and *love* of this Reconnection message. You may choose to follow a more biblical calendar; this is your choice as a believer through the liberty we have in the Holy Spirit. And new Church and Congregational groups are emerging during these days with this type of expression. *However, when you start to insist that others do the same and you become critical of the rest of the Body, you are crossing a dangerous line that should not be crossed.*

I should also make mention here of the *British and American Israel Movements*, which have more of a Church background but also look to isolate the Jewish Remnant to the tribes of Judah and Benjamin. These movements claim Israel from those who were dispersed into the nations from the Assyrian invasion and dispersion (722 BC).

At that time, up to 80 percent of the tribes of Israel were dispersed into the nations and never came back (see 2 Kings 17). So some credence is given to their physical dispersion—certain Gentiles in both the East and West might actually have physical Jewish roots. However, it is impossible to trace all this and to make blanket statements that some of these nations are actually now Israel. This does not make sense.

This group has also failed to recognize that when the two Kingdoms of Israel separated after Solomon's reign and Jeroboam set up two golden calf altars to replace worship at Jerusalem (see 1 Kings 12:28), there was an exodus of many people in all the tribes of Israel to live in Judah to separate themselves from this idolatrous act. So from this point on, even though a Remnant of Israel was represented in Judah, all the tribes of Israel were represented there during that time.

What is missing from all these types of splinter groups who are earnestly seeking and searching for their roots is that *The Reconnection* in *TONM* between Jew and Gentile is not even on their radar. Rather, they are focused on a strict code to break away from the rest of the Church and adhere to the biblical calendar.

THE RECONNECTION RESTORES TONM

With *The Reconnection* in the *Father's Heart*, we look to restore the spiritual health of the love of the family. Our goal is not necessarily to find a perfect theology between Israel and the Church, wipe out the call of the Remnant of Israel, or ignore the call for His children from the nations through the Church. Rather, we are to honor and uphold both. We are all called into a Kingdom and priesthood to rule and reign with Mashiach/Christ (see Revelation 5:10). Yeshua's reign will go out from Jerusalem into all the nations.

God's Heart for us, on both sides of the family, is to operate in a place of love and liberty, as I have been emphasizing. But we must never enforce our views so rigidly that we divide and separate the Body. This is a mistake and a breach of the love of God we are all called toward, and it plays right into the enemy's hand!

THE HOLY SPIRIT AND JEWISH IDENTITY

One of the greatest dangers for Jewish believers in seeking Jewish identity is that it should never precede our identity in Yeshua/Jesus and in the Holy Spirit. This must always come first; otherwise, it can become idolatrous.

One of the greatest dangers for Jewish believers in seeking Jewish identity is that it should never precede our identity in Yeshua/Jesus and in the Holy Spirit. This must always come first; otherwise, it can become idolatrous.

Because of our isolation and the rejection we might have experienced, this has become a major issue for us in the Messianic Body. Often the identity issue ends up taking precedence, diminishing the presence of the Lord among us.

I am reminded of the Lord's Words to the prophet Zechariah: *"Not by might, nor by power, but by My Spirit, says the Lord Almighty"* (Zech. 4:6). One of the main aspects of the New Covenant through Yeshua/Jesus is that it is supposed to bring us into a beautiful intimacy with God, where each of us knows Him for ourselves (see Jeremiah 31:34). But just how spiritual are our worship services and observances, and just how strong is His presence manifest in all we do in our Messianic services? It is the Spirit and the power of God that will ultimately touch and change our people. We must look to foster this before anything else and to treasure Him above the rest. I am not coming against our view and attachment to liturgy in this place; rather, I urge that it would flow out of the presence of God rather than the other way around, which can quench the Holy Spirit and limit His presence among us.

MY OWN PERSONAL JEWISH EXPERIENCE

I am speaking personally now. I first found the Lord in the 1980s and was supernaturally overwhelmed in my new-found relationship with Yeshua/Jesus and the Holy Spirit, with the freedom I was experiencing from within. I visited a Messianic Congregation, and it was so religious that it reminded me of my childhood synagogue. I honestly wanted to run a million miles away from it. Later on, in the 1990s, the Lord opened the door for me to minister to the Jews of the former Soviet Union. And this is when I began to connect with my Messianic family.

Plus, as the Messianic Body has matured, there are many good Messianic Congregations that have found this balance in the Spirit and Jewish identity. This is vital for Jewish believers, especially to be able to reflect this back into their own Jewish communities to help promote Yeshua as Messiah. However, many Congregations are still struggling with this issue. It greatly weakens us as a movement and reduces the role and liberty that the Holy Spirit wants to have in our midst.

I am personally not very liturgically driven because for me it can be too legalistic. However, a good number of Jewish believers not only love the richness of liturgy but also find a wonderful connection to God through it. And when the Holy Spirit is in the midst of the liturgical experience through Hebrew prayers, it is beautiful.

My good friend, Ron Corbett, is a Messianic rabbi from the Tikkun Global Apostolic Network that I am associated with. He oversees a Messianic Congregation on Long Island, and whenever we fellowship with him and his Body, the dimension and presence of the Holy Spirit in the liturgy is awesome because he has found this special place with both. If the Spirit is first in our hearts, then

He is the source, and our expression and love for God flows from this place into everything we do.

Similarly, this became the main focus of Dr. Daniel Juster's Messianic Congregation, Beth Messiah, finding this balance, which he founded in the 1980s as he was evolving in his understanding of the Holy Spirit. And just look how the Spirit of God has developed this Body of believers and the outgrowth from there into the Messianic Body at large. It is a network of fivefold Congregations based in Israel that also has a global presence that is moving in the gifts of the Holy Spirit (Tikkun Global Ministries).

We can also learn from our believing family in Israel, where in most Messianic Congregations, there is a much greater emphasis on the presence of the Holy Spirit than the liturgy. Could it be that as Jews in the land, there is less of a struggle to emphasize our Jewishness? Naturally, this is the case and something the rest of us should be willing to look at in how we can apply liturgy into our worship. As Watchman Nee put it in one of his books, "Maturity is knowing the voice of the Spirit and submitting to it."[15]

We need to seriously look at what we are doing and what we have become if we want to get back to what is most important to reach the lost sheep of Israel. We need to refocus on the Father and Yeshua, fervent worship, intercession, evangelism, and lifestyle witness to those living around us. Plus, we must pay attention to people who are in much greater need of inner healing and personal deliverance.

Otherwise, we run the risk of being too religious. If the Jewish focus takes precedence, the service becomes dry, with a limited presence of the Holy Spirit in our midst. Then the Congregation becomes stagnant, and growth can be limited toward the next generation, whom we are not currently impacting the way we should.

How is it that in just one generation, such a thriving movement of His Spirit, reaching and awakening our Jewish family to faith, which gave birth to the Messianic Movement, has now become so ineffective in reaching our people?

We need to seriously look at what we are doing and what we have become if we want to get back to what is most important to reach the lost sheep of Israel. We need to refocus on the Father and Yeshua, fervent worship, intercession, evangelism, and lifestyle witness to those living around us. Plus, we must pay attention to people who are in much greater need of inner healing and personal deliverance.

This can also explain why more Jewish believers remain in the Church and feel more comfortable there—they are gaining a closer association to the Holy Spirit through the Church (and the subsequent inner healing) more than they are in most Messianic Congregations.

Please understand I am not downplaying our need for Jewish identity or the liberty we have in the Spirit to express it, but this focus can never precede it. If it does (and in this case, we would need to be very honest with ourselves), we would confess and repent of it. We need to earnestly seek the Lord in finding the balance between the two to become healthy in this place.

THE JEWISH APOSTLES

I truly believe God has given us a standard when it comes to the boldness and love of the apostles in the way in which they proclaimed the truth back to our people and the miracles they moved in to demonstrate the Good News. Look at the way in which they handled the Lord's persecution and the subsequent brokenness it produced in each of them. Yet from it came a boldness and authority that ultimately changed the world.

It was not only the Lord who raised a standard, but also His miracle-working power in each of these men and women who became God's example for us to follow. This beckons the question, are we proclaiming the Good News about Yeshua/Jesus the way they did? Do we have boldness with the power of the Holy Spirit they had? Or are we *getting caught up in religion*, which Yeshua/Jesus Himself took a stand against?

Avner Boskey, one of the prophetic voices from the land, has written extensively on this in his book *How to Be Messianic without Becoming Meshuggah*. *Meshuggah* is a Yiddish word meaning crazy. The title is fitting when one considers all that is going on in the Messianic Movement. I strongly encourage you to read this book; I think you can benefit from Avner's depth and knowledge of the Hebrew word. His book exposes much and helps bring light to a very necessary balance that is needed in us. Here is one of his quotes from the book: "Not all that glitters is gold, and not all that's Jewish is Kosher."

MESSIANIC GENTILES

Another delicate issue that has become challenging to the Messianic Movement is the association and participation of Gentile believers who feel drawn into it. Simply put, a Messianic Gentile is a believer in Messiah from a Gentile background and has been called of the Holy Spirit to serve the Messianic community.

My focus here does not have to do with our Gentile family per se, but rather the way in which we Jewish believers are addressing our Gentile brothers and sisters.

A Messianic Gentile is a believer in Messiah from a Gentile background and has been called of the Holy Spirit to serve the Messianic community.

I can tell you firsthand as one who has spent several years in a Messianic Congregation with a heart for *TONM* between Jew and Gentile that one of my greatest concerns when the rabbi was teaching on Jewish identity was that my Gentile brothers and sisters would invariably feel second class to their Jewish family. And I can say plainly that this is not of the Lord because while we might have different roles to play out, we are *most definitely one* in Body and Spirit.

There is a fine line in this place that is most delicate when attempting to encourage Jewish believers into their identity without offending Gentile believers. The secret to this, I believe, is twofold:

first, we must emphasize the unity and coheirship of all believers. In the Spirit, there is now no difference between us, except for our callings and current identity and ultimately where we might end up serving when the Lord returns. Second, we must teach clearly on Messianic Gentile identity, as those who have been called by the Lord to serve the Jewish community.

Gentile participation in Messianic Congregations should be seen as an asset, and a unity of love in Spirit should always be fostered between the two, including leadership. In this way, when Gentile believers understand their calling to serve beside their Jewish family, leadership can be free to emphasize Jewish identity issues to Jewish believers without anyone feeling like they are losing anything.

HASHIVENU

However, certain groups have emerged in light of the Gentile Messianic issue as it has grown from within the movement to even discourage Gentile participation. Or, for those feeling called to it, they are encouraging conversion to Judaism instead, which again goes against the mandate for Gentiles set by the apostles.

Thank God these Jewish believers have a healthier view of the Gentile Church in acknowledging its legitimacy. Although their intentions might be good in wanting to fully identify with their Jewish heritage and encourage Jewish believers to do the same, they have gone to extremes in specific areas that are in need of Realignment. First, with the Jewish identity issue, they fully acknowledge rabbinical practices and affirm its authority over Israel insofar that the Rabbinate really has received the crown (through the Levitical Priesthood under the Mosaic Law and now through Yeshua). However, this counteracts the spiritual authority that was released to Israel's new authority along with its fivefold governing focus to equip the rest of the Body for the works of the ministry (see Ephesians 2:20).

We know the broken-off branches (those included in the all Israel and yet to be saved—see Romans 11:26) are still to be reestablished into the priesthood of believers, according to Isaiah 61:6 and Revelation 5:9–10 (from every tribe and nation). But it will be under the guise and leadership of Israel's new authority (Jewish and Gentile), not the old one. Yeshua/Jesus removed this from the Levitical priesthood and released it to the apostles and prophets at Shavuot/Pentecost, along with its fivefold governing focus to equip the rest of the Body for the works of the ministry.

It is important to note that Israel's twelve sons are also included in the eternal rule of the Kingdom, along with the twelve Jewish apostles, whose names are written and etched into its foundations and gates (see Revelation 21:12–14).

It is important to note that Israel's twelve sons are also included in the eternal rule of the Kingdom, along with the twelve Jewish apostles, whose names are written and etched into its foundations and gates (see Revelation 21:12–14). There is no mention in these Scriptures, with any continuity, of the Aaronic priestly Covenant. But I should point out that there seems to be a role to play for the Levites in Ezekiel's temple, which could be included as part of the new priesthood of believers if this temple is actually physically rebuilt in the Millenium (see Ezekiel 44:15).

My brothers and sisters who follow these beliefs probably would not agree with me on this comment: Rabbinic Judaism first, Spirit second. Although this is exactly what it ends up producing. Plus, it also exalts the calling of the Jew over the Gentile, which also contradicts Scripture.

Their main focus is to shepherd the firstborn into this place. Although they try their best to be honest and open to the Gentile believers around them, Gentile believers are mostly discouraged, except those who feel called to this place. In this case, conversion is often encouraged. This approach brings offense to our Gentile family and has caused many of them to feel shunned and even to leave the movement.

In addition, because of this intensity on the firstborn with the

Hashivenu approach, they naturally lose touch with their call to unite and Reconnect with their Gentile family in *TONM*, and this continues to fuel their isolation from the rest of us.

Whenever issues of the heart and mind create separation and division among us, we must be willing to take a second look and open our minds to a new approach and a different perspective.

PRIDE AND SPIRITUAL PRIDE

There can be a spiritual pride among *traditional Jews* who think that because of our calling as a chosen people, we are better than the Gentiles. In this light, a certain judgmental or even critical spirit exists and has affected the way we act toward outsiders.

The Yiddish word, *goyim*, simply means non-Jew. However, whenever it is used or I hear it, it often conjures up certain a negative connotation because of the

There is a definite call of the firstborn and Remnant of Israel from within the family, but we will never come close to fulfilling it if we are still being deceived in this area. Our Lord was the perfect example to us in this place of servanthood for the greatest among us, He said, "will be your servant" (see Matthew 23:11).

hatred and judgment that is associated with it. As Jewish believers, we need to be sensitive and aware of sinful actions that have been passed down in our own generational bloodlines and affect the way we view and interact with our Christian family.

One such sin issue is pride. Even though most believers hopefully would have confronted this issue in their own walks with the Lord, if we have not fully dealt with it in the *generational bloodline*, then it can still have an effect on us. The enemy is then free to influence us in this regard.

This is especially true of *spiritual pride*. Some of the talk I have heard among my Messianic brethren gives me cause for concern regarding how we can sometimes view our Gentile family in the Church. It is important to consider the current separation that exists between the two groups and all the misunderstandings that go along with it. The issue of rejection can so easily connect and play into spiritual pride, so we need to become more sensitive and aware of it and how it can affect us.

There is a definite call of the firstborn and Remnant of Israel from within the family, but we will never come close to fulfilling it if we are still being deceived in this area. Our Lord was the perfect example to us in this place of servanthood for the greatest among us, He said, *"will be your servant"* (see Matthew 23:11). His own action in washing His disciples' feet should be an indication to us of exactly how God wants us to act toward our Gentile family in the faith, and vice versa.

Although the Church might not have properly understood us up to this time, this separation is not of God. Nor our own desires to be separate from them because of the way they have misjudged us and treated our people in the past. It is time for this division to be healed! The Apostle Paul wrote that all of us have been given over to disobedience (especially in this area) and that God may now have *mercy* on us all and begin to cleanse and heal the divide between us in *TONM*.

You might think as a Jewish believer that much more is needed on the part of our Gentile family in how they should reconcile with us. You might be right. However, both groups need to move in *love, forgiveness,* and *humility* with one another so that God's ultimate blessings and power will flow through us and create a renewed unity between Israel and the Church.

HEALING IS NEEDED

It might seem strange that certain Gentile believers have moved on from the Messianic Body to form their own groups, but it is not that surprising when we realize that their experience was from much of the above that I have described and not from a balanced perspective between Spirit and truth in the Messianic Body.

Could it be that in our pursuit of Jewishness in the diaspora (dispersion in the nations) and the imbalance it has produced, we look messy to the outsider?

Plus, if the strength and well-being of the Messianic Body is such a threat to the enemy in light of what it will ultimately lead to concerning the rest of Israel's salvation, don't you think he would attack it to bring all sorts of divisions and confusion? This is actually exactly what is happening right now.

> You might think as a Jewish believer that much more is needed on the part of our Gentile family in how they should reconcile with us. You might be right. However, both groups need to move in love, forgiveness, and humility with one another so that God's ultimate blessings and power will flow through us and create a renewed unity between Israel and the Church.

We must work hard to *expose* and *outsmart* the enemy instead of defending our positions and ourselves. Unless we can find the humility and honesty of heart to come into a greater place of repentance that is necessary to allow for the Holy Spirit's healing through us, we will remain separate and cut off from the very sources in God's Body that can help bring the healing and strength our Lord is so wanting to provide through *TONM*. This is the same for some of our Gentile family who are not willing to give it up. In this case, we continue to play into the enemy's hand that fosters our divisions and separation.

The rise of these splinter groups should serve us good notice that something is wrong somewhere and needs to be addressed. Plus, as a movement, it should also be a strong indicator for us to get our act together. *We need to clean up the original so that the counterfeits will be exposed.*

THE REMNANT OF ISRAEL MUST MOVE INTO THE RECONNECTION

Our separation and isolation from the rest of God's family has become so much of a norm for us in the Messianic Movement that the health and strength of *TONM* between Jew and Gentile is not on our radar, as it should be. Yet in this final stage before our Lord returns to us, it is the very *Heart of God* for His family to be one, according to Yeshua/Jesus's prayer in John 17.

We have had the time of the Jew, and we have had the time of the Gentile. This is the day of Reconciliation *for both groups to shine* and our Father's plans to finally unite His family. There is so much more for us to gain as our Gentile family is properly Reconnected to us, and we are to them. Pray to God that we will become more open to this and that the Father

The rise of these splinter groups should serve us good notice that something is wrong somewhere and needs to be addressed. Plus, as a movement, it should also be a strong indicator for us to get our act together. We need to clean up the original so that the counterfeits will be exposed.

would not have to wait until the next generation is ready, as He did in the wilderness when we came out of Egypt.

In this light, the Holy Spirit is transitioning and leading us into this period. We must be willing to adjust and cooperate with His plans, just as our Gentile family needs to do the same with us. This is a new day for all of us and a very necessary transaction that will bring us the fullness and the resurrection power that has been lacking from both groups in light of our distinct separation.

EZEKIEL'S PROPHECY WILL BE FULFILLED

We are in part two of Ezekiel's prophecies to the dry bones (see Ezekiel 37:1–14). Part one is already near completion: the land has been restored, with many Jewish people already returning (see Ezekiel 37:1–8). We have entered the beginning phase of part two (see Ezekiel 37:9–11), when the breath is released. In this phase, *The Reconnection* must take place within us as His family so the *mercy* can be released through us as *one* Body and *one* flock. This will ultimately lead us to part three of this prophecy, which ends with the resurrection of the dead and the Lord's return (verses 12–14).

God's children know His voice, and the great shepherd is calling us to Him (see John 10:16). We need to stand in the gap and call on heaven so that the *breath* can be released into the balance of Israel. This call is part of God's preparation for His return to restore His Body to Himself. This will take a new and a fresh approach in the way we petition heaven, as these battles cannot be fought in our own strength, but only through The Holy Spirit's leading.

We have entered the beginning phase of part two (see Ezekiel 37:9–11), when the breath is released. In this phase, The Reconnection must take place within us as His family so the mercy can be released through us as one Body and one flock.

Rabbi Gamaliel said, "For if their purpose or activity is of human origin, it will fail. But if it is from God, you will not be able to stop these men; you will only find yourselves fighting against God" (see Acts 5:38–39). *"As had just been said: Today, if you hear His voice, do not harden your hearts as you did in the rebellion"* (Heb. 3:15).

We will never be able to achieve the fullness of God's plans through us as His Remnant Body until we fully embrace our Gentile-believing family in the Church, loving them where they are currently and as our very own. They are not there just to help us financially either, so that we can continue in our separateness trying to reach Israel alone. This is misguided thinking.

THE POWER EQUATION

In *Romans 911*, you have learned of the great significance of our Gentile family Reconnecting spiritually with us through the *Heart of the Father* and the great power in the Holy Spirit that it will help to release. The same is true for us Reconnecting with them. In reality, neither group can totally fulfill its role without the other. This is the Father's perfect blueprint to bring us together and make us one.

As we now know, it is the believing Jew and believing Gentile, God's united family, that are the chosen instruments to bring forth for the balance of Israel's salvation and the last great harvest of souls. Through a heavenly supplication and an earthly witness, our unification will help release the mercy of God on the rest.

OUR IDENTITY WILL BE UPHELD

This does not mean we will lose or shed our identity as the Remnant of Israel as we Reconnect with the Gentile-believing Church. Instead, with their help, we will become strengthened in it. The Father's plan is for them to bless us and for us to bless them.

> *"My prayer is not for them alone. I pray also for those who will believe in me through their message, that all of them may be one, Father, just as you are in me and I am in you. May they also be in us so that the world may believe that You have sent me? I have given them the Glory that You gave me, that they may be one as we are one—I in them and you in me—so that they may be brought to complete unity. Then the world will know that You sent me and have loved them even as You have loved me"* (John 17:20–23).

FEAR OF ASSIMILATION

This brings me to some of the other barriers and obstacles for us to overcome from the Messianic side. Our fear of assimilation is very real when it comes to connecting with the Church, which is obviously far greater in size than the Messianic Body.

In reality, neither group can totally fulfill its role without the other. This is the Father's perfect blueprint to bring us together and make us one.

With this issue, let's remind ourselves of the olive-tree illustrations in chapter 6 and compare the current one that portrays our isolation to the one of Abba's illustration. Through the Father's olive tree, we are now fully strengthened, flourishing, and free flowing, not only among the natural branches but also from one side to the other. Nothing of our identity and calling has been lost; rather, it has been strengthened and healed through our spiritual reunion with our Gentile family, who has also been called to uphold us. In fact, this union has made us more effective among our own people to help win more of them to Yeshua.

When Yeshua/Jesus told the Pharisees that He had other sheep He must bring into the pen, they were most startled and had no comprehension of what He was saying. His emphasis on the oneness of flock in His Word and the subsequent unity is what He focused on in these verses (see John 10:14–17).

First it was the Jews, and then it was the Gentiles; now it's both. We are not an assimilated Body but rather a united one *into a unique oneness that blesses our diversity, through our identities and callings.* We will be priests of the most high through Israel and the nations (see Revelation 5:9–10).

If we don't have our primary identity first from within the context of *TONM* between Jew and Gentile, we are always going to have a skewed approach toward the Jewish aspect of the faith, and we will most certainly fail to find the balance our Father desires for *The Reconnection.* Now is the time that God has chosen to bring all our differences to the surface so that His *mercy* can be released on us all.

MOSES'S HANDS WILL BE RAISED

There is so much more for us to gain when coming out of our isolation and Reconnecting with our Gentile-believing family than if we don't. As I have already illustrated in earlier chapters, there is a prophetic portrait here regarding Moses, Aaron, and Hur. As Moses's hands were raised up against the Amalekites and aided by Aaron and Hur, who in this picture can represent our Gentile family, he was strengthened, his hands were raised, and the enemy was defeated.

We will be recipients of greater financial help from the Church as it recognizes our spiritual health in the overall equation of God's end-time plan. We have much to gain spiritually from our Gentile family, many of whom are more experienced in certain areas of inner healing and spiritual gifts and in the ways in which they connect to the Holy Spirit. We have so much to offer one another.

SECTION 2
RESTORATIVE PRAYER

These prayers have been written for all of us as Jewish believers so we can pray for confession, renouncement, and repentance and ask the Holy Spirit to fully cleanse our hearts and minds from anything negative toward our Gentile-believing family and the Church. We also should pray for any other issues that might be holding us back individually or corporately among the Jewish branches in *TONM*. These prayers are not just for issues that relate to us personally but are for anything in our generational bloodline and our ancestry that may still be affecting us.

May we as Jewish believers be willing to follow the example of our Lord and Savior, Yeshua HaMashiach, His apostles, and all the initial Jewish believers of the first *Ekklesia*, to lay down our lives for our Gentile-believing family, as well as those who are yet to be saved out of the nations. May we serve them and love them, as we love Him, so that His love in us will provide us the hope and the patience to see God's children from the nations Reconnect spiritually to us, as our Father has always intended them to be. May we, as coheirs with our Gentile-believing family, help our Lord prepare the way for His coming. Wow!

TESHUVAH: REPENTANCE

This requires a great act of humility on our part and servitude. May we humble ourselves in forgiveness and repentance so that we can truly be reconciled with the rest of God's family.

I wrote these prayers to address all the issues in this chapter, but every prayer might not apply to you personally. However, for the sake of the Messianic Body at large, including the

This requires a great act of humility on our part and servitude. May we humble ourselves in forgiveness and repentance so that we can truly be reconciled with the rest of God's family.

splinter groups that have gotten off track, please pray the following:

Avinu Malkeinu, Our Father, Our King, I come to in the precious name of your Son, Yeshua, and first declare my love and commitment to you as one of your Jewish sons and daughters.

> *Lord, help me forgive the Church and my Gentile-believing family for any wrongdoing or misunderstandings toward me, the Jewish people, and the Remnant of Israel. Lord, please also forgive me for any judgments toward them as my brothers and sisters and spiritual family.*
>
> *Lord, please forgive us as a Body if we have gotten off track. Forgive us for our weaknesses, our fears, our pride, and our insecurities. If any of these have enabled the enemy to lead us into the wrong direction, please forgive us.*
>
> *Lord, please forgive me if at any point I have reacted to the pain and root of rejection that has been evident in and among my people. Lord, I invite Your healing in this area and ask You to expose other influences through my generational bloodline, with all these weaknesses and sins. Lord, forgive me for wanting to control those things that I can't control.*
>
> *Lord, please forgive me for any idolatry in my heart in wanting to bring our Jewishness to the forefront and without knowingly putting your Holy Spirit in second place; forgive me for seeking traditions and laws more than the innermost issues of my heart. Lord, please*

forgive me for embracing any legalism and/or any legalistic spirits that are opposed to Your will.

Lord, please forgive me for rejecting my Gentile brothers and sisters in the Church and for any judgment I might have harbored against them. Lord, please forgive me for any anger, hatred, frustration, or resentment I have held toward any member of our Gentile family.

Lord, please forgive me for any judgment against Your Church and any harshness that might have developed in my heart as a result of the Church's position and misunderstanding against us as Jewish believers and our calling as the Remnant of Israel in Your Body and Your family.

Lord, please forgive me for imposing any rules and regulations on our brothers and sisters that are not in Scripture and for requiring either Jews or Gentiles to follow the Mosaic Law over the laws of Messiah and Torah.

Lord, please forgive me for adhering to any false doctrines or teachings concerning Israel's calling and the priesthood of believers, which has been passed on to the new priesthood in Messiah Yeshua between Jew and Gentile in TONM (see Revelation 5:9–10; Ephesians 2:14–22).

Lord, on behalf of the Messianic Movement, please forgive us from being separate from our Gentile family and from the Church.

Lord, I confess all these weaknesses and sins to You; I renounce them and break off any influences through my own actions, or through generational bloodline influences through the sins of my fathers and mothers through generational sins and any other influences. I plead Your blood over them and break off any holds that the evil one might have over them and render them powerless in the precious name of Yeshua Hamashiach. Amen.

PRAYER OF FORGIVENESS FOR THE JEWISH PEOPLE

Lord, please forgive our people for our pride, sometimes thinking that we were better than others.

Lord, please forgive our people for wanting to be like the world, instead of a people to be set apart by Yourself.

Lord, please forgive our people for forsaking You as our King.

Lord, please forgive the balance of our people for rejecting Yeshua, Your Son, and the Messiah of Israel.

Lord, please forgive our people for persecuting the initial followers of Yeshua and for the hatred in their hearts toward them.

Lord, we stand in the gap for them, asking that You would forgive their sins and remember them no more, even as You have promised to do in Your Word and to restore Israel to Yourself as Your firstborn sons and daughters.

Lord, we ask not only for the people of Israel, but also for all the other children from the nations who will call You by name; that in this Reconciliation and Reconnection, You would release a cry through us, Your Body, that will go up to the heavens in agreement with Your Spirit and release the resurrection power You have promised as you gather Israel to Yourself. I pray that You, Abba, will be glorified and that Your Son, Yeshua, will be lifted up to draw all men unto Himself.

I pray these prayers in the most precious name of Yeshua/Jesus, Your Son. Amen.

RECEIVING THE FATHER'S HEART: MY PRAYER FOR YOU

Now, Lord, please fill Your loving child with the fullness of Your Heart for the Church and for Your Gentile children, in the precious name of Yeshua. Amen.

Congratulations! You have just received the *Father's Heart* for His children from the nations and for His Church. You might feel like weeping, and if so, I encourage you to do so. However, if you do not feel like weeping, that is also okay. But do expect to see things differently from now on, not only in regard to your understanding of the Word of God as it relates to Israel and the Church, but also in the way you might feel or act toward your Gentile family.

PRAYER FOR MESSIANIC LEADERS

Messianic leaders have a greater responsibility to begin to shepherd the vision of the *Father's Heart* for His family to be one, between Jew and Gentile.

Leaders, please pray this prayer:

Avinu Malkeinu, Our Father, Our King, I come to You in the precious name of Your Son Yeshua. Lord as one of Your leaders among the Jewish branches of the faith, I confess and repent of any pride that has fueled my separation and judgment of the Church and/or my Gentile-believing family. Lord, I also confess any fear of assimilation with the Church, and I ask You to remove it and cleanse my heart from these sins. Father, as Your shepherd, help me guide Your children into Your Heart and to the love for one another that Yeshua had for You. I pray that it will Reconnect us spiritually in TONM the way You have always intended it to be. I pray that the world would know Yeshua as Your sent Son and for your family to be one through Your love and mercy in us, spilled out into a lost and dying world.

> Messianic leaders have a greater responsibility to begin to shepherd the vision of the Father's Heart for His family to be one, between Jew and Gentile.

Lord, I repent of putting my own identity before You; please forgive me. And now, Lord, rekindle me among the Jewish branches so that Your Holy Spirit will set a fire through me for Your Glory to come to the Earth, just as it was with our founding apostles. Let it start with me and spread into the hearts of the congregants You have given me to shepherd and oversee. Lord, let them shine with the light and power of Yeshua back to the rest of the Jewish community, spreading the truth and teaching of the one and only Messiah of Israel, Yeshua Hamashiach, with signs and wonders demonstrating the Word wherever we go.

Lord, give me a love for my Gentile family, and help me connect with them in our community and work together for Your Glory to come to where we live. Lord, let me receive from them all that they can help give me in the Holy Spirit, and vice versa, and let them receive from me the richness of our Jewish heritage. Together, may we both receive the richness of Messiah in TONM and the fullness thereof. Lord, may Your will be done in this area to unite us and make us one, that together we will work for the balance of Israel's salvation and the end-time harvest; to help complete your family on the Earth and prepare us for Your coming. In Yeshua's matchless name I pray. Amen.

May we as Jewish believers be willing to follow the example of our Lord and Savior, Yeshua HaMashiach, His apostles, and all the initial Jewish believers of the first Ekklesia, to lay down our lives for our Gentile-believing family.

SECTION 3
A NEW DAY

OUR CALLING AS JEWISH BELIEVERS

There is no doubt about our calling as Jewish believers into a unique identity from within the unity of *TONM*. The restored Remnant of Israel is the very beginning of the physical fulfillment of God's Covenants toward Israel's spiritual Restoration. Through this final awakening of our people, He will show His Glory to the world. This is God's end-time plan! He will transform our hearts of stone into hearts of flesh and circumcise them with His Holy Spirit that we would love Him with all of our hearts and with all of our souls (see Deuteronomy 30:4–6; Ezekiel 36:22–27; Romans 11:25–27).

We are called into a unique priesthood with a divine destiny now joined together with our Lord and God's children from the nations that will go out from Jerusalem and the land of Israel into all of the Earth (see Isaiah 61:6–7; Revelation 5:9–10).

We are nearing the time of our inheritance, as well as the inheritance of God's children from the nations. However, God has so designed this time that neither of us may come into that inheritance without each other and without spiritually uniting and Reconnecting as one family with one purpose to glorify the God of Israel.

MUTUAL BLESSING

We are called to love and bless each another. Jewish believers are called to bless their Gentile-believing family and act as bridge to help them Reconnect to their roots, to Israel as its commonwealth, into the fullness of that identity. Gentile believers are called to bless their Jewish family, to hold up their arms and strengthen them so that their hands can be raised for the battle. We can't have one without the other.

It's amusing to think of it in this light. But aren't Jews specifically called to be a light to the nations, and aren't Gentile believers specifically called to draw Jews to jealousy? (See Isaiah 42:6; Romans 11:11.) It is time for us both to complete our roles so that Yeshua/Jesus can be glorified through His Body. This is the purpose of God's mercy now, to help prepare us for His coming.

The Reconnection brings greater *fullness* and greater *intimacy*. It begins to unveil the missing elements in the Body; it breaks off all known and unknown curses from the Body, which ultimately releases greater Kingdom power upon us (see Romans 11:12–15). The fullness of this element of intimacy has been lacking in the Church since it broke away from its Jewish roots and heritage because anyone who does not bless Israel is under a curse (see Genesis 12:3). This has been coupled with the residual negative influences left on the Church from the roots of Replacement Theology that still need to be removed so that the fullness of this intimacy can be restored with our Lord. The Holy Spirit has much more to give us as we move into this Reconciliation.

It's amusing to think of it in this light. But aren't Jews specifically called to be a light to the nations, and aren't Gentile believers specifically called to draw Jews to jealousy? (See Isaiah 42:6; Romans 11:11.) It is time for us both to complete our roles so that Yeshua/Jesus can be glorified through His Body.

> *"No longer will they teach their neighbor, or say to one another, 'Know the Lord,' because they will all know me, from the least to the greatest, declares the Lord"* (Jer. 31:31–34).

Through *The Reconnection*, we can expect this fullness to be released to us from the Father and for His Body to come into much greater intimacy than we have gotten used to in the past. I believe that both groups will come into a period of greater blessing through this union and that, at least for a while, we can enjoy unity, love, and harmony before the greater persecution comes from the world onto the Body of Messiah/Christ, Who will continue to stand for His Word and Truth.

WHAT CAN WE EXPECT THROUGH THE RECONNECTION?

Through *The Reconnection*, we can expect a much closer relationship with the Father and Yeshua/Jesus, and we will become more focused on the Holy Spirit and the power and presence of God. We can expect a much greater dependency on God through more focused and experiential worship and Spirit-led intercession; the natural outflow of this is a renewed interest in power evangelism and lifestyle witness to the lost. As Jewish believers who have embraced *The Reconnection*, we would have opened our hearts to the deeper healing and deliverance issues we need as a result of our Jewish heritage. The pain and suffering of thousands of years of rejection and hatred that have been passed through the generations have affected us, and we must become more open and transparent with our own weaknesses and vulnerabilities through our humanity.

We would have received a greater washing and cleansing from the Holy Spirit through His continued help and aid to strengthen us in these areas. And we will achieve a greater focus on the transformation in the inner man that only the Holy Spirit can bring in each of us to love God and serve one another.

Avner Boskey has written, "God will ultimately transform the whole dynamic of rejection for His beloved people Israel. He will usher in the most powerful move of His Holy Spirit the world has ever seen when Israel's rejection of Yeshua turns into Israel's acceptance of Yeshua."

Avner Boskey has written, "God will ultimately transform the whole dynamic of rejection for His beloved people Israel. He will usher in the most powerful move of His Holy Spirit the world has ever seen *when Israel's rejection of Yeshua turns into Israel's acceptance of Yeshua.*"

We can also look forward to a greater boldness and depth of spiritual character that was more akin to the apostles and the initial Jewish believers when the Church first began when we bring back the Gospel to our own Jewish friends and neighbors, along with the power of God that is supposed to accompany it. We can expect a renewed cooperation and collaboration from our Gentile family to help restore Israel and help finish the job. This is not just to first-fruit finances to help strengthen the Remnant of Israel, but also to offer spiritual support through worship and intercessory prayer in the land from the nations to help open the spiritual skies and fortify the front lines of the Church.

We can expect a greater lobby and support from the Church for the Remnant of Israel in accordance with 1 Corinthians 12:12–31 as the Church moves back into Alignment with its Jewish Remnant. *The needs of the Jewish-believing Body that are addressed in these Scriptures must come first before the rest of Israel.* We can also expect Jewish believers in the Church to be encouraged and shepherded into

Asher Intrater, the founder and leader of Revive Israel Ministries, wrote a book on this topic called Alignment, which I highly recommend. It is a wonderful follow-up on The Reconnection.

their Jewish identity, which will strengthen them into their calling.

Asher Intrater, the founder and leader of Revive Israel Ministries, wrote a book on this topic called *Alignment,* which I highly recommend. It is a wonderful follow-up on *The Reconnection.* As a Jewish believer with a prophetic background in the land, he has become a scholar of the Hebrew Word of God. His Messianic insights and depth of knowledge in these times of Reconnection and Alignment into the Body are strategic and offer us a renewed perspective from the Jewish branches.

Through *The Reconnection,* we can expect to move in greater love, tolerance, and patience for the Church and our Gentile family. We will be able to cross over in fellowship, in praise, and in worship with our Gentile family without any fear of assimilation. We will bless one another!

> *"Finally brothers and sisters, whatever is true, whatever is noble, whatever is right, whatever is pure, whatever is lovely, whatever is admirable—if anything is excellent or praiseworthy—think about such things"* (Phil. 4:8).

We can further expect to overcome some of our Messianic aversions to certain Christian terminology. I am not suggesting that we use them in our Jewish witness but rather that we become more accepting of Gentile practices when enjoying fellowship with them. Although we know many Christian terms have been misused against our people, we must come to understand that these terms are still near and dear to our Gentile-believing family, who earnestly love and seek our Lord. We need to allow the Blood of the Lamb to wash away past hurts and wounds so that we can have the freedom to flow throughout both sides of the *olive tree*.

It's not possible to anticipate every change and improvement that *The Reconnection* will bring, except to say that greater fullness and greater power can only bring greater love and greater fruit.

> *"This is to my Father's Glory that you bear much fruit, showing yourselves to be my disciples"* (John 15:8).

WE MUST COMMIT TO ONE ANOTHER AS TO MASHIACH/CHRIST

For this to take place on both sides, we need to make a firm commitment to one another. Will you be prayerful about this and make a decision to willingly move into *The Reconnection* and to love your Gentile-believing family as your very own?

In a healthy Jewish- and Gentile-believing environment, both Church and Messianic groups work together for the common good of the Body. Divided houses will not stand, but God's Body will. The fruit of this will transform His Body into the *Heart of the Father* and the love of His Son so that we will be empowered and made ready for His coming.

CHAPTER 9

THE RECONNECTION AND ITS APOSTOLIC FOUNDATIONS

OW THAT WE have addressed the greater obstacles to *The Reconnection* through the Messianic and Christian lens, let us also focus on the part of the American Church that has begun to recognize the different aspects of *The Reconnection* and is already beginning to move into it. This is happening through some notable ministries.

It is not my intention to be exhaustive here but rather to provide an outline of some of the major ministries and works of the Lord that are arising to help facilitate all that God is doing with His Kingdom on the Earth. To start with, five spiritual fathers among our Gentile family immediately come to mind in the Church whom I would like to honor. They have truly helped pioneer the *Heart of the Father* to help Reconnect Jews and Gentiles spiritually and to enable the Church to gain a better understanding concerning Israel and the salvation of the Jewish people.

SPIRITUAL FATHERS

The first, Derek Prince, has gone on to be with our Lord. He was used mightily to begin to break up the ground in this area. The remaining five men, Pastor Don Finto, Pastor Jack Hayford, Tom Hess, Pastor Olen Griffing, and Dr. Ray Gannon, are still very much blowing this shofar message given every opportunity available to them. They have all helped to establish ministries that are totally focused on Israel's salvation and *The Reconnection* between

Israel and the Church. And Tom Hess started the first prayer house in Israel (in Jerusalem). All these leaders have recognized the truth about God's Word concerning the Restoration of Israel and the Jewish people, shining the light of this message and demonstrating its love during a time when most did not understand it.

I pray that the God of Israel will continue to richly bless these wonderful leaders and their ministries, plus the many thousands of unknown intercessors in the Ekklesia/Church who have helped our Lord birth this movement among us. God knows you by name.

IT ALL STARTS WITH PRAYER!

Intercessors do not usually look for recognition. They are the most wonderful type of people, usually totally unassuming, and have often carried weaknesses in their own lives that God has used to shape them into His watchmen and women (see Isaiah 62:6–7). Without them, where would we be? These prayer warriors have helped pave the way through their cries and their prayers for Israel to come forth among many other issues in the Church and world. I always say that when I get to heaven, I want to be able to visit their houses, as I am sure they will be among some of the nicest residences there.

Although there has always been a Remnant of Jewish believers in the Church, from the time of Yeshua/Jesus until this modern day (see Romans 11:1–6), I believe the Remnant of Israel has been mirrored back into the Church with a Remnant of Gentile believers who have a deeper understanding and connection to Israel, which has come to them by revelation. These believers are usually prayer people because they are closer to the *Heart of God* through their day-to-day practices and intimacy with the King.

PRAYER SAINTS: RUTH AND CORNELIUS

To help with terminology, I often refer to these prayer saints as Ruths and Corneliuses because they have a great love and respect for Israel and the Jewish people, just as Ruth and Cornelius did in the Bible.

Like Israel, they are a Remnant, yet you can find them in almost every Bible-believing Church, despite the Church's differing eschatology. Just as Israel's Remnant is growing, so are Ruth and Cornelius. At some point during their walks and intimacy with the Lord, He has made known to them the significance of Israel in His end-time plan, and the Holy Spirit has supernaturally connected them with the whole *Israel Piece* of the puzzle.

> To help with terminology, I often refer to these prayer saints as Ruths and Corneliuses because they have a great love and respect for Israel and the Jewish people, just as Ruth and Cornelius did in the Bible.

In response, they have become advocates for Israel and are filled with a supernatural love for Israel and the Jewish people. They also have a strong belief that all Covenants toward the physical seed of Israel in Scripture still apply. During these days, these watchmen and watchwomen will play a significant role to help bring *The Reconnection* forth. I will address this issue more fully in the final part of the book.

We should pay both honor and respect to these watchmen and watchwomen and to their leaders, such as Tom Hess, founder of Jerusalem House of Prayer, and Rick and Patricia Ridings, founder of Succat Hallel, who have established prayer ministries in Jerusalem crying out for Israel's salvation. We can also look to Jane Hansen Hoyt, who heads up Aglow Ministries International and the thousands of intercessors alongside her in the United States and around the world. Her ministry has strongly encouraged prayer and intercession for Israel throughout the Church.

And what about those who have gone before us? They include the Puritans and the Pietists, Count Zinzendorf, Rees Howells, and numerous unnamed saints who heard the voice of the Lord concerning Israel. Let us give thanks for these intercessors and for their faithfulness.

LIKE THE WATERS OF A DAM

The receiving of *The Reconnection* message in the Church and Messianic bodies can be compared to the blowing up of a dam, as in the 1978 movie *Force 10 from Navarone*. Hardly anyone hears or sees the initial explosion. However, the little cracks it causes gradually begin to open. Then the pressure from the water builds up, and its weight begins to push against those cracks, breaking into the thick cement walls that are holding everything together. The first hole is seen on the face of the dam, and the water begins to spurt out into the valley below. The pressure continues to build, and soon after, the dam explodes, and all the water gushes out, destroying everything in its path.

The image of the dam breaking is a good one to compare to how the message of Reconnection is being received. It begins by spreading slowly, and then picks up pace as others learn of the message. Soon enough, many more know, and then there is an *explosion*. This is when the balance of God's sheep come into the fold, fully receiving *The Reconnection* message. This is the time; this is the hour!

Keep in mind that without the original pioneers who received God's Heart and vision for the reuniting of His family (and the numerous prayers and intercession that have gone up into the heavenlies), we would not be where we are today with regard to spreading this message. As we continue to blow *The Reconnection* shofar and fuel it with the prayers of the saints to help bring it forth, God's healing and cleansing are in the winds to properly reconcile His Body unto Himself.

APOSTOLIC FOUNDATIONS

As I write this chapter and begin to acknowledge some of the leaders in the Church who God is raising up for this purpose, there is a pattern between *The Reconnection* and its apostolic foundations that I would like to bring to your attention. I do not think it is a mistake or a coincidence that at the very same time this message of Reconnection is beginning to be trumpeted in the Church, so is the movement to reestablish its fivefold ministry focus. And isn't it interesting that both of these ministry foci came from the original apostolic roots and foundation that the Lord established for His Church when it first began?

I want to be totally honest with you in that I am an advocate for the reestablishment of the fivefold ministry. I am also aware that it has it flaws currently, and like anything new, it can have bugs that need to be fixed. I think it is true to say that as a Body, we are so young in this new expression that we all have a lot to learn. Pray to God that we will be teachable and correctable so we can receive and apply all that God is saying to us during this hour toward the full Restoration of His Holy Church on the Earth.

For the sake of unity, I would be foolish if I did not mention the current division that exists in the Church over the reemergence of the fivefold ministry and the controversy it is causing through counterfeits, self-promotion, fleshly associations, and the like. These issues need to be addressed, especially to help the rest of God's Body find this new direction, if they are willing. We should hear clearly from the other parts of the Body who are holding back and have reservations because of some of these challenges.

> *I do not think it is a mistake or a coincidence that at the very same time this message of Reconnection is beginning to be trumpeted in the Church, so is the movement to reestablish its fivefold ministry focus. And isn't it interesting that both of these ministry foci came from the original apostolic roots and foundation that the Lord established for His Church when it first began?*

Just like with *The Reconnection* in *TONM*, the greater Body of the Church and Messianic bodies need to enter a deeper place of dialogue to find understanding. And the same is true with the Apostle

Paul's teaching on the fivefold gifts of the Holy Spirit to equip the saints for the works of the ministry (see Ephesians 4:11-12). Most do not question these gifts, but rather how they are applied.

Some believers are moving forward in these gifts, some are holding back because of what they see, and some are in error. Perhaps the fivefold ministry focus is one of the most controversial issues of our day, even more so than *The Reconnection*. However, should we throw out the baby with the bath water? The use and application of these gifts from within the Body could be the very source that helps break us out of our slumber and rejuvenate the Body for much greater works.

Specifically, the current pastoral model for the local Church is not based on its original apostolic foundations but rather has its roots in a Greco/Roman model that changed the Church when Rome nationalized the faith. What is it that we are holding onto so dearly here? We are doing so even amid the current failings of the Church to more effectively reach the communities around it, or where so many pastors are burning out because far too much of the ministry burden is falling upon their shoulders.

I think sometimes God allows us to feel frustrated, perhaps when things are not working the way they should in reaching the world around us. God wants to break through these boundaries to more effectively impact the world with the Kingdom of God and to reach many more souls with salvation. The great question is, how can this be done?

Doesn't Scripture show us a different way, where the Church Body has been given certain gifts in the Holy Spirit to release the rest of us into the ministry and out of the pew? Can we at least look at the positives that the fivefold can bring to us before we totally condemn it? And doesn't discernment without love and prayer bring judgment if we misjudge it, which only continues to fuel the separation and division among us? As with other moves of God in the past, this could cause us to miss all that God is saying in this hour.

Instead, could we open up and engage in healthy dialogue and debate together as God's family to love one another and explore the possibilities that might lie ahead for us. As well as some of the adjustments needed with the fivefold ministry? As one who ascribes to the fivefold and to the pursuit of truth in its application, would you allow me to share some of my thoughts and insights in this area for us to consider? It is my hope that this door might be opened to fully contemplate God's plan for us during these days. I am not suggesting a political correctness here but rather a renewed unity in the Father's love for one another to be able to work through these differences—just like with *The Reconnection*. Nor am I suggesting that I see this Restoration in all of its fullness, but if God is in it, we have to start somewhere.

First, let us try to better define how fivefold gifts can *function*, as well as ways we may consider to overcome the *titling* and *flesh* that can be associated to the naming of an apostle and prophet. This is where I believe the greatest controversy exists. Then let's explore the *benefits* that the fivefold gifts can produce in us as a Body. Discussions and dialogue among ministry leaders could really help us try to resolve these significant issues, which are greatly needed in the Church at this time.

This could help us to find a way through these challenges and open the door for the greater Body of Messiah/Christ to re-embrace the fivefold gifts.

THE FUNCTION OF THE FIVEFOLD

Truth be told, I think there is a little bit of these gifts in each one of us, especially when we move out in some kind of ministry function. And I think it is important for us to understand that the fivefold gifts can operate at every level of Church ministry—in the local Church itself, in para-Church ministries, in cities and states, regionally, nationally, and even globally. The challenge for us in this place, however, is not so much with leaders from the local Church or even with itinerant ministries (although the local Church can definitely benefit from a greater fivefold focus, releasing the saints into a greater works of ministry and especially prayer), but rather with larger ministries and with leaders who are having a greater influence and wider reach in the Church as a whole.

Most of the time, these ministry leaders in cities and regions are already functioning in these gifts without necessarily being aware of it. But some are shy to move forward in a greater way because of the title issues, and I believe this is holding us back from our full potential in loosing the Kingdom of God all around us. Those who are moving in an apostolic or prophetic anointing should never be self-proclaimed (this is an error), but rather be recognized by those around them whom they serve. For the greatest, the Lord shared is the one who serves (see Matthew 23:11).

> Those who are moving in an apostolic or prophetic gifting should never be self-proclaimed (this is an error), but rather be recognized by those around them whom they serve. For the greatest, the Lord shared is the one who serves (see Matthew 23:11).

It is this area of ministry that I believe needs to change the most in our communities and regions. If we can help empower our local leaders in cities and regions, as well as better recognize the fivefold leaders with greater spheres of influence (national and global), then we can release them with more confidence to serve the Body of Messiah/Christ into their callings to empower the rest of us into the works of the ministry. Does that make sense?

I believe this is God's plan and His design for His Church: to release a greater element of power and authority over us—especially through the emerging praise and prayer movement to expand the reach of the Kingdom of God into our communities and regions under more of an apostolic and prophetic covering.

The great question however, is, how can this be achieved in light of the resistance to the naming and claiming issue of being an apostle and prophet coming from the greater Body of believers, while still encouraging those, who are called to this type of ministry gifting to serve the Body? I don't have all the answers here, but I would like to make a suggestion that may help in this regard.

Because the naming of an apostle or prophet is so controversial to many in the greater Ekklesia/Church, could we possibly consider not calling ourselves apostles or prophets, and instead refer to the actual gift, or anointing? For example, when asked, we could say that we are moving in an apostolic gifting, or a prophetic gifting, when serving the Body in a particular area, and only when the need may arise to communicate it, and stay away from any self-proclamations. Yet we will still move into the gifting and the office the Lord is calling us into, so we can more freely move into it. Those people the fivefold leaders are serving may be freer to use these terms when describing their particular leaders. And could those of us who are already moving in the fivefold ministry consider giving up the use of these terms for the sake of unity with the greater Body? I believe the key here is to be able to move the Body successfully into the fivefold ministry, so that apostolic and prophetic leaders can come together more effectively and get the job done for the Kingdom of God. This is what really counts, don't you think?

To be honest, I have had a change of heart in this place. I am very willing to give up the use of the terms to help the Body of Messiah/Christ more effectively move into it, if that is what it will take. And I think this can make the difference.

Plus, I think it is also true to say that if we can get this titling issue resolved, there also needs to be a greater cohesiveness between apostolic and prophetic leaders because there is a healthy balance of the Lord's Heart when these two types of giftings flow together. And there is a need for the apostolic leaders to more readily recognize and acknowledge prophetic leaders in our midst so they can work more effectively together.

There is some good food for thought and prayer here. For sure, we need to find a way through the objections so the Kingdom can be released through us in a greater way. Let's take a look at some of the benefits of the fivefold.

Art Katz was an American author and a prophetic Messianic preacher who traveled the world teaching an alternative to what he called today's "make nice" Christianity. He had much to say about this, especially focusing on moving the entire Body into it. His book, *Apostolic Foundations*, helps lay a healthy foundation for returning to our apostolic roots. He wrote that book for this purpose, and is a masterpiece on the subject, like a fine vintage wine.

As it stands, in my opinion, the old local Church model is still very much divided, with some of the stronger ones thinking that they can cover every possible ministry base without needing to have the rest of the Body necessarily come together. Plus, in this model, the saints are too *pew-bound*, leaving the greater works of the ministry to its leaders. This is more reflective of the old Covenant than the new one, and it counteracts this original model set up by the Lord and the Holy Spirit in Scripture for His Ekklesia/Church when it first began.

THE FIVEFOLD CAN MAKE THE DIFFERENCE WE NEED

I believe that for us to more effectively penetrate our communities, we first have to unite beyond the four walls of our Churches and Congregations. We need to understand that *our community focus* is just as important as our own. If we do this, the Holy Spirit can release a greater element of God's authority through us so that we can take the spiritual land where we live. This can be achieved through a renewed unity, a heightened worship, and a more heavenly type of intercession. Hence the reemergence of David's Tabernacle with its 24/7 praise and worship focus, which is becoming a vital part of

> I believe that for us to more effectively penetrate our communities, we first have to unite beyond the four walls of our Churches and Congregations. We need to understand that our community focus is just as important as our own. If we do this, the Holy Spirit can release a greater element of God's authority through us so that we can take the spiritual land where we live.

this Reformation, along with the *Strategic Intercession* that will also be needed.

These ministry foci can fit and flow well under the spiritual umbrella of the new apostolic eldership that God is raising up in this hour. They can release a greater measure of His authority beyond the local Church, to help it unite around their own communities. This should not replace the function of local eldership or deaconry for the local Church, which also has a biblical mandate, but rather be supplemental to it. In many cases, this is happening already in our local communities, where God is raising up new leaders for this purpose.

I know some of these leaders in my own area. But as we will hopefully see, the recognition of these giftings is important to improve structure and order among us and for His Body to ultimately work through the issues, which might be holding us back from the fullness of God's plans through us and the communities that we can help influ-

Generally speaking, the apostles have the vision to build and implement, while the prophets can help see the issues that might surround it. The evangelist mobilizes the Body into witness and evangelism, the pastor shepherds believers, and the teacher equips and teaches the Body.

ence. If we can come into a greater understanding of how we recognize these leaders and how the local structure can be implemented in tandem with the local Church, this could help dramatically to open this door and resolve some of these challenges. Our love and unity with one another are crucial elements here, and Church leadership can play a strategic role in how this happens while also bringing greater organization to the Kingdom of God.

Right now, God is raising up new leaders. Some are local, some are regional or national, and some can have a global impact to help more fully activate God's family into the greater works of the ministry. *This is the function of the fivefold:* to equip and release the rest of the Body into the works of the Kingdom instead of leaders trying to do it for us. Their giftings should not only be seen but also witnessed and recognized by those around them, to serve the Church and Messianic bodies. Some of them are moving in an apostolic gifting, some of them are moving in a prophetic gifting, and some of them are moving in both. It is healthy for the Body when these leaders work together and with others. Generally speaking, the apostles have the vision to build and implement, while the prophets can help see the issues that might surround it. The evangelist mobilizes the Body into witness and evangelism, the pastor shepherds believers, and the teacher equips and teaches the Body. These leaders can possess different skills from within the fivefold context, but one will likely be more dominant than the others.

Similarly, these gifts can also be witnessed and experienced by the rest of us, those being mobilized into the works of ministry. Some can be apostolic in establishing new types of works; others can be more prophetic in their gifts through prayer and healing ministries; and still others can have teaching, evangelistic, and other types of nurturing gifts, similar to that of a pastor. The fivefold gifts are seen and reflected at every level of ministry.

A couple of years ago, I listened to a teaching by Peter Wagner, who was one of the modern day pioneers for the fivefold ministry. I am aware that Peter Wagner has been one of more controversial personalities in the Church because of what he believed and taught on the fivefold ministry, but being human, we often learn the most through trial and error. In this light, I am extremely grateful for the revelation that came through him; he pushed the envelope in this most significant area of ministry for the rest of us.

In this particular teaching, he taught about the differences between a Church and an apostolic center.[16] It was a brilliant dissertation and very empowering to all those present because it pointed out differences between the two models and how they might work together. Could it be in this day that God wants to bless both approaches? New ideas and leadership can bring the two together and create greater unity in the community.

Let us work to find ways through the obstacles and resistances to the fivefold ministry and create a healthy balance in some of the more delicate areas. There is an order here, providing it is processed in the correct manner, without it going to people's heads, which is obviously key. I think we will be amazed at the transformation that it will help bring to God's Ekklesia/Church and all He wants to do during these days. In my mind, this is worth fighting for.

Apostolic and prophetic leaders must act humbly and give up their rights to those they serve. The Heart of Mashiach/Christ holds that the greatest would be the servant. We should always act in service to others, for it is the will of God! For this reason, I have created a new word for this purpose to better describe this new type of leadership: "servitudel"—it should come before anything else.

Asher Intrater, who heads up the Tikkun Global Ministries (a Messianic network of ministries moving in the fivefold gifts), along with Dr. Daniel Juster and Eitan Shishkoff, puts it this way:

> The structure of the five-fold ministry is similar to that of marriage. In a marriage each person is individually called to submit to the Lord; then they are called to submit to one another; then the wife is called to submit to her husband; and the husband is called to give up his rights for his wife. (See Ephesians 5:21–33.)

There is a healthy order that brings life and sustenance to the marriage. I think the same can be true of the fivefold, which God has put in place to bring greater order and direction to His Body. However, it is important to note here that the husband is called to give up his rights for his wife, which is also the call of the apostle, the prophet, and the other fivefold leaders. They must act humbly and give up their rights to those they serve. The Heart of Mashiach/Christ holds that the greatest would be the servant. We should always act in service to others, for it is the will of God! For this reason, I have created a new word for this purpose to better describe this new type of leadership: "servitudel"—it should come before anything else.

Similarly, Chuck Pierce, who heads Glory of Zion International Ministries, describes the fivefold in this manner:

> The Bible compares members of the Body of Christ to the organs of a human Body. The human Body has many organs, each with its own function, and every organ is important. But certain organs, like the brain and the heart, are called vital organs. The other organs cannot live without these.
>
> In the same way God has placed many gifts in the Body of Christ. All the gifts are important, but the fivefold gifts are like vital organs. Their purpose is to create an environment where the other gifts are able to thrive. Where fivefold ministry is established, the whole Body is built up, and all the members are equipped to fulfill their destiny. (*The Apostolic Church Arising* — Pierce, 100)

Simply put, these men and women are called to serve the rest of us, yet with a great sacrifice. They are not lording over us in a way that is counterfeit. They are speaking the message Yeshua/Jesus taught. It is the upside/downside/right-side revelation that Yeshua/Jesus taught His apostles regarding leadership that true apostolic and prophetic leadership are called toward. *The challenge is how to implement this in the healthiest way possible.* This will be difficult without further debate and dialogue, as we have discussed.

Everyone seems to be used to the terms "Pastor," "Teacher," or "Bishop," and in the Messianic community, the term "Rabbi." Even "Evangelist" is OK, but the moment we get close to recognizing apostolic and prophetic leadership, it immediately gets controversial. But can we not start to judge our leadership by their fruit? (see Matthew 7:15–16; 2 Peter 2:1). We have been warned about false apostles and prophets, *but what about legitimate ones?*

This is especially true if we can remove the fleshly and ego associations to moving in these giftings. However, if they are moving in these types of gifts to help empower the Church, why can't we encourage them into it? Wouldn't it be more fruitful to bless them and strengthen them in their calling?

Should we ignore this recognition, in light of the challenges it presents? Or, in ignoring it, would we be diluting its effectiveness? Should we refrain from calling the husband the head of the household because he might not be able to handle it? No, we should encourage him into all humility and in the priestly role he is called to. Isn't it the same with apostolic and prophetic gifts?" This is especially true if we can remove the fleshly and ego associations to moving in these giftings. We should encourage them in their service and correct them when they are out of line. Like the husband, if it has gone to his head or his ego, and he is lording it over his wife by misunderstanding his calling, we would help bring correction to set them back on the path. But we wouldn't eliminate his role or calling in the process; rather, we would uphold it. The marriage analogy has several unique implications in this regard.

IT DIDN'T FINISH WITH THE TWELVE APOSTLES

Isn't it also evident from Scripture that there were additional apostles and prophets aside from the ones Yeshua/Jesus anointed? What about James, Jesus's brother (see 1 Corinthians 15:7) or the Apostle Paul and the prophets in Antioch (see Acts 13:1), or Andronicus and Junia (a woman) in Rome (see Romans 16:7)? I believe these leadership roles are at the heart of *The Reconnection* to our Jewish roots, and this is exactly how the Ekklesia/Church operated in the first century. At that time, the Church transformed the world.

> *"He gave some as apostles, and some as prophets, and some as evangelists, and some as pastors and teachers, for the equipping of the saints for the work of service, to the building up of the Body of* Messiah/Christ" (Eph. 4:11–12 NASB).

This did not end with the super-apostles but rather created governing eldership in the Ekklesia/Church that would oversee God's work on the Earth. I believe apostolic and prophetic leaders are vital to the Body of Messiah/Christ because it is usually through these leaders that new works for the Kingdom of God are established. From within the context of their servitude in the Spirit, they provide vision and the platform for the rest of the Church Body to act on.

I respectfully submit that the reestablishment of the fivefold and *The Reconnection* are a necessary part of the end-time Church's Reformation to move His Body into the roles He has planned for us in these days. Please prayerfully consider what I have written and the great need for Church and Messianic leadership to enter into deeper dialogue to address these issues.

A NEW WINESKIN, A NEW STRUCTURE

I also believe during this time the Lord is bringing us into a *new wineskin* (speaking metaphorically toward a renewed structure), to help restore His Ekklesia/Church. Perhaps some of the solutions and corrections to the current fivefold framework and the divisions among us might actually be found as we discover the fullness of our Jewish roots and the love and unity it releases. Could it be that, as we look to heal and restore the first division and separation in the Ekklesia/Church, we will naturally find healing and Restoration for the other parts of the Ekklesia/Church?

> *I also believe during this time the Lord is bringing us into a new wineskin (speaking metaphorically toward a renewed structure), to help restore His Ekklesia/Church.*

As we move into this final age for His Kingdom to come upon the Earth, I believe the Lord wants to move us back into the patterns He designed for His Ekklesia/Church through *The Reconnection* and its apostolic foundations. If I am correct, I don't think we can experience all that the new wineskin has to offer without embracing the fullness of its structure. It is God's design to pour into us His love, His mercy, His order, His authority, and His power.

If we can recognize and accept that the application of the fivefold gifts are for us today as in times past, then can we make more of an earnest effort to find a greater balance in how they are applied? Change is needed not only corporately in how the Ekklesia/Church functions, but also individually in how we actuate it out of the Church age into the Kingdom age.

MY PERSONAL EXPERIENCE IN THE FIVEFOLD

My own personal experience in the fivefold has been healthy. I learned early on in my faith that spiritual covering is significant and that God can do more through us if we submit to His leadership and counsel.

As the Lord moved me into a greater ministry focus with *The Reconnection*, I naturally sought out godly counsel, support, and spiritual covering beyond my ministry board. However, because my ministry focus is to both parts of the Body, Yeshua/Jesus led me to have two spiritual associations in the fivefold: a Messianic association through Dr. Daniel Juster of Tikkun Global Ministries and a Church association through Che Ahn of Harvest International Ministries (HIM).

I informed each of them of the two associations, and they immediately accepted and embraced one another in light of my focus. I can tell you quite plainly that since that time, I have never been forced or directed into anything. On the contrary, all I have ever received from both apostolic leaders has been love, godly counsel, encouragement, and empowerment to minister the assignments the Lord has given to me to help our family Reconnect in *TONM*. I have also felt safer with these spiritual coverings over me under our Lord. It just feels right in my spirit.

GOOD BOOKS ON THE FIVEFOLD

I am not claiming to be an expert on this subject, like many of these new leaders God is raising up with the fivefold vision, but I do want to raise the issue for greater consideration. Some really good books have already been written on the fivefold that I highly recommend, such as *Apostolic Foundations* by Arthur Katz, which I already mentioned, and *The Apostolic Church Arising* by Chuck D. Pierce and Robert Heidler. Other great reads include *Rediscovering Apostles and Prophets* by Doug Beacham, *The Five Fingers of God* by Mark Tubbs, *5Q: Reactivating the Original Intelligence and Capacity of the Body of Christ* by Alan Hirsch, *Apostles Today,* and other teachings on this subject by Peter Wagner.

THE TWO ARE LINKED

In my mind, both *The Reconnection* and the fivefold require God's Ekklesia/Church to reform so these principles can be received and applied. However, it is also important to note that both ministry foci came out of and from the founding apostles and authority of the Ekklesai/Church that Mashiach/Christ Himself established. In fact, I believe *The Reconnection* is at the very heart of the fivefold ministry focus, as it was in the beginning of the Ekklesia/Church. The two should actually go hand in hand in *TONM*.

As I was studying this issue for the book, I was sharing my heart with Rabbi Marty Waldman, who leads the Toward Jerusalem Council 2 initiative. He suggested Dr. Doug Beacham's book, *Rediscovering the Role of Apostles and Prophets*. Dr. Beacham serves as the general superintendent of the International Pentecostal Holiness Church and is also a board member of TJC2.

Not only is his work on the fivefold notable, but He is one of the first Christian theologians I am aware of who fully recognizes the great significance of *The Reconnection* between Jew and Gentile in *TONM*, as it relates to the fullness of the fivefold ministry. My jaw dropped, my heart melted, and my eyes welled up with tears as I read some of his comments in his book:

This fundamental unity of all things of, in, and through Christ is exhibited in the divine plan to heal the division between Jew and Gentile. In Ephesians 2:11–19, Paul emphasized how Christ has reconciled Jew and Gentile to God, "in one Body through the cross, thereby putting to death the enmity" (2:16). "Through Christ Jews and Gentiles have access by one Spirit to the Father" (2:18). Because of the revelation of this mystery of uniting Jew and Gentile into one Body, the Body of Christ, those who believe are "*fellow citizens with the saints* (Jewish believers—emphasis added) and members of the household of God" (2:19).

This new humanity and "household of God" is built on the foundations of the apostles and prophets, Jesus Christ Himself being the chief cornerstone, in whom the whole building, being fitted together, grows into a holy temple in the Lord, in whom you are also being built together for a dwelling place of God in the Spirit (see Ephesians 2:20–22).

In the Gospel, Paul understood that the death of Jesus was God's way of restoring Jew and Gentile to the Covenant promises of God to Abraham. Paul had received "revelation" of God's "mystery" (divine promises hidden in the death and resurrection of Jesus), "which in other ages was not made known to the sons of men, as it has now been revealed by the Spirit to His holy apostles and prophets: that the Gentiles should be fellow heirs, of the same Body, and partakers of His promise in Christ through the Gospel" (see Ephesians 3:3, 5–6).

I am convinced that this dimension of the Gospel has yet to be fully appreciated. One of satan's most successful ploys has been antisemitism, which has rendered the Church impotent in relation to Jews. The world has repeatedly witnessed the demonstration of this spirit that has weakened the Church's influence and power.

Apostolic and prophetic ministry has a theological dimension related to the revelation of this mystery. Apostles and prophets are foundational and revelatory regarding healing the rifts between Jews and Gentiles. Paul was convinced that the primary role of apostles and prophets is to proclaim the unity of Jew and Gentile in Christ and live in such anointing and power that both would leave their prejudices and differences covered in the blood of Christ.... "With Christ as the 'cornerstone' (that is, the stone which is the strength and source of measurement), 'the whole building [of Jew and Gentile], being joined together, grows [present tense meaning continue to grow] into a holy temple' (Ephesians 3:20, the inner sanctuary of the temple, implying a growing in intimacy with Christ). This understanding of the Gospel builds a dwelling place in the Spirit for God's presence.

What a strong discourse on the fivefold related to the Remnant of Israel and the Jewish people and our Reconnection toward them! If we carried Dr. Beacham's revelation and understanding of Yeshua/Jesus's Heart within us, how long would it take for us to truly get all this right?

As we know, this portion of Christ's work continues. Gentiles have not lived in the fullness of Christ's riches in Glory and have forfeited their primary evangelism tool to the Jews. The 'dwelling place in the Spirit' is a two-thousand-year-old construction project that has often been delayed because the Church fails to build on the foundation of the apostles and prophets.

This is the heart cry of the Spirit for the Body of Christ in the twenty-first century. Not only is the Church to rediscover apostles and prophets, but such persons are to understand the depth and expanse of their ministry. This new discovery of apostles and prophets is not about new Church order or even Reformation, or even a Reformation of the Church. It is about the Church's being fully released in power through living in the fullness of the Spirit. There is an eschatological and evangelistic imperative that relates to Jews and Gentiles behind the Spirit's beckoning the Church in this day… *"The public Restoration of apostle and prophets should repudiate this religion and beckon the Church to the promise of Reconciliation between Jew and Gentile, and Gentile and Gentile."*

Second, Paul's Churches understood the theological necessity of living in the fullness of the Holy Spirit. It was a necessity demanded by eschatological and evangelical imperatives related to the salvation of the Jews. The emerging Gentile Church lost much of this imperative and failed to comprehend the original function of the apostolic and prophetic ministries as well as the other ministries that remained actively identified in the following centuries.

Taking the Gospel to the ends of the Earth, a Christ given, Christ-inspired, and Christ-directed mandate, is ultimately not separate from the divine plan regarding the fulfillment of divine plans related to the Jews.

In the next chapter we will look at apostles and prophets within the context of Ephesians 4:1-16. But that examination must not be made in isolation from the theological imperatives evidenced in this chapter, especially the all-important issue of God's redemptive purposes related to Israel. (Beacham, 104,105,107,108)

What a strong discourse on the fivefold related to the Remnant of Israel and the Jewish people and our Reconnection toward them! If we carried Dr. Beacham's revelation and understanding of Yeshua/Jesus's Heart within us, how long would it take for us to truly get all this right?

NEGATIVES OF THE FIVEFOLD

Will there be false apostles and prophets? And can the flesh and ego of titles and self-promotion get in the way of this new move of the Holy Spirit and all that God wants to do with it? Absolutely, but equally damaging is taking a position against it because of these issues if they are holding us back from it. But let us not look at this criticism in such a negative light that shuts us down from addressing it. Rather, we should use it to expose the enemy and any flesh among us. We must also use it to help all those called to find the fullness of their gifting with all humility and love.

Let us not forget John's and James's request to sit at the Lord's side. Yeshua's response was, *"Can you drink the measure of the cup or the baptism?"* One has to be called of God to operate in these gifts at different levels of ministry, and if not, look out; we are asking for a whipping! I think John's and James's request tied into the fivefold leads one to a certain soberness concerning callings and gifts. In fact, to operate as lead apostles and prophets is a huge responsibility and should never be taken lightly. To whom much is given, much is expected (see Luke 12:48). Need I remind you of the seven sons of Sceva? (See Acts 19:13–16.)

I often think of the fivefold gifts in ministry terms in the sense that apostolic and prophetic leaders can be like majors, colonels, or even generals. I, however, could not be a general if I were not called and trained to be one, could I?

In my former life, as an entrepreneur and business founder with a lot of responsibility in the business world and having hundreds of people to manage and oversee, I can relate to a similar burden of leadership. I would not want to be in this position if I were not called to be. In this light, Church leadership is in great need of our prayer and support.

What is more important to me is to be faithful to what God has called me to and not to the quantity of cities or coins, as in the parables, but rather to be faithful to the call and to recognize it contextually as it relates to the Body, which is made up of many parts.

I am not to vie for something beyond that which I have been given because this is sometimes what can cause others to attempt to move into positions that may not have been designed for them. We call this "selfish ambition," and it is not honorable. It can be dangerous and produce the wrong results for the Body. Selfish ambition is of the flesh. True apostolic and prophetic leaders at any level are not only called but also trained individually by the Holy Spirit through their own life experiences to prepare them for these equipping roles.

THE FLESH AND THE SPIRIT

I think it is true to say that wherever the Spirit is, the flesh is not far behind, nor the devil to stir it up. This is one of the greatest struggles of our common humanity as believers, and we will be dealing with the flesh and the enemy until we leave our bodies.

Yeshua/Jesus gave us a great example of this with His beloved Peter. Literally in the same discussion, Peter claims Yeshua/Jesus to be God's Son. And for this he receives a commendation from the Lord, but then moments later he is being rebuked for moving in the flesh, wanting to prevent the cross in Yeshua/Jesus's life (see Matthew 16:13–23).

This text shows how easy it is for me to be in the Spirit and then in the flesh. And how readily the enemy looks to pounce on heavenly revelation with some kind of confusion and error. We need to be more aware of this and how the enemy works against us. But we also have to have the humility to be able to recognize it. The same could be said of us moving in our spiritual gifts, which can also get out of hand. However, do we discount them as a result of a negative experience; or rather, do we bring these experiences fully into the light to learn from them, to test the spirit, so order can follow?

Are not the gifts of the prophets subject to the prophets? God is not a God of disorder but of peace (see 1 Corinthians 14:32). And didn't the first-century Church find a way through these issues?

Another area in the fivefold that always needs to be watched is the balance we have in it. It is supposed to be a cohesive working of all five gifts operating hand in hand to complement one another, even though the apostle and prophet focus should be foundational to it. This applies more to our local and regional expressions of the fivefold ministry than to national and global foci. However, our focus on the apostle and prophet can sometimes get out of hand, especially as the Body that is immersed in it (which is not always anchored in Mashiach/Christ as it needs to be) is focusing on and running after the prophetic more than it should. I think the area that is affected the most by this is the gift of evangelism, which has obviously taken a backseat to the apostolic and prophetic giftings in the charismatic movement. Let us pray for the gift of evangelism to be fully reestablished within the context of the fivefold ministry and for greater balance to be maintained overall.

I think we could profit by being more honest with ourselves in this place because title, self-promotion, and being out of balance are issues for us to deal with as the fivefold emerges. Plus, if it is holding others back who might more readily embrace the fivefold if some of these issues were more effectively dealt with, then without question we should be addressing it. There is a greater transparency that must prevail here to help break down other barriers for the balance of our family. Those of us who are already in the movement can help to play a role in bringing this to pass.

In our love for one another and Yeshua's Heart for us to be united, let us bring these issues fully into the light through prayer and intercession, and honest and open dialogue. Let us develop good and healthy teachings that fully expose the frailties and weaknesses of the fivefold movement to equip us with the right godly character to be able to walk in these places of leadership with all humility and deference.

Let us never forget that the apostles and prophets were written into the foundations of the Ekklesia/Church. Their character and leadership in Mashiach/Christ was not to be as the Gentiles acted but in servitude to others (see Matthew 20:25–29), as I have already emphasized.

In our love for one another and Yeshua/Jesus's Heart for us to be united, let us bring these issues fully into the light through prayer and intercession, and honest and open dialogue. Let us develop good and healthy teachings that fully expose the frailties and weaknesses of the fivefold movement to equip us with the right godly character to be able to walk in these places of leadership with all humility and deference.

On this note, there is a wonderful teaching in Chuck Pierce's and Robert Heidler's book, *The Apostolic Church Arising,* on the marks of an apostle, which Robert's wife, Linda, also contributed to (Heidler, chapter 9). This chapter lays out ten points that define this type of humility and servitude. Alan Hirsch's book on the fivefold, 5Q, also does a good job on emphasizing these "servitudel" qualities.

There is no lording it over here, but rather a divine order to bring health and greater power to God's Body and family. Through His love and grace, we can become more open to the full movement of the Holy Spirit and recognize all He is doing at this time to equip His Ekklesia/Church for what will be the greatest hour on Earth prior to the Lord's return.

If God is behind this Restoration and it is His way and His plan to release a greater element of order and authority among His Body to reach a lost and dying world, then who are we to challenge it? Rather, let us be constructive and focus our time and efforts on possible solutions to the obstacles and challenges that are arising as a result of it. Let us find a way through that can bring more order and more peace to this most significant ministry focus to equip the Body for greater Kingdom works.

I leave you with one last thought concerning the controversy that exists with fivefold ministry. Without a doubt, it is the most important one. *If God is behind this Restoration and it is His way and His plan to release a greater element of order and authority among His Body to reach a lost and dying world, then who are we to challenge it?* Rather, let us be constructive and focus our time and efforts on possible solutions to the obstacles and challenges that are arising as a result of it. Let us find a way through that can bring more order and more peace to this most significant ministry focus to equip the Body for greater Kingdom works.

THE APOSTOLIC CHURCH ARISING

Having said that, and reviewing this arising apostolic movement, an interesting pattern can be seen emerging through the differences in the ministry foci. It is as if God has given each group a different piece of *The Reconnection* and the fivefold gifts to bring forth for Israel and the Church.

Although each of these ministries already carries a deeper understanding of *The Reconnection* between the Jew and Gentile in *TONM* and Israel and the Church (especially with their individual ministry foci), it is important to note that God's hand and blessing are upon them. Their ministries have not only been raised up within the past twenty years, but they are mightily blessed because the *Israel Piece* is center and foremost in most of their ministry foci (see Genesis 12:3).

> Reviewing this arising apostolic movement, an interesting pattern can be seen emerging through the differences in the ministry foci. It is as if God has given each group a different piece of The Reconnection and the fivefold gifts to bring forth for Israel and the Church.

FIVEFOLD PATTERNS IN THE CHURCH

As I lay out this pattern and example in the American Church, please understand that most of these leaders are apostolic in their own right (many have a global influence), yet they are moving in a particular focus in *The Reconnection* and the fivefold that I would like to bring your attention to. In fact, this can be seen among both groups of leaders in the olive tree, Jewish and Gentile alike. I will begin with discussion of the Gentile leadership.

Please note that the apostolic flow that is described below is not necessarily in the same order as Scripture. I believe this movement was born first through prayer and intercession, which has a natural connection to the prophetic ministry focus in the fivefold.

PROPHETIC INTERCESSION

On May 7, 1999, Mike Bickle and twenty full-time intercessory missionaries founded the International House of Prayer (IHOP) of Kansas City. This ministry, which is centered on raising up houses of worship and prayer in the spirit of the tabernacle of David, is doing a phenomenal job of laying down the foundation in the Church for Israel's salvation and the last great outpouring of the Holy Spirit throughout the nations. This is happening in the United States and around the world. Mike Bickle often speaks about God raising up *one hundred million intercessors* specifically for this purpose. IHOP KC just completed 21 years of 24/7 prayer. This is a remarkable achievement for the Glory of God.

More recently, Daniel Lim became CEO of IHOPKC to assist Mike in the overall management of the International House of Prayer. Daniel Lim has also written the foreword for the *Romans 911 Study Guide*.

PROPHETIC MINISTRY

For the past twenty years, Chuck Pierce has been blowing a prophetic shofar into the Body of Messiah/Christ concerning Israel and the Church. He has been given deep understanding of *TONM* and trumpets its message at the core of the fivefold movement and Restoration in Yeshua/Jesus's Church. He founded the Glory of Zion Ministries specifically for this purpose, and from it is emerging new and powerful teachings to train the Ekklesia/Church and its leadership in a whole new prophetic manner connected to its Jewish roots that is beginning to change the way in which we operate in the Spirit. There is a dunamis (power) on his ministry that is catching like wildfire. Robert Heidler, an apostolic teacher, who wrote *The Messianic Church Arising* and *The Apostolic Church Arising* with Chuck Pierce, is also connected with Glory of Zion Ministries and teaches extensively on Israel and the Ekklesia/Church.

David Damien, an Egyptian believer living in Canada, has been given a call of the Lord to help prepare the Bride for the Lord's coming. He carries a special burden of Yeshua's Heart of love and unity in the family of God according to John 17. He has been working tirelessly to help reunite the Body of Messiah/Christ into a global prayer movement through his Watchmen for the Nations ministry focus. More recently he has connected closely with Asher Intrater from Tikkun Global Ministries to Reconnect and Realign in *TONM*, and to promote this special bond throughout the nations.

James Goll, who was part of the IHOP movement when it started, has also been a prophetic voice and trumpet for Israel's Restoration in the Church. He has written a number of books on the subject, too. The Holy Spirit has used James to bring forth *Strategic Intercession* for Israel and the Church through identificational repentance. (See the "James Goll" reference in the Appendix.)

More recently, as apostolic and prophetic leadership is moving into this Restoration in the family of God, Lou Engle from *The Call* has been calling for greater fasting and prayer for Israel and the Church. In the spring of 2021, Lou called the Ekklesia/Church into the "Yeshua Fast," foundationally on prayer for Israel and the Jewish people. His ministry has also started a virtual house of prayer for Israel's salvation.

Cindy Jacobs and Heidi Baker, who have strong prophetic voices in the fivefold movement, are also very focused on Israel and the Church and unity in *TONM*.

PASTORAL FOCUS

Pastor Robert Morris is the founding pastor of Gateway Church in Dallas, which he started in 2000. It is now the fourth-largest Church in the United States. When asking the Lord why He had blessed him so much, God answered him, saying, "It is because you are giving your first fruits to Israel." Gateway Church understands that the Remnant of Israel must come first when wanting to bless Israel because it is part of our family and God's Body (see 1 Corinthians 12:12–27). Gateway Church is also one of the first Gentile Churches in the United States to establish a separate meeting focus for Jewish believers to encourage them in their identity, much akin to the dual-expression ministry I described in earlier chapters.

Pastor Wayne Hilsden, who cofounded King of Kings in Jerusalem, is another such leader with vision in *TONM* from the Gentile apostolic side of the family. Through the Holy Spirit's guidance, he has developed a number of other Jewish-based ministries such as One for Israel, described in the media segment, and FIRM (Fellowship of Israel Related Ministries), which is a new ministry Wayne founded to help the Church connect to and bless Israel.

TEACHING MINISTRY

The Messianic Bible Institute was established by Jewish and Gentile leadership in the Church and is training leaders to shepherd Jewish believers and Messianic Gentiles in the Church. The Institute was founded by Jonathan Bernis, Olen Griffing, Daniel Juster, David Rudolf, Roger West, Mike Becker, and a number of other apostolic Gentile leaders who have helped establish this ministry. They include Dr. Wayne Wilkes, Jr., Pastor David McQueen, and Dr. Ray Gannon. There are now schools in Ukraine, Ethiopia, Zimbabwe, and the United States. MJIB also established a graduate-school program with King's University in Dallas, Texas.

Tod McDowell, who is Don Finto's spiritual son, heads up Caleb Global Ministries, which is specifically training new leaders into

The Reconnection and fivefold gifts. Tod has a prophetic gifting and teaching ministry in *TONM*.

MORE RECENTLY

More recently, Paul Wilbur and Stovall Weems have formed an alliance in *TONM*. Stovall Weems is Pastor of Celebration Church in Jacksonville, FL, who had a personal encounter with Yeshua/Jesus while Paul Wilbur was connecting the Communion service to the Passover. And literally, within minutes, Pastor Weems was spiritually Reconnected in *TONM*. What a fantastic story, and I think we can expect more experiences like this, as the prayer intensifies for *The Reconnection* and *Alignment* message. You can view Stovall's testimony with Paul Wibur of this experience on Sid Roth. (https://youtu.be/MlO876wKaWc)

THE FIVEFOLD IS EMERGING

Several fivefold leaders are working tirelessly to bring forth this mission (see Ephesians 4:11–13). Che Ahn of Harvest International Ministries (HIM), Bill Johnson of Bethel Church, Rick Joyner of Morning Star Church, and Randy Clark are leading expansive ministries to further establish the fivefold gifts—not just in the United States, but also globally. You might be surprised to hear that this section of the Church is showing far greater growth patterns than the rest of the Church. Plus, Robert Sterns of Eagle Wings Ministry is blazing the trail to help the Church Reconnect to Israel in the political and humanitarian realms.

Through Che Ahn's apostolic gifting and network, upwards of thirty thousand Churches in more than seventy nations worldwide are associated with the HIM organization. This is happening because the children of God are being equipped and released into their divine ministry foci that the Lord has given them. They are feeling empowered by this, and it is releasing them into the greater works of the ministry. *I can tell you firsthand that the main focus of all of these leaders is to aid the Holy Spirit to equip the saints for the works of the ministry.*

In 2013, Che Ahn of HIM and Dr. Daniel Juster and Eitan Shishkoff of Tikkun Global Ministries, along with me (Reconnecting Ministries), signed a historical document in Nazareth, Israel, where Yeshua/Jesus started His ministry. *The Reconnecting Ministry Commission Document*[17] is the first of its kind in the Ekklesia/Church to unite both Jewish and Gentile believers into the fullness of *TONM* and to invite the necessary healing and ministry focus to help bring this about in the Body of Messiah/Christ.

> The Reconnecting Ministry Commission Document is the first of its kind in the Ekklesia/Church to unite both Jewish and Gentile believers into the fullness of TONM and to invite the necessary healing and ministry focus to help bring this about in the Body of Messiah/Christ.

Brad Long, who heads up PRMI (Presbyterian Reformed Ministries International), has also been blazing the trail for Church reform and has connected with Tikkun Ministries in strengthening ONM relationships. Brad has also created *The Dunamis Project*, which is one of the most thorough teaching series I have ever seen or experienced learning about and embracing the gifts of the Holy Spirit. Brad and the PRMI team are also leading the Body out in greater prayer revelation for deeper types of intercession.

MINISTRY OF EVANGELISM

Simply put, the official ministry focus of evangelism for *The Reconnection* is not recognized because the Church is not yet evangelizing the Jewish people as it should, because of the disconnection. And there are currently only a few Christian ministries operating in this most crucial area, however; evangelism and lifestyle witness are obviously greatly needed to win the Jewish people back into the faith. *It must come out of a transformed heart and a willingness and love in the Christian Body to want to fulfill the Gentile call to reach the Jewish people* (see Romans 11). A corrected and Realigned heart toward Israel, coupled with the waves of intercession going up to the heavens for Israel's salvation from the Church, will produce a natural outflow of evangelism and witness that will change the world forever.

Here are a couple of Reconnected reality quotes from Sid Roth for the Body of Messiah/Christ: "If we want more Gentiles saved, reach out to the Jews!" and "To the Jew first opens up to more Gentiles."

FIVEFOLD PATTERN IN THE MESSIANIC MOVEMENT

Before I begin to address the fivefold on the Messianic side, let me just say that it has emerged slowly. At this point, most Messianic leaders are not nearly as well known as Church leaders. Again, many of these leaders are apostolic in their own right, but my main emphasis here is their lead ministry focus.

APOSTOLIC

No one has carried this burden of Reconnection in *TONM* more than Dr. Daniel Juster. As a Jewish believer, he is one of the founding fathers of Messianic Judaism. Dan has become a master theologian in the Messianic area and has a great love for the Church. He was also one of the founders of the UMJC (Union of Messianic Jewish Congregations), an organization that helps organize and coordinate the Messianic Movement.

More recently in the past several years, Dan formed Tikkun Global Ministries, led by Asher Intrater and Eitan Shiskoff—the first fivefold apostolic network in the Messianic Movement. Dan also cofounded the Toward Jerusalem Council 2 (TJCII), which is a new group of both Jewish and Gentile leaders to unite Israel and the Church. In addition, Dan helped found the Messianic Bible Institute with Rabbi Jonathan Bernis from Jewish Voice.

Rabbi Jonathan Bernis is also moving in an apostolic gifting. Jonathan not only heads up Jewish Voice Ministries; he is actively involved in moving the Messianic Movement forward in all areas of growth. Jonathan was a key founder of Messianic Jewish Congregational movements in several countries. He is also involved in a number of other organizations that are promoting greater understanding between Israel and the Church, such as FIRM, a new ministry founded by Wayne Hilsden to see Churches partner with the Messianic Jewish movement. Jonathan has also recently started Heritage with Troy Wallace in Los Angeles, CA, which is a a One New Man-focused body between Jews and Gentiles.

Dr. Mitch Glaser, who leads Chosen People Ministries, is also moving in an apostolic gifting. Through his leadership, Chosen People has established local ministries in sixteen countries across the world, in more heavily Jewish populated areas. Their focus is to reach Jewish people with the Gospel, to equip believers in this area, and to help plant local Congregations and outreach ministries.

PROPHETIC MINISTRY

Seven Messianic leaders come to mind who are moving under the prophetic gifting in Israel and the nations, that I am aware of, on the Messianic side. Five of them are in Israel, and two are in the nations. In 2017, Asher Intrater took the helm of Tikkun Global Ministries as its apostolic leader. He also founded Revive Israel Ministries to awaken and shepherd Jewish believers in the land through apostolic and prophetic ministry. Revive Ministries also has a major focus on raising up the next generation of Jewish believers in the land. More recently, Asher's prophetic gifting has really given Tikkun Global Ministries that balance in the Spirit, helping the Church to find deeper insight and connection to Israel's Remnant. God is also opening doors for Asher and Tikkun to connect with other Church apostolic networks around the world, most recently in China.

Avner Boskey is one of the Messianic patriarchs in the land with a worship and intercession focus. He and his wife, Rachel, live in the Beersheva region of Israel and are dedicated to stirring up the creative arts, worship, intercession, evangelism, and the prophetic gifts within a Jewish and Israeli matrix. They oversee Final Frontier Ministries, whose USA administrative offices are in Nashville. Their spirits are deep in the knowledge of the love of God.

Arni Klein is deeply immersed in a passion for the Heart of God and carries a measure of prophetic insight for bringing Israel and the nations into understanding their respective places in *TONM*. Arni emigrated to the land in the early 1990s and with his wife, Yonit, founded Emmaus Way Ministries. He and Yonit are also among the pioneers of worship ministry in the land.

The Berger Brothers, Reuvan and Benjamin, are also Messianic patriarchs in the land with prophetic background. They founded one of the first Messianic synagogues in Israel, Kehilat Ha'she al Har Zion (the Congregation of the Lamb on Mount Zion), which meets at Christ Church in Jerusalem. It is the oldest mission for the Jewish people in Israel, founded by William Wilberforce in the nineteenth century. They also founded *Kehilat News*, which reports news in the Jewish nations from a Messianic biblical perspective.

Jonathan Cahn founded Beth Israel, one of the largest Messianic Congregations in the United States, located in Wayne, New Jersey. Jonathan is best known for his prophetic writings. *The Harbinger: The Ancient Mystery That Holds the Secret to America's Future*, his best-known book, ties judgments on Israel to the United States in a most revealing manner. The book has sold millions of copies. His latest books, *The Oracle: The Juliean Mysteries Unveiled* and *The Harbinger 2*, are also creating a major stir. They truly unravel some of God's deeper mysteries and are must-reads for all those Reconnecting to Israel. In 2015, *Charisma Magazine* recognized Jonathan as one of the most influential spiritual characters in the past forty years. And in 2020 Jonathan Cahn founded "The Return" with Kevin Jessip, which is a ministry especially focused to bring the Church, nation and world into greater repentance before a holy and righteous God.

I mention this not to exalt him but rather for the Christian Church to begin to recognize a shifting in the Spirit as we incorporate God's voice coming from the Jewish branches, as well as from the Gentile Church.

When the stock market fell 777 points in one day, on the eve of Rosh Hashanah in 2008, I wrote in *The Ezekiel Generation* that God was about to do a new thing to begin to sound the trumpet prophetically through the firstborn by raising up Jewish voices to help awaken Israel and the Church. This is now happening among the Body of Messiah/Christ as the Jewish branches reemerge through Messianic ministries like Jonathan's—and others will come.

When the stock market fell 777 points in one day, on the eve of Rosh Hashanah in 2008, I wrote in The Ezekiel Generation that God was about to do a new thing to begin to sound the trumpet prophetically through the firstborn by raising up Jewish voices to help awaken Israel and the Church. This is now happening among the Body of Messiah/Christ as the Jewish branches reemerge through Messianic ministries like Jonathan's— and others will come.

Furthermore, Dr. Morgan founded Howard Morgan Ministries (HMM). He is one of the pioneers of *The Reconnection* movement and has spread this message since the 1990s in the United States. His spirit is deep in the knowledge of Israel, the Church, and *The Reconnection* to our Jewish roots.

PROPHETIC INTERCESSION

I would now like to speak about the ministry focus that God is leading me in. *The Reconnection* ministry I am called to can manifest in the Church and Messianic bodies only with a breakthrough into the intercessory realm, which is why my ministry focus goes hand in hand with prayer and intercession, to help bring it to pass.

My life and ministry experience over the past thirty years has prepared me to be in the place where I am now to teach and train His Body into the depths of *The Reconnection* and to mobilize us into this fray.

> *"And His reason? To show to all the rulers in heaven how perfectly wise He is when all of His family—Jews and Gentiles alike—are seen to be joined together in His Church, in just the way He had always planned it through Yeshua/Jesus Mashiach/Christ our Lord"* (Eph. 3:10 NLT—Messianic emphasis added).

EVANGELISTS

There is a great correction coming in both the Church and Messianic bodies with regard to evangelism. We are not reaching out as we ought to be for the power and guidance of the Holy Spirit to reach the Jewish people. Although most of us are not evangelists, we are all called to share our faith.

There is a great correction coming in both the Church and Messianic bodies with regard to evangelism. We are not reaching out as we ought to be for the power and guidance of the Holy Spirit to reach the Jewish people.

In Israel, an evangelist by the name of Jacob Damkani founded Trumpet of Salvation to Israel Ministries. They train Christians from the nations into Jewish evangelism to bring Yeshua's message into the cities and streets of Israel.

In Israel, Ron Cantor serves as a senior leader of Tikkun Global, a global Messianic family dedicated to the Restoration of Israel and the Church. He hosts *Out of Zion* on GOD TV and serves as the GOD TV Israel director. He has a prophetic evangelistic focus and has emerged in this Restoration with a strong media platform. Ron is speaking boldly about all issues of Restoration in the Ekklesia/Church. He is also the author of a number of books on the same subject.

In the United States, Messianic leader J. B. Bernstein founded *Gates of Zion Ministries* and trains Jewish and Gentile believers for evangelism. Bernstein helps the Body understand the practical and hands-on aspects of "fishing for men" and seeks to restore the biblical pattern of evangelism, which according to Paul is "To the Jew first and also to the Greek" (see Romans 1:16). Bernstein has turned his website (www.gatesofzion.net) into a portal that is designed to make the least of us into effective fishers of men.

Internationally, Messianic leaders Stewart and Chantal Winograd founded Reach Initiative International Ministries. They have been spreading God's love through missions, humanitarian efforts, and evangelism in the former Soviet Union, Belarus, India, and Israel. They also established Brit Chadasa Messianic Congregation in Belarus.

PASTORS

David and Karen Davis cofounded Kehilat HaCarmel (Carmel Congregation) with Peter Tsukahira in 1991. This pioneering Israeli Messianic Congregation focuses on *TONM* of Jew and Arab. The Davises were originally sent out by David Wilkerson and Times Square Church (which I was a part of in the 1990s). David served as senior pastor for twenty-five years and went to be with the Lord in 5777/2017. Dani Sayag is now the lead pastor.

Eitan Shiskoff is one of three main leaders in Tikkun Global Ministries. Eitan truly has a pastor's heart and has founded several Congregations in Israel under The Tents of Mercy banner. He is also serving on the board of the new FIRM organization in Israel.

Guy Cohen shepherds Harvest of Asher in Acre, Israel. And more recently assumed responsibility for managing for Tikkun Israel, which are a network of Israeli Messianic Congregations in the land.

Rabbi Marty Waldman founded Messianic Congregation Baruch Hashem in Dallas, Texas. Marty was the visionary for the TJC2 and now serves as the executive general secretary.

TEACHERS

Dr. Michael Brown is one of the foremost Messianic teachers on the planet. He is the acting president of FIRE School of Ministry. He has written countless books about Messianic topics and how to equip the Body of Messiah/Christ, and he is known for debating numerous adversaries in the Jewish and Muslim communities. Most recently, he founded *The Line of Fire* radio show, which airs nationally in the United States.

Ariel Blumenthal is less known in the Messianic Body as he has spent most of his time and work connecting with the Church in Asia. Ariel is a brilliant teacher on all aspects of *TONM* between Israel and the Church. He currently shepherds Ahavat Yeshua in Israel, which is a Hebrew Speaking Congregation, and is also one of the main leaders in the Tikkun network of ministries.

More recently, Curt Landry has gained in popularity and emerged as a dynamic teacher on *One New Man* issues. His ministry focuses on various humanitarian efforts in the land feeding Israeli soldier families, and holocaust survivors. His ministry serves as a bridge between Israel and the Church.

In 2014, Pastor Mark Biltz trumpeted "The Blood Moons" teachings on the Body of Messiah/Church. Mark is an incredible teacher on Jewish roots and founded El Shaddai Ministries, a *One New Man* Congregation.

Pastor David Harwood, founder of Restoration Fellowship in Glen Cove, New York, has been given a deep teaching from the Holy Spirit on the love of God to help transform the Body of Messiah/Christ.

YOUNGER LEADERS

A number of younger fivefold leaders from the next generation are also emerging. They are as follows:

- Chad Holland, King of Kings Jerusalem
- Jason Sobel, Fusion Ministries
- Troy Wallace, Jewish Voice Ministries
- Ezra Benjamin, Jewish Voice Ministries
- Ben Juster, Tikkun Int'l
- Nathan Wilbur, Wilbur Ministries
- Joel Wilbur, Wilbur Ministries
- Matthew Smoler, IHOP
- Nic Lesmeister, Gateway Center for Israel
- Matt Rosenburg, Texas A&M Hillel
- Jacob Rosenberg, Adat Ha Tikvah
- Kevin Solomon, Beth Hillel
- Aaron Mendez, Beth Am Messiah
- Joshua Brumbach, Ahavat Zion
- Michael and Vanessa Mistretta, FIRM
- Sam and Liza Lewis, Shoresh David
- Paul Blake, Elim Messianic Congregation

There are a number of others whom I should mention who have helped pioneer or promote *TONM* in the Body of Messiah; I have listed their names and ministries below. The appendix has a complete listing.

IN THE LAND OF ISRAEL

- Karen Davis, Kehilat HaCarmel
- Peter Tsukahira, Kehilat HaCarmel
- Daniel Sayad, Kehilat HaCarmel
- Ari and Shira Sorka-Ram, Maoz Ministries
- Avi Mizrachi, Dugit Messianic Outreach
- Israel Pochtar, Voice of Judah Ministries
- Barry and Batya Siegal, Vision for Israel
- Juergen Buehler, ICEJ
- Tom Craig, ICEJ
- Chris Mitchell, CBN
- Belay Birli, Ethiopian Messianic Community
- Oded Shoshani, Melech HaMalakhim
- Leon Mazin, Return to Zion
- Sandra Teplinksky, Light of Zion

IN THE UNITED STATES

The Prophet Bob Jones was outspoken when it came to Israel and helped to prophetically seed the IHOP movement.

- David Brickner, Jews for Jesus
- Pat Robertson, CBN
- Lou Engle, The Call
- Canon Brian Cox, Washington Diplomacy Organization
- Joseph Matterra, MMI
- Dr. Michael Evans, Jerusalem Prayer Team

- Dave Kubal, Intercessors for America
- Stuart Dauermann, Hashivenu
- Robert Wolff, Majestic Glory Ministries
- Gary DePasquale, IHOP Eastgate
- John Chisholm, IHOPKC Israel Mandate
- Pierre Bezencon, IHOPKC Israel Mandate
- Myles and Katharine Weiss, House of Peace
- Joel Richardson, Joelstrumpet.com
- Doug Hershey, Ezra Adventures
- Greg Stone, Gateway Church
- Jerry and Jo Miller, Grace Empowers! Ministries
- Jack Jacobs, Beth Am Messiah
- Todd Westphal, El Shaddai Ministries
- Richard Cleary, Kingdom Living Ministries
- John Glueck, Kingdom Living Ministries
- Tom Blake, Kingdom Living Ministries
- Gary Derechinsky, Beth Ariel
- Bill McCartney, Promise Keepers
- Raleigh Washington, Road to Jerusalem
- John Dawson, Youth with a Mission
- Craig Keener, Asbury Theological Seminary
- Reuvan Doran, Metro Hope Ministries
- Eric Teitelman, House of David and Co-Mission
- Jed Robyn, Co-Mission
- Joel Liberman, Tree of Life Messianic Congregation

- Earl Clampett, Simple Truth Ministries
- Jeanne Nigro, Jeanne Nigro Ministries
- Brad Long, PRMI
- Cindy Strickler, PRMI
- Martin Boardman, PRMI
- Mark Rantz, Beit Hallel
- Michael Walker, Beth Abraham/Church in the City
- Stewart and Millie Lieberman, Or Chaim Congregation
- Brian Sanders, Why Stand with Israel

INTERNATIONAL

- Boris Grenshenko, Ukraine, Kiev Jewish Messianic Congregation
- Marcello Guimares, Brazil, Messianic Jewish Congregation Har Tzion (Belo Horizonte)
- Richard Harvey, United Kingdom, Mapping Jewish Theology
- Derek Frank, United Kingdom, Woodmont Bible Church

THANK YOU

There are many other wonderful leaders in the Body of Messiah/ Christ who are helping to pioneer *The Reconnection* in *TONM*; it is impossible to list them all. To those who have already passed on, thank you. And to those who continue this work, may God's blessing, anointing, and power be upon you to continue the great work you have started for His Kingdom and His family to be one (see John 17:22–23).

PART IV

PRAY! PRAY! PRAY!

CHAPTER 10

THE STRATEGY

WHEN I THINK of strategy for *The Reconnection* and the five-fold ministry to take place in God's family, I often think of a chess game, with our Father moving all His different pieces. Of course He is masterful and supreme; He is the ultimate brain and creative force in the universe and beyond! He is the one holy and loving God, with His Son at the forefront and His Holy Spirit everywhere. Nothing is out of His hands or control, and He ultimately knows exactly how all this will transpire for His Kingdom to come. The God of Israel is sovereign, and His timing is perfect.

However, as He moves each of the pieces into place (through the release of differing revelations to His Body), the different pieces are not always totally familiar with the other pieces' focus and purpose. Here I think of a special assignment for a military mission and how some of the soldiers are on a need-to-know basis until more is revealed.

I think this applies to all of us within the Ekklesia/Church's final Reformation, including our leaders. I'm not sure any of us see the total picture, as the Lord does. This has become more and more apparent to me as I have been writing this book. One of the things I've recognized when it comes to *The Reconnection* and the fivefold is that none of us have been given the full picture (or are yet operating in it). This new wineskin structure and the Restoration it will bring to His Ekklesia/Church is being released in different parts that actually make up the whole. *Pray to God that we will all have the humility to be able to recognize this.*

If unity is the key here, this makes so much sense from the

Father because we are actually in great need of one another to see the whole picture. It is as if God has given different pieces to different folks, and for us to see the greater picture, we must be willing to embrace the revelation coming from other parts of the Body that might not necessarily be our own individual focus. Not only is revelation given through the fivefold gifts, but also distinctions between the Jewish and Gentile sides of the family. This is vital to our unity and overall understanding.

MORE WILL BE REVEALED

We have a much better chance of seeing this together once our separation issues have been dealt with than otherwise. Hali heard a great story in this regard on Hillsong television. A soccer coach had just finished coaching a game, and he lost his wedding ring somewhere on the field. So instead of having the team look for the ring in many different directions, they joined together arm in arm and walked the entire field. In this way, with a united approach, the ring was found easily.

> One of the things I've recognized when it comes to The Reconnection and the fivefold is that none of us have been given the full picture (or are yet operating in it). This new wineskin structure and the Restoration it will bring to His Church is being released in different parts that actually make up the whole. Pray to God that we will all have the humility to be able to recognize this.

Otherwise, it might not have happened, with each one twirling around the field going in their own direction.

This is a picture of the greater unity and cooperation needed between us as a Body that will begin to make all the difference in our effectiveness with the Kingdom of God upon the Earth. Just think for a moment how much more effective we could be with *The Reconnection* and the fivefold if we were to combine the revelation that has already been given to the Body. Think of David's Tent reemerging through 24/7 worship and prayer, the prophetic intercession for Israel and the nations to come forth, the reestablishment of the fivefold gifts in the Body of Messiah/Christ, the significance of this spiritual *Reconnection* and *Alignment* in *TONM*, our connection and understanding to our Jewish roots and heritage, the Church's refocus on Israel and the nations, and the reshepherding of Jewish believers into their identity and the prophetic intercessory assignments to help bring it all to pass. *Can you imagine what might happen as we begin to put all these individual pieces together? How much more powerful and effective we will be!*

I have obviously given the strategy issue a lot of thought, prayer, and consideration. But before I begin to lay out what God has shown me thus far. Let me say that I honestly believe that the closer we come into *The Reconnection*, and the more that Jewish and Gentile leaders *unite* and *collaborate* in it, that *more* shall be revealed from heaven. God is actually waiting for this unity to transpire through us so that more of this connection will be released as a result. From one brother to another, I only know this in part (see 1 Corinthians 13:12; John 16:13).

This strategy not only relates to the unpacking of *The Reconnection* in the family of God but also to the other parts of Reformation that are necessary in His Church and Messianic bodies. These are also a natural outflow of the other vital ministry foci for the Kingdom of God in the last days. Let me first touch on the crucial aspects of *The Reconnection* strategy and then move into the larger picture, which also includes the Restoration of the fivefold gifts.

PASTORS AND RABBIS

The Reconnection unveils our spirits, but at the present time, the fullness of it doesn't come right away and numerous obstacles are preventing us from finding it. This is certainly the case with most Church leadership who have been trained in Christian seminaries and Bible colleges, where everything has been laid out so perfectly for them to view and process regarding eschatology that little is left to speculation. This is also applicable to most Messianic leadership, who has their own set of issues to deal with in this equation.

However, as you have already hopefully discovered, the Church of old does not necessarily apply here because God is moving us back into the time of unity between both groups of the faith. Plus, many Christian and Church viewpoints still come from more of a Gentile perspective instead of from the heart of *TONM*, as we have already discussed. This is how it is has been and operated for almost eighteen hundred years, as the Gentile mindset began to infiltrate the Church and then later began to separate from its Jewish roots and heritage. In this light, what has become evident to me is that our local pastors and rabbis—may God bless each and every one of them—are not necessarily the first ones to get this revelation.

It is ultimately essential for all Jewish and Gentile leadership to receive The Reconnection to shepherd the flock into it. Many will need a great deal of encouragement to embrace this time and one another from their leadership, and the mercy-healing God is wanting to pour out on us to help unite us.

Having said that, it is ultimately essential for all Jewish and Gentile leadership to receive *The Reconnection* to shepherd the flock into it. Many will need a great deal of encouragement to embrace this time and one another from their leadership, and the mercy-healing God is wanting to pour out on us to help unite us.

However, there is also a caution here for our leaders: when looking at other vital aspects of God's Restoration and Reformation to His Kingdom upon the Earth and other revivals or awakenings, many leaders and Church groups were left behind. This is because they had too easily hung their hats on where God might have moved beforehand, especially now, as we move out of the time of the Gentiles into the time of *TONM*. This is a challenge for sure. However, let this not be said of this generation of leaders and especially theologians who might need to take a fresh look to be able to process what God is doing in this hour.

The Reconnection comes only by *spiritual revelation*. It is an eye opener through His Holy Spirit, so prayer and intercession become a strategic key in God's plans to help bring it to pass. Let us pray earnestly and strategically for our leaders—not to judge them, but rather to stand in the gap for them until they are fully immersed into *The Reconnection*.

STRATEGIC INTERCESSION

This is where *Ruth* and *Cornelius* come into play—the watchmen and watchwomen upon Jerusalem's walls who stand in the gap for the Church and Messianic bodies and our apostolic foundations. They are to intercede for them to receive the fullness of *The Reconnection* and the emerging fivefold ministry focus. When Jew and Gentile Reconnect in the Spirit, as one Bride, the barriers and obstacles will be brought down for the full Restoration of *TONM*, which will begin to prepare us for the Bridegroom.

> This is where Ruth and Cornelius come into play—the watchmen and watchwomen upon Jerusalem's walls who stand in the gap for the Church and Messianic bodies. They are to intercede for them to receive the fullness of the Reconnection and the emerging fivefold ministry focus. When Jew and Gentile Reconnect in the spirit, as one Bride, the barriers and obstacles will be brought down for the full Restoration of TONM.

Current levels of understanding among watchmen and watchwomen related to the fullness of *The Reconnection* can be varied and need to be expanded. If the *Father's Heart* for the unity in *TONM* is a ten, most current levels of understanding can range from a two to a five on that same scale.

I believe that these precious saints and the worshipers, watchmen, and watchwomen among them will play a strategic role in God's end-time plan to help transform the rest of God's family and release the fullness of *The Reconnection* to the greater Body through Spirit-led prayer and intercession. *They are the first group from within the Church whose hearts have been awakened back toward Israel. In a sense, they are the first fruits to help enlighten the rest of us.*

THREE FOCI FOR THE RECONNECTION

In my mind, three new points of focus are needed here to improve our intercession on *The Reconnection,* as well as other significant ministry issues that are in need of targeting, which are vital for the Kingdom of God.

First, we need to *reprioritize prayer ministry* in the Church and Messianic bodies because it is essential to all. We need to give prayer a much greater prominence in our local bodies, as is beginning to happen through the Coronavirus epidemic. And we need to more fully recognize the strategic intercessory focus, along with the prophetic intercessory gifts given to many of these prayer warriors who carry this burden (from within the context of the fivefold ministry). We need to help train them, along with younger believers who are also called, so they can be equipped to more effectively use their gifts.

Second, we need to *increase their knowledge and understanding* of *The Reconnection* and *Alignment* so they know how to pray more effectively for it.

And third, *we need to train them for a new type of Spirit-led intercession* for these days that can more effectively get the job done.

WE MUST TAKE THE GROUND

While intercession can be lifted up anywhere, there is something significant to be said about where our feet are actually planted. This is true especially for our local communities, regarding the strongholds of resistance that the Holy Spirit is wanting to break down and the individual grounds and land that need to be taken back spiritually for His Church and Messianic bodies in this most strategic area. This is significant for the Kingdom of God on the Earth, and our local focus is essential to it. Wars are never won with major assaults all at once, but rather through many smaller battles.

This strategic intercessory principle is the same here for all seven spheres and is supplemental to the 24/7 approach. In this final Restoration of the Ekklesia/Church, God has given us two major prayer foci, which we will discuss in more detail in the next chapter. There is one prayer focus for 24/7-type worship and prayer—for *Harp & Bowl*—and one for *Strategic Intercession*. We call this type of prayer, "Pure Intercession." It is important for us to define the two and begin to equip the Church and Messianic bodies for these roles. The Holy Spirit is working in different ways to take back the Earth around us for the Kingdom of God through our local communities. This will require a united approach at all levels (locally, regionally, nationally, and globally). This is one of the main reasons why the fivefold gifts are so strategic right now and why we need them to carry out God's plan to establish greater order throughout the Church and mobilize the Body into the works of ministry and prayer.

A TIME OF MERCY

We are now in a time of mercy for God's family to receive *The Reconnection*. In this light, Ruth and Cornelius need to have love, patience, and respect that comes through that mercy, through the *Father's Heart*, to stand in the gap for their Churches, their Congregations, and their communities. The idea is not to judge here, but rather to pray and intercede for our pastors and rabbis, for our Churches and Congregations that do not yet see *The Reconnection* the way it has been shown to us by

> There is one prayer focus for 24/7-type worship and prayer—for Harp & Bowl—and one for strategic Intercession. We call this type of prayer, Pure Intercession. It is important for us to define the two and begin to equip the Church and Messianic bodies for this additional prayer focus.

the Father, so that the balance of God's family can be fully unveiled to these truths. There is a plan, a purpose, and a process here. Hallelujah!

Mike Bickle, who is the founding apostolic leader at IHOP Kansas City, has spoken prophetically about this, referring to a hundred million intercessors globally whom God is touching and raising up for this very purpose.

THE BODY OF MESSIAH/CHRIST IS THE CHOSEN VESSEL

If the current Body of Messiah/Christ *on the Earth is the chosen vessel to pour forth the supplication into the heavens for Israel's spiritual awakening, then shouldn't our focus in prayer and intercession begin to change for the Body first to receive this revelation?* This is not to say that prayer for Israel is not required, but if the Church is the chosen vessel of God to help lift the veil from Israel, shouldn't the veil be lifted first from the Church? This is a key point to our understanding here, especially for the watchmen and watchwomen.

As we have discussed, nearly all Church eschatology is still missing the mark and fullness of *The Reconnection* revelation for the reasons already described. However, in this place comes the need for the intercessor: the watchman and watchwomen and the worshipers to stand in the gap for the Church and for Israel. *This is the call for Ruth and Cornelius in God's end-time strategy to help to usher in this transformation through worship and prayer.*

This principle of intercession not only applies to *The Reconnection* but to all the other aspects of Reformation that God wants to bring at this time, including the fivefold gifts and all other ministry foci that need to be put under the feet of the Lord.

ISRAEL FIRST, THEN THE NATIONS

The Reconnection shifts us back into our original identity and all that means to be coheirs together with Israel. It also awakens us to the reality of the battle and where the front lines are located. If you were the enemy and you knew the Lord was to reestablish His throne in Jerusalem, where would you put your greatest resistance?

Here we will need to properly support the Remnant Body of believers in the land, both Jews and Arabs, who are in great need of the Church's help. We need to lift their arms and first-fruit our worship and intercession into the land so that the spiritual skies are properly prepared for what is about to take place. Because the principle of the Gospel is to the Jew first and then to the nations, *I believe that, as we put our feet in the land with a mission's approach to help strengthen the Kingdom there, the natural outflow will be an increase of power into the harvest of the nations.*

This same principle also applies to Reconnecting with the Remnant in the nations as we work to help strengthen them to be the best possible witness back to their own people. Right now, Jewish believers need to have the boldness of Peter to proclaim the only true path of Judaism, which is through Yeshua (see Acts 2:14–41).

EVANGELISM, THE NATURAL OUTFLOW

Wasn't it interesting to note, as we discussed the revelation of the *Israel Piece* in the fivefold ministry on the Gentile side, that the evangelism piece was still missing? This is because the Church is not yet moving to draw Israel to envy, as it should. But as we begin to move into a greater focus of *The Reconnection* burden through intercession, this will obviously begin to change. Until it comes, it must remain one of our greatest foci to awaken the Body to much greater Jewish witness and evangelism. Even then, we will need provide the spiritual fuel that is always necessary for effective witness and power evangelism.

DAVID'S TENT

This brings me to the next major point in the strategy, which is the reemergence of David's Tent with 24/7 worship and praise. It is no coincidence that so many reforms are happening at the same time and will become the central hubs for this transformation. *A prayer revolution has already begun, and we are just beginning to get a small taste of it!*

A NEW HEAVENLY TYPE OF WORSHIP

In 2017, Hali and I took a small group of watchmen and watchwomen to the Galilee Worship Center in Israel, led by Arni and Yonit Klein. For ten days, our directive was to do nothing but sit before the throne of the Lord and worship Him. The worship we experienced during that time was off the charts and definitely a part of this new wineskin in the Ekklesia/Church. A new style of worship from the Holy Spirit is wanting to pour out through His Body as we connect more closely to the Heart of the Lord. Arni and Yonit have a strong calling in this area to educate the Body for this purpose. And there are others whom the Lord is obviously raising up all over the globe to do the same.

What will sustain this Reformation will be its consistency to always have praise, prayer, and worship at the altars of the living God through a united effort that is inclusive of a Kingdom strategy to properly affect and influence the world around us.

Beautiful new worship styles are coming out of the Church through ministries like Hillsong and Bethel Church. Many other wonderful, new, talented worship leaders are arising as well, bringing us so much closer to the Heart of God.

It is never teaching or preaching that brings revival and awakening, but rather prayer and praise, which as a foundation should always be the outflow of any type of ministry. What will sustain this Reformation will be its consistency to always have praise, prayer, and worship at the altars of the living God through a united effort that is inclusive of a Kingdom strategy to properly affect and influence the world around us. The 24/7 houses of worship and prayer are just perfect for this focus and in this light are emerging all around us. They are a perfect venue for all believers, Churches, and Messianic bodies to support because we all love to worship.

However, the Church does not yet fully recognize the David's Tent movement (24/7 prayer) or the fivefold ministry focus, which can more effectively help position it in the local community. This prayer movement is not being properly supported and funded, as it needs to be, or will be in

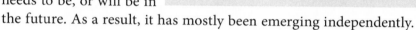

While intercession can be lifted up anywhere, there is something significant to be said about where our feet are actually planted. This is true especially for our local communities, regarding the strongholds of resistance that the Holy Spirit is wanting to break down and the individual grounds and land that need to be taken back spiritually for His Church and Messianic bodies in this most strategic area.

the future. As a result, it has mostly been emerging independently.

Much of the 24/7 ministry focus is already happening overseas in Asia, Korea, China, and India as many new and wonderful works of God are being raised up to impact a lost and dying world. Many of these areas are seeing huge spiritual awakenings and unprecedented revival. The common denominator among them all is their total and utter commitment to God through 24/7 prayer and worship to properly support their ministry focus and the breakthrough from the Lord in the heavens that is coming as a result. These new focuses on 24/7 praise and worship and on *Strategic Intercession* will become the vital link for the local Church and Messianic bodies to more effectively reach their communities.

OUT OF THE PEW FOR THE WORKS OF GOD

It all starts with prayer, yet prayer is often one of the weakest links in the Church. This obviously needs to change. These new prayer focuses will give opportunity for all believers to get involved and to help unite their communities. It will also help to undergird *The Reconnection* movement and further establish the fivefold ministry.

This is God's plan and His strategy, but it will take change on our part to break down the walls of the local Church in the Western world and unite the Body as a whole with a Kingdom purpose. As Yeshua/Jesus reminded us, *"My house will be called a house of prayer"* (Is. 56:7; Matt. 21:13).

SEVEN SPHERES OF INFLUENCE

Within this context, we should not only be praying for souls to come forth and for the spiritual atmosphere to change where we minister, but for the Lord to properly reestablish the fivefold ministry, which will bring a keener focus into our local, regional, and national efforts. This will aid in God's plans to more effectively release the power of the Holy Spirit to break through to the spheres of influence in the world around us, as well as to strengthen all other ministry foci. This seven spheres strategy, which was founded by *Youth With A Mission* leader Loren Cunningham and *Campus Crusade* leader Bill Bright (1975). It truly gives God's Body the wider picture of spiritual influence for breakthrough in a 24/7 focus on worship and prayer.

These seven spheres of influence are religion, family, education, media, arts, entertainment, and business. Simply put, the more the Kingdom of God can break through to these areas of influence, the more effective we will become with the Gospel.

As you will see, through the power of the Holy Spirit, both the *Harp & Bowl* and *Pure Intercession* focuses will not only serve to help break down most of the spiritual barriers around us as greater Kingdom authority is released through them; they will also help bring a greater unity and community focus among us, which is essential for this to take place.

LIGHT OF THE WORLD PRAYER CENTER

I have a dear friend whom I met through the 10 Days prayer movement. His name is Jason Hubbard, and he started the Light of the World Prayer Center in Bellingham, Washington. Jason gives all credit and honor to Yeshua/Jesus. Bellingham, Washington, is not a strong Christian area. As a result, the Church is very much of a Remnant in the overall community. However, something quite wonderful has happened there with the Body of Messiah/Christ and the emergence of this new 24/7 praise and worship focus. Seventy percent of the local Churches have united to support this praise and worship center, taking daily,

This brings me to the next major point in the strategy, which is the reemergence of David's Tent with 24/7 worship and praise.

weekly, and monthly shifts so that everyone in the local Church has an opportunity to pray and worship. Plus, the local Churches are now sharing the financial burden to support the prayer focus and effort.

It is seen and recognized as a vital ministry to help mobilize believers into a greater worship focus and to participate in spiritual battles to win over our communities with a greater praise and prayer focus. But that's not all! Here is the fruit of it in Jason's own words back in 2017:

- Forty Churches each take a day of prayer once a month every month to pray

- Forty weekly prayer sets at the prayer center (eighty-plus hours per week at the prayer center), people coming from different local Churches to pray together across denominational lines

- Nine thousand water baptisms of new believers since 2009 (about one thousand-plus per year on average)

- Twelve hundred of these were new Hispanic believers

- Eleven Hispanic Church plants in the last six years

- Eighty new Church plants in ten years

- Seven new Whatcom County Church plants this last year

- Seventy out of one hundred Bellingham pastors praying together once a month

- En Gedi (safe house for women coming out of trafficking/ prostitution), twenty-five of them have come to Christ, 90 percent rate of women getting back into healthy living

- Abortion numbers dropped every year since 2007, nationally numbers of babies aborted in college towns (one baby saved for every fifty abortions); in Bellingham, one baby saved at our clinic for every two abortions.[14]

Dick Simmons was a spiritual father to many of the prayer leaders in the United States that are emerging in this new movement. Dick passed away in 2020. He was a notable intercessor in the Body of Messiah/Christ for more than fifty years. Here's what Dick Simmons had to say about the stirring in Bellingham and what he believes is from the Lord when I saw him last year in Washington, DC: "The prayer awakening that started through Light of the World Prayer Center in the Northwest will spread to the rest of the country." I believe this because it is the correct framework and unity for the Holy Spirit to pour through His love, His mercy, and His power. Through His Body and Holy temple, the world will be changed. More recently, Jason joined with Brian Alarid and Pastor Trey Kent to form America Prays,[18] which has a vision to unite and equip forty thousand Churches in 24/7-type prayer for a national spiritual awakening. Jason has also joined John Robb at the *IPC* (*International Prayer Council*), as their Executive Coordinator, and plans are in place for Jason to assume full management in 2021. The *IPC* has a fantastic reach and is connected to prayer ministries all over the world.

CHURCH DOORS OPENING FOR EARLY-MORNING PRAYER

We can also expect one of the most basic things to happen in this Reformation, which is really quite simple when you think about it. That is the regular opening of Church doors for early-morning prayer. What does it actually take for a Church, or a Messianic Congregation, to cover each day of the week so the doors of the Church are opened for prayer

We can also expect one of the most basic things to happen in this Reformation, which is really quite simple when you think about it. That is the regular opening of Church doors for early-morning prayer.

and worship? I believe this will be one of the first changes for the Body of Messiah/Christ to make as we begin to reprioritize prayer to its proper place.

PRAYER MOVEMENT

Another very relevant prayer movement that is arising is the *10 Days of Prayer,* [19] mobilizing the Ekklesia/Church to pray around the Feasts of the Lord. Hali and I are personally very involved in the 10 Days of Prayer Ministry, and I serve on the board.

The 10 Days of Prayer movement is catching quickly and as of 2019, was already in more than seventy cities nationwide, with numerous doors opening internationally. In 2020 we formed an alliance with "The Return" ministry with Kevin Jessip and Jonathan Cahn both focused on moving the Ekklesia/Church and the world into much deeper repentance, which greatly expanded the 10 Days Prayer ministry into over 150 cities world-wide, and helped to launch a new 24/7/365 Global prayer focus now known as Global Family 24-7 Prayer.

I believe this will become a global movement in His Church and Messianic bodies to move us into a deeper and more sincere prayer focus around the Feasts of the Lord, which is part of *The Reconnection* and *Alignment* focus.

Jonathan Friz, who founded 10 Days, received a specific word from God that led him into this prayer direction: *"Babylon refuses to mourn, but my people will mourn before I return."* Jonathan has also had dreams and visions of complete cities shutting down for 10 Days of Prayer. Mourning in this context through the Holy Spirit is not a negative, but rather an impulse to move our hearts closer to God without condemnation.

The 10 Days of Prayer focus also complements 24/7 praise and prayer. What better way to pray than through the Feasts of God, which are appointed days for reflection in God's own calendar? They are a natural way to keep our hearts in check with God. (See Leviticus 23:1–2.)

Jonathan Friz, who founded 10 Days, received a specific word from God that led him into this prayer direction: "Babylon refuses to mourn, but my people will mourn before I return." Jonathan has also had dreams and visions of complete cities shutting down for 10 Days of Prayer.

Through the 10 Day Prayer Movement and the guidance of the Holy Spirit, we are experiencing a New Covenant type of approach to the Ten Days of Awe through a heartfelt personal repentance and cry for our nation and world to return to God. This comes from the original purpose and function of this special ten-day period between Rosh Hashanah and Yom Kippur for reflection, repentance, and introspection; to earnestly seek God to bring about change. When you think about this from God's perspective, what is the main purpose of connecting us to His Feasts? It is to be more focused on and closer with Yeshua/Jesus.

Awakening The Dawn is another prayer movement emerging in these days, founded by David Bradshaw. Its focus is to set up prayer tents in every state capital in the country to worship, pray, and share the Love of Yeshua/Jesus during and around Sukkot/The Feast of Tabernacles. In 2016, Awakening The Dawn was launched on the Mall in Washington, DC, with every state represented. And in 2019, the group initiated its college-campus strategy to ultimately set up a tent on every college campus in America.

Finally, *The Day of Repentance* is an additional prayer initiative that is petitioning Washington for a national day of repentance for our country to be held on Yom Kippur. There is no mistake here, as all three of these prayer initiatives are in and around the Feasts of The Lord. In my view, they provide an organic way for the Gentile Church to connect more with its Jewish roots and heritage. This is a good thing, as the Feasts of the Lord are divine appointments from God for us to connect more intimately with Him, as well as with His plans and purposes in these end times.

> *I am fully convinced (assuming our continued humility) that the Holy Spirit will use these new prayer and worship initiatives to lead us into some of the greatest spiritual battles ever fought for the Kingdom of God on the Earth. They will open up Heaven's doors to all kinds of Glory and power that is to be released upon His end-time Body to achieve His plans and purposes.*

As we have discussed in earlier chapters, there is liberty in the olive tree for Jews and Gentiles to enjoy their unique celebrations that lift up our Lord. But in my mind, this is God's own chess move to bring His Body to Reconnect without any foreknowledge of the greater picture. He wants us to be able to experience and connect with the depth in the Heart of God through His Holy Feasts.

GLOBAL PRAYER INITIATIVES

Global prayer initiatives are also arising, connecting prayer leaders and groups with an international focus. One such group is the *IPC (International Prayer Connect)*, which I already mentioned, is led by John Robb and Jason Hubbard. Their goal is to mobilize and equip worldwide prayer for the blessing, healing, and transformation of the Church and nations. Another such ministry is *The Watchmen for The Nations*, led by David Damien. Both of these ministries have experienced dramatic expansion as a result of the Coronavirus epidemic.

PRAYER LINES

Prayer line ministries have also been emerging, like *Prayer Surge Now* headed up by Dai Sup Han, who mobilizes watchmen and watchwomen to pray together nationally on all sorts of significant Church ministry and national and global issues. *Prayer Surge Now* is very focused on Israel's awakening and the Church's connection to it.

A NEW WINESKIN AND A RENEWED STRUCTURE

The Glory is coming! We can look forward to a new wineskin, a renewed structure in the Church, a new anointing, a new government, and a new authority for the Restoration of *TONM*. David's Tent is arising with new types and styles of 24/7 worship and prayer and with financial reform to fund it. This will prepare the Bride for the Lord's return. A praying Ekklesia/Church with mighty watchmen and watchwomen pulling down the strongholds through the power and the leading of the Holy Spirit!

The Glory is coming! We can look forward to a new wineskin, a renewed structure in the Church, a new government, and a new authority for the Restoration of TONM. David's Tent is arising with new types and styles of 24/7 worship and prayer and with financial reform to fund it. This will prepare the Bride for the Lord's return. A praying Ekklesia/Church with mighty watchmen and watchwomen pulling down the strongholds through the power and the leading of the Holy Spirit!

This is an unprecedented move of God's Spirit, and it will usher in major Reformation to His Ekklesia/Church. It will transform the way it operates and functions in many areas, so as to release the greater element of God's power and authority on the Earth.

The new wineskin is already apparent. God is doing something new as we begin to move into this final stage to prepare the Bride. We know it; we can feel it in our inner man; that something is definitely on the horizon. And God will move natural events into play to bring these changes about. This is already beginning to happen.

The Restoration of *TONM* between Jew and Gentile releases a renewed *dynamic* through the *Father's Heart* that in turn releases greater unity and greater love for one another. We are witnessing John 17 in action!

SPECIAL ASSIGNMENTS

Of course, *The Reconnection* is not the only strategic intercessory assignment. There are many other issues in the Ekklesia/Church the Holy Spirit wants to target that are in need of *Pure Intercession*. However, I do believe *The Reconnection* in *TONM* is such a large issue in and of itself that a separate intercessory focus is required to help bring it forth in *TONM*.

RECON WARRIORS

We have named these separate groups, "Recon Warriors" (Reconnecting Warriors) and/or "*Pure Intercession*," and they have already begun to emerge.

CALLING ON ALL INTERCESSORS

In light of *The Reconnection* and *Alignment* focus and the great need for it in the Body of Messiah/Christ, the Lord is looking to raise up an army of prayer warriors for this purpose through these groups. We are calling on all intercessors and all 24/7

We are calling on all intercessors and all 24/7 praise and prayer houses to put aside one meeting a week, or even once a month, and dedicate it to praying for The Reconnection and Alignment focus in TONM—for the Church and for Israel.

praise and prayer houses to put aside one meeting a week, or even once a month, and dedicate it to praying for *The Reconnection* and *Alignment* focus in *TONM*—for the Church and for Israel.

Will you please pray and seek the Lord regarding how you can adopt the *Pure Intercession* approach and begin to put it into action in your local group and community? The next chapter is dedicated to establishing pure intercessory groups all over the nation and throughout the world.

CALLING ON ALL THEOLOGIANS

We are also putting out a call to all Christian and Messianic theologians to lovingly put the issues of *The Reconnection* and *Alignment* on the table. I ask you to willingly take a fresh look at all issues between Jew and Gentile, Israel and the Church, in *TONM* and to go back to the days and times that the Church began to embrace Replacement Theology and thinking. Please do this not only with the intent to cut off this root of deception, but also to bring us back to Israel the way that God intended us to be.

CALLING ON ALL APOSTOLIC LEADERSHIP

We are also putting out a call to all global, national, and regional apostolic fivefold leadership, not only to embrace the fullness of *The Reconnection* but also to more readily embrace each other's vision for us to embrace the whole. We need to come together in a round-table format and engage in dialogue so we can fully re-embrace *TONM* between Jew and Gentile in the family of God. There is a huge need for this presently! Please be prayerful about this.

This is no easy challenge for us, but one nonetheless that is now necessary for the Church and Messianic bodies to release us into our destinies. Glory to the God of Israel!

A DECLARATION OF FAITH

I think it's true to say that any word, message, or direction from God that has not yet been fulfilled must begin with prayer. Prayer is the very foundation of any new ministry focus to bring about its very fulfillment. However, it is my sincere hope that this new prayer and worship focus will not only be used to initiate this

Reconnection ministry focus but that we will allow these prayer and worship ministries to become foundational to everything else we do and learn that the power from the fount always comes when we stay on our knees.

I am fully convinced (assuming our continued humility) that the Holy Spirit will use these new prayer and worship initiatives to lead us into some of the greatest spiritual battles ever fought for the Kingdom of God on the Earth. They will open up Heaven's doors to all kinds of Glory and power that is to be released upon His end-time Body to achieve His plans and purposes. Through these prayer initiatives, more will be revealed to us about how we will achieve these goals through His directives. But first we need to prepare a place for Him, both individually and corporately, for the fire of God to arise.

Father, I believe these things are going to happen and indeed make a declaration of faith into them to help bring them to pass! In Yeshua/Jesus's most precious name. Amen.

CHAPTER 11

THE BATTLE BELONGS TO HIM

A S WE HAVE discussed, the final Restoration of the Body of Messiah/Christ has already begun. There are movements to reestablish the fivefold ministry, movements to reestablish 24/7 worship and prayer, movements to refocus on Israel, and movements to foster greater love and unity for the Kingdom of God on the Earth.

THERE IS AN ORDER

What we have yet to discover is that there is an *order* for us to follow that is foundational to the rest. While the *Israel Piece* is already on the radar, we are still to lock it into its rightful place. This will become our greatest prayer and intercessory focus to help *midwife* this transformation in the Church and Messianic bodies to take on Israel's awakening through the power and guidance of the Holy Spirit. The result will release the greater power of the harvest to the nations.

As I have already outlined, the *Israel Piece* in its proper place and focus will help unlock the fullness of the end-time revival the Church is so hungry for; it will not be released in any other way. This is truly a new day, and looking back to old days and old revivals will not suffice without this final piece of God's Restoration to His family in *TONM*, into the fullness of John 17 love and unity. This key in the *Father's Heart* opens heaven's doors to the rest of God's end-time plans.

Like Abel's offering and the movement of the ark, the Kingdom of God has been established with a certain order and protocol.

When we follow it, not only is the blessing released, but the end-time power to help finish the job. *The Reconnection* not only removes any old negative influences in the way; it also brings about this spiritual Realignment in us to help complete the family of God for Yeshua/Jesus's coming. To emphasize this, let's take a deeper look at His prayer for the family of God in John 17.

JOHN 17—UNITY IN TONM

The *oneness* of John 17 with the Father and the Son is not just about unity among believers, as the Church has understood up to this point in time. It is also about the unity in *TONM*, which is *foundational* to this text and crucial to our understanding.

Yeshua/Jesus's first prayer immediately focuses us on unity with a special relationship between the Father and the Son, Who is the ultimate source. Verses 2–4 focus on Yeshua's Gospel mission to the world, His authority, and His purpose to reveal eternity to humankind. From a family perspective, these verses relate to all of us who would accept Him and His message, both Jew and Gentile alike. And in verse 5, we return to the unity between the Father and the Son and the reality and significance of that relationship. The word *Glory* is key here, as you will see.

The oneness of John 17 with the Father and the Son is not just about unity among believers, as the Church has understood up to this point in time. It is also about the unity in TONM, which is foundational to this text and crucial to our understanding.

However, in verse 6, Yeshua/Jesus shifts back to the family and to the way in which the Kingdom of God and the Gospel are positioned: *"first to the Jew, then to the Gentile"* (Rom. 1:16). Verses 6–8 focus on the Jewish apostles believing and following Him. In verse 9, Yeshua/Jesus states that He is praying specifically for them.

As I have already illustrated from the fig-tree experience in chapter 3, God had called Israel to be a *light* to the nations to bring His Gospel to the four corners. In calling the apostles to Himself (as well as all of the other Jewish believers who founded the Ekklesia/Church), this was a part of that fulfillment so that the rest of God's children could be grafted into the same (see Isaiah 49:6). This is a prayer for Israel first, all of whom were Jews, to fulfill their calling to take the Gospel out to the world.

In verse 11, Yeshua/Jesus prays for their protection and their unity. Verse 12 retells us of Judas's doom, the loss of one of the twelve disciples, and his prophetic destiny through Scripture (see Psalm 41:9; Psalm 109:8; Zechariah 11:12–13). Then in verses 13–19, He prays for their protection, their sanctification, and their commission. But again in verse 20, Yeshua/Jesus *shifts* His focus. This time, however, it is toward His children from nations: *"My prayer is not for them alone. I pray also for those who will believe in Me through their message, that all of them may be one, Father, just as You are in Me and I am in You."*

Yeshua/Jesus did not say *"My* message"; *He* said, "those who would believe in *Me,* through *their* message." Wait a moment—*their* message? Yeshua/Jesus is our message; however, *He* gave this commission to His Jewish apostles (renewed Israel) to take it out to the nations, so God's other children could be grafted into the same olive tree (Israel) to become *One New Man* united in Spirit with the Father and the Son. This special union made up *TONM!* This means Jews and Gentiles are living, loving, and operating together in the unity and harmony of the Holy Spirit. What is key is that it was Israel who took the Gospel out so that God's children from the nations (His other sheep in John 10:16) could also be grafted into it.

Three key words in verses 22 and 23 (NIV) are "Glory," "complete," and "brought." Yeshua/Jesus releases His *Glory* to the Jewish believers who God uses to bring *His* message to the Gentiles, *"that they may be one (Jew and Gentile), as We are one,"* which is integral to His next statement: "I in them and You in Me"—*so that they may be brought to complete unity* and so that *His Glory* would be seen through this special unity between them. The word "brought" implies *action* of some kind for this to take place.

It puts a whole new light on this text when we understand how critical Jewish and Gentile unity are to the plans of God and to the health, blessing, and power that are associated with this equation in the Kingdom and Heart of God. And especially now that Israel's awakening is upon us, it changes everything!

Then look what it says: *"That the world will know that You (The Father) sent Me and have loved them even as You have loved Me."* And look what happened in the first century and how this love and unity changed the world through the *Glory* of God as *TONM* operated in this love and harmony in the family of God.

Three key words in verses 22 and 23 are "Glory," "complete," and "brought." Yeshua/Jesus releases His Glory to the Jewish believers who God uses to bring His message to the Gentiles, "that they may be one (Jew and Gentile), as We are one," which is integral to His next statement: "I in them and You in Me"— so that they may be brought to complete unity and so that His Glory would be seen through this special unity between them. The word "brought" implies action of some kind for this to take place.

Well, similarly, as God looks to reunite us again between Jew and Gentile and Israel and the Church—look out! As we once again Reconnect to Israel's Remnant first-born children who are now being awakened, we can see exactly what that complete healthy, loving unity between us will bring.

This is why the *Israel Piece* and our spiritual Reconnection to the Remnant of Israel is at the *heart* and *center* of this revival and awakening. It is the connection and *power source* to the rest—the fire, as we Reconnect the wire and the greater riches and life from the dead (see Romans 11:15). The devil will do anything and everything he can to stop it because he knows when we get the *heart* of this message and begin to move into *The Reconnection*, it is the beginning of the end for him.

Then in verses 24–27, Yeshua/Jesus focuses us on the greatest commandment to love, which is the natural outflow of the *Father's Heart* for His family to be one: *"I have made You known to them, and I will continue to make You known, in order that the love You have for Me may be in them and that I myself may be in them."*

In this Reconnection, we must come to understand that the *fullness* of the Glory of the Father and the Son is at stake here. This is why we need to repair this breach and fully correct it so that His Glory and the fullness of His love and power may flow through us so we can reach a lost and dying world.

A SMALL TASTE

The Lord gave me a small glimpse of this as I attended the 10 Days of Prayer leaders' conference at the Moody Campus in Massachusetts in May 2017. I was asked to speak on *The Reconnection*.

The transition in the spiritual climate of the room from the time we arrived on a Tuesday afternoon to the time we left was nothing short of miraculous as the *fullness of love and joy* swept through us by the power and Glory of the Holy Spirit. It was like a little touch of heaven, and everyone who was present experienced it.

I was one among a few other leaders who brought teachings on the unity and love associated with John 17 that the 10 Days prayer movement is fostering. The two main characteristics of John 17 are unity and love, and Gaylord Enns brought His teachings on *The Love Revolution*. The power of love in the Body to transform and reestablish the greatest and newest commandment of Yeshua/Jesus, to love. In fact, Gaylord Enns is on a mission to have Jesus's only new commandment reinstated into the Church's creed, because it is missing—if you can believe that! *"A new commandment I give you: Love one another. As I have loved you, so you must love one another. By this everyone will know that you are My disciples, if you love one another"* (John 13:34–35).

We were all impacted through Gaylord's teachings on love. However, as the Lord led me to bring this foundational message in *TONM* as part of its source, something greater was released into our midst. It was as if the *Father's Heart* for His family was being poured out, and it caused the presence of love we were already experiencing to intensify.

As the Holy Spirit brought this revelation to us through *The Reconnection* in *TONM*, it was like another door opened up in the heavens with fullness of love and joy. Then on Friday morning, when Gaylord brought his second teaching, there was an amazing presence of love in the room, such that few of us had ever experienced before. Plus, the power of God also increased as we were praying for others at the conference. As the Holy Spirit put the *Israel Piece* back into its proper place, we felt *the greater riches and power of God's Glory* through the love of God. This is why we *cannot* let up until the Church and Messianic bodies understand the fullness of *The Reconnection message* and all that it means to us and the Kingdom of God at this time.

LEADERS MUST GET THE FULLNESS OF THE RECONNECTION

This is why we also cannot let up when we see leaders in the Body who begin to Reconnect with some form of a burden for Israel, but then make the classic error of treating it like just another ministry focus, which it is not. Or, when they just look to bring Jewish Roots into the Church without this deeper connection; it misses the mark.

This is why we also cannot let up when we see leaders in the Body who begin to Reconnect with some form of a burden for Israel, but then make the classic error of treating it like just another ministry focus, which it is not. Or, when they just look to bring Jewish Roots into the Church without this deeper connection; it misses the mark.

What usually happens in this case is that ministers look to plug the *Israel Piece* in equally with other ministry foci, instead of recognizing the fullness it brings to everything else. This spiritual Reconnection in *TONM* becomes a great source of outflow for all other ministry foci.

I write this with the full permission and blessing of my two dearest brothers, Jonathan Friz and Gregg Healey, from 10 Days of Prayer. When they first received *The Reconnection* message, they began to track in this direction, which is honestly very common for God's children and leaders from the nations, especially because of this disconnected path we have been on for most of the Church's past.

Jonathan, Gregg, and I have often taken field trips together with 10 Days, helping grow and expand the ministry focus. During some of these trips, we would have heavy conversations about *The Reconnection* that may have been challenging to them at the time. But I would not let up on this particular issue, as I honestly love them too much to allow them to fall into this trap, as so many other leaders do presently when first beginning to embrace Israel, trying to keep it in perspective with the rest. In time and even through the reading of this book (with the editing help they have both contributed), they began to understand what I was trying to explain to them about the *centrality* of *The Reconnection* that I explained previously in the section titled "John 17—Unity in *The One New Man*." We must also learn that the fullness of *The Reconnection* message does not come overnight; it is a process for sure.

MEN

Similarly, the absence of men in prayer and intercession needs to be addressed. I don't have all the answers regarding what is keeping men from this most vital ministry, except to say that it is a missing link to all God wants to do through us during these days. There is something significant to be had in the Spirit through male participation that completes the human element before God. This is likely one of the reasons why the enemy does all he can to keep men away from prayer.

God gave me a vision concerning this issue that I'd like to share. It was of a battlefield. The left and right flanks of the military force were filled with able and willing sisters, but the front rows, where the men were supposed to be, were empty. This prevented the army from moving forward as it should.

Dick Simmons from Men of Nations has stated unequivocally that the revival is not coming until men come into full repentance, not only as the priests of their homes and families, but also in prayer and intercession for the issues of God. Our greatest call as men is to serve those around us like Yeshua/Jesus did. We are also

to be intimate with the Father, as He was, and to do His bidding as the warriors He has called us to be. Believe it or not, this calling on men comes in

There is something significant to be had in the Spirit through male participation that completes the human element before God.

the Spirit first, before anything in the natural realm, and it should never be in reverse. Otherwise, we miss out on the full anointing and blessing on our lives and the lives of our families.

Like *The Reconnection*, this issue needs to be addressed more fully in prayer and intercession to help facilitate this change. *Men of God, leaders, and pastors, please lead by example, respond to this challenge, and take your rightful places alongside the women in God's end-time plans.*

I needed to address this final teaching in John 17 on the positioning of *TONM* for us to understand the totality of what God is expecting before I discuss the new intercessory prayer focus that it will require. So the question now becomes, what do we do with all this information?

NO ONE IS MORE EAGER THAN THE HOLY SPIRIT

We must learn that this is God's battle to navigate; it is His timing. Yet our *agreement* and *connection* to it are crucial to His overall plan to break off the enemy's holds. We need to come into agreement with His plans on the Earth for this to take place. At times, we will be swept up into the heavens by the power and leading of the Holy Spirit, where these powers and principalities are dealt with. These battles can be addressed *only* in the spiritual realm and through His leading. *"The weapons we fight with are not the weapons of this world. On the contrary, they have divine power to demolish strongholds"* (2 Cor. 10:4).

This can be compared to walking in a minefield full of obstacles on both sides of the family (Jew and Gentile). There are strongholds that need to be broken off those whom we are praying for, to bring them into *The Reconnection* fullness in *TONM*. When we have broken through on an issue, praying and interceding for a particular group or focus, new resistances can arise. This is by no means a one-shot deal; the enemy has his land mines all over the place to prevent *The Reconnection* from taking full root among us.

We must learn that this is God's battle to navigate; it is His timing. Yet our agreement and connection to it are crucial to His overall plan to break off the enemy's holds.

This is why we need a greater dependence on the Holy Spirit, as it is only in His timing and His strategy that the enemy will be outsmarted.

This war and these battles will be tricky to navigate, and we will not achieve them in one day! However, no one is more eager to address these changes than the Holy Spirit Himself, who stands waiting for us with an increase in our revelation and theological understanding and also with His guidance and help to bring it all to pass.

In this light, greater *training* and *discipline* will be required through His praying saints. This is obviously where the prayer and intercessory focus come into play in *The Reconnection* strategy and how necessary it will be for these changes in the family of God to take place.

The Holy Spirit can produce these prayer and intercessory foci in any number of ways, when worship and prayer are being offered: through regular prayer meetings, 24/7 worship, and prayer sessions through *Harp & Bowl*, as it is more commonly recognized; and any one of us as believers can be involved in these prayer initiatives. However, I think it safe to say that during this time, a greater focus will be required through prophetic intercession that God is placing on the walls to help bring this to pass.

Not only are we heading for some of the greatest battles in the Spirit, but also for some of the greatest victories for the Kingdom of God on the Earth. Although we might be able to suit up and prepare, this is a *heavenly battle* and will require a *heavenly approach*.

The Apostle Paul's comments on how the mystery was unveiled to help bring in the Gentiles in his letter to the Ephesians is most appropriate as a prayer here. As God now unveils the mystery to restore Israel and complete His family on the Earth, readied for His coming.

> *"And to make all see what is the fellowship of the mystery, which from the beginning of the ages has been hidden in God who created all things through **Messiah Yeshua/ Jesus Christ**; to the intent that now the manifold wisdom of God might be made known by the Church to the principalities and powers in the heavenly places, according to the eternal purpose which He accomplished in **Messiah Yeshua/Christ Jesus** our Lord, in whom we have boldness and access with confidence through faith in Him"* (Eph. 3:9–12 NKJV—Messianic translation added).

TWO PRAYER DIRECTIVES

> *"I have posted watchmen on your walls, Jerusalem: they will never be silent day or night.*
>
> *You who call on the Lord, give yourself no rest, and give Him no rest till He establishes Jerusalem and makes her the praise of the earth"* (Is. 62:6–7).

JERUSALEM FIRST

First, let us understand the declaration here, with both directives, which is to give both God and ourselves no rest *until* He fully establishes Jerusalem. This is a huge shift in our thinking, as we have already discussed. We must comprehend the centrality of this focus as we reprioritize our *prayer* and *intercession* toward Israel so that the *natural outflow* of the Kingdom's heart and power is from this place—*not just for Jerusalem, but also for everywhere else.*

There is also a very real wake-up call for us that as we Reconnect with Israel spiritually, we also Reconnect with our Jewish-believing Body and their very own fight to win Jerusalem and Israel back to the Lord. This is now our *fight* and is the very *greatest battle* of them all.

TWO PRAYER FOCI

From within this context of the final Restoration in the Body of Messiah/Christ, regarding prayer, I believe there are *two distinct* initiatives: one for all of us and one for prophetic intercessors. Not all of us are evangelists, but we are all called to share the Gospel with those around us and give witness to our faith. Similarly, not all of us are prophetic intercessors, but we are all called to prayer and to watch. And there can be variances in our giftings in the Holy Spirit with prayer, just like with prophecy and healing, we are all called to prayer and to watch. Some have more of one gift and more of another. What counts is that the Body of Messiah/Christ is built up and that His purposes are achieved.

However, up to this point, prayer is still one of the weakest links in the Church. Some of our Church programs are truly wonderful (to bring forth greater healing in our lives), but in the scheme of things, they should never take precedence over prayer. Too often, our Churches have many of us so busy going from one meeting to the next that we lose sight of what is most important—that we must not focus only on our own needs but also on the needs of others and impact a lost and dying world around us. This really needs to change if we want a greater breakthrough in our local communities.

24/7 WORSHIP AND PRAYER

This is where the 24/7 worship and prayer focus can truly make a difference. As all of us believers love to worship and fit easily into this type of an environment, where we can also offer up our prayers to God. We need to pray and encourage our leaders to Churches and Congregations to move in this direction to support the local 24/7 prayer initiatives that are developing from within our communities and are not necessarily connected to any one Church/Congregation group, but rather have been placed there by the Lord to serve their local areas, communities, and regions.

This not only breaks down our individual Church/Congregation walls, but if led and encouraged properly, it mobilizes believers out of pews and into the *action* of *worship* and *praise* that can and will begin to affect the local communities around us.

We need to pray and encourage our leaders and Churches/Congregations to move in this direction to support the local 24/7 prayer initiatives that are developing from within our communities and are not necessarily connected to any one Church/Congregation group, but rather have been placed there by the Lord to serve their local areas, communities, and regions.

Of course, 24/7 is not the only way to pray corporately. There are weekly prayer meetings, monthly prayer meetings, early-morning prayer meetings, all-night prayer meetings, house gatherings, and prayer lines that also have a wider reach. And now, through virtual video calls. These all serve well to petition God for our needs and causes. The biggest difference with the 24/7 praise and prayer initiative is that it broadens our local focus from our immediate Churches/Congregations to include our local communities and regions. This unites the local Church/Congregation and Messianic bodies into the effort. Wouldn't it be great to have regular local Church/Congregation gatherings of prayer and praise from within each of our own communities? This is where ministry foci like 10 Days can make such a difference to the Body of Messiah/Christ; they are communal efforts of prayer for the local Body.

These prayer leaders are priests, just like our local pastors, rabbis, and teachers, and should be included in the tithe from the Ekklesia/Church, with each local Church/Congregation contributing to the costs to make up the whole. Pray to God for this to change.

What's interesting about the 24/7 prayer movement currently is that it is arising independently of any one local Church/Congregation. And often, these most blessed prayer leaders are still struggling to make ends meet because the local Church/Congregation is not yet helping to fund and support the movement as it should. *These prayer leaders are priests, just like our local pastors, rabbis, and teachers, and should be included in the tithe from the Ekklesia/Church, with each local Church/Congregation contributing to the costs to make up the whole. Pray to God for this to change.*

1 CHURCH, 1 DAY

Tim Taylor is the founder of the *1 Church, 1 Day* initiative, an amazingly simple method for all local Churches/Congregations to get involved with 24/7 Praise and Prayer, which is now being developed further by the 24/7 movement.

This can work in two ways: one with a separate location given just for 24/7 praise and prayer or with each Church/Congregation committing to the time frame but meeting in their own buildings. Either way, if thirty Churches/Congregations in any local area will come together and commit to one day a month of praise and prayer, or if fifteen Churches/Congregations commit to two days of praise and prayer a month, a new 24/7 praise and prayer initiative can be born and established near you.

For it to function well, it will require a leader who should be properly funded by the same Churches/Congregations (as a prayer leader). This will require an adjustment in most Church/Congregation budgeting but one that will ultimately make a huge difference to all the local Churches/Congregations participating in it. Plus, it will begin to draw together the local Churches/Congregations into a greater united effort to reach their communities for the Kingdom of God. This is God's plan for all of us during these days and part of the same fivefold Reformation that can help bring a greater order to it after 10 Days and Awakening the Dawn, which can help create greater unity among us.

Personally speaking, I like the separate location idea better because it helps break down the Church/Congregation walls to focus on the greater community. Through the Holy Spirit's leading, we will need to target the fears that are holding back some of our leaders related to the tithe.

STRATEGIC INTERCESSION

Another natural outflow of the 24/7 praise and prayer initiative is the further development of *Strategic Intercession* to more effectively gain deeper insights from the Lord and to *target the strongholds in each area through the leading of the Holy Spirit.* This is not only true for *The Reconnection*, but also for the many other prayer issues that might be required. Many of these intercessory prayer foci with *The Reconnection* and *Alignment* issues are listed at the end of this book.

SPIRITUAL AUTHORITY

In this *crucial* area of intercession, it is most important for us to understand the realms of our spiritual authority. Please understand that in and of ourselves, we are no match for the enemy, who still operates in one of the heavenly realms and has huge spiritual influences all around us, influencing and controlling his various strongholds that are still in place and need to be brought down.

However, greater is He who is in us than he who is in the world. Through Mashaich/Christ, we not only know he is a defeated foe, but also that we have all we need according to the marvelous riches of Messiah Yeshua/Christ Jesus.

However, we must tread with caution. Several years ago, a number of new books and teachings arose on spiritual warfare, and many teachers were encouraging believers to name and target strongholds as they began to recognize them and then go after them in prayer. However, it wasn't long after this period of teachings that we began to hear stories of how some of these teachers and individuals had come under major counterattacks that nearly destroyed them. We cannot just name targets and pray without following the correct procedure set up in heaven for us to follow here on the Earth. Regarding intercession, we must accept what is in place to know how to operate in and around it to achieve God's plans and purposes for the Kingdom of God.

First, *spiritual warfare should always be of the Holy Spirit's leading* so that we are properly protected under the shadow and shelter of His wings when in this type of intercession. Second, I believe the Holy Spirit releases greater authority to us for various purposes, both individually and corporately, to achieve the necessary goals of prayer. The same could also be said of spiritual anointings released on those for ministry purposes.

Individual spiritual authority is given to us for each of our own walks and lives. Parental authority is given to parents when they pray for their marriages, their families, and their children. Corporate authority is given to us to pray for our Churches/Congregations, our communities, and our regions. And spiritual authority is given to us to pray for our nations and for our world.

Similarly, His intercessors are given *realms of authority* to pray with—those that are local, regional, national, and global. It is important for us to know who we are in this regard so we do not step into a realm that we are either not yet prepared for or not yet called toward. The Holy Spirit will lead in this area and you will know your place from Him.

Then there are ministerial realms of authority given to those with certain callings to achieve God's plans and purposes in His Body and in the world. *The Reconnection* ministry focus is one of these, and there are many others. Praying and interceding for those hundreds of millions of souls caught under Islam, Hinduism, Buddhism, and other false religions. Abortion and sexual immorality issues, politically focused ministries, evangelism ministries, and teaching ministries are examples that are in great need of additional support and focus in intercession.

The Holy Spirit equips us from heaven with the spiritual authority we need to help us get the job done here on the Earth, but *nothing is more important than our prayer focus* because it provides the needed fuel to complete the mission.

Strategic Intercession requires more effective training for prophetic intercessors—first, to properly recognize these precious saints from within the Church/Congregation and the 24/7 Prayer movement and how they move and operate within the fivefold ministry. And second, we need to train them to become more effective in their roles to serve the Lord in this crucial area.

PURE INTERCESSION—STRATEGIC PRAYER

Pure Intercession and *Harp & Bowl* worship and prayer are different to other normal types of prayer focuses, and they require greater preparation. *Harp & Bowl* fills up the bowls through worship, prayer, and the Word, releasing a greater spiritual atmosphere helping to clear the skies. *Pure Intercession* releases greater insights and directives from heaven, helping remove obstacles that are in the way. These two prayer and worship strategies for intercession work in *tandem* to achieve God's plans and objectives and to release greater authority over the enemy throughout our communities.

In the initial stages of the emerging prayer movement, *Harp &*

Bowl has been the dominant prayer model, and there has been a trend to move entirely in this direction for the watchman focus, without the added element of *Strategic Intercession*. However, both are needed to achieve God's plans and objectives. This is why *Pure Intercession* must now come forth to bring the balance.

> *Pure Intercession and Harp & Bowl worship and prayer are different to other normal types of prayer focuses, and they require greater preparation. Harp & Bowl fills up the bowls through worship, prayer, and the Word, releasing a greater spiritual atmosphere helping to clear the skies. Pure Intercession releases greater insights and directives from heaven, helping remove obstacles that are in the way.*

During these days, there are various prayer targets that God wants us to focus on to advance the Kingdom, but it is only through the Holy Spirit's guidance, leading, and covering that we will be able to achieve these goals. As a result, it will require a much greater dependence on the Holy Spirit to bring it forth.

Pure Intercession is the spiritual environment (or prayer meeting) needed through the watchmen involved to bring it about. While *Strategic Intercession* is the type of prayer experienced and offered through it, all of which is led by the Holy Spirit as much as possible.

Pure Intercession can be compared to a *fine orchestra*, with the conductor being the Holy Spirit and His intercessors being the instruments. The musicians have become skilled in their individual talents and gifts, yet their music flows so masterfully with the rest. The end result is a beautiful harmony for all to hear. The same is true

> *Pure Intercession can be compared to a fine orchestra, with the conductor being the Holy Spirit and His intercessors being the instruments.*

with intercessors who have learned their individual spiritual gifts through experience in prayer (through trial and error). As such, they can hear and discern the Holy Spirit's guidance and timing when praying and prophesying with others into *His plans; His Heart* and *His purposes* come to them through intercession.

Pure Intercession is learned through the prompting of the Holy Spirit, Who gently guides and teaches us without condemnation. Quieter warriors have learned to overcome through finding greater boldness, understanding that their own individual sound in the prophetic or prayer moment can affect the overall harmony. More confident warriors have contrarily learned the art of self-control to allow others into the same prayer subject matter to maximize its effect.

ESTABLISHING A PURE INTERCESSION GROUP

To initiate a Recon Warriors or *Pure Intercession* group, we have two main foci to train prophetic intercessors: *one is to increase their revelation and understanding on all Reconnecting Alignment issues so they know how to pray more effectively for it.* There is no greater issue currently for prayer purposes than with our understanding to switch our focus to prayer for the Church and Messianic bodies to be awakened into this cause. Not to take our prayer focus away from Israel per se, especially the Remnant of Israel, but if the Body of Messiah/Christ is the chosen catalyst to help bring this new life forth for Israel, then there is a great need to reprioritize our efforts in this regard.

The second focus is to equip and train intercessors to move more effectively with the Holy Spirit to achieve these goals. This is a new day that will require a deeper, more concentrated effort and focus on Spirit-led prayer through our gifts. There will be battles for us to fight through the Holy Spirit's guidance that will require greater individual preparation and preparation for the group we are praying with, in how we flow with the Spirit and with one another.

I will be the first to tell you that I do not necessarily have all the answers on this new Spirit-led directive, except to say that I am learning like everyone else as we go along. Please understand that the Holy Spirit is our teacher, and this is a new place of dependency that He is looking to develop through His prophetic intercessors to accomplish His end-time goals. But I do want you to know that *Pure Intercession* is not totally new, and I am sure over the centuries the Lord has moved amongst His saints in this manner as and when necessary.

I encourage all the intercessors I work with to read the book on Rees Howells's life, *Rees Howells, Intercessor*—especially the second half of the book, which is focused on *Pure Intercession*. There are some strategic keys to faith in the way he prayed and how the Holy Spirit led him that can truly make a great difference to us through our intercessory efforts.

The Holy Spirit is most eager to create a spiritual intercessory environment where He has full and utter control. This is the goal of Recon Warriors and *Pure Intercession* groups. Let us become the grip on His sword so that the Holy Spirit can guide us wherever He wants us to go. As He develops each group, He will definitely test us (to mold and to shape each group He is working through). This will prepare us for the battles that are coming; they will make all the difference to the Kingdom of God on the Earth. We will be able and ready to do His bidding and come into agreement with heaven's plans.

> The Holy Spirit is most eager to create a spiritual intercessory environment where He has full and utter control. This is the goal for all of the Recon Warrior and Pure Intercession groups. Let us become the grip on His sword so that the Holy Spirit can guide us wherever He wants us to go.

In addition, we should not think that an exact pattern (in our approach) with *Pure Intercession* will necessarily get us there. There are two reasons for this. *First*, each group develops its own characteristics dependent on the various gifts that might be present through each intercessor, so in a sense, each group has its own harmony. *Second*, the focus and the various strongholds that each group is dealing with in their individual areas are different. The Holy Spirit is keenly aware of this reality. There are however, general outlines that we can follow to help foster this special environment for the Holy Spirit's leading. More specific details are covered in *The Ezekiel Generation* (chapter 10).

TRAINING IS REQUIRED

Before any Recon Warriors or *Pure Intercession* group is initiated, proper *training* is required in both of these directives, to train intercessors into the Recon Warriors focus. If you are interested in learning more or starting a group of your own, please visit Reconnectingministries.org, where you can download these teachings to prepare for this focus. I strongly suggest that all participants take the training first before any group is started. It is very important to ensure agreement and unity before any prayer focus commences. Your group will also need time to get used to one another and get familiar with each other's gifts.

Before any Recon Warriors or Pure Intercession group is initiated, proper training is required in both of these directives, to train intercessors into the Recon Warriors focus. If you are interested in learning more or starting a group of your own, please visit Reconnectingministries.org, where you can download these teachings to prepare for this focus.

DISCERNING THE VOICE AND TIMING OF THE HOLY SPIRIT

Hearing and *discerning* the Holy Spirit's voice in *Pure Intercession* is crucial through the thoughts, images, and impressions that we receive from Him while in prayer. This is like a spiritual muscle that needs to be developed and exercised. I often refer to this as a "spiritual antenna" to symbolize not only how we might pray, but what prayers we pray and when we pray them. This comes with a constant deference that is developed with the Holy Spirit in *Pure Intercession*. The *timing element* of our prayers is crucial to the flow of His prophetic harmonies through us and the group we are praying with, which we learn through experience. Please also remember that *unity is key* to all we do in intercession.

When I teach on this, I often refer to the beautiful harmony between the Father and the Son. Yeshua/Jesus never kept the Glory for Himself; He always released it back to the Father, and the same in return. The same can be said of our *spiritual discernment* in *Pure Intercession*, through the Holy Spirit and what we might receive in prayer and then either asking for more understanding on what we are receiving from Him, or for the timing to release it in our intercessory session.

This can be delicate at times, as often Holy Spirit does not always give full pictures and only pieces that can be built upon and developed in the meeting as it goes along. For sure He is masterful and most creative in this place and takes pleasure as we dig deeper to find His directives. Rest assured though as He leads into these places, His guidance is there to direct us into it.

In *Pure Intercession* we do not jump from one prayer subject to another without first finishing what the Holy Spirit has already started. Nor do we pray for Aunt Sally's cat to be healed, as this is not the correct venue for these types of prayers. So if Sue is praying about a specific topic concerning Israel, which was already prompted by the Holy Spirit, and you received a word or insight about your Church/Congregation that also requires prayer, which can happen at the same time (because the Holy Spirit can be readying the next subject, while still in the first one that He raised), it wouldn't necessarily be the right timing to release this prayer until you know the Israel prayer topic is finished. So when to pray and the timing of it becomes a necessary part of our prayer disciplines to help us flow more effectively with the Holy Spirit as a group.

YOU SHOULD FEEL CALLED TO THIS OBJECTIVE

The Reconnecting Warriors and *Pure Intercession* focus is not for baby believers as a certain amount of spiritual maturity is necessary to be a part of *Pure Intercession*. One should also feel a calling toword it from the Holy Spirit, Who gently makes this known to each of us.

A group leader is required for *Pure Intercession* not to head up the group per se, but rather *to humbly serve and lead it through the bidding of the Holy Spirit.* Everyone is important in the group, and all should contribute equally as they are led by the Holy Spirit, which is quite different from a leader giving the directives. As with the orchestra, the various parts of His Body create a harmonious melody when they work together.

WE NEED TO BE COMMITTED TO THE CAUSE

When first called to a Recon Warriors or *Pure Intercession* group, emotions can run high. It is exciting to be involved with this most crucial prayer initiative for the Body of Messiah/Christ, but feelings can only take us so far. *Dedication, discipline,* and *commitment* are necessary parts of our involvement with any group because it is important to retain the unique gifts of each group. Of course, the Holy Spirit can work around this; there should always be liberty because things do come up in our lives when we cannot make a particular meeting date. However, our hearts should be in the right place, committed to the cause. Let us run the race to finish and complete the task at hand.

A group leader is required for Pure Intercession not to head up the group per se, but rather to humbly serve and lead it through the bidding of the Holy Spirit. Everyone is important in the group, and all should contribute equally as they are led by the Holy Spirit, which is quite different from a leader giving the directives. As with the orchestra, the various parts of His Body create a harmonious melody when they work together.

YOUR SPIRITUAL LEADERS' BLESSING

In Recon Warriors and *Pure Intercession*, we strongly recommend that each participant receive the blessing from his or her local pastor or Messianic rabbi, to be involved in the group to pray for Israel and the Church. They may not need to know the full details. But in light of The Recon mission to help spiritually Reconnect us in *TONM*, a submitted, respectful, loving heart to the authorities God has placed in each of our lives is important.

CONSECRATION

Before a group begins, it is a good idea for us to be consecrated unto the Lord for the spiritual task ahead of us. Washing of the feet is a good example for what can be done during this time, as the Holy Spirit leads you. Dedicate, pray, and prophesy over each individual so that he or she will be blessed into your group.

KEEP THE MEETING CLOSED

Recon Warriors and *Pure Intercession* intercessory groups should not be open meetings. This does not mean that new people cannot join them. However, they first need to feel called to it by the Holy Spirit. Then they must be trained like everyone else in the group so that they enter at the same level of Spirit that the group is already operating in.

We need to be careful here because with *Pure Intercession*, one person's spirit can quite easily break up the flow and unity of Holy Spirit by not being in the same place as the others. The devil will always try to get in somehow if you are not aware of some of the principles that keep him out. We should be protective of what the Holy Spirit is building through us as a united group.

COMMUNION

Communion is a wonderful way to start a meeting. Nothing is mandatory here, but connecting with God in this way so easily brings each of us into a right and proper spiritual place before a meeting is to begin.

SPIRITUAL WARFARE

Each individual Recon Warriors and *Pure Intercession* group needs to be readied and prepared for the spiritual battles that lay ahead of them so the Holy Spirit can break through with *The Reconnection* focus in the Body of Messiah/Christ around them. Here, we need to be totally dependent on the Holy Spirit's leading and timing with spiritual warfare. We need to allow the Lord to properly prepare us as individuals and as a group so we can best serve this mission.

Each individual Recon Warriors and Pure Intercession group needs to be readied and prepared for the spiritual battles that lay ahead of them so the Holy Spirit can break through with The Reconnection focus in the Body of Messiah/Christ around them. Here, we need to be totally dependent on the Holy Spirit's leading and timing with spiritual warfare. We need to allow the Lord to properly prepare us as individuals and as a group so we can best serve this mission.

As I already mentioned, there needs to be an element of spiritual maturity in each individual in the group. We also need to be open to further and deeper cleansing within ourselves to be properly prepared for what the Holy Spirit wants to do through us. The sanctification process takes a lifetime, and God never stops working on each of our souls for more of Him to be developed within us and less of our flesh. In our own *Pure Intercession* group we have chosen to embrace individual restorative prayer sessions for each participant to help break off any negative influences that may still be affecting us from the generational bloodline, or any other influences that we may not even be aware of. This is always a good move beforehand, as the Lord takes us deeper into spiritual warfare.

You will find that as you move forward with a Recon Warriors and *Pure Intercession* group in your area, often God is more interested in each of us individually than in the very cause He has called us to. It is important to give time and liberty in the group as He leads to allow Him to minister to each of us. This is a beautiful outflow of the *Father's love* for His children, which naturally builds up the love and the unity of the group. I am reminded of Yeshua's Heart, who left the ninety-nine for the one who needed attention. We should be the same here. This love will shape the group as it grows. God knows what He is doing, and His Holy Spirit is the ultimate leader through His saints. Amen.

You will also find that *Pure Intercession* is one of the closest ways to touch heaven—even more than worship because it includes all the elements of spiritual intimacy with God. Your Recon Warriors group will become the spiritual highlight of your week or month, whenever you decide to meet.

Do not be overly ambitious in wanting to go after strongholds, for you might need to surrender in this place before you are actually ready. God knows the need is there, but first allow Him to prepare you for the battles so that when they come, you will be readied both as a group and individually to be properly protected and under the shadow and shelter of His wings when being drawn into the fray.

DEBRIEF

Since nearly all of us are new to *Pure Intercession*, we are learning as we go along. For this reason, it is essential to remain humble, teachable, correctable, and transparent, especially through the Holy Spirit's leading and guidance, but also with one another. There is no room for pride or defensiveness in this type of environment. For this reason, I always encourage a *debrief* session at the end of each prayer time to be a regular part of *Pure* and *Strategic Intercession*.

In the Debrief, you can discuss and comment on the flow of the Holy Spirit inviting His guidance and input. Were you on track, or did you miss in certain places, and what can you learn to do better the next time. And before you close, always end the session with prayer, pleading the blood of Yeshua/Jesus over each of you present, families, and children, health, houses, and possessions included. And always seal the prayers, not allowing the enemy back into those places. I often pray a covering prayer, being under the shadow and shelter of His wings (see Psalm 61:4; 91:1–16).

BREAKING OFF GENERATIONAL BLOODLINE ISSUES

We might need cleansing and healing from generational bloodline influences or past sin issues. In the training for Recon Warriors and *Pure Intercession*, you would have dealt with and broken off any generational bloodline influences of antisemitism. Yet there might be other areas from generational bloodline and sin influences that need to be broken off from your life spiritually. Some have had Freemasonry or even witchcraft in their family lines without even knowing it.

It is a good idea to devote time to this in your group. We should not fear the things we might not be aware of in our hearts, but rather be open to the Holy Spirit's leading if He wants to clean us in certain areas to prepare us for a deeper place of intercession. This might be necessary to fully protect us from the enemy's influences when entering battle spiritually. None of us is perfect, and His grace is fully sufficient for us, but we should be as prepared as we can be. This is a word of caution and wisdom for us all.

You will know and begin to experience the timing of your group's readiness to enter spiritual warfare through the Holy Spirit's leading. Comfort will be felt by all. And you might have already been trained as an intercessory group outside of *The Reconnection*; *The Recon* is obviously not everything God is doing in this hour for the Kingdom of God. In this case, though, you should still enter the same training and preparation period for *The Reconnection* and not assume you are already ready. It is a different spiritual focus. *Every intercessor needs to complete the training for Pure Intercession before he or she begins.*

One of the greatest foci of *Pure Intercession* is to be led into spiritual warfare by the Holy Spirit. Please understand, as a rule, that we do not run after demons or principalities. These are spiritual beings and forces in the heavenly realms that need to be addressed through God's leading. However, there are specific times when the Holy Spirit will lead you into spiritual warfare to begin to break down the enemies' holds in certain areas.

Most of the time, this will be through the gift of tongues in the group, and through the prayer experience, it can be like ascending into heavenly realms, where the Holy Spirit is leading us into battle. Under God's leading, this is a most powerful place. Sometimes you can feel and sense the enemy on the run, like dark forces are being chased and defeated. Ultimately, the devil and his demons are no match for God.

This type of intercession is most necessary in *Pure Intercession* because this is how the enemy gets defeated so that the negative evil forces that are affecting and influencing the world around us can be broken off. It is here and with this type of intercessory prayer focus that the battle for *The Reconnection* will be fought and won. We want to effectively put all aspects of resistance and demonic influence under the Lord's feet, which ultimately is the call of the watchman and watchwomen in *Pure Intercession*. It is also important to know that when you are led into this type of intercession, you are fully protected under His blood and under the shadow and shelter of His wings.

Similarly, when you come out of a place of spiritual warfare and the meeting is over, it should be sealed off and closed properly. You do this by pleading the blood of Yeshua/Jesus and invoking His covering and protection over each person in the group and by sealing off the prayers that were prayed and for the ground that was taken. You can also ask the Lord to fill those places with the fruits of righteousness. For more on this, please refer to the training video, which you can access on the website.

It is important for all of us who come into this ministry focus to understand that God has given us what is necessary, along with the anointing and spiritual authority that goes along with prayer and intercession for *The Reconnection*. Through the Holy Spirit's leading to break through in the heavenly realms, the family of God will begin to receive this spiritual Reconciliation in *TONM*, between Jew and Gentile in our local Churches and Messianic bodies. This is no small feat, and God knows there is work to be done here.

This is one of the reasons I want to encourage all intercessory prayer groups who want to address *The Reconnection* focus in their area (in whatever country they are in worldwide), to set a date and time specifically for this prayer ministry focus and dedicate it as a Recon Warriors or *Pure Intercession* group. Let us build unity among all of our groups to help strengthen this most crucial ministry focus. And let us all come under the Holy's Spirit's umbrella in this area.

Imagine not hundreds but thousands upon thousands of watchmen and watchwomen in Pure Intercessory prayer groups sending up their intercession from their own lands and territories, going up into the heavens and fueling them for these changes to take place here on the Earth, where we live. I can see an image of thousands of spiritual lamps being lit all over the Earth, releasing light and spiritual incense. What a picture! The more *Pure Intercession* groups we have, the better. Praise God!

These are the battlegrounds we are being called toward to help prepare the Kingdom of God for His coming. Great victories await us for what might be one of the most exciting times to be on the Earth in the Body of Messiah/Christ.

I am truly honored to be a part of this Reconnection effort and to serve God's family in any way I can. I am humbled to be able to achieve the Holy Spirit's bidding in this area. The changes it will help to bring about include a transformed Church and Messianic body readied for His coming, along with a changed world influenced by that same Body. Glory be to the God of Abraham, Isaac, and Israel.

SPIRITUAL MAPPING

There is one other significant aspect of spiritual warfare that is worth noting in our pure intercessory approach that is not written about in *The Ezekiel Generation*: "spiritual mapping."

There are some good books and articles on *spiritual mapping*. Basically, it is a relatively new technique used to recognize spiritual strongholds associated to particular land areas that may be controlled and influenced by demonic forces and then to target them through prayer and intercession. The objective is to bring down their influences and to put them under the Lord's feet— to loose God's will and spiritual sovereignty over those places.

These are the battlegrounds we are being called toward to help prepare the Kingdom of God for His coming. Great victories await us for what might be one of the most exciting times to be on the Earth in the Body of Messiah/Christ.

As I've already stated, we do not run after demons or principalities, or target them in our own strength. These are spiritual beings and forces in the heavenly realms that need to be addressed through the leading and guiding of the Holy Spirit. The ideal way to accomplish this is through *Pure Intercession*, which also can be addressed through spiritual mapping.

However, it is true that the enemy not only has and places strongholds over physical areas and land ties, but his influences can also affect the family of God in the Ekklesia/Church when we have opened ourselves up to extremes or mistruths. Think of legalism, for example, or cults, and how they can affect certain bodies and groups of believers. This is also the case in preventing *The Reconnection* from coming forth where there is great resistance over the family of God that needs to be removed to free up the Body of Messiah/Christ.

For this reason, only through the Holy Spirit's leading do we encourage spiritual mapping for *The Reconnection*. Here, we encourage all individuals in the group to know their spiritual place within this context. Some, not all, will be called and led into a spiritual-mapping focus for their local Churches, Messianic bodies, and communities, and others may be called to support them in prayer while it is happening. I call these prayer warriors "anchors."

In our approach to spiritual mapping through *The Reconnection,* we encourage both focuses at the same time so that those who are called to pray where their feet are placed are properly supported by the others in the group. In a business context, this would be like a home office and field operatives working together toward the same goal.

As I write about spiritual mapping in this book, we are just beginning to be led into this most important area of prayer for *The Reconnection* in the Connecticut area, so more is to come. I believe strongly that The Holy Spirit will use this effort to achieve His goals and purposes through us for *The Reconnection.* We must take back our Churches and Messianic synagogues for this spiritual Reconnection and Realignment in *TONM* to take place. There are many resistances to this, all of which are listed in the appendix at the end of this book.

These are the battlegrounds we are being called to during these days to help prepare the Kingdom of God for His coming, and all that must take place beforehand.

Great victories await us for perhaps what will be one of the most powerful times to be on the Earth for the Body of Messiah/Christ.

I am truly honored to be a part of this transformation and to serve God's Body in any way I can. I want us to be able to achieve the Holy Spirit's bidding in this Reconnection area and all the changes it will help bring about: a transformed Church and Messianic Body readied for His coming and a changed world influenced by that same Body. Glory be to the God of Abraham, Isaac, and Israel.

SUPPORT THE RECON WARRIOR MINISTRY FOCUS

When you think of all that is at stake here, this is most probably one of the most important ministry focuses in the Body of Messiah/ Christ *presently.* Yet because *The Reconnection* is still mostly unseen and not yet fully understood, it is not being properly supported or funded as it will need to be in the future to come to completion.

The Reconnection ministry obviously needs money to support its growing focus in the United States and in the world. However, from the outpost, the unveiling of this revelation is not coming through traditional means, and neither is its funding. This is not to say that God is not touching people's hearts and spirits, Churches, and Messianic Congregations along the way to give to this cause, but there is a plan to help unite and strengthen it through those He is raising up to build its foundation.

Here I think of the widow's might, when Yeshua/ Jesus was watching the place of offering in the temple as He said she gave more than all the others

Will you pray with us and ask God to lift up an army of intercessors who fully catch The Reconnection vision? Will you pray for those who will become Reconnection ministry partners to help us to fund the work and complete the task? Would you pray to give Chai (life) to The Reconnection?

(see Mark 12:41–43). And here I think of so many intercessors who are so very close to the Lord's Heart. They do not have great material wealth of their own but still give so generously to His causes.

Imagine thousands upon thousands of prayer warriors committed to this cause. Think of how God could use the widow's strength to support its focus. Will you pray with us and ask God to lift up an army of intercessors who fully catch *The Reconnection* vision? Will you pray for those who will become Reconnection ministry partners to help us to fund the work and complete the task? Would you pray to give *Chai (life)* to *The Reconnection*?

CHAPTER 12

THE PREPARATION OF THE BRIDE

THE NEXT JUBILEE

In 2017, 5777 in the Jewish calendar, we entered a new Jubilee period (fifty years—see Leviticus 25:8–12). At the beginning of the last Jubilee period in 1967, Jerusalem came back under Israeli control, and Jewish people began once again to awaken to the Lord in a greater way. On the Jubilee before that, General Allenby (a devoted Christian man) of the British forces freed Jerusalem from Muslim control. In fact, on December 11, 1917, he dismounted his horse and walked into the city on foot out of respect to the Lord and the holiness of the city. And in this current Jubilee, President Donald Trump recognized Jerusalem as the official capital of Israel on December 6, 2017.

Jonathan Cahn has written a fantastic book on the revelation of the Jubilees called *The Oracle*, which I highly recommend. It is a fun read but very cleverly reveals some incredible truths to the Body of Messiah/Christ during these days, which are crucial to our understanding of God's plans and commitment to Israel and the Jewish people. And especially the Jubilee of 1867 that brings to light the fulfillment of keywords and prophecies related to the Jewish State's re-birthing.

These are not coincidences, and these dates and Jubilee periods are significant to the Kingdom of God. Israel's spiritual awakening has now entered its second Jubilee period since the retaking of Jerusalem. This is just the beginning, just to touch the hem of His garment when it comes to Israel's awakening and salvation. Despite the fact that most Jewish people have no great desire to be awakened, their spiritual Restoration must take place before Yeshua/Jesus can return. *As the Body of Messiah/Christ awakens and moves fully into her end-time role to help release this life, this will become one of our greatest battles.* Let us pray continually for Israel's salvation.

> *As the Body of Messiah/Christ awakens and moves fully into her end-time role to help release this life, this will become one of our greatest battles.*

It is interesting to note that at the beginning of this next Jubilee period in 2017 at our Rosh Hashanah service, we celebrated at Messiah's House in Greenwich, Connecticut (which we shared with the emerging 10 Days prayer movement in the Church to pray for and intercede around the Feasts of the Lord). *Rainbows* were given as a *sign of God's Covenant* to us, and a *prophetic shofar* was blown at our service. The Holy Spirit led us to proclaim *three* directives for His Church and Messianic bodies to move into the new Jubilee. Intercessors came from all over the state of Connecticut for this meeting. The proclamations were as follows:

1. The Restoration of *TONM* between Jew and Gentile

2. The Ekklesia/Church moving into the fullness of the fivefold ministry

3. The Preparation of the Bride for the Lord's return

We are living an end-time period before the Lord returns, and we are now moving towards these three directives, for God's family to be properly prepared with all that He is going to do during this time. God will affect and prepare the natural circumstances around us, for these transitions to take place.

These are the final stages of Restoration for the Body of Messiah/Christ to help prepare His Bride for His coming. We are preparing for God to move and prepare His Body into a greater position and element of power on the Earth for this transformation to take place. This will not be without challenge, especially to the status quo.

Simply put, Church as usual will not do in every case. This is going to change.

If we are to begin to break through some of the strongholds and resistance currently in place through the enemy, then our approach will need to change and become more heavenly.

> *"For our battle is not with flesh and blood, but against the rulers, against the authorities, against the powers of this dark world and against the spiritual forces of evil in the heavenly realms"* (Eph. 6:12).

Nothing could be truer today than this Scripture from the Apostle Paul. However, with these types of battles that are ahead of us, we are no match on our own for the evil forces aligned against us. The Ekklesia/Church is not ready, either. It is mostly divided and separated from its communal, fivefold approach and attachment to Israel's people and its Jewish roots and heritage.

As a result, these changes, adjustments, and transformations among us are most necessary to prepare us for what is to come. We will need to become more dependent on the Holy Spirit, His guidance, and His ministry models through reformed government, increased praise, worship, and intercession. We have already addressed these changes from a *corporate* perspective in this book. This chapter is more focused on our individual walks: to help prepare us *personally* for all that is coming.

THE FEAR OF THE LORD

There is a healthy balance between God's *grace* and the *fear of the Lord* that we will need to get back to in the Body of Messiah/Christ. Although Yeshua/Jesus is our greatest friend, we should never forget that the God of Israel is a consuming fire that calls each of us into a holiness and

> There is a healthy balance between God's grace and the fear of the Lord that we will need to get back to in the Body of Messiah/Christ.

purity of heart that can never be brought about through the gifts of the Holy Spirit, but rather only through the cross of Mashiach/ Christ. We must be fully committed to the pursuit of godly character before anything and everything else, just as Peter has written, *"Be ye holy; for I am holy"* (1 Pet. 1:16).

This is one of the greatest reasons why our non-charismatic brothers and sisters have such great challenges with us charismatics. But let us live such godly lives in character and witness that our very testimonies will help to naturally pull down their fears and resistance to the gifts of the Holy Spirit and allow Him more freedom to move in our midst.

CLEANER VESSELS

As we enter this time of mercy from God to clean up and restore the family to Himself in *TONM*, I think it is a fair statement to make that as we more fully break off all the past influences and residual curses (that have been upon us in the family), we can experience greater levels of intimacy, revelation, and power with God. This will be one of the greatest fruits of this transformation.

The very promise of the New Covenant prophesied to Jeremiah is one of greater intimacy where each of us know God for ourselves. *"'No longer will they teach their neighbor, or say to one another, "Know the Lord," because they will all know me, from the least of them to the greatest,' declares the Lord"* (Jer. 31:34). I think a good deal of that intimacy has been lacking in the Body in light of some of these past issues and residual curses and that during these days He is drawing us nearer to Himself. This is especially true for some of the more traditional denominations in which religion promotes a separation from that type of intimacy. It is as if "He is too holy for us commoners, so let's leave it to the leaders." This type of approach is much more of an Old Testament model. Although we should never forget the *holiness of God* and our *reverence* for Him, Yeshua/Jesus died to tear down these religious walls.

WE MUST HEAR GOD FOR OURSELVES AND KNOW HOW TO SEEK HIM

Some of this can be seen and felt in our own charismatic movement, with people running from prophet to prophet to hear God's direction for their lives. Not that hearing or receiving prophecy is a bad thing, but most of the time, these prophetic words should really only be confirming what God is actually saying to us directly through His Spirit and His Word. But if we are not personally taking the time to yield our hearts and spirits into His Holy Word and through personal prayer time, then we will be lacking in the very intimacy that has been promised us, and the fullness thereof. Nothing can replace this time spent with God alone.

There are some wonderful outlines and teachings on the Lord's Prayer. I highly recommend *Could You Not Tarry One Hour?* by Larry Lea as well as Bill Johnson's book, *When Heaven Invades Earth*.

Pray to God that we will be reminded that *self-control* is one of the fruits of the Spirit, especially when it comes to our personal prayer time (see Galatians 5:22). Our own personal disciplines in connection to our Lord and Savior are always a crucial part of that intimacy and connection. *We must be hearing God for ourselves*, as this is the very cornerstone of our faith. Days are coming that will be difficult to navigate without it.

HEARING THE VOICE

I teach a class in *Pure Intercession* in our intercessory and evangelism clinic called "Hearing the Voice." In it, we separate people into pairs—preferably men with men and women with women, and we try to group people with those they do not know. Each pair takes turns in two ten-minute segments and ministers and prays for one another. Those in the clinic are not allowed to start until they have had direction from the Holy Spirit and heard from Him in one form or another about the person they are praying for. Some hear voices, some have impressions, and some see visions given by the Holy Spirit. The key to the exercise is to personally tap into exactly how they are hearing or seeing the voice of the Holy Spirit for themselves so they can recognize how He communicates directly with them. It helps us better understand how individually each of us hears, sees, and tunes in to the Holy Spirit in each of our hearts.

It is interesting to note that no one is more eager to train His saints in hearing His voice and direction than the Holy Spirit Himself. Without fail, within minutes, the room is always transformed, as God has begun to minister to each of our personal needs—often straight to the heart.

Hearing His Voice is the central theme to all the gifts of the Holy Spirit. This same voice of the Holy Spirit is how we hear prophecy and His direction to praying Spirit-led intercession and how we hear words of wisdom and knowledge for healing and evangelism purposes. They all stem from this relationship of hearing and sensing His voice from within.

The discipline in the exercise, however, is not so much to focus on what God does or says, which is always the reaction (as it is personally very exciting), but rather to understand and tune in to exactly how God spoke that direction to us. This exercise enables us to better understand how each of us hears, sees, and tunes in to the Holy Spirit in each of our hearts.

Hearing His Voice *is the central theme to all the gifts of the Holy Spirit.* This same voice of the Holy Spirit is how we hear prophecy and His direction to praying Spirit-led intercession and how we hear words of wisdom and knowledge for healing and evangelism purposes. They all stem from this relationship of hearing and sensing His voice from within.

Hearing His voice and direction of the Holy Spirit is like training a muscle in your Body. This needs to be exercised regularly to be able to discern the voice and guidance of the Holy Spirit, which should be crucial to each of us in how we live out our faith. Plus, the Holy Spirit will test us to fine-tune us in this direction, as we become more open to it. After all, who is in charge now? And if we do not yet know how God speaks to us personally and individually, where are we going for that direction, which must always come from God first, before anyone else?

I was personally very blessed to be put on this path from the outset of my faith by a young pastor who directed me to seek out the Holy Spirit's voice and direction for my life. This helped me better understand my very own personal spiritual journey (and adventure) that I was now on with the Lord when I gave Him my life. But this obviously needed to be developed and strengthened through time in the Spirit and disciplines in the Word as I was walking and growing in His grace. Discipline is not a negative, but rather one of the major keys to any successful walk and relationship with God. An old classic, *The Celebration of Discipline*, by Richard J. Foster, helped me in this regard.

WE HAVE TO GET IT RIGHT

Similarly, our own personal victories through our individual walks become a necessary part of our faith. Through the process of sanctification, where God works to transform us, many times through our own weaknesses, a lot of us get entangled along the way. This can shut us down to the fullness and power of the Holy Spirit in each of our lives, especially through fear, doubt, and depression. This is also seen when we value our own desires over God's.

The devil's goal is to keep the saints focused on our failings and weaknesses, so we remain on the defensive, not bearing the full fruit of the Kingdom that God has intended for each of us. *"The Kingdom of heaven suffers violence and the violent take it by force"* (Matt. 11:12 KJV).

Paul was not ignorant to the enemy's devices (see 2 Corinthians 2:11). We should not be ignorant, either. But most of us are not aware enough of how the devil attempts to work against us, which can give him too much free access to move in our lives and ensnare the very things God is wanting to transform and set us free from. A lot of the time, we do not fight against these things as we should.

In this pattern, we can enter an ongoing negative cycle connected to those weaknesses (like Israel walking around the desert), which gets us nowhere. One of the devil's goals is to keep us shut down from rightfully taking what belongs to us in God.

Does fear ensnare us, or does depression, for example? In the Spirit, these things do not exist, and Yeshua/Jesus has the power to deliver us from all flesh. If we are walking with the right heart, we will learn to overcome. We must also be willing to face our weaknesses and allow the Holy Spirit into our pain. When I am experiencing these negative emotions, I no longer try to run from them, but rather invite the Holy Spirit into the midst of them so they begin to dissipate.

The devil's goal is to keep the saints focused on our failings and weaknesses, so we remain on the defensive, not bearing the full fruit of the Kingdom that God has intended for each of us. "The Kingdom of heaven suffers violence and the violent take it by force" (Matt. 11:12 KJV).

I think it is important for us to be more aware of this whole process so that the enemy is properly exposed. The Kingdom of God is not about us being defensive all the time, but rather taking back from the devil what rightfully belongs to us. This applies both personally through our own individual walks and corporately, as we have already discussed in chapters 10 and 11.

Through Yeshua/Jesus, we have become a living form of God's Temple on the Earth (see 1 Corinthians 3:16), which He achieved for us through His death and resurrection. This is the power of the New Covenant in us, and during this time we must get more in touch with a greater knowledge of exactly who we are in His Holy Spirit. We have not been born just for our own wants and desires, but rather to live out and reflect heaven here on the Earth. We are to be the salt and light in a dark world that is passing away (see Matthew 5:13–16).

Our lives are no longer our own and should not be if we are walking rightly with the King. We have been bought at a price. Praise God that we have been delivered from the curse of sin and death to live out and reflect life, truth, and righteousness here on the Earth! But just how much is that light shining? *We will not be judged by what we have done if it has already been brought into confession and repentance. But we will be judged by what we do with what He has given us to bring forth.*

CORRECT PRACTICE

I took a motorcycle training course a couple of years ago, and something one of the instructors said really struck a chord in me. We have all heard the phrase "Practice makes perfect," but this instructor emphasized that this is not correct; it is only the *right type of practice* that makes things perfect. This same principle can be applied to how we walk out our faith with some of the disciplines and practices we bring into our lives to ensure the correct fruit will be produced from them.

THE GALATIANS PROCESS

Yeshua/Jesus's desire for us all is that we would bear much fruit. This does not come without major personal battles, breakthroughs, and victories. I often say that if we truly understood the full authority of the Kingdom of God within each of us, the world would be a different place. However, God is also keenly aware of everything we go

For me, this is where The Galatians Process has come into play to dramatically help my own personal walk, which I would like to share with you.

through, sometimes by His own design. He also uses these struggles for His Glory in each of our lives. The flesh will be with us until we leave the Body. During these days, we must improve on our individual approach and personal dealings with both the enemy and the flesh. For me, this is where "The Galatians Process" has come into play to dramatically help my own personal walk, which I would like to share with you.

For the greater part of my walk in Mashiach/Christ, I found myself on the defensive when spiritual attacks would come. I have always been focused on maintaining the peace of the Holy Spirit in my heart. In the beginning of my faith, I listened to a message by Pat Robertson on the perfect will of God for your life, which focused on the peace of the Holy Spirit as a guide and indicator. Since then, I have looked to defend and protect that peace in my heart.

However, when the attacks would come, either of the enemy or the flesh—most often of both—my immediate posture was to go on the defensive and start fighting to maintain that place of peace in my heart. This is good because most of our spiritual armor is for our defense and protection.

In our own personal spiritual warfare, we need to discern what is going on before anything else. Is this an attack coming from the enemy, or is there something in my flesh that is in need of sanctification? Is this something that God might be wanting to change and transform? It is important for us to ask the Holy Spirit what is going on so we know how to properly address what is coming against us.

For example, if I felt or experienced fear, I would use the tools of confession and repentance to fight the fear. Anything that God has equipped us with to maintain a healthy walk can be considered a tool in the Spirit. But it was never an easy process, especially if the fear was strong or attached to something I didn't really want to let go of.

In our own personal spiritual warfare, we need to *discern* what is going on before anything else. Is this an attack coming from the enemy, or is there something in my flesh that is in need of sanctification? Is this something that God might be wanting to change and transform? It is important for us to ask the Holy Spirit what is going on so we know how to properly address what is coming against us. Then we need to be able to hear the voice and the discernment of the Holy Spirit from within. This is most crucial as we grow in our faith. Then at that point, I would take out the shield (faith) and sword (the Word of God) and use them to reclaim my peace, but I wouldn't say that I was always joyful after the fact; it was if something was still missing sometimes.

Peace and joy are rightfully ours in the Kingdom of God, and they belong to all those who call on the Lord. However, as His children, we must often fight to maintain their status quo within our hearts and spiritual walk. This is where the revelation of *The Galatians Process* came into play for me through the Holy Spirit later in my life and walk, and it has become a major blessing for me to overcome with fullness of joy.

I discovered *The Galatians Process* in the Holy Spirit with my dear friend, Richard Davis. As brothers, we were seeking greater joy, greater faith, and greater victory in each of our lives through personal prayer. One day on a prayer walk together, the

I always focused on going after the issue that was coming against me to stay in the Spirit, but I never looked to fill it afterward with whatever might have been taken away from me. This was the revelation. There is a counterbalance when it comes to replacing the negatives with the positives in the Spirit. The following is an example to illustrate this welcoming of the Spirit.

Holy Spirit dropped this deeper understanding of Galatians 5:16 into our hearts and spirits: *"So I say, walk by the Spirit, and you will not gratify the desires of the flesh."* This is a promise!

As I have already stated, up to this point in time, I always focused on going after the issue that was coming against me to stay in the Spirit, but I never looked to fill it afterward with whatever might have been taken away from me. *This was the revelation.* There is a counterbalance when it comes to replacing the negatives with the positives in the Spirit. The following is an example to illustrate this welcoming of the Spirit.

AN EXAMPLE

The easiest way for me to describe this process is through the emotional experiences of fear and love, or doubt and faith. After recognizing fear in my heart and that I was not trusting God for my sustenance and provision, I would confess and repent of it. In this process, I would come against the condemnation the enemy was using to keep me ensnared on top of everything else that he was throwing at me at the same time. I would then break it off by rebuking it in Yeshua's name.

As we know, there is no *condemnation* in the Lord, but the devil uses this and the guilt we sometimes feel from experiencing negative emotions to hold us back. After I am successful in this regard, I then take a stand with my shield (faith) and attack with my sword (the Word). However, to reclaim my peace and joy, I would ask the Lord to fill that place in my heart with the exact opposite emotion I was experiencing with the fruits of the Spirit (see Galatians 5:22). In this case, as I was experiencing fear, I would invite His perfect love into my heart to wash me clean so that I could return to where I was before the trial began. If I was in doubt, I would ask for faith. I am *right* to want to feel this joy and peace, they belong to me in Mashiach/Christ, but at the same time, I must always be willing to fight for them.

Sometimes, those deeper places in our hearts are closed to the Lord, as they are simply too painful to face. In such a case, I would ask the Lord into the pain rather than just fighting it off, as before this, the deeper wounds in me would remain untouched because I was missing the Lord's direction and touch in the process.

However, if the issue I was dealing with was more deep-rooted, or one that perhaps I may have been blinded to in the past (we all have blind spots), I would ask the Holy Spirit if there was an area in my heart that was in need of healing and then invite Him into it, to open up that place to the Lord's inner healing in me.

Sometimes, those deeper places in our hearts are closed to the Lord, as they are simply too painful to face. In such a case, I would ask the Lord into the pain rather than just fighting it off, as before this, the deeper wounds in me would remain untouched because I was missing the Lord's direction and touch in the process.

There is always a place in the beginning of healing that is painful, but instead of running from it, we must actually do the opposite and allow the Lord to bring healing in us. This is where our trust and faith come into play. Ultimately, we know that our Father knows best and actually knows us better than we know ourselves.

One final thought on this, which the Lord had to correct me on, is that sometimes, we can be too quick to move into the whole process and miss the healing the Lord wants to bring to our hearts. We apply the tools and get back to peace but miss the Master who is knocking on the door of a deeper place in us that needs His touch. Be discerning here. Personally, *The Galatians Process* has been a major blessing in my life. It has also blessed those I have shared it with. This is just one of the examples and insights of the Holy Spirit, who wants to equip us with the necessary tools in the Spirit to overcome whatever may be coming against us. The hope is that all of us would have greater victory in our lives and begin to move more offensively into the world so we are able to take back what belongs to God—both individually and corporately as the Body of Messiah/Christ.

My good friend Pastor Dwain Wolf from Tacoma, WA, has written a wonderful book, called *Move Your Mountains,* on using and maintaining the tools of the faith, which God has given to each of us through the Holy Spirit. I would highly recommend his books, DVDs and teachings on self-deliverance and walking in greater personal victory in each of our lives.[20]

YESHUA/JESUS DID ONLY WHAT HE SAW THE FATHER DOING

Hearing and discerning the voice of the Holy Spirit in each of us is key to how we live out our walks of faith in Mashiach/Christ. Learning this principle of being led and doing only what the Father wants is vital to our success in the Spirit (see John 5:19–20).

Hearing and discerning the voice of the Holy Spirit in each of us is key to how we live out our walks of faith in Mashiach/ Christ. Learning this principle of being led and doing only what the Father wants is vital to our success in the Spirit (see John 5:19–20).

As God continues to release this ministry focus to me, He has been working a lot with me personally on this principle. I am to only walk through the doors He is opening and not worry about the ones that are still closed. This is particularly true with *The Reconnection*, as it only comes by spiritual revelation, and it is only God who is totally aware of the timing of it all. Unless He builds the house, we labor in vain (see Psalm 127:1).

The Reconnection ministry focus is His before it is mine. It is His Heart for His family to be one, and I must allow Him to have full reign over it and to more fully submit to His direction. This also helps me with the burden of it all, as it is not mine to carry, but rather His yoke to lead me through it (see Matthew 11:28–30). The same is true for each of our lives when we have yielded our hearts to the King. I can honestly say at this point that I would be lost without this direction and squashed by the enemy with the burden of it all. Hence, I need His most crucial insights and guidance to me at this time to help me personally walk with Him in this place. Praise His Holy name!

BE TRANSFORMED

We must come to understand that no one is more eager than God to move us into more aggressive roles for His Kingdom upon the Earth. All of us are supposed to be equipped for the works of the ministry (see Ephesians 4:11–12). We will become the fruits of a transformed Body. Let's all say, "Enough of the pew," except for the equipping and worship it brings forth. Let's get God's job finished here on Earth!

This means that all of us who call on the Lord will need to go into a deeper place of intimacy and transformation in our lives, including our leaders. We need to set the examples along the way to serve the rest of the Body and move more effectively into those works of the ministry, which is the true and proper function of leadership.

This end-time Body of Messiah/Christ and family of God is going to be an overcoming and victorious Body that will be more able to face the opposition that is coming. It will be a glorious time and a glorious Ekklesia as we come down to the end before Yeshua/Jesus returns. As we move more and more into this Reformation, submitting

> *This end-time Body of Messiah/Christ and family of God is going to be an overcoming and victorious Body that will be more able to face the opposition that is coming. It will be a glorious time and a glorious Ekklesia as we come down to the end before Yeshua/Jesus returns.*

ourselves to the will of God, the power and demonstration of the Kingdom of God within each of us will be ever-present. But it will also be challenging to many of us without the extra closeness and intimacy, and some will fall away (see 1 Timothy 4:1).

If our faith has been focused too much on ourselves and the personal improvement in each of our lives drinking milk and not solid food (see Hebrews 5:12), instead of acting as a living sacrifice for His Glory, then we will be greatly challenged. Nothing can substitute the cross and the suffering that we sometimes experience in our walks and the character it builds. We should not be looking to escape these things, but rather to fully embrace them. *Always remember that after the cross is the resurrection* (see Hebrews 5:8; John 15:18–20; Hebrews 12:5–7)!

Sometimes, in my own struggles with my flesh, in my imagination,

I take hold of a large wooden cross and hug it tightly with both arms, pulling it into my Body and not letting it go. Because I know and trust that in this process of death in me, new life and transformation are coming. *I have learned over the years that Father knows best!* This is where we can agree with Jacob/James when he writes in his epistle, in the second verse, *"Consider it pure joy, my brothers and sisters, whenever you face trials of many kinds, because you know that the testing of your faith produces perseverance. Let perseverance finish its work so that you may be mature and complete, not lacking anything"* (Jac./Jas. 1:2–4). Many of our trials are needed because they develop godly character in our lives; we should be thankful for this.

This is what I believe Jacob/James is referring to when he says to give thanks in all circumstances and why we should be preparing now, when it is easier, rather than later, when it becomes more challenging (see 1 Thessalonians 5:18). Let us be like the virgins whose lamps were full and readied for His coming (see Matthew 25:1–13). Thus, when the greater testing comes (along with His grace released to us at that time), we can take our stand and position ourselves as the salt and light to all those who are around us, not so much thinking of an escape, but rather to take what belongs to God. We want His Gospel to be released into its fullness so that the end may come. This is how the apostles lived out their faith, and we should do the same.

This is quite different from a lot of current Christian theology, and adjustments are definitely needed, as I have addressed in this book. None, however, are more personal than through our own walks of faith.

ROMANS CHAPTER 12

I think it is most fitting that the Apostle Paul ends His dissertation on Israel and the Church in the book of Romans, chapter 12, with this same focus on transformation and maturity in the Spirit. Paul said that, in view of God's mercy to wash and cleanse our hearts, we would be willing to offer our bodies as a living sacrifice that is holy and pleasing to God (see Romans 12:1). We do this so we can taste and know the full will of God in our lives.

I believe there is a place here in our character that we can work toward. It is a place where we become more effective, have more peace and joy, have more faith, and overcome more adversity and where God's character is made manifest more in each of our lives. However, we must be willing to give over and open up those weaker, more vulnerable places in our hearts that have many of us trapped. *We must always be willing to search our own hearts before a holy and righteous God.*

Paul goes on to say that this is true and proper worship: *"Do not conform to the pattern* (and thinking) *of this world*, but be transformed by the renewing of your mind. Then you will be able to test and approve what God's will is—*His good pleasing and perfect will"* (see Romans 12:1–3—emphasis added by Grant Berry).

There is a process here that most of us know as *sanctification.* This change takes place through our minds and souls that they would be washed and cleansed through His Word and Spirit. What is key to note in this text is that there is a *transformation* that takes place through our obedience to be changed. We will be able to test and approve God's perfect will for each of our lives. How else can we know God's will for our lives?

LOVE WILL HAVE ITS WAY

Finally, let *love* have its way. When we meditate on the Apostle Paul's dissertation of love in 1 Corinthians (13:4–7), looking to apply each of those individual directives into our lives and walks, something greater happens with our ability to discern and hear the Holy Spirit's directives. In this case, think of Yeshua/Jesus with the adulterous woman, or, when he was under pressure from the Pharisees constantly trying to trap him. Here we see an incredible combination of the Master in action. We see the processing of His Spirit, hearing His voice, and the incredible timing of His movement in

His Father's will, but without the anchor of love, we could miss the rest. *"And now these three remain: faith, hope and love, but the greatest of these is love"* (1 Cor. 13:13).

LET FREEDOM HAVE ITS WAY

You know, the amazing thing that happens when we fully surrender to all of these issues and struggles in our hearts is that we become free from within! It is for *freedom* that Mashiach/Christ has set us free (see Galatians 5:1). Let us allow God to have full and complete reign over every issue in our hearts and trust Him to sanctify and transform us that we may bear great fruit and live the abundant life He has planned for each one of us. In the words of the psalmist worship leader, Jason Upton, "It's a holy thing to be wild and free!" Let us live this out in such a way that our light would shine in the darkness and that more would be drawn to the great freedom Yeshua/Jesus brings to each of us in the Kingdom of God. Let us act in such a way that both *religion* and *worldliness* around us would be exposed through the very examples of our lives.

RESTORATIVE PRAYER

Restorative prayer ministries can also be very helpful here. If you are not familiar with this term, "Restorative prayer" is a type of more intimate prayer ministry led by the Holy Spirit to touch deeper parts of our minds and souls for healing and cleansing purposes. Generational bloodline issues, curses, and deliverances are also dealt with in this type of an environment through the prayer counselors leading the sessions.

We should obviously pray on and check out the spiritual credentials of those who are conducting these types of prayer sessions. This is often delicate stuff, and we should have a good amount of trust in those who will be ministering to us in this place.

My own personal experience with Restorative prayer has been wonderful, freeing up many sensitive and delicate places in my heart. "Cleansing Stream" is one of the better-known ministries that focus on Restorative prayer, and I highly recommend it. Cleansing Stream is often offered through Church programs.

I think it would be helpful to many of us to look at this type of prayer like going to the doctor for a checkup. The truth is that we all have issues with negative experiences in our lives, including many that we cannot even remember or that may be in our subconscious, yet they can still affect our lives and walks with Mashiach/Christ.

The truth is that the purer our hearts are, the freer we are in the Spirit and the more effective we can become for the Lord. A strong focus on a healthy heart is the best prescription for success.

ADDITIONAL REVELATIONS

During these days, the Lord is bringing forth new revelations and greater insight as to how we can pray more effectively for the breakthrough. There are two specific teachings I would like to draw to your attention here, and I am sure more will be coming as we move more effectively in the prayer realms of heaven.

The first has to do with us personally in breaking off additional spiritual influences over us from the world. John Benefiel wrote an amazing book on this subject, exposing the demonic influences of Baal. *Divorcing Baal* discusses how we are still tied into a world system that needs to be broken off each of us spiritually. Equally, another interesting teaching on more effective prayer is *Operating in the Courts of Heaven* by Robert Henderson. This teaching unveils how the courtrooms of heaven need to be properly addressed in prayer when petitioning God for change in our own personal lives, as well as those we are praying for. These books are both must-reads for our times.

PREPARE

As we begin to enter this phase of Restoration for His end-time Body, I would like to share a prophetic vision the Lord gave to me during a time of intercession with others. In the Spirit, I saw the clouds over the horizon, and above them I saw this word in large capital letters: *PREPARE*.

I then asked the Holy Spirit how to prepare, and this is what He said:

1. Pray, pray, pray! There is a sense of urgency for us to pray for Israel and the nations.

2. Prepare the Church to Reconnect with Israel spiritually.

3. We must be filled with His Holy Spirit.

THERE IS MUCH TO BE DONE

If you have read this far, you know there is something new and strategic that needs to be birthed through *The Reconnection* message, as well as the other Reformations needed for His Ekklesia/Church—not only through the Body of Messiah/Christ corporately, but also through us personally and individually. There is much to be done!

Let us come together as one family in God and allow Him to restore His Body to Himself through His wisdom and guidance to help finish the job that Yeshua/Jesus may return to us and establish His Kingdom here upon the Earth. *Lord, may we allow You to have full rights, through Your Heart and Your love, that Your will be done here upon the Earth. In Yeshua/Jesus's most precious name. Amen.*

OUR GENERATION AND THOSE WHO TARRY

We could be the generation that sees the coming of the Lord. In reality, as believers and followers of Mashiach/Christ, we have so much to look forward to knowing this possibility. It might be challenging, but it certainly will be glorious! So let me leave you with our Lord's Words and the words of His Apostle, Paul, to God's children from the nations. Let us be the seed that fell on good soil, where it produced a crop—a hundred, sixty, or thirty times what was sown (see Matthew 13:8) and to run the race in such a way to get the prize (see 1 Corinthians 9:24).

1. *Pray, pray, pray! There is a sense of urgency for us to pray for Israel and the nations.*
2. *Prepare the Church to Reconnect with Israel spiritually.*
3. *We must be filled with His Holy Spirit.*

> *"Now to the One who is able to strengthen you according to my Good News and the proclamation of Yeshua the Messiah, according to the revelation of the mystery which has been kept secret for long ages but now is revealed and through the Writings of the Prophets has been made known to all the nations, according to the commandment of the eternal God to bring about obedience of faith—to the only wise God, through Yeshua the Messiah, to Him be the Glory forever. Amen"* (Rom. 16:25–27 TLV).

CONCLUSION

As I stated at the beginning of this chapter, President Trump has recognized Jerusalem as Israel's capital (December 6, 2017). This stands as a landmark decision for the Kingdom of God upon the Earth, along with the other strategic events that have happened during Jubilee years.

All of these acts were and are incredible breakthroughs in the

natural realm for the Kingdom of God upon the Earth. And they
have been accompanied by some kind of spiritual reaction in the
natural realm. For example, the recapture of Jerusalem by the
British was not only a breakthrough for the Jewish people, laying
the foundation for their return to the land, but also an incredible blessing to the British people, as it was a great moral boost for
the British Empire at that time. Similarly, when Israel reclaimed
Jerusalem in 1967 from the Jordanians, the spiritual awakening of
the Jewish people began through the birth of the Messianic movement with more Jewish souls coming to faith in the past fifty years
than in the last nineteen hundred years put together.

In this light, I believe we will see the same kind of response—
not just with financial blessings, but with some kind of a spiritual
release. As I have been praying and seeking the Lord on this, I have received a strong sense about this related to the Aliyah[21] (Jewish people returning to Israel) and have been meditating on one of Jeremiah's Scriptures from chapter 16, verses 14–16. In these

> *In this process, as I see it, I believe there are two periods of time in which this will occur: one for the fishermen and one for the hunters. Could it be that we have just entered a renewed period of the fishermen? Could it be that the Jewish people may return to the land with great blessings, but that a time of hunting is still yet to come?*

verses, the prophet writes about Israel's physical return to Israel,
specifically from the northern lands, as well as from everywhere
else.

In this process, as I see it, I believe there are *two periods of time*
in which this will occur: one for the *fishermen* and one for the
hunters. Could it be that we have just entered a renewed period of
the fishermen? Could it be that the Jewish people may return to the
land with great blessings, but that a time of hunting is still yet to
come? Just look at what is happening in France with antisemitism.
France had the greatest Jewish population since World War II, with

up to 550,000 Jews living there in recent years, but that has been reduced to a little more than 430,000, with many returning to Israel and purchasing property.[22]

I have always felt strongly, as the Church Reconnects spiritually with Israel's family in *TONM* and begins to take on the burden of its spiritual awakening, that we will begin to see greater pockets of spiritual openings among the Jewish people before their great and final awakening comes (see Zechariah 12:10). The Remnant of Israel must become stronger to help lay this foundation for the balance of Israel to come to faith.

I believe our focus is to be twofold in this place: first, for their *spiritual awakening* and second, for their *continued physical return* to the land. If we trust Scripture to tell this tale, Ezekiel prophesied that not *one* would be left behind (see Ezekiel 39:28). It is amazing when we think about this, as well as its consequences.

Avner Boskey speaks and focuses on the vast *army* of Israel in Ezekiel 37:10 as being a literal one that God is soon to raise up for end-time purposes.

You might not be aware of this, but in my travels, I have met a good number of believers whose hearts and spirits are already being stirred to begin to prepare houses of refuge for the Jewish people when this time actually comes.

When I discuss this currently with my American-Jewish friends,

> *So exactly who are the fishermen? We are the fishermen! The fishermen are the believing Jews and Gentiles, who in this generation and during this time have been given a commission, which is to refocus on Israel and Realign to become a very part of it. We are to cry out for its salvation to complete the family picture. This is The Reconnection!*

they honestly think I am crazy. But just look what happened to the German Jews, how secure they felt in that nation and how quickly it all came to pass. So what about us, in this twenty-first century, with the speed that we move at now? This time will not be easy for Christians, either, as the world increasingly turns against the

Kingdom of God. Perhaps it is one of the ways God brings us even closer to the Jewish people as we learn to love and bless them. I am not sure how this will all unfold, but my sense is that we should be prepared, as this chapter focuses on.

For now, let us rejoice that we are in the time of the fishermen, but let us also be sober-minded and conscious of what is to come and all that must take place before our Lord can return to us. This must include how we pray for the peace of Jerusalem; Yeshua/Jesus will not return until these things come to pass.

So exactly who are the fishermen? We are the fishermen! The fishermen are the believing Jews and Gentiles, who in this generation and during this time have been given a commission, which is to refocus on Israel and Realign to become a very part of it. We are to cry out for its salvation to complete the family picture. This is *The Reconnection*!

So I end Romans 911 with the same question and challenge to all of us as believers and lovers of the Father and Yeshua/Jesus, the God of Israel: Will you pick up this burden and join the Ezekiel Generation?

In my last book, *The Ezekiel Generation*, I made the case that this is who we are. This generation and those who will tarry are the ones whom God has ordained to stand in the gap and *"to prophesy to the breath from the four winds and breathe into these slain, that they may live"* (see Ezekiel 37:9). So I end *Romans 911* with the same question and challenge to all of us as believers and lovers of the Father and Yeshua/Jesus, the God of Israel: *Will you pick up this burden and join the Ezekiel Generation?*

As God's firstborn children, will you rejoin your believing Gentile family in the Church? As God's children from the nations, will you rejoin with your believing Jewish family and reunite in *TONM*? As God's united family, will we commit ourselves to focused prayer, intercession, and effective witness and evangelism of the Jewish people where we live? Are you willing to lay down your life for your

Jewish family when and if the time comes? *These are strong questions, but when this period of hunting comes upon the Earth, will we be ready to count the cost and assist the Jewish people to restore them to God?*

CLOSING COMMENT: TEST THE SPIRIT

In this book, you have read a lot of new information, some of which can definitely be foreign to the Christian mindset and even challenging to Jewish believers because of the renewed focus and significance of Reconnecting to one another in these last days in the Israel of God. But I want to encourage you to test these words and the spirit of this writing, as the apostle John directed us (see 1 John 4:1).

I was blessed to learn this lesson early in my walk. My first pastor always encouraged us to go back and double-check his teachings through the Scripture. I want to encourage you to do the same because I feel confident that while this Reconnection focus is new, it all comes out of the *Heart of the Father* to reunite us in Yeshua/Jesus's love for one another. And all that love will manifest in us now to help open heaven's doors for God's final plans on the Earth, and for Yeshua/Jesus to return.

I hope you are serious about *The Reconnection* message after reading this book. You have already discovered that its application is not an overnight sensation, but rather a more in-depth process that requires our full attention and a renewing of the mind in study and prayer. As *Romans 911* makes clear, the lingering effects of 1,700 years of a Replacement mindset over the Gentile Church doesn't just disappear overnight. It requires a far greater focus to eradicate all its influences. I want to encourage you to proceed to the next steps.

ROMANS 911 STUDY GUIDE

As a supplement to *Romans 911*, we have prepared a Study Guide teaching series in both book and video form that I teach, called

"*The Romans 911 Project.*" The 12-hour video Bible Study teaching series is FREE with the purchase of the books, while encouraging love offerings to strengthen *TONM* through prayer and various humanitarian projects connected to it.

While *Romans 911* spells out all of the details on *The Reconnection* and *Alignment* message, the Study Guide and the video teaching series truly helps us to move into it. The Study Guide focuses on a document the Lord gave to me in 2018, during the 10 Days of Awe called *The Reconnection Mandate*.[23] This mandate outlines five specific directives given for us to receive and embrace *The Reconnection* message. It is the next step in this process. And it truly encourages the restorative stage the Ekklesia/Church needs to enter into during these days to fulfill John 17 love and unity.

You can acquire the program on the Reconnecting Ministries website for individuals, small groups, and Churches/Congregations. There is also a free Pastoral/Leader's Guide to use in overseeing this Bible-study-series teaching. Please visit our website for more information.

ISSACHAR - DISCERNING THE TIMES

As we have already discovered in *Romans 911*, the *Israel Piece* comes by spiritual revelation. The Holy Spirit is the one who opens our eyes to this understanding. Like the tribe of Issachar who discerned the times (see 1 Chronicles 12:32), may we not only come into a complete knowledge of this Reconnection message. But may we seek the Lord for the wisdom of how to apply it into our everyday lives and walks with the Lord, into our Churches and Congregations, and learn how to communicate it to others.

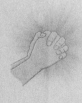

Like the tribe of Issachar who discerned the times (see 1 Chronicles 12:32), may we not only come into a complete knowledge of this Reconnection message. But may we seek the Lord for the wisdom of how to apply it into our everyday lives and walks with the Lord, into our Churches and Congregations, and learn how to communicate it to others.

CLOSING PRAYER

For both Jewish and Gentile believers, may the God of Israel richly bless you as you commence this journey and discover the fullness of *TONM*. And if you are already on this path, may He deepen your spirit and understanding for you to fully connect with one another.

I leave you with this final prayer:

"The Spirit and the Bride say, 'Come!' And let the one who is thirsty come; and let the one who wishes take the free gift of the water of life" (Rev. 22:17). So let us say together, *"Come, Lord Yeshua/Jesus!"* and unite in His love for one another and God's end-time plans so that the Peace of Jerusalem may be realized.

SUMMATIVE RESOURCES FOR PRAYER AND PETITION

FOR THE RECONNECTION IN THE ONE NEW MAN

Please note:

Praying for *The Reconnection* **in** *TONM* **is a significant part of praying for the peace of Jerusalem,** as it moves the Body of Messiah/Christ into our roles to help bring it to pass. The list contained here is not exhaustive. It is designed to give an outline of the many prayer issues the Holy Spirit is leading us to pray about for *The Reconnection* in *TONM*.

PETITION GOD FOR THE FOLLOWING:

- For the *Father's Heart* to be released for His firstborn, to His children from the nations

- For *The Reconnection* in *TONM*

- For the family of God to be reunited—believing Jews and Gentiles

- For the Remnant of Israel (in Israel) to awaken to *The Reconnection*

- For the Remnant of Israel (in the nations) to awaken to *The Reconnection*

- For God's children from the nations to awaken to *The Reconnection*

- For the Church to embrace the Jewish-believing branches

- For the Messianic Body to embrace the Gentile-believing branches
- For the Church to Realign toward Israel, specifically its Remnant
- For the Messianic Body to Realign toward the believing Church
- For Israel's spiritual awakening and Restoration
- For the breath of God to be released into the Jewish people (Ezekiel 37:9–10)
- For the end-time harvest of souls
- For the nations to connect with Israel
- For the Church in the nations to connect with Israel and specifically its Remnant (Jewish believers)
- For those caught under the spirit of Islam
- For those caught under other religions
- For the local Church to connect with HOP
- For all believers to commit to *Harp & Bowl* sets in their local communities
- For *Pure Intercession* to expand in the Prayer Movement
- To call the Watchmen forth across the nations to raise up Pure Intercessory prayer cells across the Globe
- For the fear of the Lord to return to His Ekklesia/Church
- For revival

- For the Preparation of the Bride in accordance with chapter 12

- For the Lord's return—"Come, Lord Yeshua/Jesus!"

- For the Remnant of Israel (in Israel) to find greater unity

- For love and unity between Jewish and Arab believers in Israel

- For unity between Jewish and Palestinian believers

- For peace between Israelis and Palestinians

- For greater unity in the Messianic Movement in the nations

- For the Church and Messianic Movement to embrace the fivefold gifts of the Holy Spirit

- For more Jewish people to make Aliyah (to return to the land) from the nations

- For Jewish believers to be accepted as Jews in Israel

- For Jewish believers to be able to make Aliyah. (*They are currently no longer considered Jewish by the State of Israel, and as a result, are not accepted as citizens.*)

CHRISTIAN OBSTACLES TO THE RECONNECTION

Spiritual Issues

Demonic forces aligned to prevent *The Reconnection* in all areas

To Break Away From:

- Antisemitism

- Generational antisemitism

- Legalism

- Worldliness

To Release:

- Forgiveness
- Love
- Repentance
- Identificational repentance
- Reconciliation
- Blessings on callings of Messianic Gentiles
- Greater finances to support the Remnant of Israel and Jewish focused missions
- Funding for *The Reconnection*

To Restore:

- The Church to connect with the Remnant of Israel
- The Church at large, all denominations
- Desire for unity in *TONM*
- Reconnection in the Holy Spirit
- Jewish identity for Jewish believers in the Church
- Blessings for one another
- Love for one another—John 17 unity
- Working relationship to embrace one another—For local ministries to work together
- Love and desire to reach out to Jewish friends and neighbors
- A desire for Jewish evangelism
- Support for the Body of Messiah/Christ in Israel and Diaspora

— Unity in the Body

— Spiritual health

— With the gifts of the Holy Spirit

— With finances to the believing Body first before any other issues

— Unity with Palestinian believers through identificational repentance

— Unity with Coptic Christians through identificational repentance

— Unity with any other Arab and Middle-Eastern believers through identificational repentance

Emotional Issues

- Lacking ability to forgive

- Sibling rivalry

- Jealousy

- Fear of all kinds

- Indifference

- Pride

- Arrogance

Theological Issues

To Break Away From:

- Supersessionism

- Replacement theology

- Fulfillment theology

- Dual Covenant theology

Related to Separation:

- God's Covenants to Israel, not the Church
- No Jew, no Gentile
- Connection to Abraham but not to Israel
- Church separation from Israel
- Church separation from Jewish roots

To Adjust Eschatology to Include Messianic Views and The Reconnection and Alignment:

- Preterism
- Partial preterism
- Futurism
- Historism
- Dispensationalism
- Kingdom now
- Dominion
- Rapture theology
- Amillenialism
- Premillennialism
- Postmillennialism
- Any other eschatology not in line with *The Reconnection* in *TONM*
- Splinter groups with incorrect Israel perspectives

JEWISH OBSTACLES TO THE RECONNECTION

Spiritual Issues

Demonic forces aligned to prevent *The Reconnection* in all areas

To Release:

- Forgiveness
- Love
- Repentance
- Identificational repentance
- Reconciliation

To Restore:

- Great unity in the Messianic Movement and greater understanding
- Greater unity between the Messianic Movement and the Church
- Desire for unity in *TONM*
- Reconnection in the Holy Spirit
- Blessings for one another
- Love for one another—John 17 unity
- To embrace our Gentile-believing family
- Working relationship to embrace one another
- Support for all local believing Churches
- Desire to reach the lost
- Desire for evangelism

Emotional Issues

- Lack of ability to forgive
- Rejection issues from ancestry
- Rejection from Church
- Anger
- Pride
- Spiritual pride
- Jealousy
- Fear—all kinds
- Indifference
- Arrogance

Theological Issues

To Break Away From:

- Rejection of the Church
- Jewish identity issues
- Fear of assimilation
- Messianic Gentile issues
- Rabbinical authority
- Jewish Roots Movement
- One Law theology
- Ephraimites
- For Hashivenu believers to find greater balance towards Messianic issues

Pray for the Balance of Israel:

- To repent of their sins
- For the breath of God to be released
- To be awakened
- To be free from blindness and deafness
- To be free from religious spirits
- To break off the Rabbinic deceptions of good works and deeds, replacing blood sacrifice, which is ultimately fulfilled through Yeshua Mashiach
- Not to love things of this world
- To be free from idolatry and the love of money
- To break off the secular, liberal mindset that controls their thinking
- To not have pride
- To avoid selfishness
- To not sin in anger
- To not harbor hatred
- To practice forgiveness at all times
- To not have an anti-Christ spirit
- To not reject Jewish believers
- To not reject Gentiles
- To not reject Christians
- To not have the arm of the flesh (Daniel 12:7)
- To contemplate Aliyah returning to the land
- To support Israel's final awakening

Prayer Movement

- Pray for *Harp & Bowl* worship and for *Pure Intercession.*

- Pray for the prayer Body in the land to be strengthened and protected.

- Pray for greater connection to the prayer movement in the nations toward Israel.

- Pray for First Fruits of worship and prayer to be commissioned from the nations into Israel to help clear the spiritual skies.

- Pray for greater development of *Pure* and *Strategic Intercession* in the prayer movement in the nations and Israel to develop for *The Reconnection* and Alignment, and for the final Restoration and Reformation of the Church.

Reconnecting Ministries, 2021

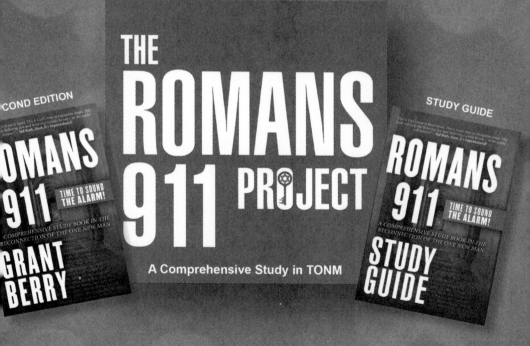

Reconnecting Ministries

- Sign up to Reconnecting Ministries Email List
- Become a Give *Chai/Life* Reconnecting Ministries Partner

Get involved with *The Reconnection*...

- Join us to Pray in the Shabbat

- Join our Feast Celebrations

- Join in our ONM + National prayer meetings

- Join the *Romans 911* Webinar Bible Study

- Listen to the *Romans 911* Podcast

- Join the Global 10 Days of Prayer movement

- Join the 24/7 365 Global Prayer Room

To contact Grant: www.Reconnectingministries.org (Click "Contact")

HELP US PROMOTE THE RECONNECTION

There are several ways you can help me get the word out about the message of this book...

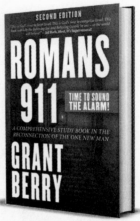

- Post a 5-star review on Amazon

- Recommend the book to friends – word of mouth is still the most effective form of advertising

- Write about the book on your Facebook, Twitter, Instagram – any social media you regularly use!

- If you blog, consider referencing the book, or publishing an excerpt from the book with a link back to our website. You have our permission to do this as long as you provide proper credit and backlinks.

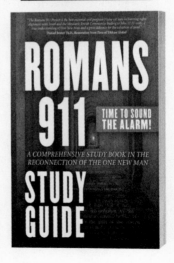

- Purchase additional copies to give away as gifts

- Purchase a copy for your pastor or Messianic rabbi

OTHER RESOURCES FROM GRANT BERRY

The Ezekiel Generation

The New Covenant Prophecy

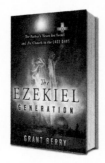

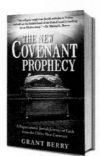

To order these books and learn more, go to:

http://www.Reconnectingministries.org/about_the_books.html

- To read Charisma Online Magazine articles on *The Reconnection*

- To watch or listen to interviews

- To watch and listen to sermons and additional teachings on *The Reconnection*

- To download *Pure Intercession* Teaching Series

- To download *The Romans 911 Project*: www.Reconnectingministries.org/media.html

- To contact Grant for interviews or speaking engagements: www.Reconnectingministries.org (Click "Contact")

Visit our websites for more information:
www.Romans911.org or
www.Reconnectingministries.org

REFERENCES

1. Antisemitism. https://www.holocaustremembrance.com/sites/default/files/memo-on-spelling-of-antisemitism_final-1.pdf

2. Blumenthal, Ariel. "One New Man: Mystery of the Messiah." *One New Man: The Mystery of Messiah*, July 21 2017, reviveisrael.org/archive/ language/english/2017/07-21-One-New-Man.html.

3. Paganism in the Church. Saint Augustine, *The City of God*.

4. Anti-Semitism of the 'Church Fathers,' Yashanet.com, http://www.yashanet.com/library/fathers.htm.

5. Ambrosio, Alicia. "What You Need to Know about the Orthodox- Catholic Split," Aleteia, September 13, 2017, https://aleteia.org/2017/09/13/what-you-need-to-know-about-the-orthodox-catholic-split-and-hopes-for-reunification/.

6. B. Bagatti. *The Church from the Circumcision*.

7. Cornelius - https://biblehub.com/acts/10-3.htm.

8. Early Church Persecution of Jewish roots. https://www.curtlandry.com/how-the-jewish-roots-of-the-christian-faith-were-removed-from-the-early-Church/

9. Kinser, Mark. "Messianic Judaism." Wikipedia, Wikimedia Foundation, March 30 2018, https://en.wikipedia.org/wiki/Messianic_Judaism.

10. "Oneg Shabbat." Dictionary.com, www.dictionary.com/browse/oneg-shabbat.

11. "Messianic Jews: A Brief History." Jews for Jesus, 2015, jewsforjesus.org/jewishresources/community/messianic-jews-a-brief-history/.

12. "What Is 'Replacement Theology'?" *The Ezekiel Generation*, page 71.

13. Susan Torregrosa, November 2016. New Forensic Evidence Validates the Shroud of Turin. Shroud video link. https://youtu.be/UT4WXW6A0gA

14. Juster, Daniel C., Th D. Written for *Romans 911*.

15. Ferguson, Gordon. "What About Watchman Nee's Teaching on Soul and Spirit?" Gordon Ferguson, Garber Consulting, http://gordonferguson.org/articles/what-about-watchman-nee-s-teaching-on-soul-and-spirit/.

16. Wagner, Peter teaching. https://kgministries.com/index.php/blog/67-how-an-apostolic-center-is-different-from-the-local-Church

17. "Reconnecting Ministry Commission Document." Reconnecting Ministries. https://reconnectingministries.org/ministry-reports/

18. Americaprays. https://Americaprays.org

19. 10 Days of Prayer. 10days.net

20. Wolf, Dwain – www.restoredlifepress.com

21. "Definition of 'Aliyah.'" *Collins English Dictionary, Collins Dictionary*, www.collinsdictionary.com/us/dictionary/english/aliyah.

[22] French Jewish Population. https://en.m.wikipedia.org/wiki/Jewish_ population_by_country

[23] https://reconnectingministries.org/reconnection-mandate/

BIBLE TRANSLATION:

KJV Bible. Zondervan, 1995.
NIV Bible. Hodder & Stoughton, 2000.
TLV Bible. Baker Books, 2015.
NLT Bible. Tyndale House, 1996.
NASB Bible. Lockman Foundation, 1995.

RECONNECTING MINISTRY RESOURCES

MINISTRY GROUPS:

Beth Israel
http://www.bethisraelworshipcenter.org/

Carmel Assembly
http://www.carmelassembly.org/

Cleansing Stream Ministries
https://www.cleansingstream.org

Chosen People Ministry
https://chosenpeople.com/site/

Dome of the Rock
http://www.islamic-awareness.org/History/Islam/Inscriptions/DoTR.html

El Shaddai Ministries
http://www.elshaddaiministries.us/

Fellowship and International Revival & Evangelism School of Ministry
http://www.fire-international.org/

Final Frontier Ministries
https://davidstent.org/

Gate of Zion Ministries
http://gatestozion.net/

Harvest International Ministries

harvestim.org

Howard Morgan Ministries

https://howardmorganministries.org/

IHOP Kansas City

https://www.ihopkc.org

Messianic Bible Institute

http://mjbi.org/about

MJAA: Messianic Jewish Alliance of America

https://mjaa.org

King of Kings, Jerusalem

http://www.kkcj.org/

FIRM

http://firm.org.il/

Toward Jerusalem Council II

http://tjcii.org/

Trumpet of Salvation to Israel

https://trumpetofsalvation.org/

Reach International Ministries

https://globalawakening.com/network/members-directory/item/reach-international-ministries

Revive Israel

https://www.reviveisrael.org/

Tikkun Global Ministries

http://www.tikkunministries.org/

Union Messianic Jewish Congregations

https://www.umjc.org/

MINISTRY LEADERS:

Aliyah: Exodus International

a. www.operationexodususa.org

b. www.aliyahusa.com

Heidi Baker:

www.irisglobal.org/

Doug Beacham: *Rediscovering Apostles and Prophets*

John Benefiel: *Divorcing Baal*

The Berger Brothers, Reuvan & Benjamin:

a. http://kehilanews.com/

b. http://tjcii.eu/messianic-jews-key-to-christian-unity/

Jonathan Bernis: Jewish Voice Ministries International

https://www.jewishvoice.org

Grant Berry:

a. *The New Covenant Prophecy*

b. *The Ezekiel Generation*

c. *Romans 911 Study Guide*

d. *The Romans 911 Project*

Mike Bickle: IHOP Kansas City

https://mikebickle.org/

Craig Blaising: Essay: *The New Christian Zionism*

Avner Boskey: *How to Be Messianic without Becoming Meshuggah*

David Brickner: Jews for Jesus

https://jewsforjesus.org/

Manny Brotman:

http://www.sandrasheskinbrotman.com/manny.htm

Dr. Michael Brown: Fire School of Ministry & Line of Fire Radio Show

a. http://www.fire-school.org/author/drmlbrown/

b. http://thelineoffire.org

Dr. Michael Brown:

a. *The Real Kosher Jesus*

b. *Our Hands Are Stained with Blood*

Jonathan Cahn:

a. *The Harbinger*

b. *The Mystery of the Shemitah*

c. *The Paradigm*

Ron Cantor: Tikkun Global

https://www.roncantor.com

Martin Chernoff:

https://www.charismamag.com/blogs/standing-with-israel/18351-martin-chernoff-the-father-of-20th-century-messianic-judaism

David Chernoff:

cby.org

Joel Chernoff:

https://www.lambmessianicmusic.com/

Earl Clampett: *The Blueprint*

Harold Eberle and Martin Trench: *Victorious Eschatology*

Gaylord Enns: *The Love Revolution*
https://www.loverevolutionnow.org/

Barry Feinman: Jezreel International Ministries
http://www.jezreelinternational.org

Don Finto:
  a. *Your People Shall Be My People*
  b. *Prepare*
  c. *God's Promise and the Future of Israel*

Don Finto & Tod McDowell: Caleb Global Ministries
https://calebcompany.org

Kobi & Shani Fergus:
  http://yeshuaisrael.com

Richard J. Foster: *The Celebration of Discipline*

Joseph Frey:
  https://en.wikipedia.org/wiki/Joseph_Samuel_C._F._Frey

Dr. Ray Gannon:
  https://www.destinyimage.com/products/the-shifting-romance-with israel?variant=630893772825

James Goll:
  a. *The Coming Israel Awakening*
  b. *Praying for Israel's Destiny*
  c. *The Prophetic Intercessor*
  https://www.godencounters.com/

Daniah Greenberg: The Tree of Life Version
https://www.tlvbiblesociety.org

Boris Grenshenko:
https://kemokiev.org/about-us

Olen Griffing:
http://gatewaypeople.com/profiles/olen-griffing

Dai Sup Han: Prayer Surge Now
www.PrayerSurgeNOW.net

David Harwood:
a. *Love of God*
b. *For the Sake of the Fathers*
www.loveofGodproject.org

Jack Hayford: Jack Hayford Ministries
https://www.jackhayford.org/

Gregg Healey: Impact Connecticut
nhcap.com — newbreed.co

Robert Henderson: *Operating in the Courts of Heaven*

Alan Hirsch, 5Q
alanhirsch.org

Tom Hess:
http://www.jhopfan.com

Jane Hansen Hoyt: Aglow International
https://www.aglow.org/

Rees Howells:
Rees Howells the Intercessor

Jason Hubbard: Light of the World Prayer Center
lowpc.org/

Asher Intrater:

    a. *Alignment*

    b. *Covenant Relationships*

    c. *Israel, the Church, and the Last Days*

Cindy Jacobs:

    https://www.generals.org/home/

Bill Johnson:

    www.bethel.com/ministries/bill-johnson/

Rick Joyner:

    https://www.morningstarministries.org/

Dr. Daniel Juster:

    a. *Passover: The Key That Unlocks the Book of Revelation*

    b. *Jewish Roots*

    c. *Israel, the Church, and the Last Days*

Arthur Katz: Art Katz Ministries
http://artkatzministries.org

    a. *Apostolic Foundations*

Arni Klein & Yonit Klein: Emmaus Way Ministries
http://emmausway.org

Larry Lea:

    Could You Not Tarry One Hour?

Lisa Loden & Salim J. Munayer:

    https://www.worldwidemission.org/year/2017/people/lisa-loden

    a. *Through My Enemy's Eyes*

    https://www.worldwidemission.org/year/2017/people/salim
-j-munayer

Gerald R. McDermott: The New Christian Zionism

https://www.thegospelcoalition.org/blogs/evangelical-history/
the-new-christian-zionism/

Howard Morgan:

https://howardmorganministries.org/
So Deeply Scarred – A History of "Christian" Anti-Semitism

Robert Morris:

http://gatewaypeople.com/profiles/robert-morris

Chuck D. Pierce & Robert Heidler: *The Apostolic Church Arising*

Derek Prince: Derek Prince Ministries

https://www.derekprince.org

Joseph Rabinowitz:

https://jewsforjesus.org/blog/joseph-rabinowitz-and-the-messi-
anic-movement-the-herzl-of-jewish-christianity/

Rick & Patti Ridings:

https://www.succathallel.com

John Robb: International Prayer Council

www.ipcprayer.org

Pat Robertson:

CBN.com

Moishe Rosen: Jews for Jesus

https://jewsforjesus.org

Sid Roth:

It's Supernatural
www.sidroth.org/

Kirt Schneider:
discoveringthejewishjesus.com/

Eitan Shishkoff:
www.tentsofmercy.org/

David H. Stern: *Complete Jewish Bible*
https://messianicjewish.net/dr-david-stern

Mark Tubbs: *The Five Fingers of God*

Peter Wagner: *Apostles Today; Apostle and Prophets*

Marty Waldman: Baruch Hashem Messianic Synagogue
baruchhashemsynagogue.org/

William Wilberforce:
https://www.cmj-israel.org

Dr. Wayne Wilks:
http://gatewaypeople.com/profiles/wayne-wilks-jr

Stewart & Chantal Winograd: Reach Initiative International
Ministries
https://reachii.org/

Robert Wolff: Majestic Glory Ministries
a. *Awakening TONM*
b. *Catch & Release*
c. *Sitting with Seamoor*
http://www.awakening1.org

Count Ludwig Von Zinzendorf: Jewish Ministry focus
https://jewsforjesus.org/publications/newsletter/
newsletter-nov-1994/zinzendorf-and-the-jewish-people

Dr. Patrick Zukeran:

www.probe.org/four-views-of-revelation/

BOOKS ON REPLACEMENT THEOLOGY:

Douglas Harrink: *Paul and the Post Liberals*

R. Kendall Soulen: *The God of Israel and Christian Theology*

Willis Beecher: *The Prophets and the Promise (1910)*

Barry Horner: *Future Israel*